The Ultimate Case Guide: How to Successfully Teach and Write Case Studies

Martin Kupp and Urs Mueller

ubiquity press
London

Published by
Ubiquity Press Ltd.
Unit 3N, 6 Osborn Street
London E1 6TD
www.ubiquitypress.com

Text © Martin Kupp and Urs Mueller 2024

First published 2024

Cover design and illustration by Amber Dalgleish

Print and digital versions typeset by Siliconchips Services Ltd.

ISBN (Paperback): 978-1-914481-56-7
ISBN (PDF): 978-1-914481-57-4
ISBN (EPUB): 978-1-914481-58-1
ISBN (Mobi): 978-1-914481-59-8

DOI: https://doi.org/10.5334/bdb

Supplementary materials:
Case Teaching Workbook: https://doi.org/10.5334/bdb.e
Case Writing Workbook: https://doi.org/10.5334/bdb.f

This work is licensed under the Creative Commons Attribution-NonCommercial 4.0 International License (unless stated otherwise within the content of the work). To view a copy of this license, visit https://creativecommons.org/licenses/by-nc/4.0/ or send a letter to Creative Commons, 444 Castro Street, Suite 900, Mountain View, California, 94041, USA. This license allows sharing and copying any part of the work for personal use, providing author attribution is clearly stated. This license prohibits commercial use of the material.

The full text of this book has been peer-reviewed to ensure high academic standards. For full review policies, see https://www.ubiquitypress.com/

Suggested citation:
Kupp, M., and Mueller, U. 2024. *The Ultimate Case Guide: How to Successfully Teach and Write Case Studies*. London: Ubiquity Press. DOI: https://doi.org/10.5334/bdb. License: CC BY-NC 4.0

To read the free, open access version of this book online, visit https://doi.org/10.5334/bdb or scan this QR code with your mobile device:

Table of Contents

Foreword	xi
Acknowledgements	xiii
Preface	xv
Supplementary materials	xviii

The case method in the spotlight ... 1

    History of the case method ... 1
    What is a case study? ... 2
    Why use case studies? ... 6
    Criticism of the case method ... 8
    What makes a good case study? ... 12
    Variety of cases ... 16
    The issue of issues ... 21
    The organizational context ... 23
    References ... 26

Teaching a case-based session ... 27

    Our case teaching beliefs and philosophy ... 27
    The case teaching process: an overview ... 32
    Choosing a (new) case-based session ... 32
    Case study selection ... 34
    Teaching plan development ... 40
    Preparation ... 48
    Opening the case discussion ... 54
    Running the session ... 61
    Closure and transfer ... 88
    Reflection and other ... 90
    Getting better at case teaching ... 101
    Using case teaching for case writing ... 105
    References ... 111

Teaching a case-based course ... 113

    From a single session to a full course ... 113
    Designing the course ... 114

Opening and running a case-based course or program	119
Grading of a case-based course	123
Ethical considerations for a case-based course	128
Reference	130

Writing great case studies — 131

Our case writing beliefs and philosophy	132
Benefits of writing your own case	134
The case development funnel	134
1. Case origin	136
2. Educational objectives	140
3. Strategic decisions	144
4. Tactical choices	153
5. Operational activities for your own case study	166
6. Test-use case in class	212
7. Finishing the case and teaching note	218
8. Publishing the case and teaching note	238
9. Promoting your case study	239
Developing alternative format case studies	241
Typical mistakes in case developments	244
Resourcing: getting support for your case development	246
Structured approach to developing your own case studies	248
References	249

Index — 251

Extended Table of Contents

Foreword	xi
Acknowledgements	xiii
Preface	xv
Supplementary materials	xviii
The case method in the spotlight	**1**
History of the case method	1
Some background	1
Continuing inspiration	2
What is a case study?	2
The metaphor of the 'patient in the room'	2
Teaching cases versus research cases	3
Plurality and diversity	4
Deep learning	6
Why use case studies?	6
The functions of a teaching case	6
The benefits of case studies for online education	7
Broadening the horizon of participants	7
Broadening the horizon of facilitators	7
Criticism of the case method	8
The potential danger of wrong syllogisms	9
Cases are unrealistic because they all have 'solutions' and usually deal with success stories	10
What makes a good case study?	12
Make sure it's a case and not just a story	12
Make sure that the case tackles a relevant, important issue	13
Make sure that the case provides a voyage of discovery – and even some interesting surprises	13
Make sure that the case is controversial	13
Make sure the case contains contrasts and comparisons	14
Make sure the case provides 'currently useful generalizations'	14
Make sure the case has the data required to tackle the problem – not too much and not too little	14
Make sure the case has a personal touch	15
Make sure the case is well structured and easy to read	15
Make sure that the case is short	15

Variety of cases	16
Case dimensions	16
Prototypical case types	20
The issue of issues	21
The organizational context	23
Familiarizing students with case method	23
Recruitment and promotion	24
Organizational support	25
References	26
Teaching a case-based session	**27**
Our case teaching beliefs and philosophy	27
Prioritize method over content	28
Elevate your participants to your eye level	29
Experiment a lot and find your own path	31
The case teaching process: an overview	32
Choosing a (new) case-based session	32
Identifying the right course	32
Identifying the right session	33
Learners and learning objectives	33
Case study selection	34
Searching	34
Selecting	37
Teaching plan development	40
Context and constraints	41
Flow of the session	41
Learning cycles	42
Orchestrating immediate and underlying issue	43
Additional material	43
The teaching plan	44
Planning the use of the board	46
Preparation	48
Know your class	48
Preparing the case and materials	51
Opening the case discussion	54
Setting the scene: at the start of the session	54
Getting started	55
Opening question	55
Additional tactics to get the discussion going	59
Dealing with participants who know the outcome and give it away immediately	60

Running the session	61
Asking great questions	61
Listening carefully	72
Orchestrating the discussion	78
Closure and transfer	88
Reflection and other	90
Typical mistakes in case teaching	90
Cultural and language aspects of using case studies	91
Using media and technology as an instructor	94
Use of board	95
Use of material	96
Thoughts on class size and location	98
Using cases for online teaching	100
Getting better at case teaching	101
Get feedback	102
Review your own performance	103
Using case teaching for case writing	105
Using case teaching for collecting material for case writing	105
Using case teaching for testing case ideas	106
When to test case ideas and how to choose the right environment	110
References	111
Teaching a case-based course	**113**
From a single session to a full course	113
Designing the course	114
Who will do the learning?	114
What are the course specifics and their relation to the overall program?	114
What is the content that you plan to cover with cases?	116
Structure and flow of the course	116
Methods and materials: case selection and mix for an entire course	118
Opening and running a case-based course or program	119
Learning contract	119
Introducing the case method to the students	120
Grading of a case-based course	123
Grading participation/contribution	124
Grading assignments and submissions	126
Grading case-based exams	127
Ethical considerations for a case-based course	128
Pretention of participant-centricity	128
Unfair allocation of airtime	129

Disrespectful treatment of participants	129
Hindsight bias	129
Ethical issues of grading	129
Reference	130

Writing great case studies — 131

Our case writing beliefs and philosophy	132
Rapid prototyping	132
Breaking the rules – but only after gaining experience	133
Focus on learning outcomes	133
Benefits of writing your own case	134
The case development funnel	134
1. Case origin	136
It is all about leads and needs	136
Identifying educational needs (content or context)	137
Finding good case leads	138
2. Educational objectives	140
Narrowing down your need for an own case study	141
Narrowing down your lead for your own case study	141
3. Strategic decisions	144
Structuring the need into a session	144
Structuring the lead into a case	146
4. Tactical choices	153
Specifying the case	153
Drafting a case teaching plan	164
5. Operational activities for your own case study	166
Drafting the case study	166
Drafting the teaching note	196
6. Test-use case in class	212
Select a safe environment to test your case	212
How to test your case draft	213
Who should test-teach the case?	214
How many times should I test the case in the classroom?	215
What to look out for	215
Learning from test use for the teaching note	216
7. Finishing the case and teaching note	218
Finishing the case study	218
Finishing the teaching note	225
8. Publishing the case and teaching note	238

9. Promoting your case study	239
Spread the news	239
Give it a try: case competitions can greatly enhance your case's visibility	240
Enhance the appeal of your case	240
Broaden your potential audience: translate your case into other languages	240
Developing alternative format case studies	241
Why a plain case might not be enough	241
Reasons to incorporate new technologies/media	241
Ways to incorporate technology and different media	243
Typical mistakes in case developments	244
Overloading your case with facts, figures and detail	244
Including too many issues	245
Being biased toward or against your protagonist and company	245
Writing to convince instead of writing to engage	246
Giving away too much	246
Using too much jargon and industry-specific language	246
Resourcing: getting support for your case development	246
Who can help?	247
What can they do?	247
Financial resources	248
Structured approach to developing your own case studies	248
Writing your first case and developing a case portfolio	248
References	249
Index	251

Foreword

As CEO of The Case Centre, I have the privilege of leading an organisation dedicated to championing the case method, one of the most powerful pedagogical learning approaches used with business and management students.

The case method is a tool that increases student engagement, makes learning flourish, and helps to create successful future business leaders. It equips students with the skills to challenge assumptions, overcome prejudices, test theories, debate solutions and develop work and life skills – an essential toolkit for navigating the complexities of the modern business landscape.

For educators, mastering the art of case writing and teaching is paramount to delivering profound learning experiences. It requires a departure from traditional academic approaches, a process that can be daunting.

Martin and Urs, two experts in the field, have dedicated much of their careers to unravelling the intricacies of the case method. They have developed practical frameworks and tools that empower educators to excel in case writing and teaching. Through the workshops and webinars that they deliver for The Case Centre they have equipped thousands of educators worldwide with the skills and confidence to harness the full potential of the case method.

I am thrilled to endorse Martin and Urs' eagerly awaited book on case writing and teaching. This comprehensive guide, accompanied by insightful workbooks, promises to demystify the case method journey, offering invaluable advice and practical strategies. With this publication, Martin and Urs are poised to extend their impact and advocate for the widespread adoption of the case method.

I invite you to immerse yourself in this book – a treasure trove of wisdom and expertise. Whether you're a seasoned case teacher or writer, or just embarking on your case journey, you'll discover invaluable insights to enrich your practice and inspire your students.

Vicky Lester
CEO, The Case Centre: the independent home of the case method.

www.thecasecentre.org

Acknowledgements

First and foremost, this book would have been impossible without the hundreds of our case teaching and case writing workshop participants. It was due to their questions, contributions, and feedback that we started to build up our repertoire of examples, ideas, solutions, and sometimes hacks to improve not only our own case teaching and writing but ultimately also that of our growing community of equally passionate case teachers and writers.

This book also builds upon the work of several distinguished experts in the field of teaching with and writing of case studies – and we are very much indebted to many different sources of inspiration. We refer to several great scholars and institutions that promoted the case method wherever possible – and we probably still missed mentioning other giants on whose shoulders we stand. One person, however, stands out for us – and this is Derek Abell who significantly shaped our understanding and case philosophy. We have had the pleasure and privilege of working with Derek for several years. Derek, a former Harvard Business School Professor and Dean of IMD in Lausanne, was the founding President of ESMT Berlin. This is where we had the opportunity to observe him teaching and got intensive and open feedback whenever he observed any of our sessions. From Derek, we learned the basic tricks of the trade and how much case study teaching and writing can be improved by receiving excellent feedback.

Ultimately, this book would have never come alive without the invaluable support of The Case Centre. Not only do we both have the pleasure of running case writing and case teaching workshops for The Case Centre, but they also encouraged us to write this book. Deborah Bennison helped us turn some of our material (which we had mainly created as slides) into wonderful text blocks. Antoinette Mills initiated and continued this precious work and supported us with her knowledge and time. We would also like to thank The Case Centre for their generous financial support for the wonderful work of Ubiquity Press for editing, peer-review, layout, and indexing.

Last but certainly not least, we would like to thank our students and executive education participants from all around the world who constantly challenged us in class, forced us to think on our feet, made us improvise and experiment, and helped us reflect on and improve our teaching. The enthusiasm of our students proved to us that case-based learning can simultaneously be highly impactful and meaningful for the participants and bring new insights to the instructors.

Preface

Dear readers,

Welcome to "The Ultimate Case Guide: How to Successfully Teach and Write Case Studies" – your comprehensive resource whether you are venturing into the world of case studies for the first time or seeking to refine your expertise further.

Who Is This Book For?

This guide is made for a diverse range of case teachers and writers. Whether you are a novice eager to draft your first case study, an experienced educator looking to enhance your classroom strategies, or a prolific case writer aiming to polish your skills, this book offers valuable insights for all. Faculty members from business schools globally, corporate trainers seeking to foster analytical thinking, and consultants dedicated to organizational development will find this book particularly beneficial.

Our Unique Approach

Our approach to case teaching and writing blends traditional methods with innovative techniques. By embracing a philosophy of rapid prototyping and iterative learning, we encourage you to apply the concepts discussed in small, manageable segments. This method allows you to adapt and evolve your case studies and teaching practices without the intimidation of a perfect product from the start.

Our case teaching philosophy is to prioritize method over content, to elevate your participants to eye level, and to embrace experimentation. The main part of the case teaching section then follows the following logic:

1. Choosing a (new) case-based session
2. Case study selection

3. Teaching plan development
4. Preparation
5. Opening the case discussion
6. Running the session
7. Closure and transfer
8. Reflection and other

When it comes to case writing, we have developed our very own approach. Many books, articles and how-to-guides on case writing follow a sequential logic, whereby authors first write the case study and then the teaching note (rarely the other way around). We do, however, fundamentally believe that the key to writing good cases is the ability to 'knead' in multiple iterations two things together: a truly relevant educational objective ("need") and an interesting managerial challenge or story ("lead"). Only after bringing these two together in several steps, will the case study and teaching note be great. Therefore, we recommend following our case development funnel:

1. Collecting possible ***Case Origins*** (leads and needs)
2. Defining ***Educational Objectives***
3. Making ***Strategic Decisions***
4. Making ***Tactical Choices***
5. Performing ***Operational Activities***
6. ***Test Using***
7. ***Finishing***
8. ***Publishing***
9. ***Promoting***

How to Best Use This Book

For Beginners: Start from the beginning and progress through the chapters sequentially. Don't yet read the chapter on case-based courses – and don't even think of writing your own case study unless you have gained a basic understanding of how to teach case studies successfully. Use the accompanying workbooks to apply concepts as you learn, enhancing retention and practical understanding. Look for icons throughout the book that denote definitions, actionable tips, and important points. These elements are designed to make the learning process dynamic and applicable.

For Seasoned Educators and Authors: Do not waste your time by reading the book from cover to cover. Instead, navigate directly to sections that address your current challenges or interests. The detailed table of contents and index facilitate this targeted approach, making it easy to find the exact content you need. To help you round-off your approach you will find a sections with icons that might be particularly relevant for you: "Ideas", "Checklist", and "From theory to practice".

Supplementary Materials: Utilize the downloadable resources (www.ultimatecaseguide.org) and the workbooks to engage with the content actively. These materials are designed to complement the theories and strategies discussed, offering practical templates and frameworks for your case writing and teaching endeavors.

Workbooks are available to download via the following DOI URLs:

– Case Teaching Workbook: https://doi.org/10.5334/bdb.e
– Case Writing Workbook: https://doi.org/10.5334/bdb.f

Community of Practice: Visit www.ultimatecaseguide.org to join our community of practice and discuss difficulties, exchange ideas, and share successes with peers. This community is invaluable for continuous learning and support.

Icons

In the margins of this book, you will find icons that aim at drawing your attention to specific parts and making navigating the book easier. Please find below an overview of the icons and their meaning:

Icon	Meaning
⚠️	Important
🧠	From theory to practice
📋	Checklist
💡	Idea
🎬	Action
📖🔍	Definition
✋	Fail-fast-pit-stop
🤝	Ask for co-creation
👹	Herertical view

Source of the icons: All icons from https://uxwing.com/; all licensed as free for use (https://uxwing.com/license/)

As you embark on this journey with us, remember that the goal is to enhance your effectiveness and confidence in using case studies as teaching tools and writing them as scholarly articles in iterations. This book aims to equip you with the skills needed to captivate your audience, whether in a classroom or a publication.

Thank you for exploring the art and science of case studies with us. We are excited to be part of your educational journey and look forward to your contributions to the vibrant world of case-based teaching and writing.

Martin and Urs

Supplementary materials

Designed to complement the theories and strategies discussed, download the following workbooks to actively engage with the content:

1. Case Teaching Workbook: https://doi.org/10.5334/bdb.e
2. Case Writing Workbook: https://doi.org/10.5334/bdb.f

The case method in the spotlight

History of the case method

'History is a set of lies agreed upon.' – Napoleon Bonaparte

It is widely believed that the case method was 'invented' at Harvard Business School, specifically in the early 1920s when Wallace Brett Donham was the school's second dean (he took office in 1919).

Well, Socrates and Aristotle and other famous instructors from history, if they were still alive, might have something to say about that! The description and discussion of a particular constellation, challenge or situation as an educational vehicle has long been part of philosophical research and instruction.

However, there's no denying that Harvard Business School's pioneering adoption and early use of the case method in management education continues to be hugely influential in many business schools across the world, as well as other professional education institutions.

Some background

So, let's unpick the history a little: It was in 1870 that the new dean of Harvard Law School, Christopher Columbus Langdell, began to teach law with cases and introduced the Socratic method of questions and answers in classes. Half a century later, this inspired Donham, a graduate of the law school, to introduce the case method at Harvard Business School. The school had been founded only in 1908, long after the foundation of the law school, which dated back to 1817.

Following a request by Donham, the marketing professor Melvin Thomas Copeland created a collection of real-life business problems that was published in 1920 (*Marketing Problems*). In parallel, Donham redirected the efforts of the 'Bureau of Business Research' to create case studies for use in class. In the early 1920s, the Bureau created a wide range of cases, with the first case, 'The General Shoe Company,' dating back to 1921. Having completed this founding work, the Bureau was later disbanded as Donham believed all faculty should begin to write their own cases.

How to cite this book chapter:
Kupp, M. and Mueller, U. 2024. *The Ultimate Case Guide: How to Successfully Teach and Write Case Studies.* Pp. 1–26. London: Ubiquity Press. DOI: https://doi.org/10.5334/bdb.a. License: CC BY-NC 4.0

Continuing inspiration

Throughout the 20th century, Harvard Business School was instrumental in inspiring other business schools (and institutions beyond business/economics) worldwide to adopt the case method. It remains a cornerstone of management education in the 21st century and, despite the sweeping cultural, historical, and technological revolutions that have taken place since Donham's day, it continues to thrive and develop.

There are certainly other ways of teaching professional disciplines such as business, but we firmly believe that the case method, by enabling participants to anticipate decisions and deal with challenges that they might face in their future careers, is one of the most powerful, effective, and inspiring, and will remain so into the future.

What is a case study?

> *'I don't pretend we have all the answers. But the questions are certainly worth thinking about.'*
> *– Arthur C. Clarke*

So, what is a case study?

This is a short question but a big one. First, let's look at a few definitions:

> *A business case imitates or simulates a real situation. Cases are verbal representations of reality that put the reader in the role of a participant in the situation. (Ellet 2007)*

> *A case is a description of an actual situation, commonly involving a decision, a challenge, an opportunity, a problem or an issue faced by a person (or persons) in an organisation. A case allows you to step figuratively into the position of a particular decision maker. (Mauffette-Leenders, Erskine, & Leenders 2005)*

> *Beginning with the very simplest definition, a case is a story. This story describes a factual series of events that occurred in the past ... the reader is expected to do one of two things: (1) make a decision or recommendation to the protagonist for a course of action to pursue, or (2) perform an analysis of the action that has already taken place. The key words in this description are story, factual, past, decision, and analysis. (Vega 2013)*

> *A case is a vehicle for learning. It can be briefly defined as: An account or description of a situation, or sequence of events, which raises issues or problems for analysis and solution. (Heath 2015)*

We do not want to add another definition and we are rather undogmatic about case studies and the case teaching method. We will therefore just consider anything to be a case study that is the recounting or description of a development or situation (real or fictional, old or recent), that – when reflected upon by participants – will allow them to learn and develop.

The metaphor of the 'patient in the room'

Next to philosophy and law, medicine has also long relied on something like case-based instruction for the development of future medical doctors. After getting acquainted with the basics (anatomy, biochemistry, etc.), medical students will learn much of their trade by dealing with real patients. They will get exposed to real patients with real issues and will then be asked what they would do now. This typically requires the combination of a diagnosis (analytical view: what is the issue?) with the proposal (or execution) of a treatment (action phase: what to do now?) – just as medical doctors will usually need to do after leaving medical school and starting their medical practice. Every day they will be exposed to new cases and will need to deal with them; especially in general practice, they might need to deal with a broken arm, a case of asthma, a patient with depression, indications of cancer, etc. And they will need to develop routines to quickly assess the situation and propose treatments.

Professionals in business also constantly need to deal with challenging constellations: Which candidate should they pick for a job? Should the company expand into a different country? What is the best way to increase factory productivity? How can they account for physical property (e.g., land) that could be sold at much higher price than the current value as recorded in the balance sheet? How do they become more innovative as an organization? And dealing with such questions also requires the combination of analysis with a recommendation/action. So why shouldn't the educational process also be a bit like medical education?

Medical schools have the advantage that they typically operate hospitals and therefore have access to many such 'cases' in reality. And, while business schools can (and sometimes do) operate businesses as laboratories for learning, it is mostly through case studies that many institutions and educators from around the globe try to bring reality to the classroom and develop the students'/participants' ability to deal with such complex constellations.

As with any metaphor, there are limits as to how comparable classical case studies for business schools are relative to patients in the medical school. But, to illustrate a few aspects, we will occasionally come back to this metaphor at various places in this book, but next we will first use it to differentiate between teaching cases and other types of case, most notably research cases.

Teaching cases versus research cases

This entire book is only about cases used for teaching, and all the types of case listed below are teaching cases. However, you may also have heard of research cases. These differ in several ways and, although a detailed explanation of their focus and purpose is beyond the limits of this book, the main differences are set out below.

A research case (usually published in an academic journal) provides a descriptive analysis of a real-life situation from a theoretical viewpoint. This means there is no protagonist or unfolding 'story,' as is usually found in teaching cases. The purpose of the analysis is to test out hypotheses and explain the 'why' and 'how' of an event or series of events. Research cases can be used, for example, to identify economic and social trends, patterns, and behaviors.

Research cases may also include the 'solutions' to any problems or challenges that are presented. What the organization did after the initial complication and how this turned out afterwards are typically the key points of research cases. This is very different to teaching cases, where participants are expected to make decisions and come up with answers as if they were the protagonist depicted in the case – usually without knowing what the organization or protagonist finally did.

We can use the metaphor of the patient in the room to exemplify this point: In the medical domain there are also multiple different types of 'cases.' Essentially, to a doctor, every patient is a case. Cases can be described in proper academic journals (research cases). Cases can be shared from doctor to doctor in hindsight. And we have the patient in the room for the medical students. All of these can be 'a case' – but they are very different purposes (see Figure 1: Types of case in the medical domain,' below): Research cases and cases that are shared between doctors (e.g., at conferences in nonscientific publications) share a retrospective focus. They describe what happened, how a situation was solved/dealt with, and what the outcome was. The patient in the room for the medical students has a very different purpose: the focus is to look forward at what should be done with this specific patient.

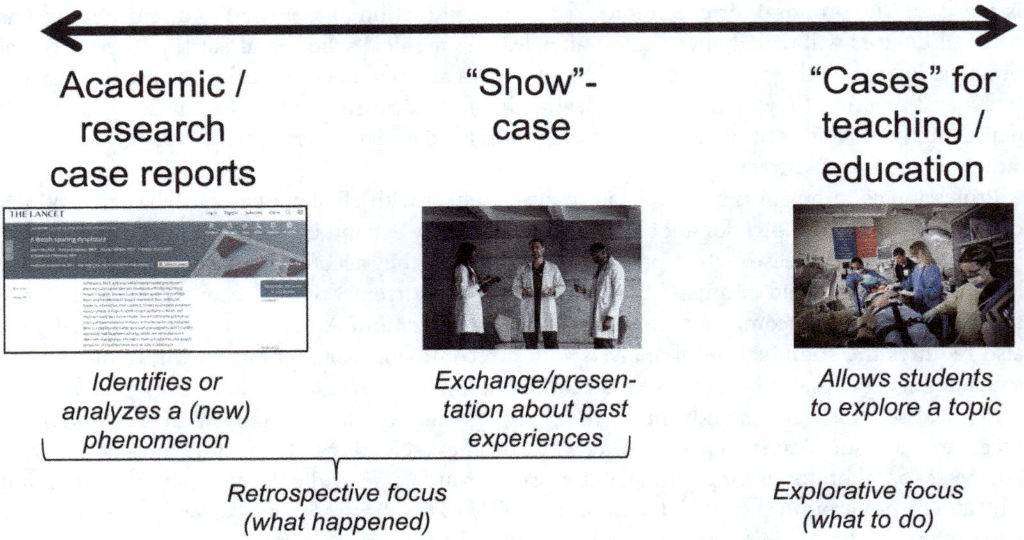

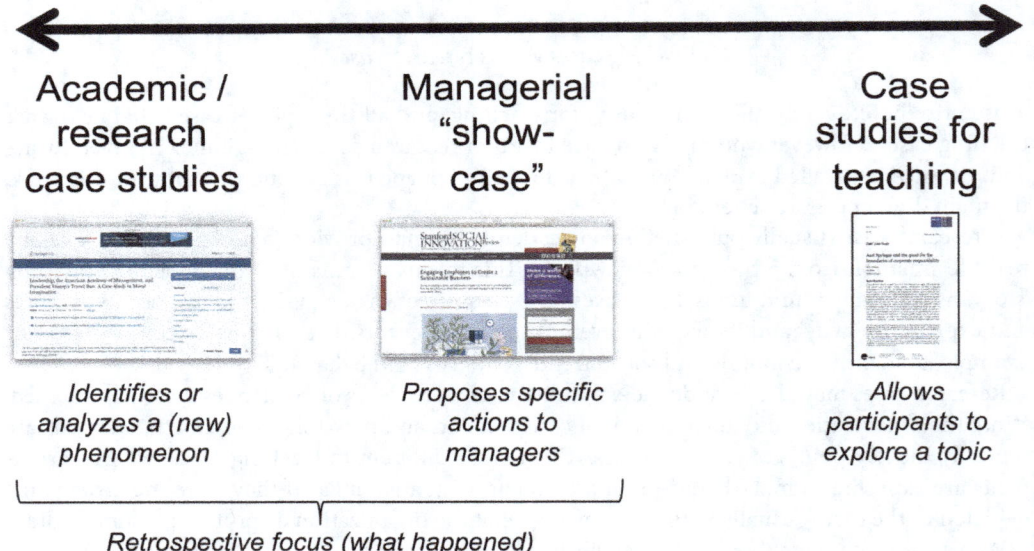

Figure 1: Types of case in the medical domain. Sources: middle: Pexels (https://www.pexels.com/de-de/foto/mann-menschen-frau-suche-5452189); right: Aspirus Health (https://www.aspirus.org/uploads/public/images/services/awh-trauma-center.jpg).

Figure 2: Types of case in business/management.

Similarly, in the domain of business and management there is an equal plurality of cases (see Figure 2: Types of case in business/management,' below): the problems professionals really need to solve, research cases for academic journals, experiences that are being shared as best practices, and case studies for educational purposes. The remainder of this book will focus entirely on cases for teaching purposes. But it will be important to keep this differentiation in mind – and to share it with your students and with potential case protagonists if you are thinking about writing a case for teaching purposes about them.

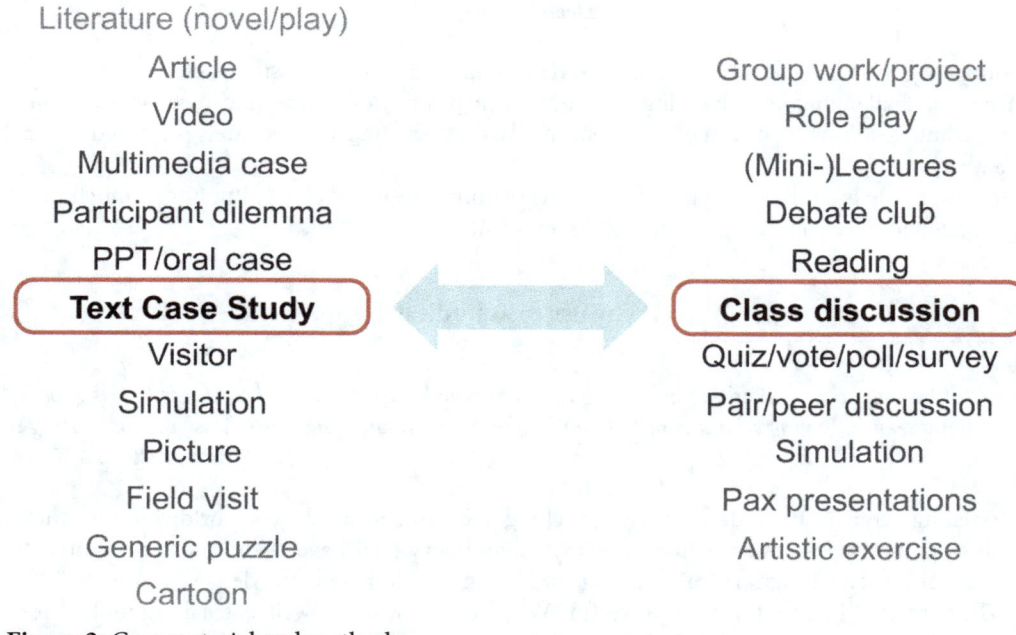

Figure 3: Case material and methods.

Plurality and diversity

We are rather undogmatic about case studies and the use of case studies for education. We believe in instructional plurality, the diversity of methods and materials. And we would also argue that it is impossible to understand the true potential of case-based instruction until you have observed or been part of a few successful case teaching sessions. This is because a classical (Harvard-style) text case study does not truly become a case until it is used in the classroom – and, even then, it becomes something slightly different each time it is taught, drawing out different responses, different opinions, different reactions. Yet, despite this unpredictability (which we would argue is itself exciting and stimulating for both participants and facilitators), a well-orchestrated session will lead to the desired and preplanned learning outcomes as intended by the case author or the facilitator.

In the figure below (see Figure 3: Case material and methods') we have visualized our undogmatic philosophy: We strongly believe that facilitators can choose from a wide range of materials that they want to use in class, like literature, articles, videos, multimedia cases, or a real manager in the room. All of this can be the 'patient in the room.' Additionally, educators can choose from a wide range of teaching formats like letting participants research something in class, running group works, orchestrating a role-play, and so on. In our opinion, skilled facilitators mix and match materials and formats according to the educational objective but also to increase engagement through the plurality and diversity of materials and methods. The traditional text case study used in a full-class case discussion is only one of many combinations possible. We think that this is important to keep in mind.

Much of our description will (seemingly) focus particularly on the use of text-based case studies in a class discussion, but we will continuously highlight how you can broaden your didactical inventory and how to use and develop exciting and relevant material for highly interactive class sessions.

Deep learning

Ultimately, a case is what it becomes in the classroom. A great case session is electric and transformative, challenging and changing perceptions, inspiring fresh ideas, and new ways of doing things, and resulting in the type of deep and lasting learning that is rarely achieved in any other way.

So, yes, a case is all those things set out in the definitions quoted above. But it is so much more than that, and only you can discover this for yourself.

Why use case studies?

> 'Not having heard something is not as good as having heard it; having heard it is not as good as having seen it; having seen it is not as good as knowing it; knowing it is not as good as putting it into practice.' – Xunzi

Storytelling is one of the oldest forms of teaching and can be traced back worldwide over thousands of years. Fables, folklore, literature, myths, and fairy tales have been used for centuries to instruct, guide, encourage critical thinking, and impart wisdom and knowledge.

Why is this? Why are stories so powerful? Why do they work so well as teaching tools? More specifically, why do case studies work so well?

Stories are compelling and engaging at many levels. They are vivid and real to the reader or listener. They trigger multiple associations, memories, and emotions. They allow us to relate new information to existing knowledge. We are drawn into previously unexplored territory, encouraged to embrace new ideas, understand from different perspectives, develop empathy, and think in fresh ways. We can be jolted out of old ways of doing things, encouraged to discard stale and tired attitudes, and be inspired to do more and be more.

The functions of a teaching case

The beauty of cases as a vehicle for learning is that they are – just like any other stories – multifunctional. They are used to:

- make content relevant for participants by infusing reality into the classroom;
- enable participants to apply and use concepts, theories and frameworks to a given situation, allowing them to relate new information to existing knowledge;
- provoke controversy and debate to increase emotional engagement and the reconfiguration of knowledge by shaking up existing preconceptions;
- excite participants by stimulating their curiosity and interest;
- improve participants' ability to deal with uncertainty and ambiguity;
- make participants aware of different possible perspectives and angles for almost any given situation (and thus develop their ability of critical thinking and creativity);
- allow participants to fail in a safe environment, receive constructive criticism and learn from the failures of other participants;
- allow a constant change in the role of learner and teacher – case discussions continuously enable participants to instruct each other;
- enable an intense social interaction with other participants leading to a significant improvement in communication and discussion skills;
- increase retention and memory, by linking academic content to an interesting and intriguing story.

The benefits of case studies for online education

When Clinton P. Biddle wrote 'The General Shoe Company' in 1921, he intended the case to be used in a physical classroom – and this is how cases continued to be used for almost an entire century. But, with the rise of online education, cases did not lose their appeal. Quite the contrary, we would argue that they even provide extra benefits when used for online teaching. Why is that? Because we all know the vicious circle of online teaching and learning: participants feeling boredom, remaining silent, switching off mentally, giving in to off- and online distractions and temptations, and their feeling of being invisible (which they often are when they shut off their cameras in live online sessions) – and, because live online teaching often slows things down, we have seen many educators moving to lecturing in online settings, which then in turn reduces students' engagement and the circle starts all over again.

So how can cases be of help in such contexts? When used well, cases will drastically enhance interaction, excitement, and participation. The use of breakout sessions and collaborative or interactive tools (more on this later in the chapter on case teaching) can help to make online sessions just as enjoyable and interactive as a classroom case discussion.

Broadening the horizon of participants

Finally, we'd like to share this great quote with you that offers an inspiring answer to the question we started with: 'why use case studies?'

> A good case is not just a well-written document and a teaching tool, or even simply an engaging story about a compelling management issue. It is an opportunity to embark on a personal journey of discovery, for the case writer, for the teacher, for the participant, and sometimes for the company. It opens horizons instead of closing them; it raises new questions instead of merely answering them, and it provides a rich forum for personal development and growth. That's what a good case is all about. (Kassarjian & Kashani 2005: p. 105)

 From theory to practice with Martin

I frequently meet with alumni of programs I have taught on. One question that I love to ask alumni is about their most vivid memory of their time at university or school. Very often the answer centers around a specific case study. Alumni answer things like 'I especially remember the case of Steinways when they were attacked by Yamaha and had to decide whether they should retreat to the premium market segment or try to attack back' or 'I will never forget the story of Damien Hirst and how he was able to find a new who, a new what, and a new how.' Cases just have the capacity to stick!

Broadening the horizon of facilitators

But not only participants benefit from the case method. The facilitator also benefits in various ways from applying the case method. For example, test-teaching early versions of your case material might benefit the further development of the material if you want to write your own case. Sometimes you can even look for stories and cases that support early versions of research papers and by discussing this with students or executives the facilitator gains additional insights and new perspectives on this material and the kind of questions he should ask in her research.

> **From theory to practice with Urs**
>
> For more than five years I have been teaching case teaching and writing workshops for the Case Centre. I always try to run these workshops participant-centered, with lots of discussions around the teaching experience of the participants. This has always been very revealing for me. While I have a background in executive education teaching, I have profited hugely from the experience in undergraduate and master's teaching of my participants. And it is due to the exchange of experiences and knowledge around challenging teaching situations (for me these are 'cases'!) that I had the chance to learn a lot from my participants. This book benefited strongly from this.

Criticism of the case method

'With no positivity, there is no hope; with no negativity, there is no improvement.'
– Criss Jami

We are strong advocates of the case method in an undogmatic understanding. We teach with cases, we write cases, we love cases. But we have to acknowledge at some point: not everyone is a fan. And we are not just talking about students who complain about having to read and prepare (often dreadfully long and boring) case studies. Relevant criticism continues to be made of the case method by educators, MBA alumni, and others who put forward reasoned arguments against its use.

Instead of simply dismissing these viewpoints as not worthy of attention, we think it is more productive to think through these negative critiques, decide if they have any validity for us, and use them to continually refine and improve our approach to teaching with cases.

Here are a few of the main criticisms commonly made against the case method (as condensed from, e.g., Hühn 2013, Khurana & Nohria 2008, and Nohria 2012, or discussions with colleagues and participants in our case method workshops):

- The case method is theory-free – we just know certain things; so why always start a case discussion from scratch?
- They just train the use of tools – they neither truly invite reflection nor do they provide education.
- Cases focus too much on business practice and not enough on key ideas, theories, and frameworks.
- Cases are presented as requiring a 'solution' but, in reality, many situations are insoluble.
- Cases claim to bring a 'slice of life' into the classroom, but in reality they can only simulate real-life situations.
- Too many cases are about success stories, which is not truly representative of the business world.
- The situations depicted in cases are being assessed with the benefit of hindsight – again, this does not reflect life in the real world.
- Because cases are taught in a safe classroom environment, they encourage a false sense of security.
- The main challenge to be addressed is immediately obvious from the case – there is no requirement to identify the problem as there would be in real life.

Of course, we have to admit that all these criticisms contain an element of truth. However, our advice is to take the criticism on board and use it positively to enrich and enhance your case teaching and writing. These objections demonstrate the importance of carefully thinking through your approach to using cases in the classroom.

> Some criticism of the case method can be rebutted or dealt with through respective use/production of case studies. A good example is the criticism that students have 'a false sense of security' (Hühn 2013) in the case method classroom. In our opinion, this is a strength, not a weakness.
>
> The safe environment offered by the case method classroom is vital to the success of a case teaching session. It is the perfect arena to test ideas, challenge opposing theories and opinions, explore potential solutions, practice persuasive and effective public speaking, and build self-confidence and develop numerous other skills that will be invaluable in the world of business.
>
> Another criticism leveled at the case method – that students are presented with an obvious problem to solve – can also be safely rebutted. It is true that most cases will present an immediate issue (problem or challenge), very often highlighted in the opening paragraph. However, a well-written and effective case will also include an underlying issue that will only become apparent with close analysis. There is a requirement to 'dig deeper' and uncover these underlying issues; this can be a tricky and demanding process – and a world away from being 'presented with an obvious problem to solve.' See page 21 for more on immediate and underlying issues.

Two powerful objections against the case method that we have heard many times concern (1) the danger of false generalizations from cases and (2) the fact that cases tend to be success stories with positive 'solutions.' Next we give some examples of how these two objections have informed our approach to case teaching (and writing) and what you can do about them.

The potential danger of wrong syllogisms

Empirical evidence that is based on one single case is usually not reliable or relevant. It is very dangerous to conclude any general rules (or advice for success) from an individual case study. And we truly believe that this is not the overall idea of good case teaching. Quite the contrary: a good case study should be able to demonstrate or exemplify theory and research results. Cases are examples of what happened in one specific company/organization in a specific situation. The reflection on whether this observation is generalizable should be informed by research, which clearly goes beyond the case and should be based on empirical evidence or existing theory.

Keeping this criticism in mind when preparing your teaching will hopefully keep you from falling into this trap. There are many ways to prevent this from happening. You can, for example, teach several cases on one topic. When teaching the subject of pricing you could use a case on a B2B and a B2C company and additionally cases from a small and a large company or from companies in different industries (high- versus low-fixed-cost businesses) of different regions. This variety will help the students to develop a broader sense of the topic and will allow you as educators to make elaborate links to proper research. Additionally, you might want to add some (short) lectures on important research results and, last but not least, you will make available pre- and postcourse readings that embed the individual case in the larger theoretical context. The discussion of the individual case is an important element of the learning but it is far from the only component. The case discussion should instead be accompanied by many other elements, like textbook readings, journal articles, and potentially additional insights from other disciplines, to avoid wrong syllogisms.

The potential danger of wrong syllogisms applies even more when you write your own case study. We will get back to this in the chapter on case writing, but we often have come across case authors who got overly obsessed with their own cases. They heard about an interesting decision or action of a company and then wrote a case that centers on this decision or action. And on the surface such cases sometimes almost seem to be convincing. Just as a fictitious example, a case author might try to write about Uber along the following argumentation:

A. Uber is successful
B. Uber did these five things
   1. Uber eliminated the middlemen/intermediaries
   2. Uber is innovative
   3. Uber's business model is disruptive
   4. Uber's business model makes use of network effects
   5. Uber was connected to startup networks (Techstars)
C. Ergo: if companies do these five things they are/will be successful

As convincing as this might sound upon superficial reading, this is a nonsensical argument – that would result in a case study with unsubstantiated lessons learned for the participants. That the syllogism above is wrong is very quickly evident if we just replace the things that Uber did:

A. Uber is successful
B. Uber did these five things
   1. Uber has a company name beginning with U
   2. Uber was founded in the USA
   3. Uber is active in the transport industry
   4. Uber quickly expanded into other countries
   5. Uber developed an app for all cellphone OSs
C. Ergo: if companies do these five things they are/will be successful

Good luck to your students if they learned in your class that they had to do these five things to be successful. And such wrong syllogisms often get amplified by hindsight bias.

Cases are unrealistic because they all have 'solutions' and usually deal with success stories

Another relevant and often legitimate criticism is related to the previous point: Most published case studies somehow deal with successes, protagonists or organizations overcoming initial challenges or obstacles, seemingly providing a blueprint for how the participants should act in the future. And, because when discussing cases we usually look back in time, participants and educators are at risk of allowing later successes to bias the discussion.

However, it is important to realize that not all cases are about success stories – and they should not be! Choose the case studies that you plan to teach and write carefully and include cases that cover failures. This can be particularly effective if the case itself is seemingly about a success story, but the company or protagonists have run into trouble because of what they did as a response to the constellation described in the case.

This is a good way to highlight that real life outside the classroom is complex, messy, ambiguous, and often frustrating: we must face facts and acknowledge that failure (although not necessarily a dead end) and dilemmas without 'good' solutions are ever-present in the world of business.

> **From theory to practice with Urs**
>
> I teach business ethics – and, to do a proper job as educator, I need to prepare participants for difficult ethical choices, i.e., for constellations in which none of the possible courses of action could legitimately be labeled as a success. But even in my domain most existing case studies describe cases of successes – e.g., how a company overcame an issue such as corruption or child labor. This is clearly important but doesn't help my participants to fully grasp my domain. And, because few organizations want to openly discuss ethical missteps and challenges, I occasionally resort to additional, alternative material for case style discussions, such as literature, history, movies, documentaries, anonymized stories from alumni etc.

So what can you do to overcome the positivity bias of case studies? Here are a few ideas:

- Make sure to include at least a few cases of failures into your syllabus.
- If an organization or protagonist later runs into problems or falls out of favor, intentionally keep the case in your curriculum – but make this a point in the session (see e.g., Yemen & Clawson 2014).
- Focus your debriefing on when/why the protagonist's course of action could have failed or under what circumstances we could label the action as not good/not optimal.
- Contrast the case with other examples of individuals or organizations that showed similar behavior but failed.

In essence, we believe that much of the criticism of case studies has a bit of truth, but that the criticisms usually relate instead to the way in which case studies are being used or written – and that all of them can be overcome through a reflective use of the method.

> **Dealing with criticism of the case method when teaching with or writing case studies**
>
> – Don't ignore the criticism; use it to improve your teaching and writing.
> – Ask key questions and review your approach to case teaching.
> – Take positive steps to counter criticisms.
> – Avoid wrong generalizations (wrong syllogisms) by clearly linking your educational objective (for case teaching) or underlying issues (for case writing) to science and existing literature.
> – If exploring an entirely new domain without existing literature: highlight what is generally accepted business knowledge and what is speculation or what might be limited in validity to a specific context.
> – Be robust in your defense of the case method: if you don't believe in it, neither will your students.
> – Check what your students learned from the cases (beyond cognitive download): if their learning is biased, change your didactics or the case study.

What makes a good case study?

'The art of teaching is the art of assisting discovery.' – Mark Van Doren

We'll start with some great observations made by J.B. Kassarjian and Kamran Kashani that appeared in a 2005 book chapter they wrote entitled 'Writing an Effective Case for Executive Programmes':

> A 'good case' is not just a well-written document and a teaching tool, or even simply an engaging story about a compelling management issue. It is an opportunity to embark on a personal journey of discovery, for the case writer, for the teacher, for the participant, and sometimes for the company. It opens horizons instead of closing them; it raises new questions instead of merely answering them, and it provides a rich forum for personal development and growth.

That's what a good case is all about.

Although these observations were made in relation to cases used in executive education, we believe they apply equally well to cases used with any level of participants, from undergraduate upwards.

Let's drill down a little more and look at some of these issues in more detail with the help of Derek Abell, who listed 10 points to look out for in a good case (IMD Technical Note 1997/2003). These should prove useful both when writing a case and when selecting one to teach:

1. Make sure it's a case and not just a story.
2. Make sure that the case tackles a relevant, important issue.
3. Make sure that the case provides a voyage of discovery – and even some interesting surprises.
4. Make sure that the case is controversial.
5. Make sure the case contains contrasts and comparisons.
6. Make sure the case provides 'currently useful generalizations.'
7. Make sure the case has the data required to tackle the problem – not too much, and not too little.
8. Make sure the case has a personal touch.
9. Make sure the case is well structured and easy to read.
10. Make sure that the case is short.

Below, we look at each of these points in a little more detail.

Make sure it's a case and not just a story

This is an interesting distinction and one we agree with. First, we believe that a good case also should be a story. Or perhaps, more accurately, an unfinished story – one that requires input from class participants until a resolution or 'ending' can be reached. It is the need for this crucial contribution that means a case becomes more than 'just' a story: learners are not passive readers; they become active participants, usually by 'stepping into the shoes' of the protagonist to make the decisions that will drive the story forward. Abell here rightly points to the fact that the text of a case study in itself is comparably irrelevant. Or, as Heath (n.d.) puts it, '[a] teaching case has little or no merit in isolation. It is simply one component within a teaching or learning situation. Its purpose is to connect with other components in the situation, to establish linkages and trigger activity within and between students and facilitator.' What is key is to provide the material for a relevant exploration, discussion, or exercise in the class – and for that a good story might just not be good enough.

As Abell notes, '[s]orting out the wheat from the chaff, getting to the essential issues, and learning to ask the right questions, are key objectives in case teaching.' (Abell 2003, p. 2)

Make sure that the case tackles a relevant, important issue

Writing or teaching a case that is irrelevant for the intended audience is a waste of time. Participants will neither engage with the subject matter nor learn anything of importance from it. The issue or issues covered in the case must have substance and address a problem, challenge, or situation that is of direct relevance and significance to your participants.

Think back to the metaphor of the patient in the room: If you train future medical doctors in north Finland, they might have less/little use from investigating malaria patients, and future dentists might not need to deal with broken ankles. Along this line of thought, just make sure to provide your participants with case constellations that they are likely to experience in a similar shape or form in their professional futures. And, if that is not the case, only pick cases that you as an expert in your domain truly believe to be important for your participants to know.

Make sure that the case provides a voyage of discovery – and even some interesting surprises

We like Derek Abell's take on this: 'Good cases are like onions – the more you peel away the outer layers, the more you discover inside' (p. 3). We could not put it any better ourselves. It is important for a case to have both an immediate issue and an underlying issue. The immediate issue is the 'hook' that will kick-start the classroom discussion. This will then lead to the discovery of more fundamental underlying issues as the 'outer layers are peeled away.' (For more on the differentiation between immediate and underlying issues see the section 'The Issue of Issues,' page 21.)

To illustrate this peeling process, let's use the famous Harvard case study 'Rob Parson at Morgan Stanley' by Diane Burton (1998). The case (and usually also the case discussion) opens with the question (or vote) of whether Paul Nasr should propose Rob Parson for fast-track promotion to managing director or not – the immediate issue. This is really an intriguing and compelling issue because Rob Parson is so incredibly successful in his task of selling and building a business. But at the same time his colleagues dislike him strongly and he has a history of breaking rules and of being perceived as uncooperative. When discussing the case students will quickly realize that the decision for or against the promotion depends on many deeper level issues (the underlying issues) such as organizational culture, strategy, and the role of HR processes and systems. And, to discuss the case, they will almost inevitably peel the onion layer by layer.

Make sure that the case is controversial

In line with our earlier discussion of the (sometimes legitimate but addressable) criticisms of the case method, a case should not have easy answers or 'solutions.' There are usually no easy answers in the real world of business, so they have no place in a case. (And, if there are really easy answers, we do not need to discuss them in class and do not need cases for them…) The best cases provoke intense discussion, disagreement, and debate, leading to deep and lasting learning. It is helpful if there are multiple, possibly legitimate responses to the immediate issue; only in this way will participants develop their ability to see alternative options and will grow the habit of creative thinking. In addition, by taking part in such passionate discussion, participants also learn a wide range of key skills such as the ability to argue cogently for or against a point of view, as well as expertise in listening, responding, communicating, and persuading.

Make sure the case contains contrasts and comparisons

There is no single recipe for success in business. That is why the best cases use contrasts and comparisons to demonstrate how different ideas, approaches, cultures, and personal styles can all lead to positive (or negative) outcomes. A family business can be as successful as a publicly listed firm. A self-made entrepreneur with humble family roots might be just as successful as a PhD in engineering with an MBA from a top school. Class participants can gain greater wisdom and perspective from such contrasting examples and find positive role models for their own approach to management and business.

And if an individual case study does not provide such comparisons and contrasts, educators should aim to achieve the same effect and learning by using contrasting case studies over the span of an entire course.

Make sure the case provides 'currently useful generalizations'

As mentioned above, a case should be relevant to the intended audience. However, the best cases also offer the opportunity to draw wider lessons from the specifics of the case. For example, can the lessons learned and conclusions drawn also be applied in a different country, culture, company, or marketplace? Often this cannot be achieved by the case alone (see also above the justified criticism of the case method) but with the help of pre- or postreadings, with small lectures during class, or with the use of additional and complementary cases in other sessions. It is your task to ensure that students reflect upon and understand the extent to which the generalized business knowledge that you explored with a specific case can or cannot be translated to other situations.

Make sure the case has the data required to tackle the problem – not too much and not too little

The amount of data contained in a case should match your educational objective – this is true for cases that you pick from others but even more so for cases that you might want to write yourself. You will probably have experienced this already when you used a case in class: how much of the information contained in the case did you or your participants explicitly refer to during the case discussion? Quite often we ask our participants to invest an hour in reading a case, without then ever really utilizing the data. Sometimes you might have the opposite experience where the case in itself does not provide all the information that is necessary to have a deep conversation. If either of the two is true for you, search for cases in which the data is more in line with what you actually need in class.

Abell notes that there are three types of data that a good case should always include:

1. Enough information to enable a meaningful debate in the classroom. This may include details about the industry itself, the company, where it is in place and time, and the historical context. These descriptions should be jargon-free and easy to follow and understand.
2. Exhibits at the end of the case, for example financial statements, growth rates, and key company announcements.

3. Biographical and background information about key players in the case to help participants understand their values, approach, and temperament. An individual's strengths and weaknesses can often have a decisive influence on the outcome of a case.

And, if you are writing a case, it is vital to include not only all the data that the students will need to discuss the case. Also think about other case teachers and all the information that they would need to successfully use your case (and include such data either in the case or in the teaching note). This will give your case wider appeal as no specialist or 'insider' knowledge will be required to teach it. At the same time, you should resist the temptation to overload your case with data. Always keep your learning objectives in mind and take out any unnecessary material.

Make sure the case has a personal touch

Cases usually center on problems (often a decision that needs to be taken). But all problems are someone's problems. Problems do not exist without a perspective – and the perspective matters to how professionals in practice can or should respond to them. Accordingly, this perspective needs to be visible in the case – and for that the protagonist is key (again both for your case selection as well as for your own case writing). A protagonist who participants can easily identify with is one of the key components of a successful case. A set of facts, figures, and events without mention of any key personnel or their reactions to the unfolding situation would be very dull indeed in the classroom.

Cases with video supplements of the case protagonists or, even better, a guest appearance by the protagonist or an expert from the industry or company in the classroom will also help the case to come alive for participants.

Make sure the case is well structured and easy to read

A potentially great case can be ruined if it is badly written and poorly structured. We offer some in-depth advice on writing cases later in this book (see page 244), but when it comes to selecting cases written by others there is a simple rule: if you do not find the reading to be enjoyable or at least acceptable, your participants will be unlikely to join your class with excitement about the upcoming case discussion.

Make sure that the case is short

We agree with Abell that cases should be as short as possible, while not leaving out key details. This is one of the fundamental attributes of a good case. When picking a case, ensure that the expected reading time is somewhat fitting to the educational objective and the time spent for the case in class. Make sure to consider different reading speeds (especially when you have participants for whom the case language is not their native language) but also different time budgets for case reading for different types of participants. We also have to remember that today's generation of learners are more used to scanning the web and dipping in and out of various websites, often within seconds of landing; they take in information differently and are often resistant to long pages of text. We have to adapt our approach rather than bemoaning theirs.

And also, when writing a case, always keep your audience in mind. For example, executives will often have little time to plow through a 20- or 30-page case, experts (or more advanced students) in a domain might need less background, etc.

> **What makes a good case?**
>
> Make sure that the case you pick for teaching or writing:
>
> – is a case and not just a story,
> – tackles a relevant and important issue,
> – provides a voyage of discovery,
> – is controversial,
> – contains contrasts and comparisons,
> – provides 'currently useful generalizations,'
> – includes the data required to tackle the problem,
> – has a personal touch,
> – is well structured and easy to read,
> – is short.
>
> Source: Derek Abell, IMD Technical Note (1997/2003).

Variety of cases

'Variety's the very spice of life that gives it all its flavour.' – William Cowper

Following our undogmatic approach, we will gladly consider many different types of educational material to be at least case-like. So, feel free to call various things a 'case study.' But at the same time it is important to clarify what we are talking about. In this section, we will propose a few differentiations and logical separations between different types of material that can be used for teaching purposes.

Case dimensions

In the heads of many facilitators, there is something like a 'classical' case study for teaching purposes. This is what many have in their minds whenever they talk, think, or write about case studies. This will typically be a 'Harvard-style' case, i.e., a rather extensive description of a real managerial challenge from the (recent) past, with lots of data and information and a decision to be taken. And cases of this type remain to be very influential and important for management education. (If you think back to the metaphor of the patient in the room, this is rightfully so. Such rich and long cases try to get close to the constellation and information that the protagonist faced in reality.)

However, case-based teaching can be done on the basis of a very broad range of different case types. We identified seven dimensions along which case material can be systematically differentiated. We think that this is important to keep in mind, as this information will not only help you to find the right case for your specific teaching objective but also to increase the variety of your teaching material and therefore ultimately engagement. (And, if you intend to write a case, make deliberate choices along all of these seven dimensions. The choices should not happen by accident but after careful reflection.)

Prospective (decision) vs. retrospective (nondecision)

 Retrospective cases invite participants to engage in a discussion about events that are – even from the time of the case – looking backward. They will usually have no or at least less of a decision/action focus. The discussion will typically focus more on how the company/person got to where she is at the time of the case than discussing how she should move forward. Typical examples for this kind of case study are 'Benihana of Tokyo' (Sasser & Klug 1978) or 'Madonna: Strategy in action' (Anderson & Kupp 2006). In both cases the teaching objective is to untangle the ingredients of the success by analyzing the history/past from the very early beginnings to the time that the case is set.

Prospective cases typically call for an action, decision, plan, etc. that is – from the point of time of the case – forward-looking. Most of the time prospective cases will have a decision focus. And, while prospective cases will still mostly be situated in the past, the discussion will typically focus more on how the company/person could or should move forward from the time that the case is positioned. A typical example for this kind of case study is the classic case 'Rob Parson at Morgan Stanley' (Burton 1998). While the case provides a lot of detail on the past performance of Rob Parson, the discussion focuses on the difficult decision of whether to promote Parson to managing director that his manager, Paul Nasr, faces – therefore it is forward-looking.

Many cases will contain both perspectives: Retrospective cases still implicitly include the question of how the person or organization should go forward and if the success can be sustained or not. Prospective cases, on the other hand, also usually need historical data because the past of an individual or firm will limit the options that are available for the future. We still believe this to be an important differentiation, as the educational objectives will have different emphases: Retrospective cases are usually great to improve analytical skills and to exercise certain tools. In comparison, prospective cases focus more on the development of decision-making skills.

Real vs. fictional

This dimension is not really a dichotomy but rather a gradation. What we mean by this is that there are for various reasons grades of fictionality of cases. There are, for example, completely fictional cases. A good example would be the 'Who's Responsible for the Drawbridge Drama?' (Müller & Schäfer 2010). The moral dilemma of this case is completely made up (with the first known publication in Katz 1978). Other cases are real but might be rather old, in some cases even historical. A famous INSEAD case study centers around Napoleon Bonaparte (Kim et al. 2008) and there are multiple cases about the race to the South Pole (e.g., Fischer, Crawford, & Boynton 2003). While these cases are based on real stories, they are historical and desk-based. Then there are more recent and up-to-date cases that for whatever reason had to be either sanitized, anonymized, or disguised. While you could argue that these cases are real as they are based on real stories and often involve field research, from a participants' point of view these cases nevertheless feel less real as they do not know the real names of the people involved and/or the real company name, location and the like. For us the next level up in terms of 'realness' is desk-based cases, e.g., cases on real people and companies purely based on secondary sources. While these cases are of course real and often contemporary, they frequently lack details and insights about the involved people. In these types of case, it is very likely that direct quotes from the protagonist or their specific point of view are missing or are less elaborated. Finally, there are real and contemporary cases based on field research and with company release. These cases are typically rich in information on the protagonist and all relevant people and specific insights into the company that would be hard to find in secondary sources.

Single text vs. several texts

There are different overall structures for case studies. Most cases are single case studies with an accompanying teaching note. But you can also decide to use a case series with an A, B, and potentially C or D case (sometimes also called 'multipart' cases, e.g., Vega 2013). Usually, the first case will be the longest part of the series, giving all the necessary background on the company, industry, protagonist, etc. It has a specific cutoff date and is often prospective with a clear decision to take going forward. Case B is then often a kind of update on what the protagonist or company decided to do after the constellation described in case A plus a new challenge. The B case is often only one to two pages long. This can then go on. Some cases have been published as a single case initially but have added a B and/or C case over time; some cases were immediately designed as a case series.

Besides a single case or case series, you can also choose to use several independent but related cases, for example cases on different companies facing the same kind of challenge or separate cases about the same organization, but looking at different topics (e.g., you can probably find accounting, strategy, change management, and operations cases about Nike). And, finally, you can decide to use an industry background note and combine this with a case study (or a case series).

Long vs. short

One of the most frequent questions we get during our case teaching or writing workshops is about the optimal length of a case. We will discuss the pros and cons of long cases in more detail in the case teaching and case writing sections. Here we just want to highlight the fact that the length of a case might matter, and that you should think about it. Most cases have somewhere between 15 and 35 pages but there are extremes in both directions. The catalogue of the Case Centre comprises more than 1,200 cases with only one page, e.g., the IMD case study 'MJ Basket' (Schmenner 2002). On the other end of the spectrum, the case 'The Mortgage for Pacific Tower' by Lynne Sagalyn and Jennifer Morgan (CCW141703) from 2014 has a length of 148 pages as it includes the full set of documents for a real estate mortgage deal. The average length of cases listed at the Case Centre is 12 pages; the average length of best-selling cases is 18 pages. When instructors search for cases, the most frequent search interval that they use is '< 10 pages.'

Complex vs. easy

The complexity of cases can vary considerably. Mauffette-Leenders, Erskine, and Leenders (2005) proposed three main factors that influence the perceived complexity of a case study (see also Lima & Fabiani 2014). First and foremost, there is the *analytical complexity* of the case study, which is mainly about the visibility of the problem that the case protagonist (and thus the students/participants) are facing. Some cases are very outspoken about the underlying issues and also the potential choices or alternatives, while others try to hide important facts and even try to lead the reader in the wrong direction. The second dimension of the case complexity (*conceptual complexity*) refers to the underlying concepts, tools, or techniques that the case study covers. These can be rather simple heuristics, checklist, or 2×2 matrices or rather complex theoretical constructs. And finally, there is the *presentation complexity*: the presentation of the case itself in terms of its volume and clarity (structure, writing style, visual presentation, etc.) will influence the perceived overall complexity of the case study for the readers.

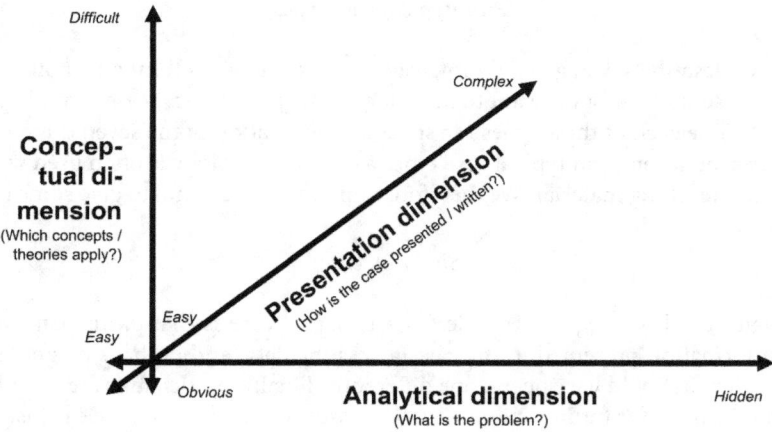

Figure 4: Dimensions of case complexity. Source: Adapted from: Mauffette-Leenders, Erskine, Leenders (2005). Learning with Cases. P.12.

Whether a case should be complex or easy along any of these three dimensions of case complexity should depend upon the intended learning outcomes – and we will come back to this aspect in the case teaching and case writing chapters.

Failure vs. success

We already touched on this topic when briefly looking at key criticism of the case method: most case studies describe situations of success (already in the case or as an update after the discussion). We believe that there are two main reasons for this. First of all, companies and also the case protagonist prefer to share their success stories and are sometimes even unwilling to talk about, let alone publish, their failures. Additionally, it is probably also driven by the fact that case studies for research frequently look at success cases. While learning from failures can be particularly powerful, there will be many fewer cases to select from.

Text-based vs. other formats and materials

The text-based case study is what most people have in mind, when thinking and talking about 'case studies' for use in classrooms. However, there are many other forms of material/content that can equally well be used to apply case-based learning methods. You might want to think about using cases from textbooks, mini-cases, live cases from your participants, video cases, multimedia cases, newspaper articles that you can enrich with more context or specific questions, literature, company or site visits, and many more.

An interesting point of view is that you can use different formats on the same underlying case idea over time. In that sense the different formats might represent different stages of adoption of the content. For example, you read an interesting newspaper article and decide to use it in class. You get positive feedback and decide to dig deeper into the story by adding more content; you might find some videos on the company. After using this material, you start to write your own short mini-case based on secondary material. Then, you might be ready to reach out to the company and conduct interviews, enriching your existing material with quotes and additional material. And, finally, you turn this into a video or multimedia case in close collaboration with the case protagonist.

Prototypical case types

While above we describe seven general dimensions to look at when thinking about, choosing, or even writing a case study, we now want to introduce some prototypical case types as proposed by Heath (2015). While each of these types is a specific combination of the seven dimensions above, we want to describe seven prototypical case types as this terminology is often used when instructors refer to their teaching material. We therefore think that it is helpful to give some background.

Situation case

Many cases fall into this category. The idea of a situation case is that participants are asked to analyze the information presented in the case, assess the data, and perhaps diagnose what went wrong or how things should have been done differently. Finally, participants are expected to make their recommendations for future action. Situation cases typically involve a clear case protagonist and some background information on other relevant people. They tend to be ambivalent between prospective and retrospective considerations, but during the case discussion a lot of emphasis will be on the retrospective analysis of the situation.

Decision case

A decision case is a situation case with a very clear decision (or immediate issue) to take (or solve) – i.e., the focus clearly shifts toward the prospective dimension (both in the case itself and in the class discussion). These cases put participants on the spot. They are expected to make a decision and come up with an action plan to implement their decision. To add to the difficulty, a number of different decisions and related action plans can appear equally reasonable and feasible.

Incident case

Incident cases are very short cases (often no longer than a paragraph or a page) that describe a single incident or event. They can be used to introduce, discuss, or illustrate a theory or concept, or to raise a particular point for further discussion. Incident cases are useful in a number of ways.

For case teachers: Incident cases can be a good option for new case teachers who want to 'dip their toes in the water' and get a feel for case teaching. They are also a useful option when introducing inexperienced students to the case method, especially as they rarely require preclass preparation.

For case authors: Incident cases often do not require an enormous amount of research and are therefore good possible starting points for first-time case authors. Because they are so targeted and focused they will also help to write cases that are perfectly suited for a very specific educational need.

Background case

A background case provides broader context and background about a specific function, industry, country, activity, etc. – but are dressed as a case. Instead of just providing facts, they adopt the narrative logic of other types of case. Background cases offer a more interesting and compelling way to provide necessary information and data than more conventional handouts (such as industry or technical notes) or reading material which students can find boring and off-putting. Background cases can be used in combination with more traditional situation cases as part of a wider course of study.

Exercise case

Exercise cases are often used when students are required to carry out quantitative analysis (e.g., for accounting, finance, statistics, or operations courses). Working with numerical data within the context of a case is more interesting for students than simply being presented with a set of statistics to manipulate as an abstract exercise. Exercise cases can be fictitious and often have no or only very little detail about the involved people.

Complex case

This is a more challenging version of the situation case. The complex case deliberately includes a lot of potentially distracting information that may look important at first sight but is in fact superficial and irrelevant. In the logic of the three dimensions of case complexity, they tend to drastically elevate complexity in the analytical and presentation dimensions. With such cases, participants face a double challenge: they need to use their powers of discrimination to distinguish what is relevant and significant before then going on to recommend a solution or course of action.

Best practice case

This is something that we do not really like, but what many outsiders to the case method often have in mind. Best practice cases tell a company success story, offering an example of best practice or a benchmark to aim for. Protagonists and firms like to be presented as such best practice cases and they can also work well from a mnemotechnical perspective: students easily remember creative approaches that made organizations successful. But beware: next to the legitimate criticism of success-focused cases (as discussed above), best practice cases will either tend to become victim to the hindsight bias or alienate students who think that the organization or protagonist should have done something else.

The issue of issues

'Leadership is the day-to-day communications about the real issues.' – Chris Argyris

Whether you are writing or teaching a case, you must be clear about the issues to be explored. This is an important aspect of the case method, and we will return to it later. But we believe that much of the success of the case method derives from the integration of multi-layered issues in a case. And for that there is an established terminological differentiation. Cases should include clearly defined:

- immediate issue(s), and
- underlying issue(s).

 Immediate issues are those issues (it might well also be just one issue) that are directly visible to the reader of the case study. They are usually presented early in the case study, frequently in the opening paragraph, and typically present the question, dilemma, decision that the case protagonist faces (you can find more on immediate issues, opening paragraph, and protagonist in the case writing chapter).

Underlying issues are usually not explicitly mentioned as issues in the case but subject areas that will need to be addressed in order to properly respond to the immediate issues in the case. They are like the bottom of the iceberg: they are not visible but are the much bigger part of the overall learning objective. (In Abell's terminology, they are the inner part of the onion that only get visible after peeling off the outer parts.) They are usually closely linked to the educational content needs that you already identified earlier.

The immediate issue in the case, also known as the 'hook,' will generally be used to get the classroom discussion going. This often works well when the immediate issue is introduced in the opening paragraph in the form of a key question facing the protagonist. This helps participants to quickly 'step into the shoes' of the protagonist and debate possible solutions. The immediate issue should ideally be controversial, offering a range of potential responses that may appear equally viable. This provides excellent material for a lively discussion at the start of the case session.

This initial debate should then lead to the realization that there are more fundamental problems affecting the immediate issue (think back to Abell's metaphor of peeling the onion). These are the underlying issues to be addressed. Underlying issues are usually difficult and challenging to deal with, often having no clear-cut answer or single solution. This, of course, reflects the reality of life in the real world of business.

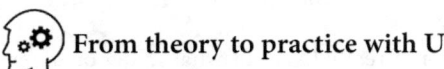 From theory to practice with Urs

In my 'Vodafone in Egypt: National Crises and Their Implications for Multinational Corporations' case (cowritten with Shirish Pandit), Hatem Dowidar, CEO of Vodafone Egypt, is faced with an immediate issue: the government has ordered Vodafone in early 2011 to suspend communication services in certain areas, including Tahrir Square, the center of protests against the 30-year rule of President Hosni Mubarak.

Should Dowidar follow this instruction? This is an immediate issue, or hook, that will get the classroom discussion going (there are also other potential immediate issues in this particular case).

The debate about this immediate issue faced by the protagonist will then lead to a more in-depth discussion of the complex underlying issues in this case. These involve fundamental and often intractable questions about, for example, law versus ethics, conflicts of interest, personal responsibility, and possible limitations to international expansion for multinational firms.

Good and exciting case discussions usually benefit significantly if the immediate and underlying issue are not too closely related to one another (this is what Abell called the 'voyage of discovery'). Sometimes you will come across a case study where immediate and underlying issues are almost identical. Just as an example, think about a possible case study with the underlying issue of the development of a sustainability strategy. The case opens with the protagonist sitting at a desk thinking about a sustainability strategy. But we would contest that you should rather select (or write) a case in which the protagonist faces a difficult choice that is then gradually leading to the underlying issue. In the example of the sustainability strategy, the protagonist might need to decide whether to use the recycled material A, which will require the application of more chemicals, or material B, which not only requires fewer chemicals but is also cheaper. But when participants then discuss this choice they will need to go back to the current state of the overall sustainability strategy and what might need to be done additionally.

> **☰ The issue of issues**
>
> - Clearly defined immediate and underlying issues are vital for great cases.
> - When teaching a case: pick a case in which the immediate and underlying issues are not too closely related so that there is enough space for the 'voyage of discovery' (Abell).
> - Use the immediate and underlying issues to orchestrate class discussion when teaching a case.
> - When writing a case: include both and make sure that they are separate from one another, but in a way that responding to the immediate issue will require touching on the underlying issues.

The organizational context

'Always design a thing by considering it in its next larger context – a chair in a room, a room in a house, a house in an environment, an environment in a city plan.' – Eliel Saarinen

Your institution or department may already fully embrace the case method, faculty and teaching staff might be actively encouraged to teach and write cases, and students/participants might be completely used to the case method as key educational mode in all programs. If not, we hope you will develop the confidence to introduce or increase use of the case method at your organization. We are passionate advocates of the case method and hope we can persuade you to become one too.

From our own experience, but also from feedback that we get during case method workshops, we believe that an organization must think through a couple of elements to be able to really embrace the case method. We will briefly discuss three of them: student preparation, HR policies, and support to faculty and teaching staff.

Familiarizing students with case method

The extent to which students in degree programs and participants in executive education will be used to the case method will vary significantly across institutions. If multiple teachers in the same program use cases, we strongly recommend that the respective schools prepare participants for the case method. Here are a few things that schools can do:

> **☰ Familiarizing students with case method**
>
> - Inform your students about the use of case studies – and about the expected benefits of the method.
> - Provide guidelines about expected behaviors from participants in case discussions.
> - Start the course with rather easy and controversial cases so that students immediately debate and start to appreciate the value of the case method.
> - Make your students familiar with the 'The short cycle case study screening' (see below).

The short cycle case study screening

Participants who are not used to the case method are often surprised by the amount of preparation necessary for a case-based session. In programs with many cases this can quickly lead to a feeling of being overwhelmed. According to our experience this is often because they use inefficient techniques to read a case – most notably, they start to read a case very carefully from the very top to the very bottom of the text. However, this is not only inefficient in itself; it also fails to achieve a legitimate and important learning objective, namely the students' ability to digest large amounts of text/data in short periods of time – a requirement that they will very likely face in their professional futures.

Raymond Corey (1976/1996) suggested starting case preparation by glancing over the entire text very rapidly. Mauffette-Leenders, Erskine, and Leenders (2005) came up with a more structured approach that we believe all educators, but also all participants, should know: the 'short cycle case study screening': They recommend the use of the following process to all participants – including the guideline that this process should not take more than about five minutes:

The short cycle case screening (adapted from Mauffette-Leenders, Erskine, & Leenders 2005):

1. Read the assignment questions (if any).
2. (Quickly) read the title and opening paragraph of the case.
3. Read all the chapter titles. Possibly skim parts of the text while looking for the titles – but only rapidly!
4. Read the closing paragraph.
5. Check all the exhibits.

(Up to this point this should not have taken more than three to five minutes.)

6. Reflect on the type of case study, summarize your understanding (who, when, what, why, how?) and reflect on the assignment question(s) (do you have an immediate reaction/recommendation?). Summarize mentally or write it down as aide-memoire for the case discussion itself (especially when preparing well in advance!).
7. Only then read the full text of the case – when you already know what it is all about. As you now know what the case is all about: try to read as fast as possible.
8. If other prereading (textbook chapters, articles, etc.) is assigned together with the case, read the prereading first and only then the case!

With this process you will make the lives of your participants much easier. But it can help also you: when screening cases for your own use in class, the process is equally helpful. And, when you write a case, present your case in a way that the short cycle case screening works well for other educators and for the students.

Recruitment and promotion

Over and over, we have asked participants in our workshops on case writing and teaching how the case method is taken into consideration when recruiting and promoting faculty. And often we get the answer that it is not. We truly believe that this should change and that this might have the biggest single impact on how a school will be able to accelerate their efforts regarding the support and integration of the case method. (You get what you measure and incentivize.)

But we have also had exceptions to the rule and there are several schools that look out for the usage and production of case studies in their recruitment and promotion processes. Quite often this was described to us as organizational campaigns in which the case method was adopted at the institution in reaction to accreditation or benchmarking efforts. Such schools would check and discuss with job candidates their teaching methods and they will have a set of questions around how to engage participants, typical material used, and of course also teaching evaluations.

When promoting faculty, it was the same. These schools had a set of criteria around teaching that included specific questions on the case method.

If a school just does not really focus on the case method as a didactical approach, if it does not select or reward people for mastery of cases, you can still keep doing it. You might have to do a bit more to convince your students that cases are relevant and helpful. But you will probably need to focus on other performance metrics (usually academic publications) instead of putting a lot of effort into writing and publishing your own cases – at least until you reach tenure. However, even if the school does not institutionalize the case method, you can still – e.g., during job talks, when being part of the hiring/selection committee – use your case method mindset and give such candidates a bit of a push.

Organizational support

A third key element is organizational support for using the case method. We think that a couple of elements should be in place. When looking at teaching with cases, we strongly encourage schools to set up teaching mentors, buddies, or small teaching support groups. These groups should meet regularly to discuss teaching methodology and even more importantly they should sit in each other's classes at least once per semester, or, better, twice. Peer feedback is extremely valuable not only to improve but to reflect in general and to get additional inspiration about, for example, great cases, good opening questions, and the like. The same goes with writing cases. Here we found that the best schools have a small unit that offers dedicated support for case writers, through copyright checking, professional editing, and formatting up to support for desk research and writing. All of this will lower the entry barrier for faculty to get started with case writing – and that might be different things in different schools.

There are a few persuasive arguments to be made in favor of encouraging case teaching and writing in an organization. The benefits of the case method for students are numerous, as explained above. To summarize, cases are extremely powerful teaching tools. They make for exciting and memorable teaching sessions, offering participants the opportunity to take on board new ideas, learn new skills, become familiar with management theory and concepts, and develop expertise in areas that are vital for a successful business career, for example listening, speaking, defending a point of a view, evaluating various options, and decision-making.

And there are also numerous benefits for the organization, starting with the fact that cases are seen as positive in both ranking and accreditation. A clear profile and strong organizational support might also attract strong candidates to the school. Finally, the case method is widely used in executive education programs and typically receives high evaluations from participants. If your school wants to grow its executive education portfolio it therefore pays off to institutionalize the efforts, mainly by being very conscious in the two areas described above: recruiting/promotions and organizational support.

Managing the organizational context for the case method

- Introduce participants to the case method at the beginning of a course/program.
- Make participants familiar with the short cycle case screening process (and adopt it for yourself).
- Gain a clear picture of where your organization currently stands in relation to the case method.
- Specifically look at the recruiting and promoting processes and whether they consider case teaching and writing.
- Support faculty and teaching staff in their effort to use or even write case studies.

References

Abell, D 1997; 2003 *What makes a good case?* IMD Technical Note (IMD-3-0731).

Burton, D 1998 Rob Parson at Morgan Stanley (A-D). *Harvard Business School Case Study*. 9-498-054 (for case A). Available at https://www.thecasecentre.org/products/view?id=43700.

Corey, E R 1976; 1996 The Use of Cases in Management Education. Harvard Business School Note 9-376-240 (originally published in 1976; revised 1996).

Ellet, W 2007 *The case study handbook: How to read, discuss, and write persuasively about cases*. Boston, MA: Harvard Business Review Press.

Heath, J 2015 *Teaching and writing case studies – A practical guide*. 4th ed. The Case Centre.

Hühn, M P 2014 You Reap What You Sow: How MBA Programs Undermine Ethics. *Journal of Business Ethics*, 121, pp. 527–541.

Kassarjian, J B and Kashani, K 2005 Writing an effective case for executive programs. In: Strebel, P and Keys, T *Mastering executive education: How to combine content with context and emotion – The IMD guide*. Harlow: FT Prentice Hall, pp. 105–117.

Khurana, R and Nohria, N 2008 It's time to make management a true profession. *Harvard Business Review*, October.

Lima, M and Fabiani, T 2014 *Teaching with cases: A framework-based approach*. Self-published. Available at https://www.amazon.com/Teaching-Cases-Framework-Based-Marcos-Lima/dp/1496137868/.

Mauffette-Leenders, L A, Erskine, J A, and Leenders, M 2005 *Learning with cases*. 3rd ed. Richard Ivey School of Business.

Nohria, N 2012 What business schools can learn from the medical profession. *Harvard Business Review*, 90(1–2): 38.

Vega, G 2013 *The case writing workbook: A self-guided workshop*. New York, NY: M.E. Sharpe.

Yemen, G and Clawson, J G 2014 When effective cases contain contradictions and paradoxes. *The Washington Post*, October 31. Available at https://www.washingtonpost.com/business/when-effective-cases-contain-contradictions-and-paradoxes/2014/10/31/b3219e2c-5eb2-11e4-91f7-5d89b5e8c251_story.html.

Xunzi 1990 A Translation and Study of the Complete Works. Volume II, Books 7–16. Translated by John Knoblock. Stanford, CA: Stanford University Press.

Teaching a case-based session

This chapter has been written with first-time case teachers in mind, but also contains multiple ideas and suggestions for educators who have some, or even extensive, experience in case teaching:

- If you are not yet experienced with case teaching: follow this chapter step by step in the correct sequence and use this book and the accompanying workbook to develop or review your learning objectives, reflect on your specific learning context, identify potential cases, and develop your teaching plan.
- If you are more experienced and are already using several cases in your classes but are still looking for ideas to further improve your teaching: use the table of content, the index, or the FAQ section of the webpage for this book to navigate directly to the relevant sections of this book.

Our case teaching beliefs and philosophy

There are several excellent (work-)books, articles, notes, and guides on case teaching. This might question the need for yet another case teaching guide. The initial idea for this book was born when we were looking for the ideal accompanying book for the case teaching and case writing workshops that we conduct either at our own institutions or for the workshops organized by the Case Centre. We quickly realized that the book that we had in mind did not exist. One of the reasons was that we developed some core beliefs around teaching in general, but even more so for case teaching. And we wanted these beliefs to be reflected in the book.

We therefore think that it is important to start the chapter on case teaching with these beliefs (or you could call it our case teaching philosophy). Everything that we write about later in this chapter, all the different elements, techniques, and tools that you can use, will play into one or even several of these core beliefs. And here they are:

How to cite this book chapter:
Kupp, M. and Mueller, U. 2024. *The Ultimate Case Guide: How to Successfully Teach and Write Case Studies.* Pp. 27–111. London: Ubiquity Press. DOI: https://doi.org/10.5334/bdb.b. License: CC BY-NC 4.0

> 1. **Prioritize method over content**
>   - Respect the social dimension of learning
>   - Beware the importance of non-technical content
>   - Make use of humor and ensure psychological safety
>
> 2. **Elevate your participants to eye-level**
>   - Be flexible in the flow
>   - Don't outsmart
>   - Take them seriously and trust the class
>
> 3. **Experiment a lot and find your own path**
>   - Observe others and get observed
>   - Bring your own personality to the class
>   - Find safe contexts to try new materials and methods

Figure 5: Our case teaching beliefs and philosophy.

Prioritize method over content

The case method is not the fastest route to convey knowledge to participants. Readings, lectures, video instructions, etc. will achieve that in a much shorter time. But the case method has the capacity to help your participants learn much and deeply. If it comes down to tradeoffs, we suggest prioritizing the method over the content. Why?

Respect the social dimension of learning

Books have been used for learning and education for centuries – but we still have schools and universities. Why? Why do people make the effort of going to school (or joining synchronous or asynchronous online classes) to learn, when they could simply read a book? Among other reasons (see below) it is because conceptual learning benefits from deliberation and discourse with others (see e.g., Asterhan 2015).

A participant's opportunity to ask questions, test assumptions, and argumentations and interact with other humans (sometimes in circles) strongly helps to deepen conceptual understanding. And we would contend that this is even true when comparing human-led or -orchestrated learning opportunities to mere interaction with artificial intelligence. Our teaching needs to take this into account and provide opportunities for interaction, exchange, and deliberation among our participants. This points to the importance of study groups before and after class sessions, group assignments, pair discussions and full-class interactions. And the case method is ideally suited to do exactly all of this.

Beware the importance of nontechnical content

Beyond the technical content and knowledge, our students have much to learn to be ready for their professional futures: creative and critical thinking, argumentation, communication (especially speaking in front of audiences), listening, dealing with diversity, digesting ambiguous material, decision-making, empathy, judgment, curiosity, etc. None of these is developed in only one case-based session, but through the use of case studies all of them can grow.

Think back to the metaphor of the patient in the room: Much can be learned about medicine from books. But when they stand around a patient with other students and are guided only through the diagnosis and recommendations by smart questions from the educator, the students can learn together – and much better and deeper. The same is true for business. Our participants will mostly end up in organizations with other people – sometimes in organizations with hundreds of thousands of others. Their ability to discuss managerial challenges with others in their jobs will be a key qualification and possibly more important than any single piece of content knowledge that you can provide them with.

So, when you run out of time or believe you need to make a content input, critically ask yourself if the content is really so important. In many cases, we would contest that you should probably prefer to stick to the case method and sacrifice a bit of content.

Make sense of humor and ensure psychological safety

Ensuring psychological safety is an important precondition for an open case discussion. If participants fear being penalized for comments or questions, they will be reluctant to contribute. The overall atmosphere in the class therefore needs to be safe, open, and transparent – the focus needs to be on deliberating jointly, not on fighting against each other. And, from our experience, humor can be an incredibly powerful way to ensure this psychological safety and to foster a class culture that really supports case teaching. We have seen many great educators in action – and, while their styles were extremely different, there was mostly an element of fun, with laughter in the class as a visible expression of this culture. And a bit of self-mockery can contribute to this a lot. We recommend giving it a try, even though Martin at least once had a (surprisingly) negative experience:

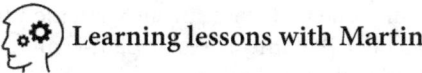 **Learning lessons with Martin**

I have learned that using humor and self-mockery when singling out participants in class can sometimes backfire and destroy trust. A class I was teaching in Portugal had begun very well with lively interaction among the students. About half an hour in, we ended up talking about different salary levels, and I asked why professors typically earn more than garbage collectors. A student responded: 'Because they are more important for society.' I believed this to be a good moment for a bit of humor and self-mockery. I laughed and asked: 'What will have the worse effect on society, if garbage collectors or professors go on a strike for a month?' A comment that resulted in general laughter of the class and allowed me to move on. The student didn't contribute again, but in a class of 70 this went unnoticed.

However, after class the student approached me to tell me how awful I had made her feel by joking at her expense and not giving her the chance to justify her remarks. As a result, she had decided to make no further contribution.

This incident brought home to me just how fragile trust can be. And it was also a salutary lesson to realize that very few participants would have the courage or take the time to confront a teacher in this way, so there have probably been many more situations where I had potentially destroyed trust without even realizing it.

Elevate your participants to your eye level

Our second core belief is that the biggest opportunity of using the case method is to completely change the learning atmosphere from the classical master–apprentice constellation to a collaborative relationship. In the classical master–apprentice relationship, the master imparts their knowledge either by telling or showing, for example by giving a lecture or running an exercise. The case method offers the chance to break with this power relationship and to explore and therefore learn together.

For this to happen, it is of the utmost importance that the participants feel enabled to shape and steer this discovery. They must be on eye level with the instructor. We know that the instructor is fundamentally in charge in the sense that they pick the topic of discussion and the case, that they have a clear teaching objective to achieve, and that in face-to-face settings they are often physically in front of the class ('in the pit'). But, at the same time, they should be flexible and open in how to achieve the learning objectives and, even more, must remain open to their own discoveries. Having observed many great instructors from a wide range of institutions, we concluded that three important elements are conducive to achieving this goal of elevating your participants to your eye level.

Be flexible in the flow

The most important element in elevating participants to your eye level is to be flexible in your flow. In later sections of this chapter, especially when discussing the teaching plan, we emphasize the importance of rigorous and detailed planning. But it is important to remember that the objective of detailed planning is not to then follow this plan rigorously but quite the contrary. The detailed plan will enable you to be more flexible. Having worked on a detailed plan will tell you which parts (and how much time you had planned for them) you might have to (or want to) skip because of an interesting discussion, a new and important point that was raised or a specific question that needs a longer answer or debate than expected. And this is exactly what we mean by being flexible in the flow.

This flexibility applies not only to the duration but also to the flow. Sometimes creative, smart participants make a comment that relates to a topic that was only planned to be discussed much later in the session. Rarely, it might be acceptable in such situation to park such comments (e.g., by writing the topic down on a board), but truly participant-centered teaching should be flexible enough to just change the intended flow and swap the sequence of topics.

Don't outsmart

The main idea of case-based teaching is to explore a topic together with the participants – not to demonstrate that you are more knowledgeable or smarter than them (this is presupposed when they join your class, face to face or online). When ending up in a situation in which a student disagrees with you – or in which you disagree with a student, resist the temptation to outsmart them. The purpose of the session is the learning of the class, not their perception of you. Instead of getting into a head-to-head debate, open the conversation to the entire class or outsource the conversation to after the session.

Take them seriously and trust the class

We recommend adopting the mindset that your students are smart, knowledgeable, and always have the capacity to add value to the discussion. We benefited personally from having done a lot of executive education – where you always need to assume to have a participant in the room who might have additional information about the case, the organization, the industry, or function. Even when teaching our own cases, we repeatedly had participants who knew more than us about the case. This is not a bug or danger to your academic credibility – you should rather turn this into a feature, by actively investigating your participants' areas of expertise and experience. Even your undergraduate students might have family members or have done an internship in the organization behind the case.

Taking the class seriously is not only limited to knowledge – it applies even more so to creativity and argumentation. For example, when a participant says something you disagree with, expect other participants to object for you – you usually do not have to do it yourself. The same applies to creative ideas that you are waiting for. And, if the class is a bit slow and not actively presenting the points you expect, do not tell them but rather ask questions. Trust the class – together they can come up with whatever you might need if you guide them through smart questions.

Experiment a lot and find your own path

There is no single way to success in case teaching. We both served as program directors for executive education and degree programs and had the advantage of getting to see many educators in action. And our key insight is that there are many different styles for highly successful case teaching. Over time and through experimentation you should work to find your own style of using the case method.

Observe others and get observed

If you were trained through case studies or have observed educators in other contexts, think back to your experience and learning: Which styles of case teaching did you like? Where did you learn most? You will probably realize that there was no single way to success. You will have had a few extroverted and a few introverted excellent teachers – and both worked. You will have had case teachers who gave much control to the class and others will have kept most of that for themselves – and both worked. Some of your educators might have been more structured and others will have improvised more – and again both worked. What works is the method in itself! The case method has been used for more than 100 years for very different participant groups in very different settings. The method is proven. Your challenge is to adapt it to you, to your personality, to your educational objectives, to your school, to your overall context. And for that we recommend trying to observe as many colleagues as possible – and to invite others to observe your sessions and collect their feedback afterwards.

Bring your own personality to the classroom

You are not a machine but a human being! This can legitimately become visible in the class – and it should for various reasons. It will help you to elevate your participants to eye level. But even more importantly it will help you to become a better case educator.

 From theory to practice with Martin and Urs

Just as a short example: In the past, both of us were asked to take over sessions from other educators – whom we had previously observed teaching exactly this session and case. The first time delivering these sessions usually felt artificial and fake when we initially tried to mimic the instructional style and process. Only after turning these sessions into 'our' sessions did they become successful. And this required us to adapt the sessions to our personalities. Both of us are more on the improvisation end, so we needed to let go of the teaching plan and exact sequence before getting comfortable with the respective sessions.

Do not try to just copy the teaching approach of even the best or most impressive educator you have ever seen. We know this feeling of being not as good – but only by adapting case sessions to your personality can you get equally good. (Also: do not simply rely on the teaching plan as proposed in a teaching note of a case study – you need to adapt it to your specific setting and to your instructor personality.)

Find safe contexts to try new materials and methods

Adjusting your teaching to your personality will likely require experimentation, but in many institutions there seems to be little space for that. We would still contest that at least some level of testing is possible in all contexts. Find less important sessions and try out new learning formats (e.g., if you have never tried a role-play), new cases, other types of material, etc. Do not limit yourself to classical text-based case studies but also test the extent to which you can use the case method's Socratic approach to enable learning by asking smart questions.

The case teaching process: an overview

'The profit we possess after study is to have become better and wiser.' – Michel de Montaigne

Effective case teaching starts long before your class begins and often goes well beyond it. Your focus might be on your in-class performance, and that is our focus in this book too. However, we believe it is important to approach case teaching more broadly and to think about it in different stages. This chapter will therefore be organized along what we call 'the case teaching process':

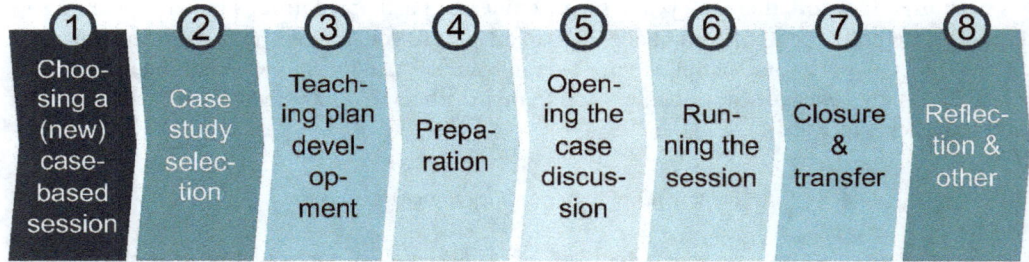

Figure 6: The case teaching process.

Choosing a (new) case-based session

Before teaching a case, you must start thinking about where and why you would like to add a case-based session to your teaching portfolio. If you do not use cases yet, you should approach this strategically by first identifying the best course for a case and then the best session within the identified course.

Identifying the right course

If you are like most of our case method workshop participants, you will teach a variety of courses for different students and will have done so for a number of years. In total you will have developed and taught many sessions and courses. Where should you start with case teaching?

We recommend choosing the right session strategically – looking mostly at factors such as where the (new) case-based session can add the highest value and where you can do so efficiently, i.e., with the least additional effort. To guide you in the identification of the session, we recommend first thinking about all the courses that you teach – and narrowing your search down to one of these courses.

> **☰ Questions to identify the best course for your (new) case-based session**
>
> - Out of all the courses that you teach, which course is worst in achieving the desired learning outcomes?
> - In which of your courses do you typically have participants (students) that might be open to a change to a case-based format?
> - Which course needs to be changed most anyway (e.g., due to a different number of sessions, bad student evaluations, new content to be covered)?
> - Which course currently has the smallest variety of different teaching/learning formats?
> - In which of your courses is the overall course content best suited for exploration, discussion, and debate?
> - **Your choice: the course for which you want to rework one of the sessions.**

Identifying the right session

After having identified a course with improvement potential, now reflect on the following questions to select an individual session within this specific course:

> **☰ Questions to identify the best session for your (new) case-based session**
>
> - Out of all the sessions that you teach in the selected course, which session works least well?
> - Which session would profit from/need most the flavor of real life (through the case study)?
> - Which of the sessions deals with concepts, theories, frameworks, tools that can best be distilled out of a case discussion (i.e., they could be the outcome of a case debate [induction] rather than being lectured and then applied [deduction])?
> - Which session deals with content that is the subject of public debate – and could therefore more easily be translated into a controversy in the classroom? For which of the subjects are there fewer 'right/wrong' answers?
> - For which sessions does the institutional context allow you to change to a case-based session (e.g., no predetermined content/material)?
> - **Your choice: the session that you want to develop as/turn into a case-based session.**

Learners and learning objectives

You are now almost ready to go on the hunt for the best possible case study for this particular session. But we would recommend you still postpone the search and first ponder the following questions that were proposed by Heath (2015):

> **☰ Learners and learning objectives**
>
> - Who is to do the learning?
> - What is to be learned?
>   - Knowledge? (knowing)
>   - Skills? (doing)
>   - Values and attitudes? (being)
> - How is it to be learned?
> - Where, and under what conditions, is it to be learned?

We will touch on some of these questions further, but it will be helpful if you have a clear idea about the session's learning objectives right from the beginning.

In the opening chapter, 'The Case Method in the Spotlight,' we discussed why cases are a great learning vehicle. Stories are compelling and engaging at many levels. They are vivid and real to the reader or listener. They trigger multiple associations, memories, and emotions. They allow us to relate new information to existing knowledge. We also highlighted the multiple functions that case studies can have and, even more importantly, how they can broaden the horizons of not only the participants but also the facilitators.

In the context of choosing a case-based session, you should now write down the specific learning objectives of the one single session that you identified earlier. What is it that you want to discuss with the participants in this session? What is it that you want them to take home and remember? This will also require you to answer the first of Heath's questions: 'Who is doing the learning?'

A learning objective might be one or several topics, theories, concepts, tools, frameworks, etc. that you would like to introduce, discuss, or apply in class, or it could be recent developments in business. And by this we do not mean the content of the overall course, let's say competitive strategy, but the content for the one single session you have chosen. For a course on competitive strategy, one session could focus on external analysis. Taking it even one step further, within external analysis, you might want to specifically teach PEST(EL) analysis or the five forces framework. This is the kind of level that you have to think of when starting to prepare yourself for using the case method – and for searching for and selecting the right case study. Sometimes (usually more rarely) the educational objective might also result from the *context* of your teaching, for example you want to illustrate some theory or concept in the context of a case with a female protagonist, or in the context of a small company or a specific country. We believe that it is necessary to be as specific as possible when defining your educational objective as this will help you to find the right case study and help you design the teaching plan later.

Case study selection

Several of the most frequently asked questions during our case teaching workshops center on searching for and selecting the right case studies. So, let's start with some practical tips around searching for cases.

Upfront, a rather prosaic point: Traditional cast studies are mostly copyright-protected. If you want to use them in your classes, you will need to acquire a respective number of licenses and if you work for a school with no or very limited budget or have large classes, this might quickly become infeasible. We therefore include comments about free options below.

Searching

One of the most obvious places to look for case studies are case repositories like the Case Centre, Harvard Business Publishing, Ivey Publishing, and others. These distributors gather many different case collections and make them available to others. ('Collection' is the term used to denote all cases from one institution or school.) The Case Centre (www.thecasecentre.org) has the world's largest and most diverse collection of cases. It holds cases written by individual authors as well as the collections of leading business schools around the world. It is also easy to search by topic and to find, for example, best-sellers, short cases, classic older cases, and translated cases. In addition, the Case Centre's free case collection offers thousands of quality cases from respected institutions, many exploring niche topics. Given the size of its collection, the Case Centre might be the best place to start if you have no idea yet what you are looking for – except for the learning objectives.

If you already have some ideas about possible cases, you could (or even might need to) look in other places, such as case platforms from individual business schools (e.g., INSEAD Publishing) or case collections from other producers of case studies that might not be available in the catalogues of the large repositories (e.g., Delta Leadership, the copyright holder of the famous Carter Racing case study by Brittain and Sitkin 1986/2006).

Another place to find teaching cases are so-called open-source educator portals, which is particularly relevant for you if your school does not have the required budget to buy licenses for case studies. There is a very fast-changing landscape of open education portals and websites. Open education is collaboratively producing and sharing knowledge. You can often find teaching cases as open educational resources (OERs). These are learning materials that can be modified and enhanced because their creators have given others permission to do so. The individuals or organizations that create OERs – which can include materials like cases but also presentation slides, podcasts, syllabi, images, lesson plans, lecture videos, maps, worksheets, and even entire textbooks – waive some (if not all) of the copyright associated with their works, typically via legal tools like Creative Commons licenses, so others can freely access, reuse, translate, and modify them (you can check https://opensource.com/resources/what-open-education).

Some platforms/distributors (either free of charge or with the usual license payment requirements) focus on collecting and providing cases focused on specific topics. One such example is a collection of case studies from the Rotterdam School of Management (RSM) Erasmus University, which produced case studies that can be used to discuss all of the 17 United Nations Sustainable Development Goals (SDGs).

There are a few academic journals that publish teaching cases, like *Case Folio, Global Journal of Business Pedagogy, IMA Educational Case Journal, Journal of Hospitality and Tourism Cases, Journal of Information Technology Teaching Cases, Sage Journal of Management Cases, The CASE Journal, The Case Research Journal,* and *International Journal of Teaching and Case Studies*. It might be worth screening their latest issues.

A few more places to search. Maybe you know from colleagues who produced but did not publish a case study. Reach out to them if their case might fit the session you selected. They might allow you to use their case free of charge. This is also true for cases that are sometimes shared at much lower or even at no license fee across partner schools from within the same network. And, finally, you could just give it a try and write your own case study – especially if you do not find a truly fitting case for the session you chose in the previous step of the case teaching process.

Where to look for traditional text-based case studies

- Case depositories (the Case Centre, Harvard Business School Publishing, Ivey Publishing);
- Individual schools or case collections (INSEAD Knowledge; Delta Leadership);
- Open-source educator portals (RSM Erasmus SDG Case collection; oikos Cases program);
- Subject specific portals and collections;
- Journals (*Case Folio*);
- Cases from colleagues;
- Cases from network schools;
- Writing own cases.

Search functions and search support at case distributors

Case distributors like the Case Centre or others have multiple possibilities to help you find the right case for your purpose. This starts with the basic search option where you can search for keywords, for example if you are looking for a case on a specific topic, company, person, region, country, etc. But very often, especially for broad search terms like 'marketing,' 'accounting,' or 'strategy,' you will have hundreds if not thousands of results. Then of course you can use the advanced search options and go into a lot more detail.

> ## 💡 How do you narrow a search to high-quality cases?
>
> Especially when starting to use cases in class, you want to be sure that they work in the sense that they are engaging and invite debate, that the case has all relevant information, and that there is a helpful teaching note. But how do you filter high-quality cases without having to read all of them? Here are four possible quality indicators:
>
> - *Going by institution:* Some schools are just famous for their case production. Even though not all their cases will be equally good, chances are at least that the case will not be extremely bad. Why? Most prestigious case collections have internal review processes – that will at least result in cases with an acceptable quality.
> - *Going by use:* Some case distributors (e.g., the Case Centre) show the use of the case over the last few years. You will get the information how many institutions or instructors have used the case in the past – and it is probably fair to assume that if a case was used more often it is more likely to also work in your context.
> - *Going by prizes and awards:* Another indicator is award-winning or best-selling cases; most case distributors clearly mark such cases separately – you could also actively search for the category winners of some of the case competitions.
> - *Going by author:* Yet one more approach is to look for top-selling case authors. For example, each year the Case Centre publishes a list of the best-selling case authors (across all their cases). You will likely find lots of great cases by starting with this list.
> - *Following recommendations from others:* Another way to find good and proven cases is to look at different syllabi from good schools. You will find syllabi from all over the world online. Just search online for them and then have a careful look for the teaching material and especially the cases that they use. You might start to look for syllabi from schools that you like or that are in the same region as yours or maybe in a region where you would like to have a case study on. If you already have a preferred case writer, check for their syllabi. And finally you should of course reach out to your colleagues who have previously taught the same or a similar course or who are teaching in parallel to you.
> - *Sticking to your experience:* Once you have found a case that works great for you, it might be worthwhile checking for additional cases from the same author. Most case authors have published several cases and, when you feel comfortable with one case study of a specific author, chances are high that her other cases might fit you as well.

Instead of searching by yourself you can also rely on support: Most case distributors offer a personalized assistance. You get in contact via phone or email, describe the course that you are teaching and the specific session that you need a case for, and they will help search for good cases for you.

Finally, you might want to consider subscribing to newsletters and updates from case collections or case distributors to stay informed. This way you will be informed not only about newly published case studies but about free cases, award winners, and upcoming competitions.

Searching for nontraditional case material

As already described in the 'Case Method in the Spotlight' chapter, we truly believe in instructional plurality, diversity of methods, and variety of the material. We suggested using the term 'case study' very broadly as any recounting or description of a situation (real or fictional, old or recent) that – when reflected upon by participants – will allow them to learn and/or develop. Therefore, we also want to highlight a number of maybe more unusual places to find good cases or case material. At all of the places listed below, you might find material that can be used as the basis for a case discussion, even if it is not a classical text-based case study with a teaching note.

Where to look for nontraditional text-based case studies

- Textbooks (often these include small cases at the end of chapters that might be very close to traditional case studies, but sometimes they just summarize [e.g., in text boxes] events or decisions that could be used for a case discussion).
- News (TV, newspapers, journals, online).
- Blogs, social media, newsletters for practitioners in your field, other sorts of webpages, etc.
- Videos (e.g., documentaries at video streaming services, YouTube, TED talks, etc.).
- Students, alumni, executive education participants sharing their experiences with you (informally or through assignments).
- Conferences, colleagues.
- MOOCs.
- Scientific journals.

Selecting

Searching for and identifying good cases is only the first step. With the vast amount of readily available cases – and assuming that you are not looking for a very niche case – you will probably still have the choice between multiple great case options for the session you identified earlier. So which of them should you choose (and on the basis of which criteria)? We therefore want to highlight some considerations that we use ourselves and that participants in our workshops told us that they have used successfully to narrow down the large number of potential cases to your final choice.

Screening

The search as described above will most likely have led to many results. Reading all of the candidates (cases and teaching notes) is probably unfeasible. We therefore propose to use the following process to quickly screen case studies for the development of a short-list of case candidates:

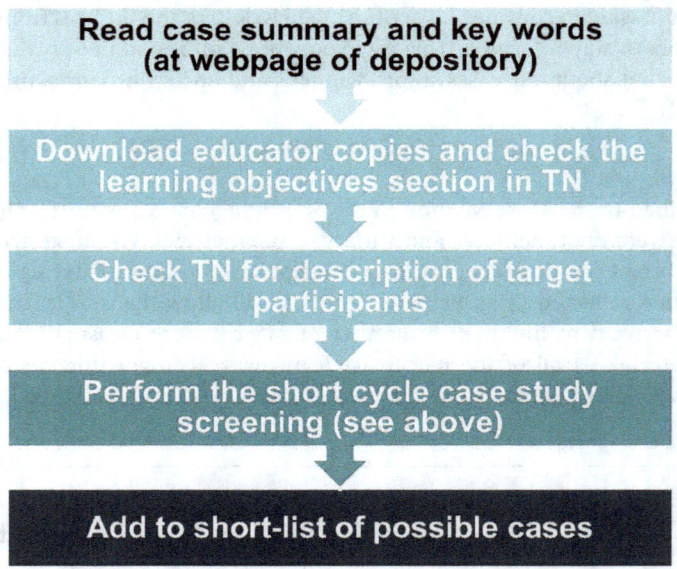

Figure 7: Screening process for short-listing of possible cases.

Be specific about your own educational objectives

Above we highlighted the fact that you should be very specific about your learning objectives. And the most obvious criterion to be used for the final selection is that the case should fit your learning objective as well as possible. Again, the more fine-grained you described your learning objective when choosing the (new) case-based session, the easier it will be now to select the matching case study. An easy way to do so is to compare your list of learning objectives with the keywords and stated learning objectives of the case, which you will usually find in the teaching note or product metadata.

The case should also fit your participant group. Undergraduates, graduates, master's students, postgraduates, and executives will react differently to cases. It is usually helpful if the participants can relate to the case protagonist (although participants might aspire to be a CEO one day, it might be difficult for them to imagine themselves being a CEO right now), the company (obviously some companies are much more known or liked than others), the industry (executives from a utility company might find it difficult to relate to the entertainment industry), or the geography (we used to teach an MBA in Portugal and we got the feedback that typical US or German cases were hard for the participants to relate to mainly due to market and company size, which were both far smaller in the Portuguese context).

But you might also want to consider elements like the length of the case (what are your participants likely to prepare? How much other work do they have to do?), the case complexity (we discussed the main dimensions of complexity – analytical, content, and presentation – in the previous chapter, 'Case Study in the Spotlight'), or how the case relates and fits with other cases/material you might use in your course.

You also might want to consider whether a teaching note for the case exists or not. A teaching note will make the preparation a lot easier, even if you ultimately decide to teach the case in a different way. The same is true for supplementary material such as videos, background notes, spreadsheets for quantitative cases, or presentation slides.

Old vs. new cases

While the age of the case could be seen as just another criterion to consider when selecting the case, we want to give a little bit of background on this question as it frequently comes up during our case workshops. We often hear (and experience ourselves) that participants complain about old cases. But there are good reasons to use old cases as some of them remain highly popular despite age (39% of the top-selling cases in 2022 were more than 10 years old, e.g., the case 'Benihana of Tokyo' by W Earl Sasser Jr and John R Klug is from 1972 and was a best-selling case at the Case Centre in every year from 2002 to 2022). Some of the reasons for their popularity are that they have meaning and relevance beyond their historical setting. They are proven to work in the classroom. But they also pose challenges for the instructor. For example, participants might google the background to the case, already existing case summaries and solutions, or just look up what happened in the meantime. As such, this is not a bad thing and could be a sign of the participants' interest. But it might also mean that participants, while looking up the solution, do not prepare properly or fall for the false assumption that what the company did is what is going to be discussed in class. There are a couple of ways to deal with these issues when choosing a rather old case. One way would be to be very proactive with the fact that the case is old. You might even want to give away what really happened in the meantime at the beginning of the session (or you could ask the participants to research the outcome and later company history). This might not only ease the discussion but prove the point that a case study is not about finding out what happened but about going on a learning journey together. You might also contrast what happened with what came up during the discussion as potential courses of action. You could also consider picking questions other than those mentioned in the teaching note to enforce thorough reading (in case you think that people have access to case summaries or solutions).

Copyright

Yet another important issue that frequently comes up in our case teaching and writing workshops is copyright. Here the main considerations are straightforward. First and foremost, you should always acquire the right licenses for cases authored by others for use in your courses. The easiest way to do this is by going through an established case distributor. Also be aware that, even if you found cases on (seemingly) public domain platforms or received cases directly from the author(s), there might still be a third party that legitimately holds the copyright (e.g., the school). Always double-check. Also make sure that the distribution of cases to participants (only paper, only via email, secure webpage, etc.) is in line with the license granted to you or your institution. Most schools have a central unit or person that deals with copyright issues and can help you to sort this out.

Sometimes it might be useful to adapt existing cases to your specific needs and context (of course not the written document, but the way you use them, for example by giving instructions to read only specific parts of the case). Sometimes it is helpful to add material to the case (e.g., technical information, updates, company information such as annual reports). Or you might want to combine two (juxtaposing) cases for one session (e.g., about same organization or with seemingly contradicting perspectives). This is not only unproblematic from a copyright perspective but we would even encourage you to think about these options, to personalize the case to your session, and to really 'own' the case.

If you actually want to abbreviate an existing case study, you need to contact the copyright holder. An alternative would be to highlight the parts of the case that participants need to read but to leave the rest of the case legible.

However, we strongly oppose case modifications like rewriting with changed timings, protagonists, perspectives, etc. There must be a considerable amount of newness to the story in order to justify this. Just changing smaller things like the timing is not enough. Obviously, we completely oppose any behavior like plagiarizing, eliminating the link to the case author, or simply not buying the adequate licenses.

Final choice

After having considered the learning objectives, the age of the case and copyright issues, it is time to bring down your short-list to one single case study. Here are the key questions that you should ask yourself if there are still a few possible cases for your chosen session:

Checklist for your final choice

- Does the case fit perfectly to your educational objective, to your participant/student group and to you?
- Is the case tested and proven to work? For example, did the case win an award or is it best-selling? Was it recommended to me by a trusted colleague? Is the case being used by others? Can I find the case in syllabi from others?
- Does the case truly fit the concepts/theories/tools/frameworks that you want to teach?
- Does the case fit well with respect to geography?
- Does the case fit well with respect to industry?
- Does the case fit well with respect to the gender, background, or seniority of the protagonist?
- Does the case fit well with respect to length? (Does the case length allow for a proper preparation? Is it in line with other readings?)
- Does the case fit well with respect to its complexity (including difficult language)?
- Does the case fit well with respect to the other cases used in the same or in other courses?
- Does the case allow you to vary the pedagogical methods?
- Do you really like the case (so that you can still teach it after a few repetitions)?
- Does the case have a (good) teaching note, a video, a spreadsheet, presentation slides, or other supplementary material?
- Can you link the case well with other readings (academic articles, textbook, technical note, etc.)?
- Is the case young? Or, if instead the case is old: Is it really so good that it should be used? Will the participants understand the context?

Teaching plan development

'By failing to prepare, you are preparing to fail.' – Benjamin Franklin

After identifying and selecting a case study for your session, it is now time to dive right into the teaching preparation. We recommend that a good starting point is to reflect upon the *teaching plan* that will describe what to include and how you want to run the actual session.

A *teaching plan* is a structured overview about the content and flow of a teaching session that usually includes information about the:

- opening question;
- introduction;
- different blocks of the session;
  - content/key learning points (e.g., tools, concepts, theories, or frameworks to be introduced or applied per session block) per session block;
  - learning formats per session block (e.g., full group discussion, small-group work, role-play, etc.);

    ◦ duration per session block;
    ◦ transitions from block to block;
  • closing section of session;
  • board plan;
  • postsession/additional activity for participants (e.g., follow-up readings);
  • overview of needed material, tools and technologies (e.g., online platforms, movies, sound, pictures, support slides) to run the session.

Context and constraints

To design a teaching plan, you need to consider the specific session context and potential constraints. Context refers to the participants (number, nationality, experience, academic background, language skills, prior performance…) and program context (where in a whole course is this specific session placed, what other topics do participants learn and discuss at the same time in other classes) but also the space that the session will take place in (classroom, online, or hybrid? Synchronous or asynchronous?). We want to focus in this part on the flow (and change) of different learning formats, the flow of session with respect to relating theory and case discussion.

Flow of the session

We believe that there are several strategic decisions to take or questions to ask when developing your teaching plan. The first is about the link between the flow of your session and your topic or underlying subject. Based on your subject, the flow of the session might be either convergent or divergent. Convergent topics or subjects start with a problem and come during the session through discussion and discovery to one specific (and correct) solution.

There are many topics where there is a correct answer, for example when working on ways to calculate rents, the optimal duration of a specific project, weighted average costs of capital, or the like. In these cases, the flow of the session will be convergent. This is important to decide upfront as this will inform your teaching plan. For convergent case topics, you will have to plan for how to react when the participants go off-trail, how to make sure that you come to the 'right' solution in time, and how to deal with potential alternative solutions. On the other hand, you might want to teach a topic that needs a divergent session flow. Then you should start with a problem and during the session the participants will develop a series of potential solutions without one being the obviously right or correct one. Often topics in strategy, leadership, entrepreneurship, or ethics follow this flow. Again, this has implications for your teaching plan as you must prepare for situations where participants might focus on only one solution or where they have problems coming up with more solutions.

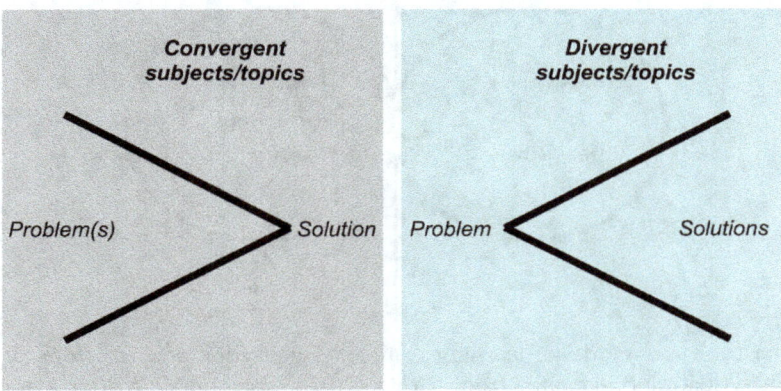

Figure 8: Convergent versus divergent subjects/topics.

Learning cycles

Besides the general flow of the session (convergent vs. divergent), it is important to think about the learning journey for the participants. In our workshops we often use the Lancaster model of learning as described by Heath (2015) or Binsted (1980) and originally developed by John Burgoyne at Lancaster University in the 1970s. The Lancaster model of learning identifies three different forms of learning and their interconnection: (1) knowledge input, (2) discovery, and (3) reflection.

The main idea of this learning model is that the facilitator should actively design a learning experience for the participants and can choose between these three different forms of learning or, even better, combine the three different forms in varying sequences. Using case studies can in our opinion support the design of complete learning cycles. Combining the three learning forms, six different cycles are possible.

1. *Input–discovery–reflection:* You would start the session with some knowledge input (for example, some frameworks, models, or theory through readings or lectures), then you let participants test those ideas through a case study discussion (discovery) and end with either an individual or group reflection on how applicable the input was for this specific case.
2. *Input–reflection–discovery:* Again, you would start the session with some knowledge input, then have participants reflect upon this input (e.g., asking them to make a conceptual/theoretical transfer of the input from one industry to another, or asking them to relate it to their own experience) and finally have a case discussion to discover the ideas or principles in action.
3. *Discovery–reflection–input:* Here you would start immediately with the case discussion through which the participants discover some ideas, frameworks, models, or theory, then jointly reflect upon the experience and end with some input on the current state of business knowledge from science about this specific phenomenon.
4. *Discovery–input–reflection:* You start the learning sequence with the discussion of a case, then provide background knowledge for example through a lecture, and end with a joint (or small-group) reflection on how this fits with previously discussed theories or past experience.
5. *Reflection–input–discovery:* In this learning cycle you could make participants reflect a specific situation that occurred to them (for example, you ask them to theorize about a question in general without a case), then present to them some background research in this field and finally end with a case discussion.
6. *Reflection–discovery–input:* Again, you start with a reflection, but then you move straight to the case discussion and only toward the end give the knowledge input on what theory has to say.

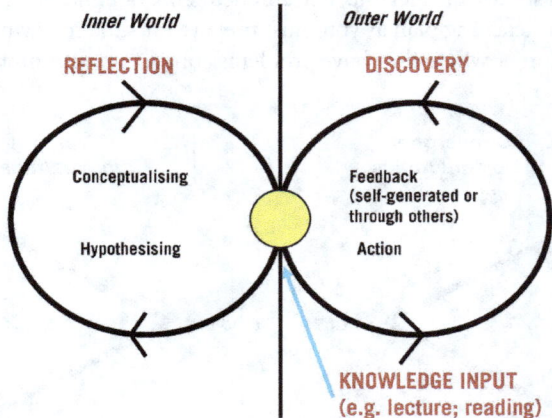

Figure 9: The Lancaster model of learning. Source: visualization adapted from Heath (2015). Source: This visualization adapted from: Heath (2015). Teaching & Writing Cases: A Practical Guide. p. 5f.; the "Lancaster model" goes back to John Burgoyne and others and can e.g. be found in Binsted D.S. (1980). "Design for learning in management training and development: a view." *Journal of European Industrial Training*, Vol. 4 Iss 8 pp. 2–32; here p.21f.

Which of these cycles is best in a given situation will depend (among other things) on the type of learning to be achieved and the participants' and facilitators' preferences. But we think that it is important to make this conscious decision, e.g., choosing which learning cycles are most appropriate to achieve your learning objective or even choosing only one or two elements of the learning cycle in a particular session. Please bear in mind that you can try to finish a cycle in one session but you can of course also use several sessions or a whole course to complete a cycle or several.

We have a separate chapter about 'Teaching a Case-Based Course,' but upfront: If you already use multiple case studies, avoid following the same pattern in all the sessions. Bring in a bit of variation to make the sessions more interesting.

Orchestrating immediate and underlying issue

In 'The Case Method in the Spotlight' we introduced the differentiation between immediate and underlying issues. This differentiation will become very important for the design of your teaching plan. The first building block(s) of your plan will usually center on the immediate issue. Should firm A acquire firm B? How should firm C react to accusations of child labor in their supply chain? Should firm D issue new equity or take a loan from a bank? These can often be the opening questions or conducted as initial votes (face to face typically as show of hands, online through polling software, etc.). During the discussion of the immediate issue, first hints about the underlying issue should either come up naturally or be solicited through respective questions. This can then be used to move to other building blocks, which will then typically focus on the underlying issues. The closing might then come back to the immediate issue or focus on reflection and transfer. You could try to visualize this for yourself by highlighting how the immediate and underlying issues are connected to one another.

Additional material

It is important to mention at this point – although maybe obvious – that the use of additional material (besides the case study) will influence the learning cycle. The link between theory and case discussion does not only relate to the actual talking in a class but also to the course context (see later) and the possible inclusion of other material. Therefore, you have to take some additional decisions in the preparation of the teaching session regarding the (1) kind of additional material (see checklist below for options), (2) whether the participants should prepare the material before or after the session, and (3) whether the material is optional or mandatory. Additional material can also support any of the three learning formats of the Lancaster model. It can be used as knowledge input (typically through readings), as reflection (e.g., through a learning journal), or as discovery (additional material on company or protagonists – possibly to be identified/ researched by the participants).

≔ Possible types of additional material for your case-based session

- textbook (entire books or only chapters/extracts),
- academic articles (e.g., *Journal of Finance*),
- managerial articles (e.g., *HBR, MIT Sloan Review*),
- technical or background notes (often explicitly linked with certain cases),
- webpages and online databases,
- newspapers (paper, online),
- videos,
- learning journal/personal reflection notebook.

The teaching plan

'It's not the plan that's important, it's the planning.' – Dr. Gramme Edwards

It is always good to have a plan – but the planning is even more important! And, especially when teaching a case study for the first time, we believe that it is important to have a detailed teaching plan. Rarely will you teach exactly according to your teaching plan. But, even when deviating from the original plan, this is done easier with the original plan on your mind as you will know which parts (and how much time you had planned for them) you might have to (or want to) skip because of an interesting discussion, a new and important idea that was raised, or a specific question that needs a longer answer than expected. But to be able to make these decisions you need a detailed plan in the first place.

The first thing that you should do is to break your session into different sections by topic. Specify the following aspects:

- *Overall session flow:* Almost like a good theater piece, your session will have an opening section, several middle parts, and a closing section. Start by writing down the key topics to be discussed with the case overall and bring them into a logical structure.
- *Learning objectives per building block:* Next up you need to define the matching learning objectives/takeaways per section. You need to be able to answer: Why do you add this element to your session flow? What are the participants going to take away from this building block?
- *Learning formats per building block:* When planning the different sections, immediately also think about the learning format of these sections (discussion, input, groupwork, individual reflection, buzz group, vote, role-play, etc.).
- *Timing/duration per building block:* Then allocate the approximate time for each section, considering the relevance of the respective building block but also the attention span of the participants.
- *Questions:* We believe that it is important to write down the most important questions per section (that will lead to debate). This could be opening questions, follow-up questions, questions in case specific topics do not come up, clarifying questions, transition questions, etc. We will get back to the topic of questions later, including a section on the particularly important opening question. But make sure that your teaching plan explicitly clarifies at least (1) the opening question and (2) questions that will help you to move from one building block to the next.
- *Board plan:* Specify what you want to add to the board in which building block. (More on this later.)
- *Additional material:* Are there handouts, videos, spreadsheets, physical sample products, etc. that you will need in the respective building blocks?
- *Link to slides:* If you use presentation slides, which slides should be shown in which building block?
- *Technological or room requirements:* Do the learning formats or additional material require specific setups, technology, or additional rooms/online breakout functionality? List all of them and check if they can be met. (For example, has the videoconferencing application that will be used for an online class got a breakout functionality and can the students be split according to the results of a vote? Is there decent sound equipment in the room so that you can show a video? Maybe you need more boards? Adhesive dots for voting or paper and scissors?) – This might sound unnecessary initially as you probably know the context of the first case use well, but it will help you tremendously when you teach the same session again in a completely different context.

Try to use the case study itself as an additional source of inspiration about the sequencing of the building blocks. The building blocks could, e.g., be organized along time (especially for retrospective cases), along a process (e.g., for operations classes), move from the issue mentioned first in the case to the issue mentioned last, etc.

 We believe that you should aim to keep all building blocks to a maximum of 15 minutes and to mix and match different formats to keep engagement high. After 15 minutes of full group discussion, you should try to insert a block with a pair or group discussion, an assignment, a vote, or role-play, and vice versa.

We recommend describing all the points from above in one big table that you can then bring to class. Below you can see a simple Excel version of a teaching plan with the key elements as described above.

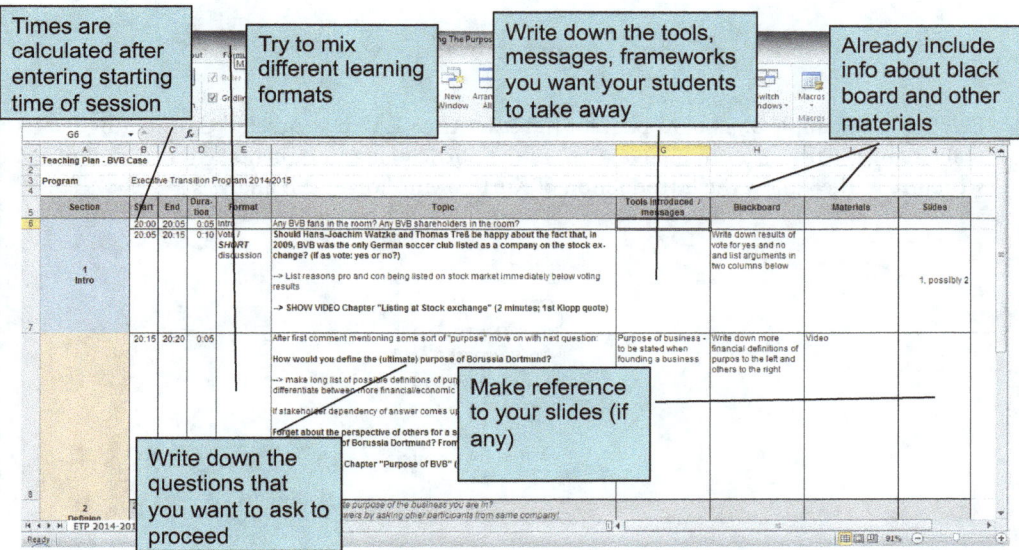

Figure 10: Example teaching plan in Microsoft Excel.

Carefully planning your session should not restrict your creativity but, on the contrary, will enable you to be more creative. For example, you may have planned five discussion sections, with each allocated a specific amount of time. This gives you a basic framework that will enable you to stay in control; you will know if one section is taking longer than planned and can then make an informed decision about whether to stay with the discussion and perhaps move one of the other planned sections to a later class. It will also allow you to realize the implications of you swapping the sequence of building blocks if a student makes a comment that 'comes too early.'

A plan enables you to think on your feet and avoids last-minute panic when you realize you have not covered everything you meant to. There is nothing worse than rushing through material toward the end of a session because you are running out of time.

But most importantly: Do not adhere to your teaching plan religiously! A truly participant-centered approach requires flexibility. As we said in the beginning, it is not the plan that is important but the planning.

Planning the use of the board

Note-taking during a case discussion is important – and we will explain and discuss this later in greater detail, focusing on how to do it during the session. Many teaching notes include suggested board plans – but not all do. And you will need to review anyway if the suggested board plan fits with your specific context and learning objectives. So, in parallel to developing your teaching plan, you should start to make a strategic plan on how to use the board for your session.

The board (could be a blackboard, a flipchart, a way to take notes in online or hybrid settings, a touchscreen in the room, etc.) will often be of critical importance to make the link between the case and the theory or concepts. If teaching in a converging/deductive approach, you could, e.g., provide a framework and ask the participants to fill out the elements. In a diverging/inductive approach, you could note the participants' comments in a way that will then allow you to add the framework later on.

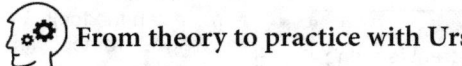 **From theory to practice with Urs**

Below is an example of a board plan for the case 'Anna Frisch at Aesch AG: Initiating Lateral Change' – this is an inductive plan, as the participants' comments will be listed in a structure to then allow the introduction of Kurt Lewin's 'force field analysis':

	ANNA's PLAN
	New marketing approach
	Targeting hospital administrators and "C-Level"
	Solution-suites instead of individual standalone products
	Shift from product to service

JUSTIFICATION	ANNA's PLAN
Buying behavior changing (administrators instead of users)	New marketing approach
Changing buying criteria (value and solutions instead of features)	Targeting hospital administrators and "C-Level"
Growth limitations in saturated German market	Solution-suites instead of individual standalone products
Upcoming health care reform with expected negative impact on industry	Shift from product to service

(Continued)

JUSTIFICATION	ANNA's PLAN	BARRIERS
Buying behavior changing (administrators instead of users)	New marketing approach	Aesch is growing and profitable: Need for change not evident
Changing buying criteria (value and solutions instead of features)	Targeting hospital administrators and "C-Level"	Timing wrong: Cost cuts at Aesch
Growth limitations in saturated German market	Solution-suites instead of individual standalone products	Germany only 6% of Aesch activities (and rather stable compared to other markets)
Upcoming health care reform with expected negative impact on industry	Shift from product to service	Others are needed to provide e.g. budget, resources, support

Figure 11: Board plan for 'Anna Frisch at Aesch AG.'

The instructor first asks participants what Anna's plan is and notes their answers in the middle of the board. Next, the instructor asks for the reasoning or justification for each of the plans and adds these comments to the left side of the board. Finally, the discussion moves on to potential barriers, and these are added to the right side of the board. The concept of the force field is then introduced and connected to the case discussion.

Depending on the technology and equipment available, plan in advance how you will use online boards, flipcharts, metaplan boards, and white- or blackboards. Important questions to consider are:

- What do you want to cover on the boards?
- What do you not want/need to write down?
- Do you want to end up with a particular structure on the board (you will have to plan for this) or do you want to capture what participants say uncensored and unstructured?
- Will you need to refer back to something during the class? If so, you will need to note that part of the discussion in a place that will be easy to find.
- How much space do you need? For example, do you capture pros and cons on one flipchart or use one for the pros and another for the cons?

Teaching plan development

- Be very specific with the learning context and potential constraints.
- Decide upon the general flow of the session: convergent vs divergent.
- Think about the appropriate learning cycles (knowledge input, discovery, reflection), which can be used as a basis for decisions on the learning process and sequence of activities and give a continuity to the whole event.
- Integrate additional material when appropriate.
- Develop a detailed teaching plan, keeping in mind that it is not about the plan but the planning.
- Make a visual map of how you plan to take notes on any type of board.

Preparation

'It takes a lot of unspectacular preparation to get spectacular results.' – Roger Staubach

Careful preparation before a case teaching session is vital if you want participants to maximize their learning and get a real buzz from having taken part. And not only do you need to know your materials well but, equally important, you must know as much as possible about who you will be teaching. This dual approach will pay dividends as you negotiate the session, orchestrate participation, and draw out key learning points.

> From our own experience, you should pay particular attention to the preparation at exactly the point in time when you believe you do not need it anymore. After you have taught a case two or three times, you will have developed confidence and experience. You might think you remember the case and teaching plan well enough – and just enter the room. Well, for us these were frequently the worst sessions of our careers as educators. If you have had such an experience, use the negative memories to put more emphasis on preparation the next time.

Know your class

It seems an obvious question, but it is a vital one: who will you be teaching? Get to know as much as you can about each of your participants and the class before the session. For example:

- What country or region are they from or do they have experience in? (And how does this link to the case?)
- What are their cultural backgrounds? (Might they be unlikely to understand certain parts of the case because they are so alien to them?)
- What business or industry experience do they have and at what level?
- What jobs have they done in the past? What jobs are they doing now?
- What roles and jobs do they aspire to? What does the program train them for?
- Are they undergraduates? Graduates? Executives? A mix?
- Are they roughly the same age group? Or very different ages?
- Mainly female? Mainly male? A mix of both?
- How large is the group?

This background knowledge is invaluable as you prepare for your case discussion. There are several ways you can use the information you gather about participants to enhance your case session, encourage participation, and introduce fresh perspectives. In both our institutions we typically receive students' profiles with pictures ahead of the first session, which is already a good start. If this is not common practice at your school, it might be worth asking for it. If learning management software is used at your school, this is also a good place to start with an introduction.

Advance knowledge of this kind will also enable you to anticipate the potential dynamics in a case session and help you create the safe environment that is necessary for an open, dynamic, and mutually respectful discussion.

So, once you have spent valuable time acquiring background knowledge about your class, how can you use it?

Nationality and culture

Is your case about a multinational company? If so, it may be perceived differently by your participants, depending on their nationality or culture. Is the advertising and marketing different across different geographical reasons? Why is a product or marketing campaign successful in one country but not in another? Why is a company making huge profits in one geographical region but struggling in another?

These are all rich seams for discussion that participants of various nationalities and different cultures can contribute to with insight, personal experience, and 'insider knowledge.' This provides another tool to ensure you can keep the discussion lively (personal viewpoints based on experience are always more compelling than abstract facts) and will not only enrich the learning experience for everyone in the class but also instill confidence and self-worth in the participant who realizes they have something of value to contribute.

Just as an example, even though cultural topics do not usually dominate thinking in operations management, it would probably be helpful to know if there are Japanese students in your session on the 'Benihana in Tokyo' case.

Cultural background can also offer an indication of the type of participant you will be dealing with. Participants from some cultural backgrounds are far more deferential toward their teacher than those from other cultures. This may not always hold true but forewarned is forearmed; if you suspect some of your participants may be unwilling to spontaneously contribute to a discussion because they feel it would be impolite to do so, you can plan ahead and incorporate tools and techniques to encourage their participation (see some tools and techniques in the following paragraphs, especially the section on participants who are too vocal or quiet).

Business and employment experience

Do not feel threatened by participants who may have more (practical) knowledge and experience than you of the topics you plan to discuss in your case session. On the contrary, this is a great opportunity to draw on their expertise for the benefit of the class as a whole. However, remember that your 'in-class expert' may not necessarily volunteer their experiences and insights, so prepare a few questions that you can ask them directly at suitable points during the discussion. This is also a great way to show respect for your participants and to demonstrate that you appreciate the opportunity to learn from others – one of the traits you will also wish to encourage in your participants.

You may have participants who have experience of working in the same industry but at completely different levels – one in management, the other on the shop floor, for example. These are gems that will only emerge from careful presession preparation and making a point of getting to know your participants.

It is a good idea to prepare a list of participants who you may be able to call on during the discussion. Make a note of roughly when and why their contribution may help to move the debate along.

Age groups

People of different ages will be able to offer different and often surprising perspectives. With a little thought and preparation this can greatly enrich your class discussion. In our experience, we have found that it is often more useful and important to be aware of the extent and type of work experience your participants have, rather than their ages. But there is one dimension in which age usually matters: the type of references to politics or culture you can make. If you are clearly older than your students, they will be increasingly unlikely to be able to understand your links to movies, books, historical events, etc. – just be aware about this and consider using it to make fun of yourself to introduce humor to the session.

Undergraduates? Graduates? Executives? A mix?

You will need to adapt your session to suit the level of the group. This may include the complexity and difficulty of the topics to be discussed as well as taking into consideration aspects such as time – executives will often have less time to prepare for a session and shorter cases will probably suit them better.

Plan to calibrate the speed of the discussion to the expected level or expertise of the group. But there is no golden rule. You will also need to test the extent of the group's appetite for discussions and how willing they are to learn from their peers as well as the instructor.

Generally, we have found that participants with sufficient work experience (MBAs and executives) tend to enjoy discussing the practicalities of applying concepts or tools, while participants with little or no work experience enjoy more theoretical discussions on the pros and cons of various concepts and tools.

With executives, it is crucial to ensure you have an in-depth knowledge of the industry or market sector and are familiar with the participants' companies. Your presession preparation should also include a clear plan to help participants relate the case discussion to their daily work.

Gender

Be wary of gender imbalance in your classes. If, for example, your class has significantly more males than females, be aware that they may find it easy to dominate the discussion. Your female participants may not get a look in! Be ready to counteract this and plan ways to include both genders in the discussion.

Class size

Make sure to know exactly how many people you will have in class. Full-class case discussions work very well with mid-sized groups (15–40 participants), but if the group is getting very small you might need to add formats, building blocks, or material as the case discussion might slow down a bit faster when participants have made their key points. On the other hand, very large groups of over 40 participants will require the addition of pair or group discussions to allow all participants to contribute in every session.

> **Preparation: your participants**
>
> – Find out as much as you can about who you will be teaching.
> – Note key aspects such as nationality, culture, gender, work experience, areas of expertise, age, and previous track record in class.
> – Make a list of why and when you will call on individual participants to contribute.
> – Prepare tools and techniques to deal with both dominant and quiet participants.
> – Always draw on the expertise of your participants during the discussion.

Preparing the case and materials

(Re)familiarize yourself with the case

If you are teaching a case that you have taught before, always refamiliarize yourself with both the case and the teaching note.

Look through any notes or comments you have made when previously teaching the case. It is a good idea to make notes each time you teach a case and keep them for handy reference in an electronic file, a physical folder, or an electronic or paper notebook. If you are teaching your own case, this will also be useful material when writing or updating your teaching note.

It goes without saying that if you are teaching a case for the first time, particularly if it is not your own, you must make sure you know both the case and the teaching note inside out. It is also vital to do some additional research about the company, industry, and market sector. Then you will not be caught off guard by sharp participants who have also been researching the case and know more than you!

Things to investigate each time while (re)reading the case study and teaching note

- What happened to the organization after the date of the case? (e.g., mergers or acquisitions, bankruptcy, growth or stagnation, rebranding, changes in product portfolio or international footprint),
  - in general?
  - specifically related to the case?
- What happened to the protagonist?
- Are there bigger changes in the overall context (e.g., the political landscape, the overall industry, new technologies)?

Review your teaching (and board) plan

During the preparation you need to revisit your teaching plan and potentially adjust it according to your audience (see above) or to different learning objectives.

The first things to look at again are your opening and follow-up questions. Based on your preparation for your audience, you might want to adjust your questions. Always have your opening question ready in advance, plus one or two backups in case the first fails to ignite any debate.

Also revisit the structure and flow of your session. Review how long you wish to spend on each section. Consider the relevance of the topics to the participants and the learning objectives.

Also reconsider the board plan – taking into account the specific context (room layout, video-conferencing software, visibility of board in hybrid setting, etc.).

Preclass preparation for participants

How much work do you want your participants to do before walking into your classroom?
You will expect them to read the case, of course, but what else? Be clear about your expectations. For example, is the presession work to be presented in class? Is it just for background reading? Do you want to see the work before the class? Is it mandatory? Does it count toward grades? Or is the presession work optional?

If you wish to assign tasks to participants, either to the class as a whole or to individuals, be sure to do this well in advance. By allowing plenty of time, you can also send out a reminder closer to the date of the session or submission deadline.

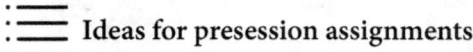 **Ideas for presession assignments**

Here are a few ideas for possible presession assignments that will help to engage and interest your participants in advance of the class:
- Recommend additional readings (e.g., traditional textbooks, academic or managerial articles, online information, news items).
- Assign videos to be watched (e.g., company presentations, commercials, publicly available interviews with board members, MOOCs, TED Talks).
- Stimulate presession discussions, e.g., through online forums or in small groups.
- Require case writeups or specific responses to questions (e.g., through a questionnaire).
- Demand that participants perform specific analysis (e.g., ratio analysis) or calculations.
- Ask for the preparation of a role-play in class.
- Ask for reflective essays/papers that move beyond the case at hand (e.g., writeups of personal or professional experiences; participants could be asked to describe a situation where they tried to convince somebody else to do something and they refused).
- Request additional research about the case or the larger context.

 What other type of presession preparation do you find works really well? Please share your experiences with us for future editions of this book.

Setting the scene: before class

Do you want your participants to be fired up and ready to go before they even reach your classroom? If so, simply telling them in advance which case they need to read is not sufficient. Some of your participants will read the case, others might scan it, and a few will not even look at it; they are intelligent individuals and will be confident they can just wing it in class. But is this what you want to be faced with at the start of your session?

It does not have to be this way.

Preclass preparation means you will have a far higher chance of running a successful session because your participants will already be inspired and ready to learn as soon as they come into the classroom.

Raise participants' expectations and excitement

 Preclass communication is key. It is possible to create a buzz of anticipation before the session, as well as ensuring that participants prepare well. Think carefully about:

- the tone and style of your communication;
- the content, i.e., the instructions and information you want to give your participants; and
- the channels you will use to communicate with your participants.

Tone and style

As mentioned above: it is one of our core beliefs that you can and should bring your personality to the class; the same is true for the preclass communication. No two teaching styles are the same and what works for one person will not work for another. The same goes for the style of communication we adopt when liaising with our participants outside the classroom. You need to decide what works for you and at what point on the spectrum between formal and informal you feel most comfortable.

However, we would say that it is important to be consistent, so your participants know what to expect. This is an important aspect of building trust.

Content

The content of your preclass communications needs careful thought. Will you focus on strict instructions? Explain the grading system? List the learning objectives? Invite preclass contributions? Or simply make suggestions rather than give instructions?

> **From theory to practice with Martin**
>
> The answers to these questions will depend to a large extent on your audience. For example, some groups will need far more guidance than others. I always give undergraduates and first-year master's participants longer and more precise instructions than other groups. This will often include the learning objectives they should be aiming to achieve.
>
> However, with more experienced or mature participants, for example final-year master's participants or executives, I provide less information and usually exclude the learning objectives. I like to introduce a little ambiguity and intrigue and also want to ensure that more experienced and mature participants are sufficiently challenged. So that they do not feel being treated as school kids, I will often decide against sending presession assignments or questions to executives at all – with the exception of a request to read the case.

Channels

The 'how' is very important and there are a number of options to choose between. These are some of the most frequently used communication channels:

- Learning management systems (sometimes also called e-learning platform, such as Canvas, Blackboard, and Moodle);
- Email;
- Messages in team collaboration software (such as MS Teams and Slack) or messengers (e.g., WhatsApp and WeChat);
- Shared online drives (such as Dropbox, MS SharePoint, Google Drive, and Notion);
- Providing hard-copy paperwork and/or informing via a physical (pin) notice board;
- Creating a video of yourself introducing the case and other required assignments;
- Making time to visit the group during a break to spark interest in the case;
- Short live online kick-off sessions in which you explain what is to come and what is expected from the participants.

> **Preparation: before class**
>
> – (Re)familiarize yourself with the case and teaching note: know your material inside out.
> – Review your teaching plan and board plan but be prepared to think on your feet!
> – Preclass communication is key.
> – Provide clear and unambiguous instructions about presession assignments.
> – Beware that your preclass communication sets the tone and style for the case discussion.

Opening the case discussion

'Give me six hours to chop down a tree and I will spend the first four sharpening the axe.'
– Abraham Lincoln

Setting the scene: at the start of the session

How do you feel if you walk into a silent room, sit down at an empty desk, and look at a blank screen? Enthused? Ready to learn? How about if music is playing, an intriguing product has been placed in front of you, images or a video clip are on display, and the instructor is welcoming all participants as they enter the room (or online session)? There is a huge difference between these two scenarios. It almost goes without saying that most of us would choose to walk into the second room or online session.

> Carefully setting the scene for our participants as they join our online session or come through the door will bring the classroom to life and make a dramatic difference to their mood, expectations, and level of anticipation.

Of course, we need to ensure that our scene setting is relevant to the case we are going to teach – and it will not be possible to include all these elements every time. Not all cases, for example, are about a product that is small, portable, and affordable enough for the facilitator to buy for every participant (though it may be worth asking the company concerned for free samples!).

However, with a little thought and imagination, some scene setting will always be possible. Even simple images of the protagonists on display at the front of the classroom plus some current news clippings relating to the issues discussed in the case will create interest and expectation.

> **From theory to practice with Martin**
>
> When teaching my case about Madonna, cowritten with Jamie Anderson ('Madonna: Strategy in Action'), I always start with an eight-minute video clip called 'Star.' This is part of a series of eight short films produced by BMW for the internet in 2001 and 2002. While the video is not directly related to the case, it shows Madonna in an atypical situation and is extremely funny. It's a very good icebreaker at the start of a session.

At the other end of the spectrum, why start in the classroom at all? It may be possible to meet participants at a location that is central to the case – more inspiring than the four walls of a classroom, perhaps. As Einstein said, 'logic will get you from A to B; imagination will take you everywhere.' We want our participants to use their imagination, so, when it comes to setting the scene, we should use ours too.

A last aspect of setting the scene is the creation of a positive climate in which participants can flourish, which invites participants to contribute and support them during the session.

Participation can be frightening and difficult for participants, especially at the beginning of a course/program: Comments in class are key to build reputation and network or, as David Garvin from Harvard said, '[w]hat you say is who you are' (Garvin n.d.). One of the principles of the case method is to make participants feel empathy, appreciation, and support. During class this can be achieved by following up with questions that frame their responses and ultimately make them better. It is also important to start with little or no judgment at beginning of a course/session. We know that this is hard sometimes, but we think that it is important to avoid judging answers or comments of participants by saying things like 'this is an excellent point' or 'I was looking for that' or to only note down certain answers on the board while ignoring and not writing down others.

Getting started

We have been there too: the start of a session, more than a few stage-fright nerves (ours, that is!), a roomful of (hopefully) expectant faces, silence – and the telltale signs that more than a few of the participants are already texting, googling, and surfing. Where to begin?

First impressions are so important. The way we open the case discussion is crucial for the success of the session. Always start on time and with a clear signal that the class has begun: make sure you have everyone's attention. Anything else might have undesirable long-term consequences.

> ### From theory to practice with Urs and Martin
>
> **Urs:**
> I like to have music playing at the start of a session and combine this with a very loud and energetic 'Good morning/afternoon.'
>
> It can be a good idea to turn up the music so it is too loud for participants to comfortably talk, and then turn it off as a signal that the session will begin.
>
> In some institutions, a formal signal such as a bell will mark the start of the class.
>
> **Martin:**
> I aim to be in class (or online) at least 10 minutes before the start. This means I can check that all the equipment I need is working and also, importantly, I can greet everyone as they arrive. Alternatively, I will quickly go around the class and shake hands with the participants.
>
> I remain standing and usually position myself in the center of the room or somewhere where everyone in the class can see me. I try to make eye contact with as many participants as possible but do not say anything at this stage. I then wait for everyone to settle and do not begin the session until the class is quiet.

Opening question

It is vital to get the opening question right. This is of the utmost importance as it will have a critical impact on the rest of the session. As case facilitators, we must always give this very careful thought.

From theory to practice with Martin

The first choice to make is: How difficult should the opening question be? If it's too easy, it sets the wrong tone for the session, and no one will be interested in answering it. For example, asking about the timing of the case or the identity of the protagonist (as I have seen from other educators) are both far too simplistic for an opening question.

But it's also vital to strike a balance, because if it's a closed question that is too difficult, participants will be afraid to answer in case they get it wrong. And it's important to note that this fear of responding incorrectly can be more pronounced in certain cultures and early on in a program or course.

Typically, the opening question should be posed from the perspective of the protagonist in the case. Indeed, the most traditional opening question is: 'If you were in the position of the case protagonist, what would you do?' But the question can obviously be finetuned to the specific case, e.g., 'If you were in the position of Paul Nasar, would you propose Rob Parson for promotion to managing director?'

The opening question should elicit a strong and ideally controversial response about the nature of the problem and how serious it is. Aim for a question that immediately prompts disagreement and discussion among participants. If implicitly or explicitly going for a vote, try to phrase your question so that you will get a 50/50 split. But there are exceptions to the general rule that an opening question should immediately provoke controversy:

 From theory to practice with Urs

An example of an exception to this general rule is when I teach 'Anna Frisch at Aesch AG: Initiating Lateral Change,' a case I cowrote with Ulf Schäfer.

The 'official' opening question for this case is: 'Is Anna justified in proposing changes to the marketing approach at Aesch AG?'

Most participants will agree with Anna's proposals as they are so convincing. This then makes the question of why she fails much more interesting. So, in this particular context, controversy is not instigated immediately but develops later in the session when the reasons for failure are being debated.

 Your opening question should usually be open, not closed. The reply to a closed question is limited to yes or no. (More on open versus closed questions later.)

 Here are some typical opening questions that can be used:

- If you were in the position of the protagonist, what would you do? (Probably the most frequently used opening question, neutral and focusing on the immediate issue.)
- Out of the three options mentioned in the case, which would you choose? (Centering the question around the immediate issue but abstract from the protagonist.)
- Is this a serious issue and who should deal with it? (This might provoke debate about the roles and responsibilities of the various characters in the case and is a mechanism to move to the underlying issue.)

- How effective will the proposed action be? (A good option for cases in which the protagonist has choices but seems to be leaning toward only one option.)
- Which specific actions do you propose for the protagonist? (This moves the attention to the practicalities of process and execution.)
- Which challenge should the protagonist deal with first? (A good way to start if there are multiple immediate issues and if you are flexible in the teaching flow, because you should probably focus next on the one challenge that most participants chose in response to your question.)
- Who (or what) is responsible for this situation/complication/problem? (A good option for retrospective cases, in which the analysis of the root causes is more important than the decision and next steps.)

Avoid using the same opening question when teaching multiple cases to the same group. Participants will soon anticipate what is coming and repetition will quickly lead to boredom.

 From theory to practice with Urs

My case 'Vodafone in Egypt: National Crises and Their Implications for Multinational Corporations,' cowritten with Shirish Pandit, is set in Egypt during protests against the 30-year rule of President Hosni Mubarak. It focuses on the dilemma faced by Hatem Dowidar, CEO of Vodafone Egypt, when the government ordered Vodafone and other service providers to suspend communication services in certain areas, including Tahrir Square, the center of the protests.

The case can be approached from many angles and so offers numerous examples of potential opening questions. Here are just some examples to illustrate the broad range of options you can choose between when starting a case discussion:

1.	What should Hatem Dowidar do?	Recommendation, participants have to put themselves the protagonists' shoes
2.	What would you do in Hatem's position?	Recommendation, but this time it is what participants would do in Hatem's position which might lead to different answers than the first question
3.	What do you think actually happened?	Analysis, very open question, the discussion can go in many directions
4.	If you were Vittorio Colao, CEO of the Vodafone Group, what would you expect Hatem Dowidar to do?	Recommendation, but this time with a change of perspective. It is about the boss of the protagonist
5.	Should Hatem Dowidar disconnect the services, yes or no?	Recommendation, but with a forced choice, narrowing down the options
6.	What is going on here?	Analysis, very open question, the discussion can go in many directions. Slightly different from question 3 as it points more in the direction of politics, emotions, underlying currents than pure facts (what happened)
7.	Which is more important: obeying the government or satisfying customers?	Either vote or opening for discussion, but with a very narrow focus and a forced choice

(Continued)

8.	Could Dowidar have prevented this situation?	Focus now shifts from prospective (what should he do) to retrospective (what should he have done)
9.	Why does the government give this order?	Diagnosis, shifting the focus from the protagonist to an important stakeholder, the government
10.	Is Hatem in trouble?	Assessment, very open and even ambiguous as there might be very different opinions on what trouble really is
11.	What is Hatem's challenge/problem?	Assessment, rather open. Could be narrowed down by simply rephrasing to '… most important challenge'
12.	Is Hatem pro or anti Hosni Mubarak?	Assessment, might come as a surprise at the beginning of the discussion as this seems to be a nonbusiness question
13.	Should Hatem try using his political connections to avoid the shutdown?	Recommendation, with a very narrow focus as the question already rules out many other options that Hatem could try
14.	What is the relationship between Vodafone Egypt and the group's HQ?	Assessment
15.	Can you define the problem/challenge that Hatem is facing?	Assessment, very similar to question 11, but forcing the participants to be very precise by using the word 'define'
16.	Should Vodafone shut down its business in Egypt?	Recommendation, but impersonal, general, not focusing on the protagonist but rather the whole company

As mentioned above, these are just a few of the multiple options available. It is useful to think about each possible question from both your perspective and your participants.' Would you be excited to discuss a particular question? Would your participants? Is the question too easy? Too hard? Will it provoke controversy and disagreement? Will it naturally lead to the fundamental questions/issues of the case?

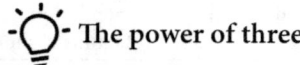
The power of three

There are three tried and tested formats to open a discussion:

(1) Open call: simply invite the entire class to respond to the opening question. It is very important not to panic if your class is initially silent – the silence is never as long as it seems to you. Resist the temptation to 'fill the gap'. Silence can be a wonderful learning opportunity so do not spoil the moment by ending it too soon. Give your participants plenty of time to think and respond; hold your nerve and wait for at least 30 seconds (count them down inwardly). This will also reaffirm your commitment to participant-centered discussion.

However, it is still a good idea to have an alternative approach ready in case no one speaks, even after you have waited patiently!

(2) Cold call: Ask an individual participant for their initial thoughts and ideas. The identification of the participant could be strategic or random. If you are met with silence, you can:

– open the discussion to the whole group;
– ask another participant to respond instead;

(Continued)

> – ask another participant to support the participant you originally picked, for example by asking: Can you please help XY by just giving him one example (or a specific quote from the case or just one word etc.);
> – allow the participant to pass this question on to a different participant;
>
> *(3) Warm call:* Warn an individual participant in advance that they will be asked for their input. This can be done well in advance (for example, after a previous class); immediately before the class (for example, as participants enter the classroom); or in class just before showing a video clip. ('Dan, after this video I would like you to…')
>
> Warm calling is good to encourage contributions from participants who already have expertise on the topic, or those who have not previously contributed sufficiently to the discussions.

Additional tactics to get the discussion going

Votes or questionnaires: Another very frequently used way to open a case discussion is to hold a class vote on a specific question (usually related to the immediate issue). This can be a very effective technique. Having responded to a vote, participants are often more willing to defend their position in class and contribute to the discussion. (This is amplified even more in face-to-face settings, where everybody can see how each other voted.) You can also ask participants to explain their decision – this can be particularly rewarding when only one or two participants vote against the rest of the class. For this to be effective you have to of course remember who voted for what. When writing down the number of votes on the board, you might want to write a couple of names (for example, very small and only readable for you or just their initials) under each number. After a vote, it is always legitimate to call on individual participants with opposing views to explain their perspective and defend their position. Try to call participants from both/all camps to balance the comments in the classroom. Voting also gives you a good sense of the distribution of perspectives in the class and enables you to stimulate the debate, e.g., by supporting the minority. In online or hybrid classes you can use online voting systems (e.g., Mentimeter, Kahoot) or simply ask participants to respond in the chat or to use the typically available reaction signs.

Small-group presentations: Ask small groups to prepare and present their ideas at the start of class. This has to be done as a preassignment (create groups upfront, give them a task, elaborate your expectations, ask them to be brief/concise). Use their input as the opening of the class. This can be very effective to ensure preparation of the case. But sometimes it might fire back in the sense that only the groups that are selected to prepare and present their ideas will actually prepare and the others will wait to be informed in class. One way to improve this is to make several groups prepare a case and select one to present their ideas and the others might add or comment. The upside of this kind of opening is that the start of the session is already participant-centered. Additionally, you will immediately get a sense of how participants have understood, interpreted, and liked the case and what kind of issues they focused on while preparing the case.

What other techniques to open a case-based session have you used in the past or observed in great teachers? Share your experience with us!

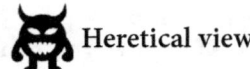 **Heretical view**

Some case facilitators open their session by summarizing the case to be discussed. We do not recommend this as it signals to participants that they can get away with less preparation next time. And, of course, it delays participant engagement (they will need to listen to the summary). The aim should be to start the discussion as soon as possible.

However, a case summary at the start of the session can sometimes be necessary, for example when participants arrive poorly prepared. This may be due to an exam, some special event, or a short-notice change to the case to be used in the session.

An introductory summary will work best if you have something a little special up your sleeve to make the session more interesting and livelier as it progresses. This might be additional material such as video clips or the presence of a case protagonist.

But starting with a case summary is definitely a technique to be avoided if possible, and only used rarely after careful consideration!

Dealing with participants who know the outcome and give it away immediately

Many of our workshop participants struggle with the problem of individual students who know the outcome of the case. This is particularly true for old cases, extremely famous cases, or cases about well-known organizations or events. Our workshop participants then frequently wonder whether the case session still makes sense if such a student simply gives away the outcome of the case early in the session (which they will then often frame as the 'solution' to the case). We strongly believe that it still makes sense to go on! And there are several techniques to deal with such situations.

We already touched on a first such technique when looking at the use of old cases: You could simply anticipate it by sharing the outcome of the case upfront at beginning of class. You could, for example, show pictures, charts, news reports, or products that illustrate the decision/action. This way you can get the 'what happened' out of the way and then fully concentrate on why and how it happened.

A second tactic is to avoid this situation from happening by using fake/sanitized cases. For example, the famous 'Carter Racing' case, by Brittain and Sitkin, deals with the issues leading up to the *Challenger* disaster from 1986 but is disguised as a NASCAR racing case. In this specific case it makes a lot of sense to disguise the fact that the data comes from the *Challenger* accident because knowing what happened to the *Challenger* will make participants look a lot more actively for problems with the data. To avoid participants googling the outcome, the case was later republished under another different name ('Speed Venture'). But, in general, there are a lot of good reasons to avoid fake/sanitized cases, so we would argue that this option should be used carefully.

Another tactic would be to use cases about less or unknown organizations and events, for which the outcome possibly cannot even be googled. But be aware that the potential advantage of participants not knowing the outcome might be counterbalanced by the fact that participants might be less willing to engage with companies or events that they do not know.

Finally, you might just as well accept that some participants know the outcome – acknowledge the fact that they did the additional research. You can see this as a good sign that people are willing to engage, to go beyond just the necessary, and to put in the extra effort to find out. We would even say that it is almost a principle of participant-centered learning that participants frequently 'know' relevant things that you might not know. Instead of fighting this, embrace the opportunity to leverage the differences in knowledge and experience to the benefit of the whole class (because in the end it is rarely every participant but just a few who care enough to find out).

> **Opening the case discussion**
>
> – Set the scene for when participants arrive/join: use your imagination!
> – Start on time and with a clear signal.
> – Get the opening question right: draft a number of options and choose wisely.
> – Always have a plan B – especially if participants are unprepared, unwilling to contribute, or surprise you with unexpected comments.
> – Decide how you will start the discussion: open call, cold call, warm call, group work, or a vote?
> – Don't be afraid of students who know the outcome.

Running the session

'For your information, let me ask you a question.' – Marshall McLuhan

While opening the session is crucial for the atmosphere and energy, the way you will run the session will be decisive for achieving your learning objectives.

The case method ultimately requires three key skills:

1. *Asking great questions:* Make sure you have a broad spectrum of different types of questions that you use in your classes. To be able to ask great question is not only a matter of preparation, but also linked to your ability to listen.
2. *Listening carefully:* Asking great questions requires you to listen carefully so that questions build on earlier questions – generating a natural flow of the session. Make sure that you stay focused on what your participants say instead of thinking about the next mini-lecture or just waiting for the keywords you expect. And next to listening to the content of the response it is equally important to listen to the social, emotional, and relational aspects (is the participant excited, is there a fight within the class, etc.).
3. *Orchestrating a discussion:* At the same time, you will have to orchestrate the class discussion with attention. In parallel to facilitating the content dimension of the case discussion, you will simultaneously need to orchestrate the discussion on a social, emotional, and relational level. We will dive deeper into these three key skills of a great case facilitator, including a deeper look at different learning formats that you can use, how important the learning space can be (if teaching face to face), and why coteaching might be a good way to deliver an extraordinary session and improve your own teaching skills at the same time.

Your job as a case facilitator is mostly to ask great questions (even in asynchronous online sessions!), so this is where we will start.

Asking great questions

Asking great questions is probably the single most important case teaching skill. You will need to prepare carefully and be ready with a broad range of questions that will advance the case discussion and encourage participation. When planning your questions, it is vital to ensure that they will help to achieve the learning objectives.

As already mentioned in the section on the teaching plan, we suggest preparing a lot of questions and quickly thinking through the potential direction that the discussion might take based on your questions. As questions are so important, we also recommend writing them down and testing them with someone. This is especially important if you do not teach in your native language. There is nothing worse than asking a question and realizing during the discussion that the participants understood the question in a different way, and you then must course-correct.

First, it is important to understand that there are various types of question that can be asked and that each type will result in a different outcome. To inspire the development of your own questions, we will first introduce a short typology of questions for case teaching and then describe all of them with various examples.

There are many possible ways of differentiating between various types of questions that usually look at different aspects and are often neither mutually exclusive nor collectively exhaustive. Also, our proposed typology is not perfect but we believe that we cover the most relevant aspects of questions for the purpose of teaching a case-based session as follows:

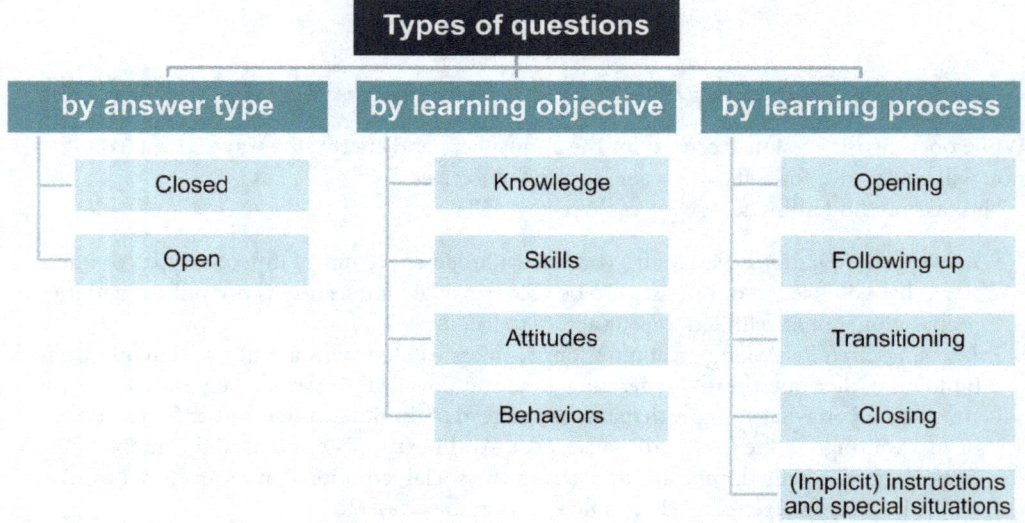

Figure 12: Typology of questions for case teaching.

 The C. Roland Christensen Center for Teaching and Learning at Harvard Business School put together a long and wonderful list of 'Questions for Class Discussions' (NN 2008), which was a source of inspiration for this entire section even though they use a different typology. The list is publicly available at http://www.hbs.edu/teaching/docs/Questions_for_Class_Discussions_rev.pdf.

Question types by answer

A frequent differentiation between types of questions (that you might know from your own survey research) is closed questions versus open questions.

Closed

 Closed (sometimes also called 'closed-ended') questions are questions that have a very limited set of possible answers. They usually result in very short, simple factual responses, e.g., a 'yes' or 'no.' Often, the answer will be right or wrong. The questioner remains in control.

Despite being closed, i.e., targeted toward a limited choice of responses, closed questions can still investigate a broad range of issues. Here are just a few examples:

- Can you tell me the total R&D spending of the company in the previous year? (facts)
- Would you fire person X or not? (opinions)

- In the position of the protagonist, would you be angry about the divestment decision? (emotions)
- On a scale from 1 to 5, is the market potential for product Z big (5) or small (1)? (scale assessments)
- The CEO knew about the ongoing sexual harassment, right? (statement dressed as question)

The benefit of closed questions is that they force participants to take a stand. This can be effective at the start of a discussion when participants can be asked to vote or express their opinion on a particular issue. You can then move from the vote to the discussion by following up with open questions, for example 'Why did you vote against giving the loan?' or 'What would make you change your mind about the location for the next production plant?'

With closed questions, educators can quickly evaluate preparation of the class or individual participants. Just cold-call a participant with a specific closed question and you will immediately know if they have read the case. You can also use closed questions to help bring a discussion back on track or to refocus when a participant's contribution becomes too broad and unspecific. (More on that later.)

However, as a general rule, closed questions should be used far less frequently than open questions during a case discussion, because they have several characteristics that are unsupportive for a fruitful and lively debate in class.

Disadvantages of closed questions for case teaching:

- Participants might be afraid about giving a wrong answer to a closed question.
- Closed questions usually do not allow space to provide reasoning behind the response which it might be important to give (e.g., why they believe that the marketing VP's actions were not racist – even though the majority of the class might have a different opinion).
- Participants might have a creative idea that just does not fit the acceptable set of responses to a closed question.
- Closed questions usually result in short responses and might not help to get the discussion going.
- Closed questions tend to simplify things through the limitation of options – which is usually not in line with the educational objective of preparing for a world of complexities.

Open

Open (sometimes also called 'open-ended') questions are questions for which respondents are not limited in their response. The questioner is less in control because the replies might go in all kinds of directions, and it is therefore not possible for the educator to (precisely) predict what the response will be and where this will lead the case discussion.

In case discussions, open questions are typically used to reflect on, diagnose, assess, evaluate, or analyze a particular situation (in retrospect) or to ask for recommendations, actions, and response strategies. Typical open questions might include:

- How would you describe the situation X was facing at the beginning of 2020? (diagnosis)
- What has led to this development? (analysis)
- How dire is the financial situation of company A in your opinion? (opinion)
- If you were in X's shoes, what would you do now? (recommendation)
- What should the specific next steps of the internal auditor be? (action)
- What could be counterarguments to what participant K just said? (invitation to object and contribute)

Open questions invite longer, more discursive replies that will often initiate alternative responses from other participants or that can open further questions by the educator. Therefore, open questions require good listening skills so you can respond appropriately to skillfully probe participants' understanding, knowledge, opinions, assumptions, or emotions and drive the discussion forward.

As mentioned before, open questions should usually be the more frequently used question style in case discussions. However, there are also a few disadvantages of open questions.

Disadvantages of open questions for case teaching:

- Responses can easily be too long, unstructured, and off track.
- The uncertainty about the direction of the response can be nerve-wracking for the educator.
- They might invite multiple participants to provide similar but just slightly varying responses that do not add value to the case discussion.
- Nonnative or introvert participants might be less willing to contribute.
- If questions are extremely open (for example, 'What do you think?' as an opening question), participants might be overwhelmed.
- When grading participation/contribution: the grading is usually a bit less objective compared to the simple check of whether the response to a closed question was right or wrong.

Despite these potential disadvantages, we strongly recommend making as much use of open questions as possible and to limit closed questions to very specific situations, such as an opening vote, the clarification of case facts, or as a way to refocus the class discussion. And, with a bit of practice, you will find it easy to ask for similar aspects through open questions.

To make the difference of closed and open questions very clear: below we provide a comparison table with examples of open-ended variants to the closed questions mentioned above:

Closed question	Open question
Can you tell me the total R&D spending of the company in the previous year?	What factors might have impacted the R&D activities of the company in the previous year?
Would you fire person X or not?	What might be reasons to fire person X or not?
In the position of the protagonist, would you be angry about the divestment decision?	In the position of the protagonist, what would be your feelings about the divestment decision?
On a scale from 1 to 5, is the market potential for product Z big (5) or small (1)?	How do you evaluate the market potential for product Z?
The CEO knew about the ongoing harassment, right?	Who might have known about the ongoing sexual harassment?

Table 1: Comparison of closed and open questions.

As you can see from the table above, the differences between closed and open questions can sometimes be very small in wording but they will move the discussion into very different directions and can elicit very different emotions and reactions from your participants overall.

And just ask yourself: Which of the two sets of questions would you have preferred to be asked as a student? So why should we treat our participants differently from how we would like to be treated?

Question types by learning objective

Questions can be used to implicitly or explicitly point toward the learning objectives of a session and to evaluate their achievement (often toward the end of a session). There is a large number of different taxonomy systems around the achievement of learning objectives (often following 'Bloom's Taxonomy'; see e.g., Anderson and Krathwohl 2001). But given the underlying complexity of human learning they tend to often be equally complex. For the purposes of this section, we will therefore just follow the frequently used differentiation of learning into knowledge, skills, attitudes, and behaviors (KSAB).

Because the three proposed main dimensions of question types (by answer, learning objective, and learning process) are quite independent of each other, just remember that the following description of questions by learning objectives will overlap with earlier and later differentiations. For example, all learning objectives can be addressed through both closed and open questions. And the same will be true below for questions by learning process. But as a source of inspiration for the formulation of your own questions, we believe this to be an acceptable redundancy.

Knowledge

Testing knowledge and the availability of information through questions is typically very straightforward. This can happen by asking for a particular piece of information, perhaps an important aspect of the case. But, while knowledge questions can be focused on the case, they could equally well go far beyond. Such questions can be used to ensure reading of the case or advancing the discussion by asking for something that may have been overlooked during the discussion so far.

Questions asking for information and knowledge are often used as a follow-up when participants express opinions but fail to back them with facts from the case. For example, if a participant argues that they would choose option A because it would be more profitable, a good follow-up question would be: 'Is there any information in the case about the level of profit that might be achieved with option A?' You could also test knowledge from earlier in the course, from other courses, or gained through comments from participants during the case session.

Examples for questions investigating knowledge and information:

- According to the case study, what are the three product ideas that person A presented in the investment meeting? (testing case reading)
- Can someone remind me about the formular for WACC so that we can calculate the expected returns for company B? (making explicit links to previous course content through a closed question)
- Which key challenges for effective team collaboration did we discuss earlier in this course that might have contributed to the team's failure in this case? (making links to previous course content through an open question)
- What are the key challenges of the automotive industry that participant C just introduced to our discussion? (testing for learning from contributions during case discussion)
- Which academic theories could provide strong support for the proposal of participant D? (inviting links to previous course content)
- We have already discussed two aspects, but which other disadvantages of the proposed marketing plan are being raised by person E in the case? (advancing the discussion to a new aspect)

As educators you are probably used to being in a position of having more information/knowledge about the subject than your participants. But the case method requires you to let the discussion flow and this lower level of control over the session can make inexperienced case teachers frightened – particularly when they have participants who have highly specialized knowledge in a field related to the case but possibly outside of the scientific domain of the educator. But through the intelligent inclusion of knowledge questions to the experts in the room you can easily deal with such issues. Here are a few ideas:

Dealing with experts in the room: Make the most of your expert by asking them specific questions that will enrich and inform the learning experience for everyone. You can frame your questions in the following ways:

- Can you please share in a few words the key trends in your industry?
- How do you organize the budgeting process in your company and how does this compare to the process described for company F in the case? (For example, when teaching in a customized executive education program for participants from only one firm.)
- Based on your experience and expertise in this field ...
  - ... would you invest in this proposal?
  - ... how would you approach this problem?
  - ... is the protagonist in the case taking the right decisions?
  - ... what would you do next?

Skills

You can also use questions to test participants' skills, e.g., their ability to apply concepts, frameworks, or tools to the specific case. Here are a few examples:

- Can you please calculate the average customer lifetime value for customer segment G of company H in the case?
- Which utilitarian arguments could person J present to seemingly justify a violation of company K's patents?
- Can you take me through the main steps of calculating total cost of ownership in general so that we can then do this for the case?
- How would you build an onboarding process for new hires at company L?

Attitudes

As a psychological construct and therefore as something deeply personal and internal, attitudes are more difficult to bring to the surface. But there are still ways to investigate your participants around their attitudes, relative to existing attitudes at the beginning of the learning as well as changes over time and attitudes at the end of the learning. And, even though the evaluation of the responses might be difficult, you might want to use questions around attitudes to clearly state that this dimension of learning matters to you. Typical questions could be:

- In the case person M shouts at N during the negotiation, how do you feel about people shouting in negotiations?
- What would you do when finding out that a colleague is underperforming like person O in the case?
- What do you think about promoting CFOs like person P to CEO positions?
- Do you think that firms like Q should follow a 'made in the USA' strategy?
- Did the discussion of this case change your attitudes about doing business in Mexico – and, if yes, in which way?

Behavior

Assessing the learning progress along behavioral aspects in a case discussion usually faces a similar but different challenge compared to assessing skills: When using questions relative to behavior during a full-class case discussion, participants will usually *not show their behavior* but will frequently be limited to *saying what they will or would do*. Accordingly, you could rely on other, case-based learning formats beyond questions to really observe the participants' behavior. Such learning formats could include role-plays, simulations, or group assignments (see below). However, asking questions related to behaviors is still relevant for multiple reasons: (1) The way in which a participant behaves in the class discussion can also be observed and become the target of questions. (2) As with attitudes, questions related to behaviors help to articulate the importance of this dimension for the achievement of the learning objectives. (3) Even though only indirect, you can still investigate likely behavior. (4) And, last but not least, you can always probe (i.e., follow-up) the response of participants to a behavior question, by inviting them to give it a try in a small ad hoc role-play with you (or another participant) during which you and the entire class can then observe the behavior.

So here are a few possible questions related to behaviors:

- In the position of R, what would you do now?
- When auditor S calls you at 8pm and wants you to come to the office immediately, what would you do?
- How would you prepare for this situation?
- Why do you only talk with me as the instructor and not with your classmates?
- You have now interrupted participant T for the second time. Do you think his comments are irrelevant?

Question types by learning process

Another useful way to think about the kind of questions you might use during the case discussion is to go by the phase of the learning process in which you might want to ask them. Such questions – though frequently formulated around the case study – often have a secondary meaning as they also structure the teaching process in parallel.

Reflect on the skills and knowledge that you want to foster, sharpen, or test in your participants – or more generally what you want to achieve with the respective questions. You can use questions to:

1. collect information to emphasize the importance of knowing the facts and figures in business (information questions);
2. probe for opinions and encourage arguments and counterarguments to develop presentation and persuasion skills (opinion questions);
3. put things in context by asking for relations and comparisons to other situations (relation questions);
4. stimulate and test participants' ability to generalize (generalization questions);
5. foster participants' ability to summarize (summary questions).

Opening

We elaborated extensively on the importance of opening questions with multiple examples in the 'Opening question' section above on page 55. We will therefore skip this critically important first step of the case teaching process here. If you have not already read that section, please go back.

Following up

Once the case discussion is off to a good start, you can use questions to keep the discussion going relative to a specific dimension of the case, i.e., usually within a building block of your teaching plan. (How to move to the next building block or topic will be discussed later.) Two main aspects (again not mutually exclusive and collectively exhaustive) are typically important in this phase:

- broadening, i.e., collecting additional information and perspectives, and
- probing, i.e., going deeper related to a certain aspect.

Broadening: collecting more information and perspectives

Broadening questions are most useful if relevant (1) *information* or (2) *perspectives* have not yet been added to the discussion. Here are a few typical questions to be asked to broaden the discussion within a building block:

- Can someone jump in and provide additional information?
- Have we missed something so far?
- What other facts might support your point of view?
- Is there anything that you would like to add?
- You mention the high overhead costs. What other costs seem to be out of hand?
- Does anyone have a strong opinion about what participant A just said?
- What do others think?
- Is there anyone who would like to build on the argument of participant B?

Broadening (just as probing below) assumes that the case discussion will not yet progress to a new building block/topic. You can use broadening questions in combination with implicit instructions to make this point:

- Before moving on to the next topic, what other obstacles to the potential market entry in Malaysia would protagonist C need to consider?
- Let's complete the marketing analysis by looking at the 'P' that we have not yet touched on. What product related aspects might have led to the success of the product launch?
- You see some black space in my 2×2 matrix; are there other possible reactions to D's dissatisfaction with his current employer?

Probing: going deeper

We believe it is hugely important to listen carefully and follow up on what participants say so you can probe for greater detail and achieve a more in-depth analysis. This is important to avoid the frequently made objection that case discussions only aim at the simple. Typical questions you can ask in response to contributions include:

- Why? Why do you think/believe that? Can you give your reasons?
- Tell me more! (not really a question – but a good way to go deeper)
- How do you conclude that the company is in trouble? What evidence from the case do you have to back up this claim?
- What is the single best argument you can make to support this position?
- Is there a conceptual or theoretical framework that supports your position?
- Would anything change your mind? Under what circumstances would you change your mind?
- How did you calculate this result?
- What would E (a stakeholder not yet considered during the discussion) think of your recommendation?
- How can we make the calculation of the potential market size by participant F a bit more precise?
- How/to what extent is that different to what participant G said earlier?
- What facts from the case support your point of view?

- What if this alternative wasn't available?
- Is participant H right in assuming that company J's fixed costs are too high?
- Could you rephrase that in simpler language?
- You mentioned X in your comment: could you explain what X is?
- Where in the case did you find that information?

Just as with broadening questions, probing questions can also be used to retain the discussion within the respective building block of your teaching plan while at the same time ensuring the necessary depth of the discussion. For example:

- You have mentioned a number of issues; could you explain Y first?
- Let's drill down a bit more. What are the specific factors influencing the throughput time in plant K?
- Leaving the two last points that you made aside, how does the credit insurance you just mentioned help company L during this crisis?
- Let's try to get a more precise estimate before moving on. Which factor might we need to consider additionally?
- Would you mind coming back to that point after we have first discussed X?

Transitioning

The subtle use of questions to move without force from one building block of your teaching plan to the next is one of the hallmarks of a great case teacher. When done well, it is through transition questions that the educator can be flexible and adaptive to participants' contributions while at the same time staying firmly in control of the learning process and timing.

Transitioning through questions requires patience, experience, and thinking on your feet. Which contributions from students will allow you to move to the next building block? What if a participant makes a comment that would allow for a wonderful transition question but it comes too early? Many things can happen in a case discussion. But, with a bit of preparation, you can increase your chances of success – even if all your prepared transition questions are eventually useless in a specific session. Here are a few examples of transition questions for your inspiration:

- You just mentioned as a side comment that the risk officer, M, seems to be unhappy in the case study. Let's explore this issue: what might be the risks associated with this insurance product? (You need to be either lucky for such a fitting comment, or you need to elicit such observations through skillful broadening questions before.)
- We have looked extensively at fixed assets. Which other assets make up more than 10% of the balance sheet and should be looked at in this particular case? (A quite focused, almost closed question.)
- Which other important aspects have we not yet discussed? (An open transition question that might move you to a topic that you did not intend to move to.)
- In our analysis of the new employee onboarding process at company N, we moved from the preparation to the first day. What should come next? (If orchestrating your teaching plan along a process, the transitions might be a bit easier.)
- Is everyone ready to move on from our external analysis? Then I would suggest looking at the internally available resources of company N. Who would like to go first? (A quite rigid and clearly marked transition with a very open-ended question to move on.)
- Are we done with the business case? Great! Let's now calculate how the case changes at different interest rates. (A hard cut but combined with praise for the achievement of the class.)

- Before moving on, are there any open questions or comments? (Not really a transitioning question but a question that clearly marks that you are ready to move on.)
- Leaving behind our discussion around customer satisfaction, what could company O do to improve its brand awareness? (The explicit mentioning of customer satisfaction and brand awareness gives the different building blocks a name – it is a bit obvious, but it might help participants to remember the key areas discussed.)
- Most of you agreed to terminate the contract with supplier P, but how else can we ensure that our raw materials don't include toxins? (A broadening question that can at the same time help you to transition to a new building block.)

Closing

When closing a case discussion, three considerations are usually key: (1) summarizing the lessons learned, (2) relating the session and session outcome to other parts of the course/program or to other business constellations, and (3) generalizing the insights from the case.

Summarizing

Summarizing questions are usually asked at the end of a case discussion to bring the session to a close. As the flow of a case-based session can be winding according to the participants' contributions, it is important to close the session with a look back at what was learned along the way. One way to achieve this is to ask summarizing questions. Typical summary questions might include:

- How would you sum up this case?
- Can someone please remind all of us about the three mistakes that protagonist Q did while trying to sell to company R?
- Based on our discussion, what is the key thing you have learned today?
- In a few years from now, what should you remember from this case discussion?
- If you were asked to write a tweet about this session, what would it be?
- Looking back at the case discussion, what seem to be the most important steps of the account consolidation process?

Relating

It is one thing to summarize (i.e., add up, bring together) the previous discussion, but often it is important to help participants to see the connections to other domains (industries, functions, countries, theories, tools…) or to their own situations (especially in executive education). The aim of relating questions is therefore to broaden the picture and to learn by comparing and contrasting. Relating questions typically come toward the end of the session but can also be used during the discussion. Typical questions might include:

- How does our case discussion compare to the experiences you have gained before coming back to school?
- Do you think that if the company was headquartered in the US, the situation would have been the same?
- How does the R&D budget of company S compare to what you know about industry T?
- How does your answer relate to the arguments of the previous participant U?
- Are there other product types for which our lessons learned might apply? Which and why?
- This case was about a luxury hotel. Do you see similar problems in other travel segments?

- How does this case relate to the research on market entry strategies as presented in the textbook?
- In which industries might our insights not be applicable?

And here are a few examples specifically for executive education or part-time degree programs (i.e., for participants who are working professionally at the same time):

- The case describes the decision process of a CEO. How does this relate to your own situation?
- How would you deal with a question like this in your company?
- What can your teams/colleagues learn from our case discussion?

Generalizing

Another classic way to close a case session is to invite participants to generalize the lessons they have learned. This can also be achieved by asking questions. Such generalizing questions can be used to inductively formulate a hypothesis out of the lessons learned. But, in line with our suggestions on how to deal with legitimate criticism of the case method, you can also use generalizing questions to help your participants explore the limits of generalizability. Typical questions might include:

- Is there anything in this case study that you think could be generalized?
- Can you draw any generally applicable conclusions from our case discussion? When do they apply and when might they not be applicable?
- If you face a similar situation in the future, what are the three main takeaways from this case that might help you avoid potential mistakes?
- This case is a very specific situation. Where do you see some generalizable principles?
- After discussing the case, what might be the three most important drivers of corporate fraud in general?
- Under which circumstances might our main conclusion not be applicable for other firms?

(Implicit) instructions and dealing with special situations

We saw with some of the questions mentioned above that you can use questions to guide the discussion (e.g., to stay at a certain topic/building block or to move on). They can also be used to deal with various types of special situations, many of which we will discuss in greater detail in the section 'Orchestrating the discussion' from page 78 onwards. But, because we believe this to be such an important feature of questions, we will now list some such situations and corresponding questions already here. (Dealing with too vocal and too silent students – just to name a few special cases – will be discussed only below.)

- Questions to deal with offensive comments or inadequate language:
  - Could you please come up with a less offensive wording of your comment?
  - Is anyone able to make the point without using such offensive language?
  - Are all of you ok with this language?
  - Is this really something you want to say – or did you mean to express something else?
- Questions to deal with contributions that are too judgmental:
  - Are you certain that there is no other way to look at the issue?
  - Would anybody else be able to illustrate why there might be other ways to look at this?
  - Could you come up with some counterperspectives/positions to your own claim?
  - Would you please find a less confrontational argument to disagree with participant V? Disagreement is important but we should keep it civil.

- Questions to deal with factual errors:
  - Where in the case study can you find support for this claim?
  - Did you have a close look at exhibit 3 in the case study?
  - How did you come up with this sales figure of 3 billion US dollars?
  - Can someone else please correct this for us?
  - Did any of the other breakout groups come up with a different result for the calculation?
- Questions to deal with excessively long contributions:
  - Sorry for interrupting, but could you please give us the executive summary/elevator pitch for this argument?
  - Participant W already mentioned three arguments; can someone else please analyze the first argument a bit deeper, before W or anybody else adds more points?

And finally, a reminder about our core belief: During the case discussion, do not stick rigidly to the list of questions that you prepared before. Some might not really fit anymore (because you might have touched the topics without even asking a question), better ones may occur to you as you go along, and participants may also come up with some great questions (that you can use in the future!). And, if you find such new/better questions: make sure to write them down during or immediately after the session – so that you can add them to the teaching plan for the next time you use the case.

Asking great questions

- Ensure your questions support the learning objectives.
- Be familiar with different types of questions and how they may affect the discussion.
- Prepare plenty of questions in advance (writing them down helps to get them right).
- Use a mix of open and closed questions but use mostly open questions.
- Use a variety of questions to advance the discussion (Why? What? Where? How? Who? Which?).
- Target specific questions at individuals when appropriate.
- Make the most of experts in your class.
- Prepare questions that will encourage in-depth probing and analysis.
- Prepare questions that will move the discussion on from one point or topic to the next.
- Prepare questions to close the session and reaffirm the learning.
- Don't stick rigidly to your list of questions: be flexible.

Listening carefully

'Listening is a positive act: you have to put yourself out to do it.' – David Hockney

Sometimes it is hard to listen. It can be even harder to listen well. But you cannot be a very good case teacher unless you are a very good listener.

Why is it hard to listen well?

Listening well in an educational context is both extremely important and at the same time very hard. As an educator you cannot simply focus on the person who is speaking; instead, you must concentrate on three things at the same time: yourself, the speaker, and the class/process.

When teaching a case, you will always be juggling various aspects of your role. Will you get through the material on time? Are the learning objectives being delivered? Have you remembered all your materials? Will the technology work? Have you got all your points across? Did you pick the right case? These are just a few of the questions that will be racing through your brain while, at the same time, you are trying to actively listen to a participant and concentrate on what they are saying.

This will, of course, affect what you hear, how you process the information, and how you incorporate it into the flow of the session. Generally speaking: the better prepared you are for the session, the more you will be able to focus on the participants, listen well, and respond appropriately and effectively.

Being aware

Listening well means doing your best to understand the motivations and feelings of the person who is speaking. For example: Why did they decide to contribute? What is their role in the class? How often have they contributed before? Do they find it difficult to contribute? Also – are they perhaps trying to convey something that is not coming across verbally? All of these factors will influence the way you process and respond to what is being said.

And, of course, you must never forget the rest of the class, even when you are concentrating on the participant who is speaking. You will need to be fully aware throughout the session: Is everyone contributing? Are one or two people dominating? Who else might have a strong opinion and be encouraged to speak? Is there an expert in the room you can ask about a particular issue?

With all this to remember, it is no wonder that listening well and taking in what your participants are saying can take a back seat. The skilled case teacher will guard against this because listening closely to what your participants are saying should be the number one priority.

If you are not listening properly, you are not teaching properly, because you would be violating our core belief of elevating your participants to eye level.

The four levels of communication

To become a great listener, it makes sense to think about communication a bit more generally. Human communication can be verbal and nonverbal, is obviously complex, and has been studied from the perspective of various academic disciplines. There are many different communication models, none of which seems to be all-encompassing or complete. For the purposes of looking at listening during case study discussions, we suggest briefly reviewing a framework developed by Friedemann Schulz von Thun. Building on earlier work by Paul Watzlawick, Schulz von Thun (1981) postulates that when people talk to each other they exchange information on four different levels in parallel:

- Factual
- Self-revelation
- Relationship
- Appeal

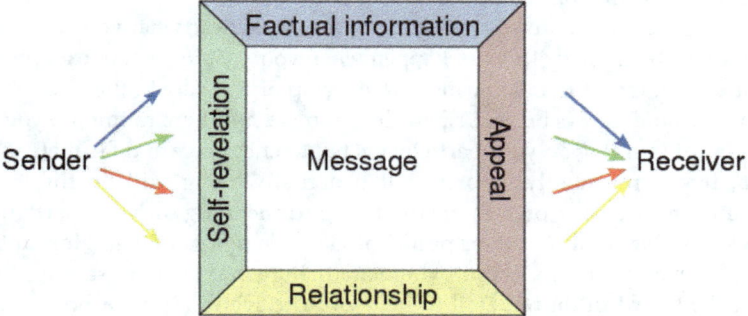

Figure 13: Schulz von Thun 'Four-Sides Model.' Source: Wikimedia Commons (https://commons.wikimedia.org/wiki/File:Four-sides-model_en.svg; author: JazzyJulius; licensed as public domain; accessed August 1, 2022).

When listening to your participants' contributions, it is certainly helpful to develop the ability to listen to more than just the content or factual information of the contribution. Also listening to self-revelation, appeal, and relationship will be important to manage the complexities of the case discussion: even though all four dimensions will not always be present or equally relevant in every statement for your case discussion, you should develop the ability to listen multidimensionally.

To illustrate the different levels, let's take a fictional example: Your name is Alexandra Perez and you are chaired professor of marketing at a reputable school. In the middle of a case discussion during your third session of an introduction to marketing course, Olena Smieshkova, one of your participants, elaborates on her ideas for the price for a new product. As she is speaking, João Martins Leite, another participant, shouts, 'Hey, Sandy, we already discussed this!' and waves with his right hand in an outward movement – obviously assuming that Sandy is your commonly used nickname. We will explain the four sides of the model in greater detail, but these could be the messages that you could hear along the four sides when João makes this comment:

- Factual message: We already discussed what Olena just said.
- Self-revelation message: I am entitled to steer the discussion, and to cut off my classmates.
- Relationship message: I, João am on the same level as you, Alexandra.
- Appeal message: Let's move on!

One small explanation: While all four dimensions are present for most communication, they can have very different salience and the way in which we can understand them will vary vastly dependent upon the context, upon us as listeners and upon our relationship with the sender – and this is often a source of misunderstanding and conflict. 'Hearing' a different appeal or relationship can easily lead to conflict. Receivers therefore need to be self-critical with their interpretation of the messages.

Factual information

At this level, your participants try to convey some sort of (usually explicit) content or information: they respond to your question or to fellow participants, they provide other types of input (e.g., by communicating factual information from the case, their experience or other sources), and they might even talk about their emotions as content or facts. For example, when someone says 'I feel pain,' the factual information is that this person claims to feel pain.

To be a good listener, you must listen to what your participants are saying on a factual level, and respond appropriately. Like this, you will be able to effectively orchestrate the discussion, e.g., through counterquestions (probing), inviting participants to expand on their point (broadening), or asking other participants to respond to them. It is only by listening carefully that you will be able to make accurate, useful, and meaningful board notes as you teach; the notes will usually relate to the factual information dimension of a contribution.

A common error on the level of factual information is to 'hear what you want to hear' rather than what is actually being said. This can happen when you are too keen to lead the discussion in a particular direction, rather than allowing it to develop organically in the classroom. The classroom discussion should always be participant-led. You are not there to impose your own understanding and way of thinking on your participants but to encourage and facilitate theirs.

In addition, if you repeatedly ignore what is actually being said on the level of factual information and impose your own interpretation and meaning on your participants' words, they will quickly understand that their points of view are not valued and lose interest in contributing. This is even more important when capturing what is being said on the board. We discuss use of the board in more detail in below in the section 'Use of board' on page 95 of this chapter.

In our example of Alexandra, Olena, and João, the factual information João seems to try to convey is that he believes that what Olena said had already been discussed. Whether or not that is factually true (i.e., if Olena might have introduced a new facet) or not is a separate point. At the level of factual information, João tries to make a point about how the world is – and from his perspective Olena seems to be adding nothing new.

Self-revelation

A good listener can learn something about the speaker beyond what they are actually saying. Does what is being said reveal something more about the speaker? Why is the speaker's contribution important to them? Why are they so keen to participate at this point in the discussion? Are they over-excited or laid back and disinterested when speaking? How does their contribution relate to what others are saying?

Paying attention to self-revelation means being alive to the atmosphere in the classroom, the tone of the discussion, and individual emotional reactions to what is being discussed. Do not forget: Your participants have a relationship to one another beyond and in parallel to your case discussion. Especially early on in a program they also position themselves vis-à-vis one another while interacting in class.

With his comment 'Hey, Sandy, we already discussed this!' João also projects that this is how he wants to be perceived by the other members of the group. His comment could therefore be read to suggest: 'I am entitled to steer the discussion, and to cut off my classmates.' But it could also mean: 'I am super-smart', 'I am impatient' – the exact understanding of the self-revelation dimension is usually more-dimensional and tricky to read. But it is there – and can have massive influence on the overall discussion.

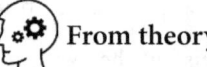 From theory to practice with Urs

I was once discussing a case that I had disguised on the basis of a real case from one of the students in the group. The case dealt with the challenge of a recently promoted manager who needed to deal with a case of alleged sexual harassment against one of her subordinates. Early in the discussion a male student commented, referring to the case protagonist: 'The girl should have done XYZ.' At that point of the discussion, the student did not yet know that the protagonist was a person in the room, but on a self-revelation dimension he clearly projected that it was ok to call a manager a 'girl.' – And I could use this self-revelation easily for a follow-up.

Relationship

The third level of communication is about the relationship between the speaker and the listener. The speaker will reveal a lot about how much they value the listener and how they perceive their relationship to the listener.

This is also very important information to take into account when orchestrating a discussion, especially as a case discussion is not a 1:1 conversation but rather an n:n communication between all members of the group. A good listener will sense the relationship between contributing participants and glean important information about their role as the listener and how they are perceived by the speakers.

This third level of communication will also give you clues about whether the discussion has become too funny, hostile, volatile, or disrespectful; if people are becoming upset; if you need to address an individual's concerns; and whether or not veiled (or open) insults are being used. It can help you decide if you need to calm things down or remind participants of the basic classroom ground rules.

In our example of João, the relationship dimension relates to both Alexandra (the professor) and to Olena (the classmate). Through the use of a nickname for the professor, João seems to project: 'I, João, am on the same level as you, Alexandra.' This might be perfectly adequate – e.g., if Alexandra introduced herself as 'Sandy' – or could be extremely rude – e.g., if all other students would refer to her as Professor Perez. And, with respect to Olena and the interruption of her contribution, João's comment clearly demonstrates the assumption of an asymmetric power/relevance relationship.

Appeal

When a participant says something there is also often an implicit call to action that is frequently well hidden. This is the fourth level of communication: 'appeal.'

By saying something in class, participants can express very different appeals. Examples of what a participant might appeal to include:

- a desire to be appreciated by classmates;
- a longing to be loved;
- an interest in getting a good grade for in-class contribution;
- a concern about being considered as being smart;
- implicit instructions about the further flow of the class (e.g., a joke can signal: please make this less boring/more fun);
- a desire to win a perceived competition with other participants by outsmarting them.

You clearly do not have to give in to such appeals but they will be implicitly present and it is helpful to be able to read them. In the example of João, he seems to appeal to an accelerated speed or at least to moving to a new topic. He does not explicitly say this – but as soon as he says 'Hey, Sandy, we already discussed this!' we can probably all understand what he had in mind.

Listen to the things that are not being said

As postulated by Watzlawick, Beavin and Jackson (1967), '[o]ne cannot not communicate: Every behavior is a form of communication. Because behavior does not have a counterpart (there is no anti-behavior), it is impossible not to communicate.'

Good listeners also listen to the things that are not being said. You should try to actively 'hear' what is being left unsaid in your class. This applies again to multiple dimensions of the communication. Why do participants not touch a certain topic? Why do some not contribute at all? Why is contribution so much lower than in previous sessions? The nonspeakers might be sending 'loud' messages on all four levels of communication as described above without saying a word. A good way to test what you sense on the four dimensions will be to ask questions. And a possible question to ask to your class is always to ask on a metalevel: 'What is going on?' and thus directly speak about the educational process instead of only talking about the content of the case discussion.

Listening through speaking: echoing

It is often tricky to avoid misunderstandings in the interpretation of the messages you are receiving, especially on the levels of self-revelation, relationship, and appeal – in addition, there is the issue of the impossibility of noncommunication. A great way to avoid, or at least minimize, such misunderstandings is often called 'echoing' – and, in case teaching, echoing is particularly helpful.

Echoing is a technique through which the educator in a case discussion feeds back something that a participant said in class just like the acoustical echo in a canyon. This can be done through statements or questions, and the wording of what is being fed back can either be verbatim or be very different from what was said originally. Essentially the educator will 'listen' (or at least ensure proper understanding) through speaking. This is a very useful and powerful tool when used sparingly and well. Echoing can be in particular very useful in building likability, safety, rapport, and social cohesion between and with the class.

The basic idea of echoing (with slight variations) probably goes back to the field of psychotherapy, where it was introduced to ensure adequate understanding by the therapist, but at the same time to abstain from judgment. When people talk about 'active' or 'reflective listening,' they occasionally have something similar in mind – and when trying to make fun of the technique it is occasionally defamed as 'parroting,' because it seemingly does not require understanding but just the repetition of words, but this is far from what we are recommending to you.

Here are some benefits of echoing:

- Repeating people's words helps with your own understanding of another person's point of view but it also sends the social signal to the other person that you are making an effort to understand. It shows that you have been listening to what they were saying, and not just thinking about what you want to say next. It also shows to the other person that there is a mutual understanding between the two of you.
- You ensure that the participant really meant what you hear. This is not only limited to the level of factual information. You can also echo what you hear on the other levels. Using the example of João saying 'Hey, Sandy, we already discussed this!' here are some possible echoing techniques:
    - Factual information: 'If I understand you correctly, you believe that Olena didn't add new perspectives and considerations. Don't you think that her use of the 4Ps was a new facet?'
    - Self-revelation: 'It seems as if you are unhappy about our case discussion so far. Can you please elaborate?'
    - Relationship: 'I might have missed something, but you seem to just have called me "Sandy," right? That is not a nickname I use or want you to use.'
    - Appeal: 'João, you seem to want to move on, right?' – 'Yes' – 'Good, but before we do so, I want to give Olena an opportunity to finish her statement.'
- The language people use reflects the reality they live in. When you use echoing in a sense, that you use their wording, you – to some degree – put yourself closer to the world that participants live in. This gives you a better chance to empathize with that person and truly understand where they are coming from and why they speak and behave in the way they do. This is why it can be a good idea to adopt the same or similar wording a person uses. Echoing signals that you are on the same page as them.
- Echoing ensures that everyone in the class hears what was said; this is especially helpful in large class, with acoustical problems, with nonnative speakers, or if the meaning of the comment was unclear or expressed in a convoluted way.

Some practical tips to start using or improving your echoing:

- Really listen to the person you are talking to. Pay particular attention to words they use frequently.
- Repeat when appropriate – but do not just be a robot or parrot. Often repeating works best when you want to continue the flow of the conversation and allow the person to give you more information.

- If the contribution was clear, use the same words and phrases the other person uses, with the same intended meaning.
- If the contribution was ambiguous, vague, or using wrong terminology/language (e.g., from nonnative speakers), modify the message and use your own (more precise) wording. You do not have to use the participant's exact words when echoing, particularly when aiming to clarify the meaning of what was said.

Careful echoing will also demonstrate that you are listening carefully and respect and value each participant's contribution. It is good practice to combine your echoing with recording the participant's comment on the board (see below for more on how to use the board). This reinforces the idea that their comment is valued as part of the discussion.

However, use echoing judiciously:

- Do not overdo echoing as this will interfere with the flow of the discussion. (Echoing tends to increase your talking time, so when the contribution was clear and others are willing to immediately follow up, go with the flow.)
- Be careful when paraphrasing a participant's comments as you may change or distort the meaning of what was said. This might confuse the issue and potentially alienate your participant ('I didn't say that').
- Do not use echoing too much as this might create the impression that you have nothing more to add other than repeating what was said before.

Listening carefully

– Be a good listener.
– Try to listen on four levels (factual information, self-revelation, relationship, appeal).
– Hear what is actually said, not what you want to hear.
– 'Listen' to the things that are not being said.
– Use echoing to enhance your listening but beware of the risks.

Orchestrating the discussion

Leading the discussion

'A conductor should guide rather than command.' – Riccardo Muti

What does orchestrating the class discussion mean? In addition to listening well and asking the right questions at the right time, you will also need to deal with different types of participants and participant behavior in the classroom and manage the discussion along your teaching plan or the flow of the class. And this is mainly what we mean by 'orchestrating the class discussion.' Just like a conductor for an orchestra, the educator will need to oversee the contribution of the various members of the class and manage the rhythm at the same time.

This can be tricky for the inexperienced teacher and is a skill that will develop over time. For example, a new case teacher may be so relieved to get a response from a participant that they then allow them to dominate the rest of the session because at least someone is talking! In addition, it is easy to miss participants who never say a word, particularly if a lively discussion is underway on the other side of the classroom.

Other issues include dealing with participants who are texting or surfing the net during the session, or those who have simply not read the case and are unprepared. It sounds like a bit of a minefield, but do not panic: there are strategies and techniques that can be used to deal with all these challenges. And, of course, you will also develop your own tried and tested methods over time.

Establishing ground rules is an important part of teaching. This will usually be done at the start of a course (and referred back to if necessary during the case sessions). We cover ground rules in some detail later on (see chapter 'Teaching a Case-Based Course' from page 113 onwards).

Some basic guidelines

Before we go into more detail about specific challenges you may face in the classroom, it is useful to summarize some basic guidelines for orchestrating a case discussion:

- Manage the allocated time well. Be punctual and expect your participants to be on time too. Do not start the session early or end it late. Keep to the timetabled breaks, although break times can be flexible with mutual negotiation.
- It is your role to steer and guide the discussion but not to dominate or restrict it. You must give your participants the freedom to take ownership of their learning (think back to the students around the patient in the room: you should allow them to gain experiences and only intervene if something goes wrong).
- Ensure the transition from one topic to the next is managed smoothly.
- Develop the skills you need to deal with participants who are too vocal and those who rarely speak.
- Do not allow 'problem' participants to take too much of your attention – this would be unfair to the vast majority of your class who will usually be motivated and keen to contribute to the discussion without dominating it.
- Use various techniques to deal with unprepared participants.
- Be prepared to deal with texters and surfers.
- Be ready to refocus participants on relevant topics and issues if the discussion strays too far from the learning objectives.
- Be prepared to challenge ideas and opinions and allow participants to question their fellow participants – this is essential for a healthy and vibrant debate.
- Make accurate board notes as the session progresses and check with participants to ensure that your interpretations of their remarks are correct.
- Make use of your participants' knowledge, experiences, and expertise in class – guided by what you learned when collecting information about them before the course or session.

Managing transitions

Moving smoothly from one topic to the next is a key skill that case teachers need to develop. Be clear about the number of topics you plan to cover in the session and roughly how long you want to spend on each. Your plan must remain flexible as you can never predict exactly how a case discussion will develop.

Each discussion section will typically have its own learning objectives (concepts, frameworks, or reflection) so it is helpful to treat each section as distinct and separate.

However, you will have to strike a delicate balance because some participants can find the transition too abrupt and forced, while others might not even notice that the discussion has moved on to another topic. There are many ways to handle a transition and you can decide which option is best for you.

Here are a number of techniques that we have used, observed, or discussed in our workshops:

- Summarize the key arguments and/or learnings from a section. This could work well as a mini-lecture of up to 10 minutes.
- Invite participants to present a summary of the section.
- Signal the end of the section by holding a vote on the issues discussed.
- Use the board to signal the end of a topic (for example, by bringing up a new board, erasing a board, turning the page…).
- Physically change your position in the room.

Always check that participants do not have any final questions or queries and make sure that everybody is ready to move on. You should prepare questions that will subtly move the discussion forward from one topic or issue to the next. (On transition questions, see page 69.)

Participants who are too vocal

Do not be tempted to rely on those participants who are always ready to offer their thoughts and opinions. This will inevitably lead to one person or a small group of people dominating the session. This is very demotivating for the rest of the class, who will feel their presence is not valued and their views are not of interest: the exact opposite of what you should be aiming for!

So, what to do? Well, here are a few tactics:

- First, remind everyone of the relevant classroom ground rules (see page 79).
- Physically turn away from the participant who is talking too much or will not stop talking! This is particularly effective if you turn away immediately after responding to them and focus on other participants in another part of the classroom.
- Make a simple, nonconfrontational statement, for example: 'Now I'd like to give some other people the opportunity to share their ideas and perspectives.'

Avoid the automatic assumption that someone who 'talks too much' always represents a problem. Use their verbal enthusiasm in a positive way! For example, select them for a role-play session. Not only will this use their talent for talking but it will also be a good learning experience for them as they will have to deal with feedback from fellow role-players.

It is possible to use humor to make someone understand that they are hogging the limelight too much. But be very careful with this tactic. It is easy to hurt people's feelings and unintentionally humiliate them. When attempts at humor go wrong you risk alienating not only the person your joke was aimed at but also the class as a whole: definitely something to avoid.

Participants who are too quiet

Your target should be for everyone in the class to contribute at least once – this will usually be possible with groups of up to 50 participants.

Always be sensitive to the reasons why some participants will find it difficult to contribute. Are the women heavily outnumbered by men? Are some of your participants from cultures where participants are expected to respectfully listen to the teacher rather than contribute their own views? Are some of your participants simply a little shy and need some encouragement before speaking up? Is an individual or small group dominating the discussion to the exclusion of everyone else? It is your responsibility to deal with this – see tips above.

Again, there are a number of techniques you can use to draw out your less vocal participants:

- Cold-calling: simply direct a question at someone who has not yet spoken. This can be more effective if you ask for their response to a previous speaker's remarks rather than bringing up a completely fresh issue for the person to deal with out of the blue.
- Announce that the next contribution to the discussion must come from someone who has not yet spoken. While saying this you can indicate with an open-palm gesture two or three participants who would be welcome to give their views.
- You can allocate a number or some other identifier to each participant and pick people to speak at random.
- Organize discussions in pairs or small groups. This can be particularly useful when teaching large classes.
- Make it clear from the start that grades will be linked with the level and quality of contributions made in class.
- Use online tools like voting apps (Poll Everywhere, Mentimeter, Crowdsignal) or even X (previously known as Twitter), where participants can engage by voting, or even posting comments.

When cold-calling a previously silent participant, be patient and do not panic if they fail to reply straight away. Understand that it may be difficult for them to 'dip their toe in the water.' So just remain calm and wait a moment or two. Be sure to note their comment on the board to reinforce the idea that their contribution is valued.

Participants who do not prepare

The first thing you must do when participants arrive at your class unprepared is find out why (some reasons are more forgivable than others). You can then decide how to deal with the problem.
Possible reasons for arriving unprepared include:

- There is genuinely too much work to get through in the course program.
- Personal problems such as family, health or work issues.
- A lack of understanding about what preparation was required.
- Participants are not interested in the case or topic.
- Participants arrive in class expecting to be 'entertained' or fed information, rather than taking responsibility for their own learning.
- Overconfidence can lead participants to believe that they are smart enough to contribute without prior preparation.
- Participants are too lazy to prepare.

If you are not clear why participants did not prepare, simply ask them. You can do this face to face or use an anonymous method such as a feedback form – you may get a more honest answer this way. Once you have established the reasons why particular participants did not prepare for the session, you can decide on a course of action.

Short-term solutions

- Ask a participant to summarize the case.
- Split the class into groups and allow a few minutes for participants to look at the case and come up with a recommendation.
- Provide a summary of the case so that everyone is quickly up to speed. You can use preprepared slides, images or video clips if you have them.
- Allow time for participants to read the case at the start of the class.

It is best not to use these short-term solutions on a regular basis as your participants will become complacent and view preparation as an optional extra.

Long-term solutions

- Communicate your expectations about the level of preparation you require before a class. Stress that preparation is not optional.
- Announce well in advance which cases you will be teaching to give participants plenty of time to read and prepare for the session. Send out a reminder a few days before the session.
- Ensure your colleagues send out a consistent message about preparation.

In addition, you can use 'pull' or 'push' techniques (or a combination of both) to encourage preparation.

Pull techniques

Depending on your teaching style and personality, 'pull' techniques may suit you more than 'push' techniques – or you may find a combination of both works well. Here are some typical 'pull' techniques:

- Support and mentor individual participants who consistently fail to prepare.
- Appeal to the pride and professionalism of participants.
- Choose short or abridged cases that participants will find faster and easier to read.
- Take the time to find cases that will more closely match the interests and concerns of your participant group.
- Encourage participants to meet in small groups in advance of the session to discuss the case and prepare short presentations on particular topics.
- Assign specific questions to individual participants in advance of the session so they are ready to answer in class.
- Use online tools to communicate and connect with participants before sessions, for example, ask them to post observations or questions about the case.

Push techniques

These are tougher tactics that can be used to send a clear message to your class. Only you can decide if any of these options will work for you and your participants. For example:

- To reinforce the requirement to prepare, explain in advance that you will be:
  ○ cold-calling participants from the start of the session
  ○ setting quizzes
  ○ allocating role-play roles
  ○ grading the level and quality of class participation.
- Carry out an initial short test about the case that participants have to pass before they can take part in the rest of the session.
- Request presession writeups, essays, or video clip presentations.
- If your participants have not prepared, immediately cancel the class or, less drastically, allow only those participants who have prepared to remain (as long as enough are left to run your session). You can also call everyone that has not prepared (once you noticed) to sit in a certain area of the classroom (first row or left-hand side etc.).

Dealing with surfers and texters

Every teacher is familiar with that heart-sinking moment when they realize that at least some of their participants are surfing the net or texting during a case session. This is a tricky situation to deal with but there a few things you can try to counteract this ubiquitous problem:

- Remind the class of the ground rules.
- Lead by example and make a point of switching off your own devices and putting them to one side at the start of the session.
- Simply ask participants not to text or surf during the session; point out that using personal devices in class is distracting for both you and other participants.
- Walk around the class at regular intervals (if the classroom layout allows) to see what is happening: participants may be taking notes on their laptops, which is perfectly legitimate, but checking out friends' Facebook pages should not be acceptable.
- Point out that taking handwritten notes leads to greater knowledge retention, although research is not really clear on this topic; compare Schoen (2012) and Smoker, Murphy, and Rockwell (2009).
- You can try a lighthearted or humorous remark to discourage an individual participant from surfing or texting during a session. But, as ever, be very careful with humor. It is easy to cause unwitting offense and alienate participants.
- You can also have an open discussion about the topic. You could, for example, just ask your students which other instructor handles the use of phones and laptops the best. Get the students to share some examples and ask why they think that this is an effective way to deal with this issue.

Orchestrating the class discussion

- Follow the basic guidelines including good time management.
- Prepare transitions and make sure that everybody is ready to move on.
- Use suitable tactics to deal with 'problem' participants.
- Do not focus too much on 'problem' participants to the detriment of others.
- Ensure participants are prepared for class.
- Minimize in-class surfing and texting.

Learning formats

> 'There's an alternative. There's always a third way, and it's not a combination of the other two ways. It's a different way.' – David Carradine

When teaching with cases it is important to use a variety of learning formats, both during a case session and over the course as whole. Evidence shows that using different learning formats has a positive impact on participants' learning. There are a number of reasons for this:

- Every participant will learn differently. By offering various formats you will be more likely to cater for different learning styles.
- Relevance is important for learning and different formats will help to highlight the relevance of a particular topic or issue.
- Different learning formats will enable your participants to take different perspectives.

- You will get the chance to use different technologies in the classroom.
- Feedback is always important and the use of different learning formats will offer participants a variety of ways to offer feedback.

A well-planned case session will include a variety of different learning formats. We hope the list below will inspire you and also encourage you to try some that you are less familiar with.

- Full-class discussion (see page 61)
- Individual presentations
- Lectures
- Guests – protagonists or other relevant individuals
- Field visits
- Video clips
- Quizzes and polls
- Simulations and demonstrations, for example, of processes
- Actors (e.g., using professional actors in class, for example for negotiation classes or storytelling having actors playing different variants)
- Group work
- Role-play

Mix it up! By changing the learning format every 15 to 20 minutes (in online formats maybe even faster) you will stand a better chance of retaining everyone's attention and interest. Using different formats will also help to actively engage as many participants as possible and will appeal to a wide range of learning styles. It is more interesting for the teacher too! However, when planning always keep your learning objectives in mind.

Let's have a closer look at a few of these options in more detail.

Full-class discussion

Full-class discussions are the backbone of the case method, and you can find more information about running a successful discussion on page 61.

Group work

Group work can be a particularly powerful learning tool. A small group can be just two people working together, a buzz group of three or four participants, or slightly larger groups. All can work well.

The location and timing of group work can be flexible too. For example, group work can take place:

- In the classroom, in breakout areas/rooms, outside (weather permitting!), or another location of the group members' choice.
- Before, during or between sessions.
- Online in advance of the session, with participants taking part in a synchronous discussion or adding their thoughts at a time that suits them (asynchronous).

You will need to decide what outcome you want to achieve from group work. Will each group present the results of their discussions? Or just selected groups? Will you ask for volunteers? Or decide based on the content of each group's discussion?

You will, of course, be limited by time, so it may only be possible for two or three groups to make a presentation at the end of their discussions. Try to select groups who will make very different presentations to avoid repetition of content. Three very similar presentations made one after the other will quickly become a turnoff for the rest of the class. This completely defeats the object of using different learning formats in your case session.

Group composition

Decide in advance how you will organize your groups. There are a number of ways to do this:

- In some programs it is common for the same groups to work together over the length of the course.
- Participants can be left to decide for themselves which groups to work in. However, be aware that this may cause uncertainty and delay that is better avoided. You may also reject this option if you do not want participants to stick together in the same 'safe' group and to ensure that quieter, or less popular participants are not excluded.
- You can simply segment the class into groups using the existing seating arrangement.
- Select group members randomly if you wish to mix up the participants and get them out of their usual seating arrangement. One way to do this is to give each participant a number (for example, from one to four if you are creating four groups) and those with the same number then work together.
- Select group members according to their expertise or background so that each group will approach the discussion from a different angle. This will also help to ensure that any subsequent presentations will offer a greater variety of content for the rest of the class.

 From theory to practice with Martin

When planning a case session, I make a note of any questions and challenges that might be suitable for group work. I can then decide during the session if it will be more useful to continue with the whole class discussion or switch to a group exercise.

For me, there are some typical signs that tell me I should switch to group work. For example:

- I feel that the energy level is dropping (often after more than 20 minutes of intense discussion).
- Only a small proportion of the participants are really engaged in the class discussion. Switching to group work will enable everyone to contribute.
- I ask a question but the answers either lack depth or are off topic. Here, group work can refocus participants.

Role-play

First, we need to be clear about what role-play actually is. Role-play requires individuals to step into the shoes of a particular character and think, feel, and behave as they believe that character would in the circumstances – not as they would themselves. This can unlock previously untapped emotions, understanding, and insights that will contribute immensely to overall learning outcomes. It is a valuable tool. In addition, role-play helps to develop skills such as listening, persuasion, negotiation, responding appropriately, and dealing with feedback.

Role-playing needs careful preparation if it is to work well, but do not let that put you off. Role-play is another highly effective teaching tool with the added bonus of being a fun thing to do. Win–win!

Here are a few guidelines for role-play:

- Clearly explain what role-play involves and what is expected of your participants – in particular, be clear about the need to 'step into the character's shoes.'
- As a general rule, do not use role-play at the start of a session. Participants will be more willing to take part once they have settled into the class and gained a little confidence.
- Always keep your learning objectives in mind. Ask yourself: will this role-play contribute to the overall aim of the session?
- Decide in advance whether the role-play can be performed while participants remain in their seats or whether they need to come to the front of the class or work in small groups.
- Decide roughly how long you want the role-play to last.
- Decide if you will take part, or if the role-play will be performed solely by participants. If participants only, what will your role be?
- Consider using participants who can be too vocal in class discussions for role-play. This will both use their verbal talents and expose them to useful feedback from the rest of the class.
- Decide which characters from the case will be part of the role-play. Consider including a minor character as this may reveal previously unconsidered points.
- Decide if the role-play will take place in small groups with only a few or no observers, or in front of the whole class.
- Consider adding interest to the role-play by giving individual characters extra information that only they know.
- Consider taking a video of the role-play. This has a number of advantages: participants can evaluate and learn from their own performance; it will help to facilitate any discussion about the role-play by reminding participants what was said; and it will help to prevent disputes about what was actually said. Also, role-play performed in small groups can then be shown to the whole class.
- Plan how the debrief will take place. This will depend on if the role-play was performed in small groups or in front of the whole class, and whether or not it was videoed. Small groups can hold their own debrief session or provide feedback to the rest of the class, either verbally or by showing the video. Whatever form the debrief takes, useful questions to ask include:
  – Which behaviors were effective and which were ineffective?
  – What should be said/done differently next time?
  – What did participants think/feel when performing the role-play?
  – Did their body language contradict their words?
- Finally, always try to ensure that those taking part in the role-play find it a positive experience that offers new insights and allows them to shine. Never allow it to become embarrassing or humiliating for anyone taking part. Always be aware that a role-play session may not work out as planned and be ready with a recovery strategy.

As a final thought, be open to spontaneous role-play opportunities, for example when two participants disagree on a fundamental point during a class discussion. One interesting technique is to ask each individual to perform a role-play in which they defend their opponent's viewpoint. This can be both fun and enlightening.

Lectures

This may seem a strange suggestion as the case method is often seen as the polar opposite of lecturing. But lecturing has its place as a valuable pedagogical tool. For example, a short lecture during a case session can be an extremely effective way to explain a relevant theory or framework, or to give some key facts and figures. And it does not have to be you who gives the lecture – this is also an ideal opportunity for one of your participants to practice their public speaking and presentation skills.

Guests

Having your protagonist in class is the most exciting way to grab the attention of your participants and reinforce the idea that the topics and issues covered in the case are rooted in the real world of business. Your protagonist can be part of the class in a number of different ways. For example, they can:

- take part as a class member;
- answer questions – either during a set time as part of the session, or at random throughout the session;
- reveal the outcome of the case at the end of the session;
- give a short presentation.

It can be very effective to bring in your protagonist as a surprise guest during a key point in the discussion. And it is not only protagonists who make great guests as part of a case session. Other possibilities include industry experts, a competitor, a consultant, or a supplier or customer of the company that features in the case.

Field visits

Arranging a field visit undoubtedly involves extra time and work but is well worth it. Visits can be made to the company discussed in the case, or to one in the same industry with similar challenges and opportunities.

On executive MBA programs, it may be possible to visit one of your participants' companies.

We strongly believe that any field visit should be closely linked to the case and add genuine value by reinforcing your learning objectives. To help achieve this and make it more than a simple visit, ensure:

- there will be enough time for a meaningful exchange with management;
- you provide clear instructions about what to look out for and observe during the visit. For example:
  – 'Observe the inbound logistics in the manufacturing plant.'
  – 'Observe the working environment and note factors that might support or hinder creativity.'

Video clips

If your protagonist cannot attend your case session, they may agree to a short video interview. Alternatively, existing footage may exist on the company website or on news sites.

Other video clips may include general news coverage of the company; presentations by other key personnel, for example at AGMs; promotional corporate videos; and company advertising.

Think carefully about how to use your video clips. You may judge that it is best to show the whole clip at a suitable point during the session. Another option is 'stop and start': show a short section of the video for discussion before going on to the next section. This can be particularly effective if you ask participants to anticipate what was said or what happens next, or what they think should be said or done next.

Quizzes and polls

Quizzes and polls can be used in a variety of ways. For example:

- In advance of the session via an online poll. You can then ask individual participants to be ready to justify their choices as a good way of kicking off the class discussion.
- As an icebreaker at the start of a session: ask for a simple show of hands to demonstrate agreement or disagreement with a particular point. You can then start the class discussion by asking individual participants why they plumped for one side or the other.
- Hold a vote at the start of the session and then at intervals throughout the session to see how many participants are 'changing sides.' Individuals can be asked to explain why they have changed their mind.
- A quiz can be used to mark the end of a particular section of your case session. This will ensure everyone is up to speed and ready to move on, as well as offering a breather and helping to break up the case session overall.

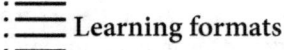 **Learning formats**

– Include a variety of elements in your case session.
– Change the learning format every 15 to 20 minutes to keep everyone's attention.
– Always keep your learning objectives in mind – make sure the learning formats you select will support the overall aim of the case session.

7. Closure and transfer

'Endings to be useful must be inconclusive.' – Samuel R. Delany

A really good case session will fly by. Try not to let the end of your session take you by surprise. Always keep an eye on the clock and aim to make the closure of your case session polished, meaningful, and memorable. There is nothing worse than ending the session and realizing that participants have not even noticed.

 Do not forget: great cases rarely have a single 'right' solution. This is one of the great strengths of the case method: it mirrors real-life business situations with all their complexities, ambiguities, and uncertainties. But be aware that some of your less experienced participants may be expecting a 'grand reveal' of the 'right' answer at the end of the session – you will need to handle their expectations in a positive way.

 It is often easy for participants to google the outcome of a case – especially if it is about a well-known organization or protagonist. This can result in participants thinking they already 'know the answer' and thus limit the scope and depth of the discussion. To avoid this, it can sometimes be a good idea to share the outcome of the case at the start of the session. This may seem counterintuitive but it can clear the way for a far more nuanced discussion. For example:

- The decisions and actions taken by the company may have worked out, but were there better solutions?
- The decisions taken worked out in the short term – but was there a better long-term solution?
- If the company made the wrong decisions, what could have been done differently?
- The outcome for the company was excellent, but was there a better/cheaper/more efficient way of arriving at that outcome?
- How does hindsight color the analysis of decisions, actions, and outcomes?

- What has happened since that makes the decisions taken seem less effective than they did at the time? Was this foreseeable?

There is no single solution to ensure a positive end to a case discussion. It will always depend on how the session went, your teaching style, and the case you have been discussing. Here are a few different options that you can 'mix and match' with the aim of 'leaving the case behind' and moving on to the lessons learned:

- Thank participants for taking part and contributing to a great discussion.
- Ask questions such as:
  - Why are we looking at this? (This aims to help participants draw generalizations from some of the key points raised in the discussion.)
  - Why should we care about these issues? (This reinforces the applicability and usefulness of the discussed topics.)
  - What other aspects might we need to consider? (A good question to check if any participants feel an important point has not been covered.)
  - Has anyone here had a similar experience to the one depicted in the case? (This is another way to highlight applicability.)
  - What is the moral of this case/story? (This will reveal what is important to individual participants and will reinforce the fact that the same case might have very different lessons for different people.)
  - To which other industries/countries/companies/functions might the lessons learned from this case be relevant? (This is another way to draw out generalizations from the case.)
  - How will the lessons learned from this case affect the way you do business in the future? (This is another way to highlight applicability.)
  - How does our discussion illustrate the concepts/tools/frameworks/theories mentioned earlier? (This is a good question to close the learning cycle.)
- Ask participants to reflect on how the discussion has influenced their thinking. For example: 'I used to think X; now I think Y'; 'Before I believed A; now I realize that B is more likely to be true.'
- Ask participants to summarize what lessons they have learned from the case. This can be done in few different ways, for example, individuals or groups can present their feedback to the rest of the class; participants can work in small groups to share their feedback among themselves; or, participants can be left to work on an individual basis (this option can be particularly effective in executive education where participants may be keen to relate the lessons learned to their own workplace).
- Ask participants to write an essay summarizing the lessons learned as a postsession exercise.
- It can be effective to end with a joke or a surprise (but make sure your joke is both funny and inoffensive, and that your 'surprise' will not fall flat because participants already know what is coming).
- Conduct an exit poll to help summarize the overall conclusions made by the class. As well as helping to signal that the discussion has come to an end, the result of a poll will demonstrate that differences of opinion remain and that different choices may be equally valid. A poll may also demonstrate how many participants have changed their mind about a particular issue. This works well if you take an initial poll before the discussion begins.

A poll can be conducted via a simple 'hands-up' exercise, or you can use online tools such as Mentimeter, Poll Everywhere, or CrowdSignal (formerly Polldaddy). As well as offering more sophisticated tools for real-time voting, they also offer the advantage of enabling participants to vote anonymously.

Do you have any great ideas for the best way to end a case discussion?

> ### ⋮≡ Closing a case session
>
> - Cases rarely end with a single 'right' solution: manage your participants' expectations.
> - Consider revealing the outcome of the case at the start of the session to enable a more nuanced discussion.
> - There is no single 'right way' to end a case discussion.
> - Select appropriate tools and techniques to ensure a great end to the session.

8. Reflection and other

Typical mistakes in case teaching

'Mistakes are the portals of discovery.' – James Joyce

No case teacher is perfect. Even highly experienced case teachers who consistently do a fantastic job in the classroom are learning all the time. And it goes without saying that we all make mistakes. The secret of becoming a good case teacher is to learn from them.

We have made plenty of mistakes ourselves over the years and have observed others making quite a few too. We can only learn by doing. Having said that, the same mistakes tend to crop up again and again, particularly among inexperienced case teachers. This list is not, of course, comprehensive, but it may help you focus on common areas of potential weakness and give you a head start in the classroom.

Teach, don't preach

This may seem an obvious point, but when you are teaching on subjects that are close to your heart the temptation to steamroller your participants (a captive audience!) into listening and agreeing with you can be overwhelming. Take a step back and remember that your job is to draw your participants out, listen to them, and get them to listen to each other. You want to hear more of their voices, not your own. Facilitate the session; do not dominate it.

Don't be a copycat

Every teacher is different; every teacher has their own unique teaching style. We can absolutely guarantee that it is impossible to copy or imitate someone else's style, however much you may admire their skills and charisma in the classroom. By trying to be someone else, you will almost certainly come across as phony and your participants will see through you instantly. By all means, pick up tips and tricks of the trade from teachers you admire, but at the same time develop your own individual approach and presence in the classroom. You will soon become one of those teachers that others will want to copy!

Prepare, prepare, prepare

Another obvious point, perhaps, but a vital one. Prepare thoroughly, then prepare some more, then do some preparation. Knowing you are fully prepared and ready for anything that your brightest participants might throw at you is a great confidence booster. Being stumped halfway through a session without a plan B or plan C is a heart-sinking and confidence draining moment that you will want to avoid at all costs.

Don't be inflexible

You have your plans A, B, and C (because you prepared so well) but do not rigidly stick to them at all costs. This may seem contradictory but flexibility is vital. You must always remember that the case method is a participant-centered learning process. Without losing sight of your learning objectives, you will sometimes need to 'go with the flow,' give your participants the space to explore, and see where it takes you. You may be pleasantly surprised!

Don't be taken too far off topic

Again, given our comments above about flexibility, this may sound slightly contradictory. However, there is a balance to be struck. It will not be possible to pursue every random thought and observation that participants make during a session. To do so risks disappearing down a rabbit hole with no way back. Always draw the discussion back to the main issues.

Lower your expectations

Do not expect too much from a single case teaching session! If you go in with too high expectations, you will probably be disappointed.

Don't pack too much into a single session

The case method is not meant to be used as a speedy way to impart lots of information; there are other ways to do this. Instead, a case session enables participants to actively participate in a gradual process of discovery resulting in deep learning. It is your job as the case teacher to provide the time and space for this learning to take place. The golden rule here is 'less is more.'

Cover less material during the session, but 'unpack' it carefully and in great detail. This approach is a fundamental component of good case teaching. As part of your preparation, you will have extra material to call on should the need arise, but only do so if absolutely necessary.

Mistakes to avoid

- Teach, don't preach.
- Don't be a copycat: always be your own unique self.
- Make sure you prepare, prepare, prepare.
- Don't be inflexible: stay participant-centered.
- Don't go too far off topic: you may not find a way back!
- Don't expect too much all at once.
- Don't try to cover too much in a single session.

Cultural and language aspects of using case studies

> 'I make a distinction between manners and etiquette – manners as the principles, which are eternal and universal, etiquette as the particular rules which are arbitrary and different in different times, different situations, different cultures.' – Judith Martin

One of the beauties of the case method is its flexibility and adaptability. It can be used to teach practically any business or management topic to participants of all ages, experience, and abilities. And it has been proven to work around the globe in a wide variety of cultural settings.

However, do bear in mind that the case method will not automatically work well in any cultural setting. You will need to address a few important points to ensure success. This may involve adapting the content of your session as well as your approach to teaching the case.

Language

Make sure you gain an understanding of which languages your participants are familiar with. You will need to know in advance if everyone will be able to understand the language your session will be conducted in. Will they all be able to follow the discussion and contribute on an equal basis? Consider whether or not you will need an interpreter.

It can be a good idea when using, for example, the English language in a session, to choose a shorter case that uses straightforward language. This will make it easier to read and understand for participants whose first language is not English.

Another very important point to bear in mind is that certain words and expressions will have different meanings in different cultures. These confusions can be amusing, confusing, or potentially offensive, so do take the time to check out both the case itself and the words and phrases you may potentially use during the discussion.

All languages have their own idioms. Idioms are groups of words that mean a specific thing but the meaning cannot be derived from the words themselves. Typical English idioms include:

- over the moon,
- raining cats and dogs,
- see the light,
- kick the bucket,
- barking up the wrong tree,
- cut the mustard,
- piece of cake,
- wet behind the ears,
- let sleeping dogs lie.

When seen as a list like this, you can easily understand how a nonnative speaker might get confused!

Remember that the common sayings and idioms you take for granted and use without thinking may be deeply mystifying to those who do not share your first language.

Cultural issues

Unfortunately, we cannot offer any simple rules that will always apply for participants from certain cultures, countries, or geographical regions. This can be a tricky area to negotiate but you will soon gain experience and develop confidence in dealing with these issues.

It is important to understand and appreciate that your participants will very often come from a wide range of cultures and that this will inevitably influence classroom interaction during your case session.

First and foremost, make sure you use this as a positive! Leverage the cultural diversity to gain a wider variety of insights and perspective. This will greatly enhance the case discussion and deepen cross-cultural understanding – an indispensable management tool in today's global business world.

However, also be aware of the following:

- Debates may become heated as differing cultural attitudes are explored. Be prepared for this.
- You may find yourself teaching a class that comprises a single cultural group – but one that is different from your own and unfamiliar to you. Do your homework in advance and be prepared.

- Some classes will have a dominant cultural group (either in numbers or vocally). Take care to include those whose culture differs but find it difficult to have their say. It is particularly important to bear this in mind when the dominant culture in a class matches your own. Make sure no one is excluded.

You may need to adapt the content of your session and the way you teach it to suit different cultures. Here are some potential issues to be aware of:

- Participants from different cultures and countries will not be familiar with all the same companies and 'well-known' people. Do not assume that your participants will have even heard of a company or chief executive you read about every day in your newspaper.
- Some cases rely on a close familiarity with certain stories and myths that are associated with particular cultures. But these will be much less meaningful for those cultures that do not share this knowledge. For example, there is a famous case based on Robin Hood but it only works well for those who come from countries where Robin Hood stories have been familiar since childhood (Lampel J 2003).
- Every culture has its own sense of humor. You and your peers might find something hilarious – but do not expect participants from a different culture to laugh or even understand the joke. To be on the safe side, use humor sparingly and judiciously.
- Different cultures have different expectations of the instructor's role. It is very important to be aware of this. Participants from certain cultures are very deferential and respectful toward teachers and believe it is their role to listen and not interrupt or speak up. This can be particularly difficult when participants from other cultures are happy to interrupt and make their opinions known. One way to deal with this is to make your expectations explicit at the beginning of the class, for example:
  – be very clear about what you expect from participants in terms of participation; or
  – jointly define expectations with the participants.
- Be aware that people from different cultures are comfortable with differing levels of personal space. Do not invade your participants' expected level of personal space, and try to ensure that fellow participants respect others' personal space too.
- Do not expect people from different cultures to have the same regard for punctuality. You may think 10am means 10am, but someone who does not share your culture may genuinely believe that 10.15am is just as good. Again, we strongly recommend being explicit about your expectations. However, also remember that – depending on the class – these cultural differences can become an important part of the overall learning experience and may be usefully included in the case discussion.
- You may have to develop different ways of challenging participants and dealing with conflict in the classroom, depending on which culture or cultures your participants are from. Often small changes in your approach will make a big difference. For example, asking participants what they would do if they were the case protagonist is very different from asking them what they would do personally. In the first case, participants can take on a different role which may make it easier for them to contribute and test out ideas and proposals. You can then interact with the protagonist (as represented by the participant), rather than the individual. This approach can help to create trust and openness in the classroom.

Other cultural considerations

Finally, when considering cultural issues, remember that this does not only apply to the different cultures of participants from various countries around the world. A 'culture' can also refer to the characteristic attitudes and behavior of particular groups. So, for example, there will usually be a great difference between a corporate culture that will dominate in an executive education session and a participant culture that will prevail in an undergraduate session. And, of course, corporate cultures will vary from one organization to the next. It is therefore good to be prepared.

> **Language and cultural aspects**
>
> – Find out in advance which languages your participants are familiar with and plan your session accordingly.
> – Understand and appreciate that your participants will come from a variety of cultures and make it your business to understand the issues involved.
> – Leverage cultural diversity in the classroom to gain positive advantage.
> – Be aware of the issues and potential problems/challenges that may arise from cultural differences.
> – Plan ahead: have strategies in place to deal with issues such as cultural conflict in the classroom, different attitudes to learning, and individual cultural preferences.

Using media and technology as an instructor

'Yes, kids love technology, but they also love Legos, scented markers, handstands, books and mud puddles. It's all about balance.' – Unknown

One of the hot issues in our workshops is the use of technology by the instructor and ultimately by the participants. As we have already stressed in different parts of this book, teaching is about reaching learning objectives and teaching style and therefore the use of technology also has to fit the facilitator. While in the end this is a very individual decisions, we think that there are some common themes worth exploring.

As a first remark we think that it is necessary to be explicit about the facilitator's expectation regarding the use of technology, both by themselves and by the participants. There are several ways to make this explicit. You might choose to have a chapter in your syllabus on the use of technology (what kind of technology will you use, what kind of technology do you expect the participants to bring to class, what do you not want to see, etc.). Additionally, or alternatively, you should make the use of technology part of your learning contract, most likely the explicit learning contract that you set up typically during the first session of your course.

When it comes to the use of technology by the facilitator, we just want to highlight that technology can play a major role in achieving your learning goals and in mixing and matching different learning formats. In your teaching you might want to include research elements (participants might have to research competitors, for example) or you might use technology for voting (e.g., Mentimeter or other applications) or even for participants to express their views (e.g., a Twitter feed or some other form of feed). There are many learning platforms available, and more and more schools are using them. These platforms often have chat functions and the like that could also be integrated into the teaching.

Technology might be important to support participants with language problems in the form of translation software or for note-taking. Most people can type faster than they can write, and this might be important especially in a fast-paced setting like face-to-face teaching.

So overall there are many good reasons to integrate technology into the teaching. But it has to fit your personality and serve your learning objectives. And, last but not least, it is about finding the right balance.

Use of board

'Visualizing information can give us a very quick solution to problems. We can get clarity or the answer to a simple problem very quickly.' – David McCandles

The use of a board (we use this here as synonym for any kind of writing support like a flipchart, metaplan, whiteboard or the like) is (or can be) an important element of a case discussion. Ultimately this is of course the choice of the facilitator if and how to use the board, but from our own experience and discussion in our workshops we think that it is important to highlight the general purpose and potential issues when using the board.

The first and foremost use of a board is to document what has been said during the discussion so that everybody understands (e.g., despite acoustic or language issues). As we discussed above in the section on preparing the teaching plan, the facilitator often already has a board layout in their head when starting to use it in class. This brings us to the first important decision. You can write down what participants said exactly how they said it, e.g., using their words, or you can decide to adjust (for example, someone says 'We have to talk to everybody that is impacted by our decision' and you note on the board 'Stakeholder analysis'). While we acknowledge the usefulness of using proper terminology, we generally advise sticking to the participants' wording. We think that it is better to make participants use the proper terminology themselves first, before noting it on the board (for example, by a follow-up question like: 'What else can you call this?' or 'What is the specific terminology for what you just described?').

The next decision you have to take is whether you want to end up with a particular structure on the board or just note whatever is being said in no particular order or format. If you use a predetermined board structure, your aim is not only to note participants' comments but the way you use the board will ultimately help participants to distill concepts, theories, frameworks, and tools by developing them out of the comments from the participants.

 From theory to practice with Martin

I use my case study on Damien Hirst to discuss with students the concept of strategic innovation. In the first longer discussion section we discover the three fundamental dimensions of innovation: customers (new who), processes (new how), and products/services (new what). I start this discussion by asking participants 'What are the key elements of Damien Hirst's success? What does he do differently from other artists?' Whatever the participants come up with, I sort into three columns on the board (new who, new how, new what) without identifying the columns. When the discussion slows down and most of the elements of Hirst's success are on the board and there are a good number of elements in each of the three rows, only then do I turn to the class and ask 'All of the things you said basically fall into three categories. That's why I sorted them into three columns. What would you call each of these columns?' Participants will immediately see that the first column mainly has examples or elements concerning identifying new customer segments, the second contains elements of his products (pieces of art and services), and the last column is concerned with the way he produces, distributes, and markets his work. So, I note 'New Who,' 'New What,' and 'New How' on the top of each column. We therefore distill the framework of strategic innovation by using the board.

Yet another important consideration is how you will use the board over the course of the whole session. When planning your session, you might plan to come back to certain elements of the discussion or to earlier solutions. You might also plan to park certain discussions if they come up too early. Here the board can be used very effectively to support this. You should decide where on a board you note elements that you plan to come back to, so that when the time is right you can easily find them and do not have to flip through a stack of flipcharts or lose time searching for these elements.

Below you will find two sample board plans. You of course have to adapt according to whatever you have as boards, whiteboards, flipcharts, metaplans, etc. We have taken a typical layout of three boards horizontally with a second board that you can pull up or down. The central idea behind both plans is to think ahead how you want to structure the discussion.

In the first plan you would most likely start the case discussion either with a vote or by teasing out the options for the protagonist. After listing all options, you would then continue by listing all arguments for each option (you might also first list all potential options but then let participants vote for the best ones and only continue with discussing those). So, the first and second boards clearly belong to each other and should be right next to each other or at least close. The third board is most likely the result of the next discussion around who would be involved in the various options, e.g., the stakeholders. In the second row we have listed a couple of additional options. You might want to discuss how to get to some results or even how you have reached consensus in class as a kind of process description. You have an additional board for the central framework that you want to discuss, and you should also have planned for some space for potential quantitative analysis. Having a dedicated board for quantitative analysis allows you to come back to these calculations in case new arguments, facts, or assumptions come up during the discussion.

The second board plan starts with a description of the potential solution or target situation. What does the protagonist want to achieve? You would then have two boards to list all driving and hindering forces. In the second row you would still have some dedicated space for potential alternative solutions/approaches that come up during the discussion, the proposed implementation approach, and a parking lot for ideas that you want to follow up later on or potentially even in the next session.

1	Options (e.g. with result of vote)	Arguments	Stakeholders
	Process description	Central framework (to be provided at beginning and filled during session)	Quantitative analysis
2	Target situation	Pro-arguments / Driving forces	Contra arguments / Hindering forces
	Alternative approaches/solutions	Implementation approach	"Parking lot" (for ideas that will be followed-up later on)

Figure 14: Sample (generic) board plans.

Use of material

Another important decision to take is how to use additional material to support the case discussion and ultimately your teaching objectives. Basically, you have to think through two decisions: when to use material and what kind of material you want to use.

Timing of material

Fundamentally the alternatives are to send material ahead of the session, typically in the form of prereadings, to hand out additional material during class, or to send out material after the session as postreadings.

Prereadings have the advantage that the discussion can start right away and that participants come prepared and with the same level of information. Typical prereadings are, for example, the case study itself, but it can also be additional material on the case like press articles, the company's website, or textbook chapters, academic journal articles, and the like. The challenge with prereadings is of course whether participants actually read them and how carefully. There are many ways of potentially enhancing the level of preparation or even assuring it, which we discuss in more depth (short-term, long-term, push, and pull techniques) in the chapter on running the session.

Additional material during class can allow you to dig deeper into certain topics and enables you to switch the teaching format. For example, you might start with the general case discussion, then switch to a mini-lecture, use a buzz-group format, and then hand out additional material like a very short press release, a short article, or a video. This allows you to highlight a certain aspect within the case discussion and add more content to then have another discussion.

 From theory to practice with Martin

When discussing my case study on Damien Hirst I want students to discover the three fundamental dimensions of innovation: customers (new who), processes (new how), and products/services (new what). Often participants come up with a lot of facts and examples for the process and product dimension but somehow neglect the customer dimension. When this happens, I show a video that I found, which shows an art critic interviewing an important art collector who also collects Damien Hirst. The video is only three minutes long but gives a lot of insights on why collectors might be interested in collecting Damien Hirst. The final question in the video actually is on why he collects. While this is partially covered in the case study itself, this interview highlights the customer dimension of strategic innovation and allows for a deeper discussion on identifying, segmenting, and serving customers.

Postreadings or in general material that is made available after the session often serves for covering aspects that were less covered during class or to follow up on questions that came up during class. As already mentioned in the section where we discuss the use of boards, sometimes topics or questions get parked during the case discussion. One way to follow up on these parked issues, especially if time in class does not allow us to actually come back to the issue, is to send out additional material to cover these questions. Other typical postreadings might concern what actually happened to the protagonist or company, background readings on the discussed frameworks or concepts, or maybe some controversial/contrarian point of view.

Kind of material

Obviously, there are an infinite number of different materials that you might want to use before, during, or after class. Here we just want to highlight a few and potentially give you some additional inspiration. Most of these suggestions we have used ourselves or became aware of during our workshops.

Material to bring the case alive

One of the reasons that cases work as a learning format is that they make content relevant for participants by infusing reality into the classroom. It might be a good idea to support this by enriching this experience by bringing for example products, samples, artifacts, videos either of the site, the protagonist, or other relevant actors, or product brochures to class. This might not always be possible, but with a little bit of creativity you can come up with surprising ideas.

> **From theory to practice with Martin**
>
> When using my Madonna case study, I use a range of music videos and also interviews with Madonna in class. When discussing my case study on Damien Hirst I show a whole range of his artworks, and pictures that I took when visiting his exhibition at the Tate Modern during the Olympics in 2012. For my Bosch case I show pictures that I took of the newly built R&D campus in Renningen.

Material to bring support preparation, discussion, and reflection

There is a whole range of more traditional materials to support either the preparation, the discussion, or the reflection after class. The most obvious ones are the slides that you might use in class (you can decide to distribute them beforehand, during, or after class) but also your documentation during class on the board or flipcharts (you can make a photo documentation and share the photos after class). You can use optional or mandatory pre- or postreadings, like book chapters or journal articles. You might also want to think about how to involve students, for example by selecting students to capture the class discussion and then sharing their notes (either checked by you or unchecked) with the class.

 Do you have any suggestions for unusual and very impactful material to support the case discussion?

Thoughts on class size and location

While often not in the hand of the facilitator, group size and location are important context factors for case discussions. Over the years we have tried and tested different group sizes, in both class and group composition for various forms of group work. Often the general framework is set by the institution a facilitator is working for, but there are nevertheless a lot of deliberate choices to make. Therefore, we would like to discuss some ideas about the general group size for a class, then some ideas about group sizes for group work and finally some additional thoughts and general remarks on the physical location (and how they are interdependent).

Class size

In the chapter 'Case Method in the Spotlight' we introduced the different functions of the case method, specifically enabling participants to apply and use concepts, theories, and frameworks to a given situation, provoking controversy and debate to increase emotional engagement, allowing participants to fail in a safe environment, receiving constructive criticism and learning from the failures of other participants, and enabling an intense social interaction with other participants leading to a significant improvement in communication and discussion skills.

For these objectives we believe that class sizes of 20 to 30 participants are ideal for the case method. Having fewer than 20 participants significantly limits the potential for controversy in the room. There will be also limited total experience in the room, and limited opportunity for networking. This will lead in our experience to a lower level of energy.

Having significantly more than 30 participants bears the risk of decreasing the learning effect due to a reduced level of interactivity. Not every student might have the time and chance to be able to contribute and say something in every session. It is also significantly easier to 'hide' in a larger group and to potentially 'switch off.' All this might lead to lower levels of energy.

In our experience, class sizes of 20 to 30 participants guarantee a broad input for mutual learning owing to a sufficient amount of real-life/business and leadership experiences in the room. We also found that classes of this size bring out a lot of alternative solutions to case studies. In general, every student has the opportunity to contribute in every single session. And a broad range of different group compositions for interactive program elements (optimal adjustment to type of exercise) can be easily organized in groups of, for example, 24 participants (you can easily split the group for debate, have four groups of six or six groups of four, or have buzz groups of two or four).

But case studies also work in (very) large groups (see e.g., Michael Sandel's famous 'Justice' course, with more than 1,000 students). Large groups frequently cause the same challenges as small groups, but the challenges get magnified, especially issues such as participation, wanted or unwanted use of technology, or dysfunctional behavior of individuals in the group. Ultimately it comes down to the fundamentals of a good case discussion, the participation of everybody. The larger the group, the more important our general suggestions are: try to change formats frequently within and between every session. In large groups we feel that it is especially important to get everybody involved, and buzz groups/pair discussions are a very good way to do that. Also role-plays and debates between selected participants representing opposing views work well in large groups.

Location

The classroom is another important context factor. As the case method is all about engagement and participation, it is important to accommodate this when setting up or choosing a room layout. Fundamentally the room layout should enable all participants to see and hear each other. While this sounds obvious, in reality most plenary layouts are designed so that everybody can see and hear the teacher or facilitator but not necessarily so that the participants see and hear each other. But, even if the room layout is not ideal, there are many small tricks a facilitator can use to improve the situation.

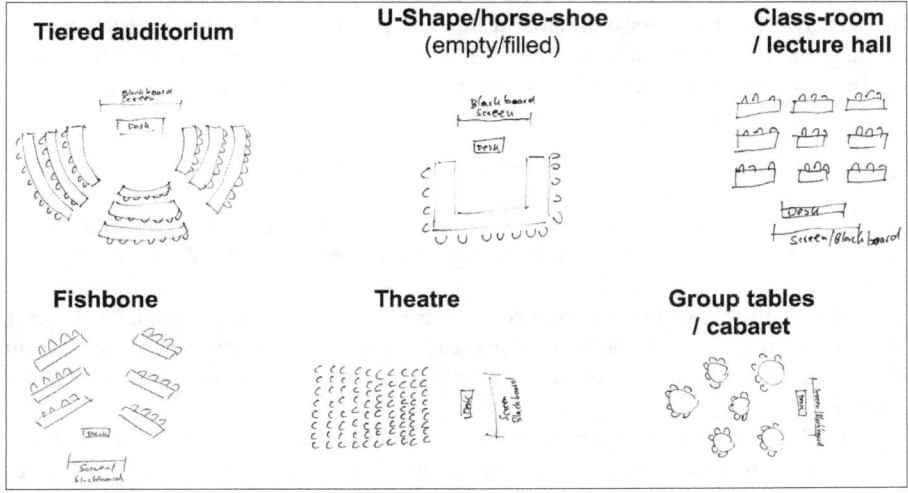

Figure 15: Sample room layouts.

The most common classroom layout for case discussions is the tiered (horseshoe) auditorium, where participants are seated in a half circle or half ellipse with the teacher's desk in the middle. Typically, the rows get higher toward the back and students sit on chairs that they can easily turn and roll around with. Participants can easily see each other and most of the time also hear each other well. If participants in the back speak too softly, resist the temptation to move closer to the participant to better understand her but instead move away as far as possible as participants then typically start to talk louder to reach you.

Variants of this classroom layout are tables set up in a U shape, often used in flat rooms or a fishbone setup. Both generally work well. In a U shape, participants on the same row might have difficulty seeing each other; in a fishbone, the first row often have a hard time looking backward when someone from the last row is speaking. Keep this in mind and, in the event that you want to use a role-play or debate between two groups, take the time to quickly get the participants of the role-play or the two groups in a good position (for example, get the opposing parties on the different sides of the U or in the fishbone set up in a middle row left and right).

For sessions with intense group work, a cabaret style with round group tables or two square tables put together might be a good solution. While the interaction between these 'islands' might be more difficult, the interaction on these group tables is very good. Just make sure that nobody sits with their back to the front of the room or wherever the facilitator is positioned.

Slightly more difficult for case discussions are traditional classroom setups with long rows of tables or theater style (long rows of chairs without tables). In both cases the interaction between participants is difficult.

Another important element of the classroom that you should take into account and get yourself familiar with is the general acoustics of the room. Sometimes high ceilings or a lot of curtains and material that dampens sound might make it very difficult to understand both the facilitator and often even more so the other participants. Noise from the air conditioning, the projector, the heating system, or any other electronic equipment might be very disturbing. Make sure to know in advance and guard against it.

Check how many whiteboards, blackboards, flipcharts, metaplans, etc. there are in the room. In general, we advise the more the better. How easily can you change the room layout (see above)? Sometimes tables or chairs are screwed to the floor. If participants do not know each other, they should be able to see the name tags (if you chose to use them). If you want them to use their laptops for group work or taking notes, check whether access to electricity is available and potentially access to Wi-Fi/internet. Also, make yourself familiar with possibilities to dim or darken the room for showing videos. We recommend that based on your teaching plan you come up with a list of items or elements that the classroom should be equipped with to be able to teach according to your teaching plan. This way you can either check yourself easily or write down what you need in the event that you are invited to teach in a new place, a different school, or a hotel.

Using cases for online teaching

> *'The most important principle for designing lively eLearning is to see eLearning design not as information design but as designing an experience.'* – Cathy Moore

Distance and/or online learning can take very different forms. Whole programs, courses, or just single classes can be taught online. This online teaching can be synchronous or asynchronous. It can involve real-time interactivity or not. We believe that in any of these forms, case studies can have their role.

The biggest difference is that in general online learning happens asynchronously. Therefore, the very typical format, the synchronous discussion in class, cannot happen or be easily transferred to an online situation. But the discussion can of course happen asynchronously and typically over a longer period of time. And this can have a lot of advantages. Participants will have more time to reflect and can potentially be more precise in their comments, answers, or analysis. So, instead of having one discussion of 30 to 75 minutes, this discussion is typically broken down into several sections over a longer period of maybe several days or weeks. An online discussion of a case study can be started by a written question on the course platform with precise instructions on what is expected, not only in terms of content but also, for example, if you expect participants to answer in a certain order or not. You can also explicitly demand that students refer to previous comments/answers. The facilitator can highlight certain comments and take those as the starting point for the next discussion section.

Online teaching can also contain webinars or video lectures, web conferences or conference calls and chats. Again, case studies can be a part of these tools and techniques. Additional tools like voting applications can easily be integrated into the learning format.

We would like to highlight two thoughts on this topic. The first is that every facilitator has to find the right balance of different formats, tools, and techniques and online teaching can be one of those. The second thought is that we see a clear trend toward online teaching or at least online elements in teaching. We think that it is therefore important for educators to get familiar with this format and to test and try different things.

 From theory to practice with Martin

In 2016 I was asked by my school to teach a course on digital transformation in our pure online master's called EMIB. This was completely new territory for me. Initially I thought that I would now have to record video lectures but I quickly found out that the EMIB is designed so that the facilitator curates content for students and tracks progress by giving assignments. The content that the facilitator curates can be of any type, like articles, book chapters, websites, videos, or self-created video lectures. But the key element of the EMIB is the assignments, which are designed to allow the participants to apply the knowledge they gained through the curated content and to allow the facilitator to track participants' progress. Of course, I immediately thought about how to integrate case studies and I tested two different ways. In the first week of the course, I used a case study (my own case study, which is not published) as an individual assignment. Participants had to read the case study and then use concepts and tools from the curated content to answer three questions. Instead of asking participants to hand in a written document with the answers, I asked for a three-minute video. This gave me the chance to get additional impressions from the participants and forced the participants to be crisp in answering the questions. In week 6 of the course, I used a case study as a group task. Participants had to work in virtual teams (sometimes distributed across continents) on a case study. They then had to hand in a power point presentation of 10 pages maximum with a clear recommendation for the case protagonist.

Getting better at case teaching

'Everyone has a chance to learn, improve, and build up their skills.' – Tom Peters

You will never stop learning how to teach. Always be open to new ideas, new approaches, and new ways of doing things. Do not assume that one day you will 'finally crack it' and become a great case teacher. It is just not like that – because being a great case teacher means constantly looking for ways to improve, to be better, to do more and achieve more for your participants.

Humility is essential: If you think you are a great case teacher, there's a good chance you might not be. At the very least, you will be missing chances to make improvements and enhance your participants' learning experience.

Being open to criticism is also essential – although, we acknowledge, often difficult. This can be particularly hard if you believe you have just taught a great case session but your participants or an observer think differently. But do not become defensive or downhearted. Always learn from feedback; accept it as a gift. Indeed, you should seek it out as it is one of the best ways to build on your case teaching skills.

Get feedback

There are a few different ways you can get feedback. As the case method is participant-centered, the most obvious opportunity to get feedback is to proactively ask your participants for feedback after the class. You can do this informally during a postclass chat, or more formally with a questionnaire distributed afterwards. Participants may be more honest if they can be anonymous! You may also be able to add your own questionnaire to any formal course evaluation used at your institution. Sample questions to ask participants include:

- Questions about the case itself (How interesting did you find the company/industry? Was it easy for you to identify with the protagonist? Was the case easy to understand? How much preparation time did you invest in the case? etc.)
- Questions about the discussion (Was the case discussion engaging? Was it easy for you to participate? What if anything hindered your participation? Did you feel left out? Did you feel that some participants dominated the discussion? etc.)
- Questions about the learning objectives (Did you get new insights from discussing the case? What specifically was new for you? What if anything is generalizable from the case discussion? etc.)

In addition to more formal and questionnaire-based feedback you might also want to consider picking individual students (and different ones over the course) to give you feedback about a specific session. In this more informal setting you might also explicitly ask for things that the participant liked about other sessions and/or other instructors. Be aware and do not get confused by individual opinions – but rather consider the big picture. Ignore very hostile comments – they are usually not driven by the educational process but by other factors. And do not forget to write down your ideas for improving your overall teaching and for this particular session – store them so that you will find them again when preparing for the next repetition of this session.

Another very valuable source for feedback is your colleagues. Ask a colleague to sit in on one of your sessions (or only part of your session) and observe you teaching. You can provide them with an observation checklist to use that will structure and ease the feedback.

 From theory to practice with Martin

Whenever I can, I ask colleagues to sit in my class, even if it is just for the first 10 minutes or the last 10 minutes. Do not forget to ask your observer to take notes because you might not have time to discuss their thoughts and impressions straight away.

Also, ask them to note both specific observations (voice, gestures, body language, etc.), as well as the overall flow of the case session, including the level and quality of engagement, discussion, and participation.

(Continued)

> I still remember very clearly the first feedback I received. I discovered that I tend to focus much more on the right side of the classroom, which can be frustrating for people sitting on my left side. I also have a tendency to spend too much time with people who disagree or have minority opinions in an attempt to change their minds. This type of feedback is invaluable and continues to inform and – hopefully – improve my teaching.

A third way to get feedback is to video yourself teaching. This can be difficult to watch back but very revealing, and we strongly recommend it. Brace yourself and watch the video through carefully, making notes as you do so. You could also ask a colleague to watch it with you and offer feedback. In addition, it can be useful to watch the video in fast-forward as this will reveal aspects of your body language that have become an unconscious repetitive habit. Videotaping a whole session can be distracting and perhaps irritating for participants and will need to be addressed.

Review your own performance

Do not rely solely on feedback from others. Carry out your own thorough review too. For the best results, do this in a systematic way (see a suggested checklist below). You should note what went well and areas that need improving. If you used a teaching plan, add your immediate postsession notes to it so they will be easy to find again. It is also a good idea to take photographs of your board and flipchart notes.

Making notes in this way will not only help you when teaching the same case in the future; it will also help you improve as a teacher overall, whichever case you are teaching.

Review your own performance checklist

This checklist will help to ensure you do not miss anything important. Try to be as honest with yourself as you can. The checklist is not set in stone and you may find it useful to add your own points to the list as you gain more experience.

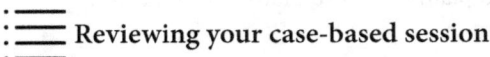 **Reviewing your case-based session**

Overall evaluation
- Did the case discussion meet your educational objectives and offer participants a meaningful and relevant 'takeaway'?
- Did the classroom discussion enable the discovery, application and critique of relevant theories, concepts, and frameworks?
- Would this case be more meaningful and relevant if taught earlier or later in the course?

The case
- Did the case itself meet your expectations?
- Did it inspire excitement and engagement and lead to key learning outcomes?
- Was any key information missing from the case?
- Were there any mistakes or inconsistencies in the case, for example facts, figures, dates?
- Did participants understand the case, or did it cause any unintended confusion?
- Do you need to find a better case? Or – an exciting thought – write your own? (See page 134.)

(Continued)

Timing
- Did your timing go to plan or did you try to cover too much or too little? (This applies to the session as a whole and individual sections of it.)
- Note which sections took longer than you thought, and which took less time so you can make adjustments next time.

Content
- Did you try to include too much? Too little? Or was it about right?
- Decide which topics to leave out next time if necessary.
- Decide which topics to add next time if necessary.
- Make a note of any unexpected topics that came up during the discussion so you can be well prepared if it happens again. Depending on its relevance, you may wish to incorporate this additional content in your next session.

Questions
- Which of your questions worked well and advanced the discussion?
- Which questions were less successful? For example, did any cause confusion? Encourage irrelevant discussion? Interfere with the flow of the discussion?
- Make a note of additional questions that would be good to ask next time; these may be questions that occurred to you afterwards or good questions that were asked by participants (never be too proud to learn from your participants!).

Sequence and flow
- Did the flow from one topic to the next seem effortless and natural in class, or did it seem like hard work?
- Should you try rearranging your teaching plan to encourage a more natural transition between topics?

Participation
- Did all of the participants take part in the discussion at some point? (This should be possible with up to 50 class members.)
- If not, how can you improve participation levels next time? (See page 59.)
- If you had a call plan, did you follow it?
- If you didn't have a call plan, should you have one in future?

Materials
- Did the materials you used in class, such as handouts, products, and videos, add value to the discussion? Were there too many? Not enough? The wrong kind?

Board notes
- Do your board notes make sense when you look back at them? (This is why it is a good idea to take a picture of the board at the end of the session – you have a permanent record for reference.)
- How can you improve your board notes in future sessions?

Your performance
- Were you fully prepared for class?
- How well did you:
  – ask questions?
  – listen?
  – manage the discussion?
- Did you speak too much and dominate the discussion as opposed to facilitating and enabling your participants to take part?

- Use 'safe' environments such as low-key events to experiment with different ways of teaching and find out what works best for you.

- Work on one aspect of your teaching at a time; do not have a list of three or four points to work on during one session. For example, plan to work on your body language or your questioning or your timing. Not all three at once!

Do not be too hard on yourself. You will not become an outstanding case teacher overnight – no one ever does. You will gradually improve over time with practice and experience. Be patient!

> ### Getting better at case teaching
>
> – Always be open to new ideas and fresh approaches.
> – Proactively seek feedback.
> – Assess your own performance against a checklist.
> – Practice in 'safe' environments.
> – Work on one aspect of your teaching at a time.
> – Do not be hard on yourself: be patient!

Using case teaching for case writing

The following chapter is partially taken from a book chapter that we were asked to write on how case teaching and case writing influences each other (Mueller & Kupp 2017). We were asked to contribute to an edited book on case studies as a teaching tool in management education by one of our former workshop participants. At the time we felt that a lot of the general issues around case teaching and case writing were already covered in one form or the other in different books. But case teaching and case writing were always treated as two seemingly independent domains. Contrary to this, we felt not only that case teaching and case writing belong together but also that they can also support and inform each other in many ways and should be combined in new and creative ways.

Using case teaching for collecting material for case writing

An obvious – but perhaps the most impactful – way to leverage case teaching for case writing is to use case-based and participant-centered teaching methods to generate leads about interesting stories that can be used for case teaching, and subsequently for case writing. For example, this could be done by asking students to write up relevant decisions from their own (professional) experiences and then use them in class.

> ### From theory to practice with Urs
>
> For my classes on business ethics, I have asked hundreds of MBA students and executives to write up the most difficult ethical decisions that they have faced and to submit them before the start of the course. I read them carefully, group them into subject areas, and discuss them in class when appropriate.
>
> The idea and story behind the case study 'Anna Frisch at Aesch AG: Initiating Lateral Change' (Müller & Schäfer 2010), which won the Case Centre's Human Resource Management/Organisational Behaviour award in 2014, was generated using an EMBA student's essay in a change management course.

Obviously, this is highly applicable to courses offered for executives, or MBA students with at least a certain level of professional experience. However, dependent upon the subject/discipline, this could even be a feasible approach for undergraduate classes. For example, teachers could ask students to present difficulties in their group work when teaching organizational behavior. Case teaching could be combined with active learning methods by first asking the students to search the news for current developments and to turn them into small cases that are then subsequently discussed in class.

Using case teaching for testing case ideas

Once you have found the inspiration for a case study – by using students/participants as described above or by just stumbling upon it in newspapers, conversations, social media, through own observations, through requests from companies, etc. – the question of whether to use this 'case lead' (we describe case leads and needs in more detail in the chapter on writing great cases) should mainly depend upon on two aspects. On the one hand, the case lead needs to fit the educational needs of the course. On the other hand, the efforts in writing this particular case study need to be balanced with the benefits. Obviously, writing a case study is resource-intensive, as one has to research the topic, conduct desk research, potentially conduct field interviews, develop an outline, write the first draft, and one day finalize the case, the teaching note, and then even get permission from the company and protagonist(s) described in the case. This is quite a bit of work, and there are many unknowns, among others:

- Is this an interesting company from a student perspective?
- Is the industry interesting?
- Will students engage, that is, is the issue controversial enough to stimulate a lively debate in class?
- Is the 'solution' sufficiently complex to justify an extended discussion of this topic?
- Are there enough questions in the case?

It would be useful to try to eliminate as many of these unknowns as possible, as fast as possible, and with as few resources as possible. This is where teaching comes into play because the classroom is, of course, the most natural and realistic place to test the idea. Below are some ideas on how to rapidly test the initial case ideas very early in the process, and for quite a low cost.

Using a newspaper article, video, blog, or other publicly available source

The first possibility for testing the case idea is to use an existing, publicly available source, such as a newspaper article, a short video or documentary, a blog entry, or the like. Depending on the initial inspiration, a quick search of archives, webpages, social media, etc. for some background information on the case should suffice. If someone mentions an interesting story, the chances are high that something can be found on the internet that relates to it. This often does not take longer than an hour or two. Sometimes an article can be found that does not require any editing.

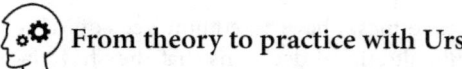 **From theory to practice with Urs**

The idea for the case study '"Do You Really Think We Are So Stupid?" A Letter to the CEO of Deutsche Telekom' (Korotov, Müller, & Schäfer 2009) resulted from an article quoting the entire letter; a quick test of this article in the class environment confirmed the viability of the case lead for a great case discussion.

Alternatively, active learning activities could be used, whereby students prepare a certain case by actively searching for information themselves before coming to the next class session, or a sanitized version could be used if the information is received in confidence.

Independently of the material provided as input, the most important part is to think through the session and to come up with the right questions to open the discussion and lead through the session. This will provide early feedback about whether it is worth investing the necessary time, effort, and possibly even resources into the research for the case study.

Using a short presentation

With a little more work, a short (for example PowerPoint) presentation, that is, a few slides, could be generated. Instead of using the original sources, a very short presentation (this does not need to be longer than four or five pages) could be created that presents the key fact of the story, already structured in a way that will help in starting and moderating a discussion. This short presentation (as opposed to just an article etc.) allows the instructor to make use of visual materials (pictures, organizational charts, tables with data, process presentations, etc.) – various elements to be considered as possible exhibits for a final case study. The presentation should have a very similar structure to a typical case study, with one page dedicated to the problem, one page on the background of the company, one on the industry or wider context, and a final page to either flesh out options or to serve as a kind of wrap-up. Depending on the topic, more details on numbers and background can be offered. As with a case study, the idea is to create a level playing field for the discussion. Of course, although this will take longer than if the original source(s) were presented, in our experience the instructor will be able to create a good presentation in only a few hours – a lot faster than a case study.

The benefits of using a presentation compared to just using the original sources are that the case story can be shaped to fit the educational objectives. Existing articles frequently present the case lead in ways that are not optimal for teaching purposes:

- They are frequently written from a (seemingly) objective, independent perspective, whereas cases usually present the issue from the perspective of one clearly identified individual.
- They frequently present the results after the decision, that is, the events and consequences of the decisions that were made by the main actors.
- They frequently contain some of the reflections and considerations that educators usually want to bring up during the discussion.

Using mini-caselets

Another format to test case ideas in the classroom is the so-called mini-caselet. The main idea is to write up a very rough and brief version of the case idea. Often, mini-caselets focus on the problem description and just offer some basic background information. The level of detail is quite low, and authors do not provide a lot of data or exhibits. Again, the idea is to just deliver the basics to ensure an informed discussion, but things such as quotes, various perspectives, and detailed figures are not added.

What to test for and what insights can be gained

Testing obviously only makes sense if there is a clear objective about what to test. Although you might already feel very confident about how to use the case and how participants will react, we believe that there are at least five good reasons to go down the testing route. Testing will help you to check: (1) what additional information is needed, (2) whether the topic is controversial and engaging, (3) whether the right perspective and protagonist have been chosen, (4) whether the immediate issue works, and (5) what level of breadth and depth is needed. Last but not least, (6) testing will provide a lot of data that might be needed for writing up the teaching note.

What additional information is needed? Is it already complete?

The most obvious test is to check what additional information is needed. Especially in cases where testing involves using a journal article or a few PowerPoint slides, the instructor will quickly realize where the discussion might get stuck or where students will ask for additional information to be able to answer questions, to formulate a recommendation, or to make a decision. A situation in which students ask for additional information is actually a great opportunity. Even if the information is not readily at hand (e.g., because instructors have not yet started to do interviews and dig deeper), an instructor can use this moment in class to start building hypotheses with the students. So, if someone asks for additional information, the instructor can ask: 'What do you assume?' or 'Does anyone know the answer?' or 'Why do you think you need this information?' Case study teaching offers this opportunity to actually develop, discuss, and challenge the different assumptions in the classroom.

Is the topic controversial and engaging?

Already when handing out a newspaper article or when starting to tell a story – for example, with the help of a few (PowerPoint) slides – you will immediately get a sense of whether the topic engages the audience. Can people easily relate to the case? Do they engage? Do they understand the situation and the context? Are they excited to talk about the specific case and the topic in general? But you can go even further and test, for example, what kind of opening question triggers the most controversial debate, and whether bringing a sample of the product helps people engage with the topic. You will also experience whether there is some kind of natural way in which the discussion can unfold. If so, this will provide an idea about what kind of information needs to be added to make it easier for participants to follow this path.

Has the most promising perspective/protagonist been chosen?

Sometimes a case can be written from the perspectives of different people (e.g., headquarters versus business unit perspective; marketing versus finance perspective; company versus stakeholder perspective; more senior versus less senior protagonist). Presenting different perspectives in different courses will give a potential case writer a good feeling about which perspective is leading to the most fruitful discussions.

 **From theory to practice with Urs**

For my case study 'Vodafone in Egypt' (Müller & Pandit 2014) we had to choose between the perspective of the local management in Egypt and the perspective of the Vodafone group headquarters. We tested both ideas/perspectives and immediately realized that each perspective would lead to a different discussion. Testing using the case as a mini-caselet in class, we realized that the local perspective was much more engaging and controversial.

Does the immediate issue work?

One of the trickiest things about writing engaging case studies is finding the appropriate immediate issue. The immediate issue is the hook into the case that is supposed to engage the reader (we discuss this in much more detail in the chapter on writing great cases). The objective of the immediate issue is to lead the reader into the case with a small and concrete issue, such as a question about whether to hire externally for the new sales executive position or to promote an internal sales manager. These kinds of questions are engaging, as they require an immediate action or decision and ultimately lead to the more fundamental issue as the discussion unfolds in class.

But, for each fundamental issue, there are, of course, many different possible immediate problems to choose from. It is therefore advisable to think of at least four or five different immediate issues, list them, and write matching opening questions for them. In one session, an instructor can try to test two or three of them by quickly discussing them at the start of the session and testing for levels of controversy, engagement, and emotions.

 From theory to practice with Martin

For the case study 'Team Wikispeed: Developing Hardware the Software Way' (Kupp, Dahlander, & Morrow, 2013), which is about the fundamental issue of organizing agile product development, there were several potential immediate issues. We came up with the following opening questions:

- Should Joe Justice allow the team to set its own agenda?
- Should Joe Justice cut and weld the existing axle or press for the development of a proprietary axle?
- How could Joe Justice improve the performance of his team?

By testing these questions in class, it became clear that question one was too closely linked with the fundamental issue of agile product development, and question three was too broad and unspecific, thereby making participants uneasy and slowing the discussion. Question two worked best: it was specific enough and it was controversial, as it offered two options and split the class.

Breadth and depth

A classic beginner's mistake in case writing is to overload the teaching objectives; we have seen countless case studies written by quite inexperienced case authors in several different case writing competitions – one of the most frequent problems is that many cases try to kill too many birds with one stone. Instead of clearly centering on sales management, a case might, for example, simultaneously include strategic, cultural, change, and leadership issues. In very specific situations, this might be acceptable, for example when intentionally making a case complex. However, in most situations, case authors will quickly realize that cases that have too many learning objectives, cover too much content, and/or address too many concepts, theories, or subjects will make the case discussion in class significantly less effective. Case authors should therefore test the necessary level of concentration, for example by eliminating aspects in iterations after each test use in class. This can even be done after publishing an initial version of the case, e.g., by adding an abridged version of the case, as is frequently done by major case distributors.

Conversely, some (but usually much fewer) cases are written with a scope that is too narrow. They focus so clearly on one single, specific issue that the first use of the case in class quickly reveals that the case does not have the necessary breadth to allow it to be used for an entire class/session. When faced with a fading discussion in the middle of the session, the case author might want to consider including (successively) more facets to the case. Alternatively, it can be most appropriate to keep the case focused – but then the author should advise other educators in the teaching note about additional exercises, discussion points, etc. that would complement the short discussion of such a highly focused case.

Collecting data for the teaching note

The last reason why it is useful to test case ideas by teaching them is that a lot of data and ideas will be generated. Such data and ideas will be very helpful when writing the teaching note. Although the main objective in writing a teaching note is to put the case into a research or teaching field context, the second objective is to help potential users (other teachers) of the case study prepare and to create an engaging atmosphere when using the case. To achieve these objectives, it is very helpful to: state the actual reactions of participants who were exposed to the case study (so that other educators can anticipate the main points of the discussion); offer guidance on board layouts; give information about what kinds of topics typically come up during the case discussion; and also offer advice on how to deal with typical questions or requests of participants. The more detailed this information is, the better.

When to test case ideas and how to choose the right environment

By now, some of the benefits of using case teaching to develop high-quality case material should be clear. But questions remain: When and how to test case ideas? For example, how can one choose the right environment? And what should be done to get the most out of these tests?

First, there is the question of timing. From experience (our own experience as well as from observing, talking to, and coaching many other educators), we fundamentally believe that the earlier the ideas can be tested, the better. Of course, the earlier the testing is started, the less the teaching process and outcome can be predicted and controlled. It is therefore important for instructors to choose the right environment and to prepare both themselves as well as the participants for the testing. The best preparation for educators is for them to be very clear about what they want to test and then choose the right audience. If, for example, the instructor wants to test for breadth and depth or relevance, a more mature audience might be the better testing ground. So, when looking for the right environment to test case ideas, you should be clear about what needs to be tested for and what audience is the right one for helping to answer this question.

The next thing to think about is how to create a safe teaching and testing environment. Whenever possible, even beforehand, you should explain to participants why certain materials are being used. Sometimes this is not possible, as it would spoil the results of the test. But it is still advisable to explain the approach at the end of the test, for example the session, and to leave enough time for everyone to discuss what they have observed.

It might also be a good idea to have a short discussion with a group of participants – for example, at the end of a course or the end of a day seminar with executives – to conduct a short feedback session, not only about the actual learning but also the process and the materials used. By explicitly exploring the learning process as well, you will gain additional insights into the teaching's effectiveness and how it relates to the materials and processes.

At many institutions, educators can also find a broad range of low(er) risk/low(er) visibility teaching opportunities that – dependent upon the testing idea mentioned above – could work well for some testing. For example, this could be, among other things: conferences, marketing events/roadshows, alumni meetings, open houses, class sessions outside of the normal curriculum (e.g., voluntary classes), electives, or internal meetings dedicated to educational purposes.

Using case teaching for case writing

- Case teaching and case writing belong together; they can also support and inform each other in many ways and should be combined in new and creative ways.
- Use your teaching to collect ideas for new case studies from participants.
- Test case ideas in early stages in class.
- Be rigorous in testing by applying a structured approach.
- Chose a safe environment for testing or create one yourself.

References

Anderson, L W and Krathwohl, D R (eds.) 2001 *A taxonomy for learning, teaching, and assessing: A revision of Bloom's taxonomy of educational objectives*. Allyn and Bacon.

Asterhan, C S C and Babichenko, M 2015 The social dimension of learning through argumentation: Effects of human presence and discourse style. *Journal of Educational Psychology*, 107(3): 740.

Binsted, D 1980 Design for learning in management training and development: A view. *Journal of European Industrial Training*, 4(8): 2–32.

Heath, J 2015 *Teaching and writing case studies – A practical guide*. 4th ed. The Case Centre.

Lampel, J 2003 Case Robin Hood. In: *The strategy process: Concepts, contexts, cases*. London, United Kingdom: Pearson, 2003, pp. 388–389.

Mueller, U and Kupp, M 2017 Combining case teaching and case writing creatively. In: *Case studies as a teaching tool in management education*. IGI Global, pp. 121–140.

Schoen, I 2012 *Effects of method and context of note-taking on memory: Handwriting versus typing in lecture and textbook-reading contexts*.

Smoker, T J, Murphy, C E, and Rockwell, A K 2009 Comparing memory for handwriting versus typing. *Proceedings of the Human Factors and Ergonomics Society Annual Meeting*, 53(22): 1744–1747. Los Angeles, CA: Sage.

Schulz von Thun, F 2008 *Miteinander reden 1. Störungen und Klärungen : allgemeine Psychologie der Kommunikation*. Reinbek: Rowohlt.

Watzlawick, P, Beavin, J H, and Jackson, D D 1967 *Pragmatics of human communication. A study of interactional patterns, pathologies, and paradoxes*. New York, NY: W. W. Norton & Company.

Teaching a case-based course

From a single session to a full course

'If you don't know where you are going, you'll end up someplace else.' – Yogi Berra

It is important to understand that preparing an entire case-based course is different from preparing a standalone case-based session. There are several additional factors to consider, and to ensure success you will have to do some careful designing. Basically, this is like taking case teaching to a meta level, e.g., you move from orchestrating a single session to orchestrating a whole semester. While the kinds of questions remain the same – for example, questions around the audience, the learning objectives, or flow of the session – you now have to think with a longer time horizon and have therefore other opportunities and constraints. In this chapter we will therefore highlight some of the questions that you have to ask yourself but also some of the tools and concepts that you might want to use. First, we will talk about some fundamental ideas about designing a case-based course, like considering the overall course setting within the larger program, case selection, additional materials, and the like. Then we will talk about managing the learning contract and introducing participants to the case method. Next, evaluating and grading your course are key and we will discuss how the case method can be used. We will close this section of the book by highlighting some key ethical considerations you should take into account when using the case method to deliver a course. This is very important and something that you have to think about upfront.

Designing the course

'Plans are of little importance, but planning is essential.'—Winston Churchill

In the paragraph on 'objectives, context, and case study selection' in the case teaching chapter, we expressed our belief that effective case teaching starts long before your class begins and often goes well beyond it.

And this is even more true when preparing a whole course. As with the preparation of a single session, you have to start thinking about who it is that you will have in your course, the teaching objectives that you want to reach by the end of the course, how you will assess the participants, and the kind of materials that you want to use over the whole course. The following five questions are a good guideline for preparing your case-based course:

1. Who will do the learning?
2. What are the course specifics and their relation to the overall program?
3. What is the content that you plan to cover through cases?
4. How do you want to structure the flow of the sessions?
5. What kind of methods/materials do you want to use that you feel comfortable with and that will support the achievement of your learning objectives (e.g., textbook, pre- and/or pos-treading, online courses, web-based training…)?

Who will do the learning?

We already covered this question extensively in the previous chapter on 'How to Teach a Case-Based Session' (page 27). Please go back and quickly check. It all starts here and cannot be emphasized enough.

What are the course specifics and their relation to the overall program?

The learning context and specifically the overall course setting and the position of the course in the overall program are very important and require the facilitators to prepare accordingly. After defining the learning objectives, you should start thinking about the learning context. When thinking about a whole course, a couple of questions or different settings come to mind. This is in no means a complete list of different settings; it just represents typical settings that we have encountered while discussing this topic during our case teaching workshops.

Core versus elective

Whether the course is a core course or an elective might have a number of implications regarding the preparation and actual delivery of the course. In general, your degree of freedom will be a lot bigger for an elective than for a core course. Often core courses, at least in bigger schools, will run in parallel and have therefore to be aligned carefully. At ESCP Europe, for example, the strategy core course has about 12 sections in the fall semester. And, while we do not impose the number of cases that have to be taught or the exact cases itself, the school expects the instructors to align. This alignment is in general achieved through the learning objectives. But the school offers time for the instructors to meet in good time before the course starts and one of the topics that is regularly discussed is the cases that could or should be used. During my time as the coordinator for the strategy course, we have developed an overview of the different cases that we regularly use per session or learning objective and update this document after each semester with new material.

In elective courses the possibilities to experiment (one of our core teaching beliefs) are typically greater. Electives are often very close to the facilitators' research agenda and teaching an elective is therefore a great chance to test but also develop new material.

 From theory to practice with Martin

In my electives I typically invite more external speakers to come and share their point of view than in a core course. These speakers can be both research collaborators but more frequently executives. Therefore, the number of living cases, basically executives bringing their actual problems and cases to class, is higher. This is a great way to test ideas and materials and to see which problems and stories stick with students and might be worth developing further.

Weekly vs blocked courses (part-time vs full-time)

The main difference between weekly and blocked courses is the time between the single sessions. In general, so-called executive programs like an executive MBA or other executive master's programs are organized in very intense blocks of several days of up to one, two, or three weeks. Even in regular, full-time programs, certain courses might be offered as a block course, for example in two consecutive days (12–15 hours) or one whole week (up to 30 hours). Therefore, a whole course of 12, 15, or even 30 hours might be taught in a single block. This will mean that there is little or no time between each single session.

The time between sessions is an important element in the planning of the course as it influences the amount of preparation that participants can dedicate to each session. While preparation is a difficult topic in itself, making participants prepare for example four cases for a whole day of teaching is to say the least challenging. But blocked courses also offer a lot of opportunities as it is easier to escape the strict boundaries of, for example, 75-minute sessions. In the section 'Teaching Plan Development' in the chapter on 'Teaching a Case-Based Session' we introduced the Lancaster model of learning and proposed that facilitators should actively design the learning experience for the participants by making participants' experience the whole learning cycle. For blocked courses, this would mean that the facilitator has more freedom to choose the amount of time they want to take to actually complete a whole cycle. In a weekly course, the facilitator has to bring each session to an end and therefore close a learning cycle. In a blocked course the facilitator has more freedom in choosing the appropriate time to complete such a learning cycle.

Position in the overall program

The position of your course in the overall program is also very important. Is your course at the very beginning of the participants' program or more toward the end? This will have an influence on how acquainted participants might already be with the case method (or even overexposed) or the potential danger that they might have already had the same or a similar case study. It is therefore always good to check these things before designing the course.

> ### From theory to practice with Martin
>
> For several years I taught a course called 'Strategic Innovation and Creativity' in an MBA program. This was a 20-hour course, delivered in 10 sessions of two hours each. I was using seven case studies over the whole course. The first two years I got really good evaluations from the students and also the atmosphere in class was very good with lively discussions. The third year was much more difficult. Participants seemed less enthusiastic, discussions were sometimes lingering on, and the overall level of attention seemed lower. What I had not realized was that the MBA program director had shifted my course from the beginning of the MBA program toward the end of the program, and this changed the whole dynamic. At the beginning of the program, participants were quite new to the case method and engaged very easily with the cases and the discussions. Also, the level of preparation was very good. When the course was moved toward the end of the program, the dynamic was different. Students were much more used to the case method, maybe even a little tired of it. Preparation was not as good, maybe because some colleagues had either overdone it with required preparation work or not followed up closely. What I learned from this was to make sure to get as much information as possible from the program director to be prepared or at least to be aware of these issues.

What is the content that you plan to cover with cases?

The degree of freedom that you have with regards to using the case method is obviously much higher when designing a whole course than with just a single session. Within a whole course you have multiple sessions and therefore a lot more time overall. You have to decide what content you want to cover with cases versus other methods and also reflect upon your overall learning objectives.

As we already described in more detail in the 'Case Method in the Spotlight' chapter, we are quite undogmatic about case studies and the use of case studies for education. We believe that facilitators should choose from a wide range of teaching formats like classical lectures, group work, role-play, simulations, and so on. In our opinion, skilled facilitators mix and match formats according to the educational objective but also to increase engagement through a plurality and diversity of methods. The traditional text case study used in a full-class case discussion is only one of many combinations possible. We think that this is important to keep in mind.

When it comes to designing a course, this plurality and diversity becomes even more important and you also have more room to maneuver. It is therefore important to think through all the sessions and then decide which content in which session you will develop with the case method or other methods.

It is helpful to go back to the functions of a case study. We have dealt with this point in more detail in the 'Case Study in the Spotlight' chapter. Taking from the long lists of functions, especially those where we see differences and sometimes advantages over other methods, it is mainly the ability of cases to infuse reality into the classroom, to enable participants to apply their knowledge and experience, to have controversial debates, and to link academic content to an intriguing story that is key. Looking at your course from this perspective, you can now ask yourself for which parts of your course you would like to use cases, how many you want to use, and at what point in time.

Structure and flow of the course

When designing a case-based session, you have the choice between a convergent and divergent flow of the session (see for more detail the sections on 'Teaching Plan Development' and here specifically the 'Flow of the Session'). This decision is based on the specific subject of the session. When designing a course, you cover several subjects and topics, some of which might be convergent in nature and some more divergent. If you have the freedom, you might want to make sure that you first have a good balance, and second that you change between the two options several times over the whole duration of the course.

Another aspect to take into consideration is the learning cycle. We then discussed learning cycles and introduced the Lancaster model of learning (see the section 'Learning Cycles'). When designing a whole course, the question of learning cycles has at least three aspects.

First, you have the choice to keep one specific learning cycle per session but to switch between different learning cycles from session to session. As in the example graphic below, you could, for example, have a first session with the learning cycle case discussion–reflection–closing lecture. For the next class you could ask the students to read an article before the session, start with a reflection, and end with a case discussion. A third session could again start with a case discussion, followed by a reflection, and then the participants would have a postreading.

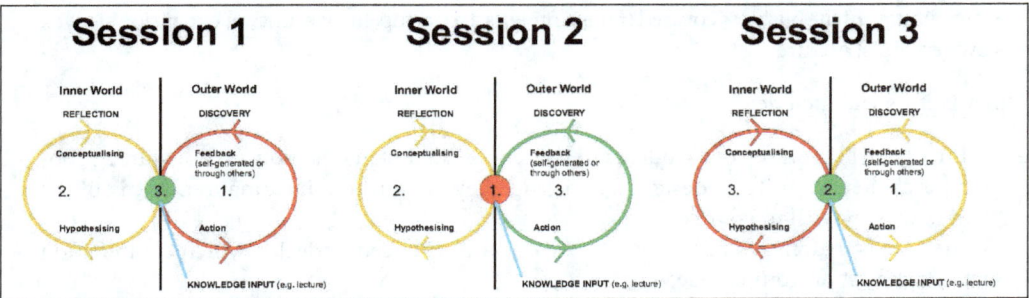

Figure 16: Structuring the flow of sessions within a course.

But designing a course gives you even more options. You can also think about using several sessions to complete one single learning cycle. So, instead of closing one learning cycle per session, you could extend the learning cycle over several sessions. You could, for example, use a whole session for a case discussion, followed by a whole session used for a reflection on the case study. The third session you would use for more theoretical input. But you are of course not restricted to using three sessions to close a learning cycle; you can also do it in two or, at the long end, maybe four or five sessions.

You should think about the whole course as one learning cycle. This change in perspective will make you think about orchestrating different learning modes throughout the whole course.

Last but not least, you will also need to consider how your course will adapt over time to meet your students' needs as they become more confident and knowledgeable. For example, case difficulty is likely to increase throughout the course, while your input as teacher should ideally decrease as students are enabled to think independently and learn from each other. The diagram below shows how this might work over a 10-session course:

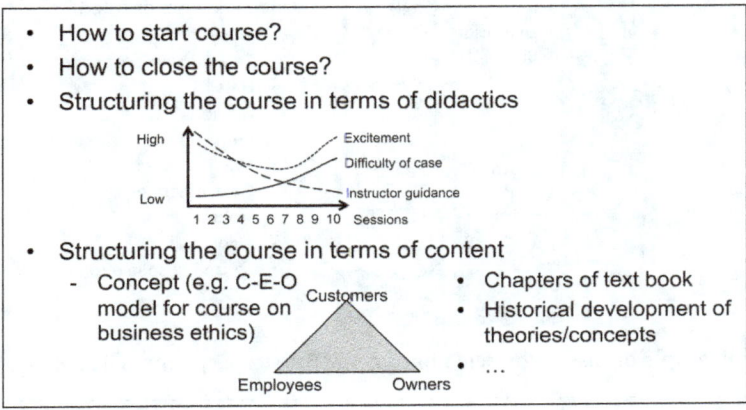

Figure 17: Thinking about a course as one learning cycle.

Methods and materials: case selection and mix for an entire course

When selecting cases for your course, you will need to take into account a number of factors to ensure that the case selection will support your overall learning objectives for the course, the content you need to cover, and also take into account the specific context of the course. While the first two are quite obvious, the last is especially important to remember when designing a course. Depending on the overall program that the course is part of, in your case selection criteria you will need to consider (this is by no means an exhaustive list):

- industries,
- geographical locations,
- functions,
- company size,
- current state of the business covered (for example, is it a startup, turnaround, or expansion story?),
- ownership structure.

Other factors will include:

- If the case will require your students to come up with a plan of action to deal with a problem or challenge, or if it is designed to provide key background information. A mix of the two may work well in your course.
- If the case is fictional or based on fact. Again, you will need to decide which combination will work best on your course.
- The age of a case. A mix of tried and tested classic cases and new cases may be most effective.

 From theory to practice with Martin

For several years Urs and I taught a strategy course in an MBA program in Portugal. After the second year we received the feedback that our cases were too focused on large multinational companies, often employing several hundred thousand people and operating globally. At the time, the largest Portuguese company employed roughly 60,000 people and was operating in a few European and African countries. This gave us the opportunity to rethink our material. We started by listing all cases and then grouped them according to different criteria. We started to look for better-suited cases and also wrote some new ones. After this overhaul, our case portfolio looked like this:

			Industries represented:
Big companies	• Ikea • Lufthansa • Sonae	• Wal*Mart	• Music • Telecommunication/Media • Retail • Airline
Small companies	• Virgin • Aesch • KTM • Robin Hood	• Celtel • Prohibition • Madonna	• Furniture • Medical devices • Conglomerate • Motorcycle • Alcohol • …. and of course robbing
	European	Non-European	

Figure 18: Example of case study selection for EMBA strategy course in Portugal.

(Continued)

> Our main criteria were company size (big/small) and location (European/non-European). Additionally, we also looked at the industries covered. In total we covered music, telecommunication/media, retail, airline, furniture, medical devices, conglomerate, motorcycle, alcohol, and of course robbing (the Robin Hood case).

Course preparation

- Teaching a case-based course is very different to teaching an individual case session.
- Create a detailed plan to cover every aspect of your course from start to finish.
- Use a mix of teaching methods to ensure deep learning.

Opening and running a case-based course or program

In this section, we focus on, in our opinion, two important aspects to think about when designing a course that uses cases. First, you will have to think about the learning contract that you want to have with your participants and how this learning contract reflects the use of cases and, second, you have to make sure to set the right expectations regarding the use of cases and you have to potentially introduce your participants to the case method.

Learning contract

> *'We don't need to share the same opinions as others, but we need to be respectful.'*
> *– Taylor Swift*

A *learning contract* sets (implicit or explicit) expectations for yourself and your participants, and specifies behaviors and habits for success. A learning contract is formed at the beginning of a semester, course, or session, often within seconds or minutes. It should ensure that everyone is treated with respect, good relations are maintained, and a positive learning atmosphere is created.

Whether you actively design and communicate a learning contract or not, there will always be a learning contract between the facilitator and the participants as learning contracts can be implicit or explicit.

Implicit

An implicit learning contract is created mainly by your own behavior and by how you react to the behavior of your participants without explicitly referring to a learning contract. If you come to class prepared and on time, if you ask challenging questions, if you treat your participants with respect etc., this will create an implicit learning contract as you will implicitly expect the same behavior from your participants. The same is true if you come late and unprepared, ask superficial questions, and are rude.

Explicit

An explicit learning contract is best created at the end of the first session or during sessions two or three. By this time, you can reflect upon observed behavior and integrate these observations into the way you want to talk about the learning contract and into the contract itself.

When it comes to the case method, several aspects are specifically important regarding the learning contract. As cases set out to enable a joint learning journey, the degree of preparation, the interaction during class, and the individuals' participation are extremely important.

For case-based courses it is very typical that participants are expected to read and prepare the cases before coming to class. But what do you do when participants come unprepared? In the previous section on teaching a case-based session, we have a whole chapter on dealing with participants that are not prepared (page 81). But here it is not so much about your immediate options around how to react but what the effect on the learning contract is and how to deal with that. A learning contract, even when set up explicitly at the beginning of the course, will change over time based on the actual behavior in class and more importantly on your reactions to the behavior. So, whatever tactics you choose when dealing with participants who are not prepared, also think about the long-term consequences and the consequences for the learning contract. We therefore believe that preparation should be part of an explicit learning contract and should be revisited in the case of problems.

The interaction between the facilitator and the participants, and – equally important – the interaction between the participants themselves, is crucial for the success of the case method. After all, the case method sets out to enable not only one-directional learning from educator to participant but should also enable participants to learn from each other. How participants treat each other, listen to each other, and engage with each other is therefore important and will be an important element of the learning contract (implicitly or explicitly).

And, last but not least, when designing a case-based course, you need to think about how you envision participants will participate. This will of course largely depend upon the overall setting of the course (face to face, online, synchronous, asynchronous). Depending on the setting, you need to make sure that you have thought about the way you want your participants to participate. You will also need to be clear about how issues such as late submission of assignments and nonattendance at sessions will be dealt with.

The importance of the learning contract

- Class relations depend on contract.
- Contracts are implicit and explicit.
- Implicit contracts in particular are done within minutes (not only over sessions).
- Contracts can change over time (external environment).
- Mechanics are important (first/last question, transition, time-outs…).
- Explicit contract might be best at end of first, in second or third session (after first experience with case method and teacher).
- Cover the 4 Ps: preparation, presence, promptness, participation.
- Create a safe environment: respect and protection.

Introducing the case method to the students

>'They know enough who know how to learn.' – Henry Adams

It is vital to remember that many participants will either have no knowledge of the case method or inaccurate preconceptions about it. Newcomers to the case method may be disconcerted by the lack of definite information and answers of the type usually given in traditional lectures. The idea of participating in a case method session may seem a daunting prospect and there may be little understanding of the benefits of doing so.

However, there are a few steps you can take to introduce the case method to your participants before the course starts; this will help to ensure that they come to the first session in a positive and receptive frame of mind.

You can then build on this in the first couple of sessions to consolidate their understanding and encourage them to get the most from the case method. A little careful planning should ensure you will soon have a class of enthusiastic 'case method converts.'

Before the course starts

Students who have never previously participated in a case discussion may find it very useful to watch a case class in action. There are many excellent examples online that can be found via a Google search. It might be a good idea to find case sessions that cover similar topics to those you will be covering in your course. You may even have video clips of your own teaching that would be helpful to share with new students before the course starts.

At the start of the course

You may wish to offer a brief introduction to the case method when you first meet your students at the start of the course. We have developed a short presentation to introduce the case method. It starts with highlighting the fact that learning actually takes place on several dimensions: The mind (cognitive), the guts (intuition), and the heart (emotional). There are a lot of ways to describe these dimensions, but for the sole purpose of introducing the case method we feel that these three dimensions and their easy visual representation work very well and are convincing.

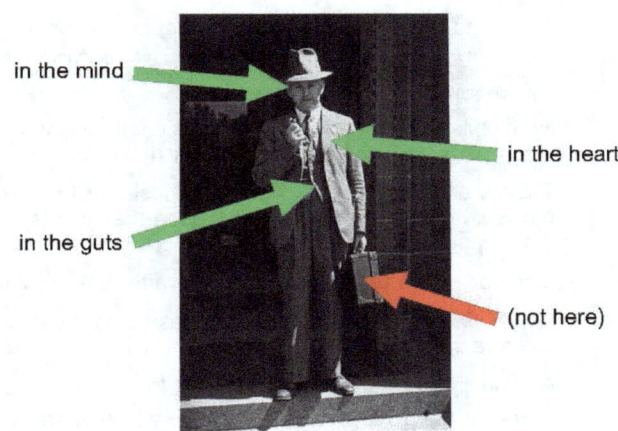

Figure 19: Where learning sticks.

We then immediately turn to the common complaints about the case study method. This is described in detail in the 'Case Method in the Spotlight' chapter (page 1) of this book if you want to go deeper. The case method is often described by its critics as lacking clear answers, having ambiguous and contradictory information, having redundant and irrelevant information, and being inefficient, just to name the most important ones. We think that it is important to start with the common complaints and to actually give participants the possibility to also voice their concerns.

Then we discuss the best ways and principles of how to learn from case discussions. We focus on the following points:

- Prepare and force yourself to commit to your personal answer!
- Learning does not (mostly) come from the instructor but is rather an effect of the class discussion.
- Participants contribute to the discussion from different points of view.
- For all really interesting issues: Different perspectives are possible and important – controversy is good! Only simple problems have simple and one-sided answers/solutions.

- Active participation of all participants is key: the learner is not a sponge but an active element of a joint learning process – 'Share your experiences.'
- Imperfect information and the role of assumptions play an important role – just as in 'regular' life.
- There are no 'right' or 'wrong' answers or contributions. Whatever adds a new aspect to the discussion is helpful. The same is true for business, management, and leadership: they are not exact sciences – 'telling the truth as a set of clear rules' is impossible.
- Draw your own conclusions (e.g., for your business).

We often end the presentation by asking the participants to come up with their own rules for the course, typically with a focus on case discussions. We capture these rules on either a slide or a flipchart. It is important to capture these rules and to have them to hand for later sessions if participants start to break the rules or the learning atmosphere is degrading. The following screenshot is from an actual session that Urs did with an EMBA class.

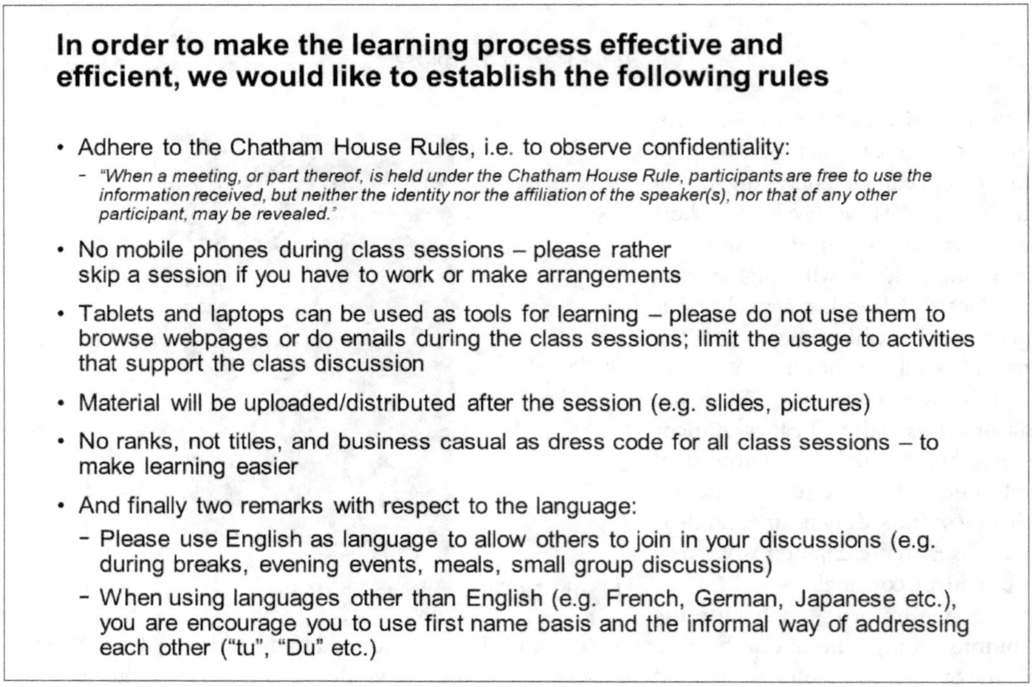

In order to make the learning process effective and efficient, we would like to establish the following rules

- Adhere to the Chatham House Rules, i.e. to observe confidentiality:
  - "When a meeting, or part thereof, is held under the Chatham House Rule, participants are free to use the information received, but neither the identity nor the affiliation of the speaker(s), nor that of any other participant, may be revealed."
- No mobile phones during class sessions – please rather skip a session if you have to work or make arrangements
- Tablets and laptops can be used as tools for learning – please do not use them to browse webpages or do emails during the class sessions; limit the usage to activities that support the class discussion
- Material will be uploaded/distributed after the session (e.g. slides, pictures)
- No ranks, not titles, and business casual as dress code for all class sessions – to make learning easier
- And finally two remarks with respect to the language:
  - Please use English as language to allow others to join in your discussions (e.g. during breaks, evening events, meals, small group discussions)
  - When using languages other than English (e.g. French, German, Japanese etc.), you are encourage you to use first name basis and the informal way of addressing each other ("tu", "Du" etc.)

Figure 20: Screenshot of slide with rules for an EMBA class.

Please note that the 'rules' go both ways. Some clearly address the participants ('No mobile phones'), others the facilitator ('Material will be uploaded'), and others go both ways ('No ranks,' language).

The beginning of the course might also be the right time to introduce the short cycle case screening approach, which we have already introduced in the 'Case Method in the Spotlight' chapter (page 1) of this book. Please go back to the 'Introducing the Case Method to the Students' section for more information.

During the course

Once the course has started, the selection of your cases will have a great impact on how your participants will adapt to the case method. Thinking about the best sequence of cases is critically important. The content of the cases is less important than their complexity and length, for example. If possible, it may be a good idea to select shorter cases for your first couple of sessions. There are many excellent cases of five pages or fewer that will appear less intimidating to students who are new to cases. (The Case Centre, for example, lists these shorter cases as 'compact cases.')

You could also kick off the first session with a 'caselet' to introduce students to full-class discussion. Caselets are short summaries, perhaps a paragraph or two, of a tricky workplace problem or challenge that needs to be addressed. These do not require preclass preparation by students and can be used as initial 'icebreakers' at the start of the course.

Over time you can then increase the complexity of the cases. We talk about materials and the flow of the sessions in more details above in the 'Structure and Flow of the Course' (page 116) and 'Methods and Materials' sections (page 118).

Introducing students to the case method

- Remember: many new business students will be unfamiliar with the case method.
- Prepare them in advance with video clips of case sessions.
- Offer a brief presentation about the case method at the start of the course.
- Make sure your students understand how to approach a case; explain the 'short cycle reading' method.
- Consider using caselets to introduce your students to case discussions.
- Consider using shorter cases at the start of your course.

Grading of a case-based course

Grading is a very important and often difficult topic. In general, it is very important to be specific about your approach to grading. You should be transparent from the start about how you will grade your students, so they have a clear understanding of what to expect and what they need to do to ensure good grades. Clarity and openness will result in fewer (if any) complaints from puzzled or disgruntled students. And, if individuals raise any queries, you will be able to refer back with confidence to your established grading criteria and justify the grade you have given. Your students should have no doubt that they will all be treated equally.

But this of course is true for any kind of grading, not only for grading of case-based courses. The specificity of case-based courses is the participant-centricity and the typically increased interactivity. And your grading should reflect this.

Depending on your school context, your participants may have no previous experience of being evaluated on the basis of their contribution in class, so you will need to be crystal clear about what is expected and what they can do to ensure the best possible grades. It is therefore even more important that you explicitly define and communicate your evaluation criteria, especially for participation and contribution.

If your students are not used to case-based courses, we recommend reminding them regularly of the importance of class contribution. We have had good experiences with directly contacting participants who are not participating in the first two or three sessions. As we explain in more detail below, we suggest taking notes immediately after each session. These notes will help you to spot these students early on. If possible, find out why they are not doing well and if there is anything more you can do to help and support them in class.

Resistance to using the case method frequently often comes from the fear that grading case-based courses is more difficult and can actually never be really specific and ultimately objective. The argument is that cases aim at controversy and good cases do not have a single 'correct' answer or solution. But this is in our opinion are rather short-sighted point of view. So, let's look at the different ways to grade in case-based courses. The main elements are:

- grading participation/contribution,
- grading assignments and submissions,
- grading case-based exams.

Grading participation/contribution

General ideas for grading participation/contribution

While grading in general is difficult and requires a lot of rigor from the facilitator, in the case of grading participation in a case-based course it can actually be a good way to stimulate the case discussion. It forces students to prepare, it forces students to contribute, and it allows you to specify and incentivize certain types of contributions (e.g., not quantity but contribution to class learning).

 If you chose to integrate grading of participation in your case-based course it is important that you follow some ground rules:

- Make sure all students are aware participation/contribution is graded.
- Explicitly define and communicate what and how you evaluate/grade (activity, participation, contribution, progress etc.)!
- Put emphasis on fair opportunity to contribute (beware of calling patterns [left/right] and blind spots in seating).
- Make selective use of methods that give more introvert students options to contribute (e.g., cold-calling, reports from individuals).
- Prepare yourself about the class and each individual student:
  - Try to remember all names.
  - Ask students to have (readable) name tags in front of them or, if online, ask them to add full names.
  - If possible, use a class map (ideally with photos!).
  - When you do not have a class map or a student booklet with pictures, make one – have students hold up name tags and take a picture (see Anderson & Schiano 2014: 43) – or take screenshot in an online setting.
  - Take pictures of class/screenshots at the beginning of each session as proof of absence/presence when starting.

On a more general note, we would advise you to always evaluate participation directly after each class, either still in the classroom if possible or back in your office if students are still around or the classroom is already booked for the next class. While it is in our experience very important to have notes for every single session, the depth and breadth of these notes do not have to be very detailed. We have had good experiences with simple scales such as:

- −1: comments that hindered the discussion,
- 0: not present,
- 1: present,
- 2: participated,
- 3: good comments,
- Exc: excused.

A small but important point: always make a note of any nonattendees. A quick way of doing this is to take a photograph at the start of the class. In this way you will have proof if a student claims they were present on a date you have down them as absent.

- Evaluate participation **directly after each class** (go to your office)!
  - Use a scale such as: -1: comments that hindered the discussion, 0: not present, 1: present, 2: participated, 3: good comments, Exc: excused
- Consider additionally collecting **self-assessment** or **feedback from classmates** (e.g. cross-participant feedback/assessment)

See also excel template for grading oral participation

Figure 21: Grading participation/contribution.

Consider additionally collecting self-assessment or feedback from classmates (e.g., cross-participant feedback/assessment). We collect the notes in a straightforward Excel table like the following one.

Make sure you discriminate between quantity and quality when awarding grades for classroom contributions. One participant may make lengthy contributions but add nothing of particular value to the debate, while another participant may offer a single sentence that leads to a vital 'ah-ha' moment for the class as a whole. A long monologue is not in itself worthy of a good grade; participants need to demonstrate that they are fully engaged in the debate: listening carefully and responding in a considered way to both the instructor and their peers in a way that moves the debate forward and increases understanding.

During class, you will have to take proactive steps to ensure everyone receives a fair grade. Here, your background reading about each participant will be invaluable as you will know in advance of any potential barriers that may prevent an individual from contributing, for example if they come from a culture where students are traditionally deferential, or if there are only a few female students, who may find it harder to make their voice heard.

You will need to place great emphasis on ensuring that everyone has an equal opportunity to contribute. This means you will need to be very aware of your own classroom habits. For example, do you tend to direct questions more toward the right or the left of the classroom? If so, you will need to ensure your calling patterns are evenly distributed across the room. Are there any blind spots in the seating arrangement that make communication with some students tricky? If so, you will need to find a way round this.

You will also need to ensure that quieter and more introverted students are given the chance to shine, for example by cold-calling; warning them in advance that you will be calling on them, so they have time to prepare; or asking them in advance to prepare a report or analysis for presentation during the session.

Bear in mind that you will probably be awarding participants a final overall grade that reflects the quality of their class contributions throughout the course. At a suitable point, perhaps a third or halfway through the course, it can be a good idea to make contact with any participants who have not done well so far. If possible, find out why they are not doing well and if there is anything more you can do to help and support them in class.

Grading participation/contribution in online courses

While the general comments on grading participation can in most cases also be applied to online courses, owing to the specificity of the online context there are additional elements to be considered.

Let's first look at the specific online context of an online synchronous class where you want to grade oral participation. While this does not sound very different to a face-to-face session, there are some particularities that you need to take into account:

- Faces online look different from in pictures (as you get them in class lists). We therefore advise taking screenshots (also to capture attendance at beginning/middle/end of sessions – and students who do not join breakouts).
- Check participation by observing activity beyond talking:
  - Contributions in chat functions or online polls (some participants feel more comfortable writing, e.g., due to language issues).
  - Do participants join breakout rooms?
  - Do they have their cameras on? What do they do?
  - Do they use reaction symbols/emoticons?

And there are also a number of advantages when grading online participation. In our experience it is easier to remember names as you see the names more often as they are displayed on the picture/video. Participants sit in very different locations and have therefore different backgrounds, which often helps to memorize them. Some systems move participants with a higher level of activity higher up in the list. You can also record the session, which will give you the possibility to do a check of all contributions, for example in a fast-forward mode.

Additionally, in an online context there are more opportunities to contribute. While oral participation during a synchronous online session is in fact not very different from a face-to-face session, students have more forms to contribute, for example through chats, polls, quizzes, and forums/discussion boards.

The benefit of these types of contribution is that you will have a record of them. This will make it a lot easier to review them and to take them into consideration. We advise being very explicit about your expectations and to explicitly include contributions to chats, forums and discussion boards, etc. in your participation grading.

Grading assignments and submissions

Cases are also a very good vehicle for (written) assignments and submissions. We put 'written' in brackets because you are of course not limited to written assignments anymore. Very often we ask our participants to upload videos or audios or create website content or other electronic documents. As cases are typically handed out before class and are supposed to be read before class, a classic form of assignment is presession case writeups or targeted essays. This not only offers you another grading element in your course; it might also positively impact the preparedness of your students. When it comes to the grading criteria for such assignments, we had made good experiences with the following criteria:

- *Focus:* The issue must be defined clearly; the analysis should stay sharply focused on the issue at hand; use of evidence and scope of discussion should reflect the participant's ability to see and concentrate on what is important.
- *Structure:* The case write-up or essay should be well structured; the presentation should be a neatly arranged flow of arguments leading to conclusions.
- *Argumentative quality:* the work should reflect rigorous use of facts and logic; the essay should demonstrate the participant's shining brainpower.

- *General relevance* of essay to the specific task.
- *Language* correct and understandable (grammar, spelling, etc.).
- *Formal criteria:* Delivery within time and word limits, explicit references to all used sources.

In addition to presession case writeups, you can of course also use postsession assignments. While all of the above criteria would typically also apply to postsession assignments, there are at least two additional criteria that you could and should use after you had the case discussion in class:

- *Link to course content:* Meaningful application of tools/frameworks/theories that were introduced/used in the context of the course.
- *Multi-perspectives:* Ability to (1) include different relevant perspectives in your analysis and (2) assess stakeholder interests and the legitimacy of their claims.

Grading case-based exams

In a case-based course it might make sense to use a case study for the final exam. After all, students should be case experts by the end of the course. There are a number of different options (again, this is by no means an exhaustive list and we welcome feedback and additional experiences/ideas):

- Students can be asked to analyze a case that has not been previously discussed in class.
- They can be asked to work on a case that has already been discussed in class.

For both alternatives there are a number of general principles and suggestions to ensure a fair and transparent process and ultimately student satisfaction. Above and beyond, there are many options that you have, and we will outline a number of those below.

- You can decide whether or not you will allow preparation time before the exam, for example time to read the case and background material.
- They can be set an 'open book' exam, meaning they have access to various materials that can be used to support their arguments and analyses.
- You can set exams to be taken on an individual basis or as a group.
- Exams can be written or take the form of a presentation to the rest of the group. You may choose to include peer evaluation of presentations as part of your grading.

The advantage of using a case for the exam is that it is a very versatile instrument. When you developed the course and decided to make it case-based, you already reflected upon the learning objectives of the course. We previously mentioned at several points the broad categories of learning objectives: knowledge, skills, and behaviors. When designing a case-based exam, you need to come back to the learning objectives and think about the right kind of questions and activities that your students are supposed to work on regarding the case study, so that you can actually evaluate if the learning objectives are achieved. We have found the following formats good examples for achieving the different overarching learning objectives:

- Closed questions that can be used to validate knowledge, for example: The protagonist thinks about entering a new industry. What kind of analysis should he perform to assess the attractiveness of the industry?
- Open questions to validate skills (for example the application of a specific framework), for example: Please perform a five forces analysis for the transportation industry in Germany at the time of the case.
- Open questions to validate behavior, for example: What would you do if you were in the shoes of the protagonist?

Make sure your suggested exam questions are not just duplicates of the assignment questions for the case that you plan to use for the exam:

1. If the exam case is quite long and you decide to hand it out before the exam, the participants might just google the assignment questions and standard responses.
2. The suggested participant assignment questions are written with class interaction in mind. They will frequently be very open-ended, whereas good questions for exams should include some closed questions to ease the grading process.

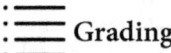 **Grading**

Grading oral participation in class
- Make sure participants understand that their contributions in class will be graded.
- Be clear and transparent about your grading criteria.
- The quality of contributions is more important than the quantity.
- Familiarize yourself with your students' background and experience in advance.
- Encourage and support students who are not doing well.
- Record grades immediately after class while everything is fresh in your mind.
- For online classes think about integrating additional elements like chats, polls, quizzes, and participation in breakout rooms.

Grading assignments and submissions
- Define your grading criteria and apply them consistently when marking work.
- Assignments can be presession and postsession.

Grading case-based exams
- You can use a new case or a case that you already discussed in class.
- Design the exam questions with your learning objectives (knowledge, skills, behaviors) in mind.

Ethical considerations for a case-based course

Ethics and ethical consideration in teaching could fill many books. There is abundant literature on ethical dilemmas in educational contexts and we do not want to review or just repeat these elements. In this chapter we want to only focus upon some specific ethical considerations when using the case method. In 'The Case Method in the Spotlight' we already outlined criticisms of the case method and acknowledged their arguments and point of view. Here we want to add some of our own observations of potential ethical dilemmas that a case teacher can run into. The following list is based on our own experience and by no means exhaustive:

- Pretention of participant-centricity,
- Unfair allocation of airtime,
- Disrespectful treatment of participants,
- Hindsight bias,
- Not evaluating the learning objectives.

Pretention of participant-centricity

At the heart of the case method lies participant-centricity. If you do not truly believe in participant-centricity, then you should not use the case method in your course, because that would give participants the false expectation that the course will be participant-centered when in reality this is not your interest. The following questions are a good test to probe your own take on customer-centricity:

- Do you try to get to know your participants already ahead of your course?
- How much flexibility does your course and your teaching plan offer?
- What are specific questions or exercises used to find out what your participants are interested in?

As mentioned before, we do not want to force you to be participant-centered and there are many great teaching formats that are not participant-centered by default. But you need to believe in the participant-centered philosophy – that does not mean that you cannot or should not steer the process but you need to allow for some leeway, i.e., do not fake an interest in the contributions of your participants if in reality you only want to bring across your point.

Unfair allocation of airtime

Almost as a consequence of being participant-centered, the case method also calls for a strong involvement of the participants in the learning process. It is therefore very important that all participants get an equal opportunity to contribute. You should make sure your calling pattern is not influenced by factors such as:

- seating order,
- introversion versus extroversion,
- gender,
- cultural background,
- previous education,
- conformity with your own opinions,
- ease of pronouncing names,
- liking

Disrespectful treatment of participants

You should be aware of the potentially devastating effects of negative, belittling, sarcastic, or humorous reactions to contributions by students. One single negative experience can lead to the complete disconnection of a participant from the session or even the entire course. Additionally, this might affect the overall learning atmosphere and trust between the facilitator and the participant group.

Hindsight bias

Case studies typically deal with events from the past. It is important to acknowledge to ourselves as facilitators and to the students that the 'real' events do not necessarily reflect optimal decisions and that luck might have played a significant role.

Ethical issues of grading

Grading on the basis of case studies requires particular attention. Cases aim for controversy and good cases do not have a single right answer/solution – accordingly you should not grade participants by their recommendations but by their ability to base a recommendation on sound analysis and the application of theories, concepts, and tools discussed in class. We give some advice on good practice when grading in a case-based course above in the section 'Grading of a Case-Based Course.' But we decided to mention this point here too when discussing ethical considerations, as it is easy to fall for biases like confirmation bias, where we value answers that confirm our own opinion higher than answers that go against our opinion. Of course, case-based discussions should not be based only on opinions but also on knowledge and analytical skills, but the case method is certainly much more prone to also including opinions in the discussion.

Reference

Anderson, E and Schiano, B 2014 *Teaching with cases: A practical guide*. Boston, MA: Harvard Business School Press.

Writing great case studies

This chapter has been written with first-time case authors in mind but it also contains many ideas and suggestions for educators who have already produced multiple, possibly even great, and successful cases:

- If you are not yet (very) experienced with writing cases: follow this chapter step by step in the correct sequence and work on your case study and teaching note in parallel to reading.
- If you are more experienced, and just seek guidance regarding individual challenges: use the table of contents, the index or the FAQ section of the webpage for this book (include link) to navigate directly to the relevant sections of this book.

To complement this book, we have developed an accompanying workbook to support you in your case writing effort. The workbook follows the creation of a case study for teaching purposes from the very beginning to the finished and published case study and teaching note. We have developed this document over many years while working with participants in our case writing workshops run by the Case Centre. According to our experience, it is particularly helpful for inexperienced case authors – the type of users we had in mind when designing most of the sections of this workbook.

Experienced case authors might find it unnecessary to go through the entire workbook. But we have often received the feedback that even veteran case authors got a number of ideas for their next case study from the process-oriented structure of this workbook. Experienced case authors might consider using the case and teaching note review sections for their critical self-assessment, or to collect structured feedback from a peer.

You will find downloadable PDF versions of the workbook on the webpage for this book.

How to cite this book chapter:
Kupp, M. and Mueller, U. 2024. *The Ultimate Case Guide: How to Successfully Teach and Write Case Studies.* Pp. 131–249. London: Ubiquity Press. DOI: https://doi.org/10.5334/bdb.d. License: CC BY-NC 4.0

Our case writing beliefs and philosophy

There are many excellent (work)books, articles, notes, and guides on writing cases. Is there really a need for yet another case writing guide? Well, you decide for yourself – but this chapter is driven by a few convictions (shall we call them philosophies?) that we developed over many years during which we not only wrote many (some not so good, but also several award-winning and best-selling) cases ourselves but also ran case writing workshops and coached less experienced colleagues from a large number of institutions and disciplines.

On the basis of these experiences, three aspects are particularly important for us and will go a long way to dealing with the most common obstacles and problems case authors face:

1. Rapid prototyping,
2. Breaking the rules – once you master the fundamentals,
3. Focus on learning outcomes.

1. Prototype rapidly
- Start to write immediately (e.g. opening paragraph)
- Work in fast iterations ('quick and dirty')
- Stop soon if you reach a dead-end

2. Break the rules – once you master the fundamentals
- Write one or a few simple and rather traditional cases first
- Learn the craft through experience
- Once you know the conventions – feel free to break all rules

3. Focus on learning outcomes
- Don't fall in love with your case lead (the story)
- Only write a case if you have already a bit of experience teaching with cases
- Ultimately a case is only a vehicle to reach a learning outcome

Figure 22: Our case writing beliefs and philosophy.

Rapid prototyping

This chapter applies the approach of agile methodologies, design thinking, etc. to case writing. Several other case writing instructions are also driven by a pragmatic philosophy but we deeply believe in the idea of working in multiple, short iterations and a 'fail fast' philosophy.

 We designed this chapter so that you do not have to read it in total before starting your own case production. Rather, we invite you to embark on a journey with us. The entire chapter is designed to be read in small increments and to start and stop your reading to immediately get into action (usually marked with an 'action' icon).

Start working immediately – do not push this back or procrastinate. Some of the great cases that you might have used in your own classes are the result of enormous amounts of work, but if you follow the proposed approach of this chapter you will get quite far with only limited effort!

Get into working mode early and with a 'quick and dirty' attitude. Great cases always require multiple rounds of improvement anyway. Do not even aim for perfection from the beginning – just get going and aim for rapid development of what startups would call prototypes or minimal viable products (MVPs). Throughout this chapter we alert you to tactics that will prevent initial activism from being futile. If you follow our approach, your early labor will almost never be useless – even if you make major changes later.

Of course, there is always a risk that your initial work will not lead to a published case study. There are many possible traps and roadblocks on the way. As you invest more and more into your case, you increase the risk of falling into the sunk-cost fallacy: you just proceed because you have already invested so much time and energy. To minimize this risk, we have included several 'fail fast pit stops.' We invite you to critically review your previous work and to consider stopping entirely or going back a few steps to avoid a late deadlock: fail fast to fail cheap!

Breaking the rules – but only after gaining experience

'My propositions serve as elucidations in the following way: anyone who understands me eventually recognizes them as nonsensical, when he has used them—as steps—to climb beyond them. (He must, so to speak, throw away the ladder after he has climbed up it.)' – Ludwig Wittgenstein
(Tractatus Logico-Philosophicus, 6.54)

Great ideas, innovations, literature, music, art, research, etc. – they all tend to break (at least some) rules and conventions. The same is probably true for case studies. Even though there are several aspects that many of the world's best case studies have in common, they will frequently be violating some if not many of the established, traditional ways of writing cases. Both of us have produced cases that deviate from the traditional case study scheme – some of them worked (extremely) well; others failed big time. As our lesson learned, we advise new case authors to first produce a few cases that follow the established patterns. Only after having produced a few conventional cases can you really get a good picture of when, why, and where you should be disruptive and innovative – only then should you move on and throw away the ladder of the conventions.

Accordingly, we invite our readers to stimulate their critical thinking while working their way through this chapter. We will present many of our recommendations apodictically – and, if you have not produced a couple of cases yet, we believe that you will be better off following them closely. But, once you have stepped up, feel free to throw away the ladder and violate any of our recommendations.

Focus on learning outcomes

Last but not least, a strong warning (that we will reiterate multiple times later on): Do not get too excited by a specific story or case opportunity. The single most common mistake we have observed with new case study authors is their missing distance to what is usually called the 'lead': a story that they picked up or a connection they happen to have. If you are anything like many people we coached over the last years, you might be obsessed with the idea of writing your own case study in combination with an almost romantic love for an individual story.

The danger of this combination: You risk losing sight of what is most important – the educational context! Make sure to always keep the intended learning outcomes in mind! When following our approach (and our 'case development funnel'; see below), you are much less likely to commit this cardinal sin of case writing newcomers.

And here comes our first fail fast pit stop: if you do not yet have at least some experience in teaching with cases, do not even try to write your first case study (at least not alone/by yourself). We have read quite a few cases that were produced by professional writers or students as sole authors. In the best case they are well-presented descriptions of interesting situations – but they will almost inevitably lack clarity regarding the educational outcome and focus on the learning process in class. If you fall into this category, try to gain case teaching experience first or at least make sure to have an experienced case teacher as coauthor, who should work with you intensively regarding the learning objective and teaching process.

Benefits of writing your own case

Why should you even consider writing your own case study? There are already thousands available; surely everything's been covered by now? So why do the work? (And make no mistake, writing a case that really works well in the classroom is hard work.)

The enormous number of existing cases would probably not have emerged if there weren't several significant benefits from writing cases. Here are a few of them:

- Teaching your own case will enhance your status with students; you will be respected as someone with expert 'inside knowledge' and connections with key figures from practice.
- Your in-depth familiarity with the subject will boost your confidence in the classroom; you will typically know much more about the situation than you write down in the case and this will reduce any insecurity, e.g., if you have only limited work experience outside of academia.
- Your passion for the subject will enthuse and inspire your students.
- You can rightfully take great pride in discussing your own case in class.
- Writing a case can be an element of or a link to your research, as you will typically investigate a real-world situation and apply academic theories, concepts, and frameworks to it.
- Writing cases might help to fulfill your individual (e.g., publications) or institutional (e.g., accreditations) targets.
- Case writing and case teaching are two complementary sides of the same coin. The insights you will gain when teaching cases will help enormously when writing cases, and vice versa. By writing case studies, you will almost automatically become a more reflective and better (case) teacher.

The case development funnel

Great cases usually (1) recount a truly interesting development, decision, or story and (2) allow the exploration or application of relevant theories, concepts, frameworks, or tools. Cases from beginners frequently lack one or the other. We have observed that many case-writing novices fail to produce great cases because they get overly excited by a story they learn about or by a connection to real-life business they happen to have – but then they often fail to turn this into a vehicle for a meaningful educational process. Inversely, but less frequently, new case authors sometimes fail because they are so driven to achieve a learning objective that they miss producing a case that is intriguing and engaging for the participants.

While mentoring and guiding colleagues through the process of producing a case study, we initially struggled to apply the frequently propagated logic of case production: some guides and textbooks on case writing (e.g., Leenders, Mauffette-Leenders, & Erskine 2010; Naumes & Naumes 2006; Roch 1989) tend to follow a more or less sequential logic, according to where one first writes (most of) the case study text and only then starts producing the corresponding teaching note. Others propose to first write the teaching note and only then write the case study (reverse engineer) (this was for example proposed by Marika Taishoff in an interview on case writing published on The Case Centre website in 2019).

 Marika Taishoff of the International University of Monaco believes that the teaching note should be drafted before the case is written. She says:

First and foremost, one should NOT start by writing the case, but by drafting the teaching note. I have found that this is the best way to articulate and structure the key learning points that you want students to come away with. It also facilitates the case writing process because the writer becomes very clear about the main messages and arguments that need to be developed in the case. (Taishoff 2019)

However, we have concluded over time that the focus should shift (ideally in many iterations) from case to teaching note and back – minor changes to the case study can fundamentally impact the educational options and small shifts in your learning objectives might require a completely different case.

Therefore, we propose an alternative interwoven case development process, which we can illustrate through the metaphor of two-component glues: two materials that remain liquid as long as separated but become a very powerful glue as soon as they are properly mixed with one another. And the same is true for cases. To produce a truly sticky case study, you will need to combine and knead (in iterations) two ingredients to get the desired result: an interesting story with a demand for a specific educational outcome.

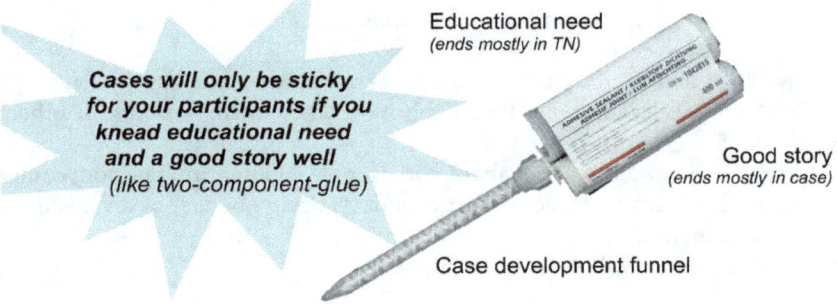

Figure 23: The two components of a sticky case: need and lead. Source: Adapted from Wikimedia Commons (https://commons.wikimedia.org/wiki/File:2-part_silicone_adhesive_sealant .jpg; author: Cjp24; licensed as: CC-BY-SA-3.0; accessed May 18, 2024).

This idea led us to the development of our 'case development funnel' – a nine-step process through which case authors will gradually work their way toward a finished case study and teaching note, moving from the more strategic and important decisions to the more operative choices and activities:

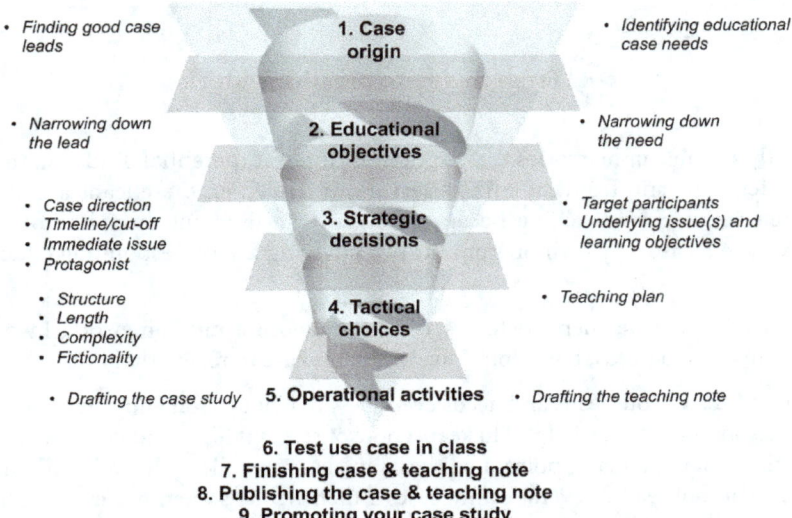

Figure 24: The case development funnel.

The remainder of this chapter follows the logic of this case development funnel. The accompanying case writing workbook can be used to work (individually, in pairs, groups or during workshops) your way through the funnel, leading to the development of a case that will make the learning really stick.

1. Case origin

'Amateurs sit and wait for inspiration, the rest of us just get up and go to work.' – Stephen King

The first step toward producing your first case study is simple and does not require a lot of time: just collect ideas, namely needs and leads for your case. Even if you are not yet sure if you really want to invest the time and effort into producing your own case, just start to collect ideas – and postpone the production of a case until you have found what you were really looking for. Borrowing the terminology of Leenders et al. (2010: 31), we call this stage of the case development funnel 'case origin.'

It is all about leads and needs

Almost all case writing guides agree: The best cases are created when you have a matching pair of an interesting 'lead' *and* a relevant 'need.' If you only have one of them, wait for the other before starting to write a case!

A *lead* is a 'story' that you want to write about, for example an interesting person, company, or development. A *need* is a learning objective that cannot (yet/fully) be met by an existing case or alternative educational method.

You can start with either but will always need both:

- A leads-based approach gives you the opportunity to leverage a real-life dilemma or challenge.
- A needs-based approach allows you to target a specific learning objective.

Be critical: you might have a great lead, but is there really a corresponding need? You should ask yourself: would my students truly benefit from discussing a case on the basis of this particular lead? And the reverse is also true: you might have a need, but no real lead; does it really make sense to write a case with an artificial or second-class lead?

However, if you have both and they are a good fit, you are in the ideal position to start work on what should result in a truly great case. Exciting!

 From theory to practice with Urs

I frequently stumble upon stories that capture my interest (potential 'leads') in the news, from participants, and from my own observations. However, these leads are often initially irrelevant for my teaching because they cover a different discipline or because I already have a case (my own or from others) covering the corresponding educational need.

The opposite is also true: there are topics, concepts, theories, and frameworks I would like to discuss in class (a need), but I don't have a suitable case to match that need.

Sometimes these various leads and needs eventually match up (somehow magically) – and for that reason I find it very helpful to keep a note of relevant leads and needs, so that I can come back to them at a later point. I cultivate an electronic file with leads without needs and needs without leads. Several of my cases I then wrote, sometimes even many years later, when suddenly lead and need matched (e.g., through a change in the lead or through a new need).

To ensure that your lead truly matches your need, we propose to first step back a little bit and to reconsider all possible leads and needs first. To highlight our emphasis on the importance of a great educational need (versus the usually dominating lead), we will always start with the needs-based perspective in the first three steps of our case development funnel.

Identifying educational needs (content or context)

How do you identify relevant and valuable educational needs? And what is a need really?

A need could, for example, be one or several topics, issues, theories, concepts, tools, frameworks, etc. that you would like to introduce, discuss, and apply in class but for which you are currently lacking an adequate case. This will be particularly true for the most recent developments in business, but also for (new) theories that are not yet sufficiently elaborate. In both situations there will probably be no (good) cases yet. Here it is the *content* of your planned session that provides the educational need for the case.

Sometimes (usually more rarely) the educational need might also result from the *context* of your teaching. There is a seemingly infinite number of cases about change management and many of them might allow you to perfectly discuss the theories, tools, and concepts that you want your participants to discuss. But maybe the context of your teaching requires a case with a female protagonist, leading a change in a small team in a finance department in a sub-Saharan family business. How likely will you be to find something that fits this need in existing case collections?

In a nutshell, there are different reasons to *need* a case. See below for an incomplete list of possible case needs:

Types of case needs

- *Educational content needs:* you need to teach a certain *content* but do not have a matching case, e.g., you need a case in order to introduce, explain, illustrate, review, apply, critically reflect, etc. theories, issues, frameworks, academic concepts, tools, etc.
- *Educational context needs:* you teach in a certain *context* and need a case that will suit this particular audience and/or program, e.g., regarding
  – geographical and/or cultural setting of the case;
  – industry or market sector;
  – firm size;
  – type/ownership structure of the organization (not-for-profit vs family business vs publicly listed vs government owned);
  – functional setting;
  – gender of the protagonist;
  – protagonist's level of seniority.

The key is to be absolutely clear about your reasons for writing the case and what you want to achieve. And, while we suggest starting to build a long list of potential needs, it is also important to be critical with your case needs early on in the process. This will ease your decisions later.

Critical questions for your case need

Did you describe your potential case needs clearly enough?

- Which theories do you want to cover?
- What should be the three/four takeaways for your students?
- What should their notes say?
- How does your presentation look like?

From theory to practice with Urs and Martin

Urs:
Several years ago, a colleague of mine asked me whether I knew about a case about B2B sales in professional services contexts that would allow discussion of the need to map buying and selling centers (following Frederick E. Webster and Yoram Wind's influential paper in the *Journal of Marketing* from 1972). I did recall a few great cases about B2B sales, but no case came to my mind with this particular setting. (Using the terminology from above, the need was an educational context need rather than an educational content need.) But upon further reflection, I remembered a case from my own experience: About a year earlier, I had tried to sell an executive education program to a large company – but I failed miserably. Given my colleague's need, I quickly wrote down the main aspects of the story, but at that time the need was not my need and so I never finished the case. A few years later, my colleague Johannes Habel joined my school. Johannes is very much focused on teaching and researching sales and sales management – and, again, he needed such a case for some of his courses. It was only then that the two of us decided to try the case in class (see below section 6, on testing the case) and – given the success of the case in the classroom – finished the case and teaching note. 'ESMT's pitch to EAD Systems' was born, about nine years after the initial idea.

Martin:
When I heard about Kiva, a nonprofit organization with a mission to connect people through lending to alleviate poverty, I was immediately impressed and wanted to write a case about this amazing story. I wrote an initial version but realized that I was missing a clear teaching need: none of my classes at that time focused on nonprofit organizations and developing markets.

I had almost dismissed the idea when I stumbled across Zopa, an organization that was supporting Kiva. I realized that this was the story I was looking for in the first place: a very innovative and disruptive for-profit startup, based in the UK. I called the company and arranged to interview key people. Not only were the topics and geographical location a good fit but Zopa was at the very start of its journey and so it was a great time to get involved.

I published my first case on Zopa in 2006 and have since updated it three times so far, most recently in 2014. I have traced Zopa's story from its early beginnings to its current position as an established player in the financial service industry only eight years later.

Finding good case leads

Always be alert to potential leads – become a story collector! Anything from a casual conversation with a student to a breaking news story may lead to the creation of a prizewinning case (we like to aim high!) – or, at the very least, to a case that works well in your classroom. Just stay alert and keep a list of interesting leads. And beware: leads do not need to be very specific – and you do not have to specify the educational need immediately. Whatever you hear about can start a process of associations or reflections or initiate the search for other cases/leads that might fit your need better. Many former case writing workshop participants described how they managed to develop a case mindset/radar over time: once you start looking for case leads, you will see them almost everywhere.

Here are just a few possibilities you can explore to identify good leads:
How to find good leads

- News stories, magazines (e.g., trade magazines) and journal articles, television/radio programs, and trending topics on social media.
- Textbooks.
- Your own (prior or current) experiences in the world of business as an employee or consultant.
- Your personal experiences with a company or organization (e.g., as customer, shareholder, or any other type of stakeholder).
- Stories and experiences shared by family, friends, and (former) colleagues.
- Client contacts and guest speakers.
- And finally: do not overlook the many ideas that might come from your students, participants, and alumni:
  - This is especially true when teaching executives who will have numerous stories to share both informally and in the classroom about their experiences.
  - Students' written work, for example, course work or thesis material, can also be a rich resource, and may even become the basis for a cowritten case.
  - Alumni frequently want to give back. Make sure to stay in touch!
- Great opportunities can also arise if a company approaches you to discuss the possibility of writing a case about some aspect of their business.

Also think back to examples and stories that you have already used in class. You chose these stories probably because they somehow fitted into whatever you were teaching! They can therefore be easily connected to an educational need.

 From theory to practice with Urs and Martin

Urs:
When I was given the opportunity to teach at a business school in Portugal, I chose a novel about the Portuguese sailor Ferdinand Magellan as spare-time reading for the flight. I was immediately intrigued by the story and formed the belief that it would be possible to teach almost any subject in business administration or management based on this story about the first circumnavigation of the world. I felt it would be interesting to use the information about the expedition to teach accounting and finance, economics, strategy, or cross-cultural management. I immediately realized I had a great lead – but initially I didn't have a need!

Several years later, I was asked by a client to run a customized executive education program on business ethics. My client's observation was that the organization's middle managers showed too much obedience and didn't voice their concerns and disagreements frequently enough with top management decisions. Immediately, the story of the mutiny against Magellan (April 1520) came to my mind. I finally had a very specific educational need to my lead – and immediately wrote the case 'Magellan versus Quesada: To Mutiny or Not to Mutiny?'

Should you follow a specific lead?

Before following up on a specific lead (and before 'falling in love' with it), try to be objective and ask yourself two critical questions:

- If someone else wrote a case based on your lead, would you choose to use it?
- Will your (planned) case really meet your learning objectives better than any other case that is currently available?

If the answer to either of these questions is no: look for a different lead! Taking a critical approach to your lead early will help you avoid wasting time and energy. It is always best to anticipate and preempt the reactions of colleagues and students, who will almost certainly be very critical of any shortcomings in your case.

If you have the case writing workbook (see page xviii for where to find this), you can now take the time and use the tables provided in the first chapter to start your own list of case leads and needs. If you do not have or want to use the case writing workbook, simply start your own list on a piece of paper, in a notebook, or as an electronic document. Start your own needs and leads collection right now. It will only take a few minutes but will make all the difference!

2. Educational objectives

If you followed the advice from the last section, you should now have two (possibly long) lists with interesting case leads and educational needs. Ideally you will have identified your optimal way of keeping them for long-term usage, e.g., in an (electronic) notebook, in separate files, or in the case writing workbook.

To get started with your own case, it is time to find the magically matching pair of case lead and case need – or, in other words, to narrow down a specific set of learning objectives for your case lead or vice versa. But as you do so: constantly (or in iterations) challenge yourself regarding the quality of the lead and need as well as their fit to one another. Earlier we described three such situations when for us, sometimes after many years, a specific lead and educational need finally matched.

When to write your own case

- Don't reinvent the wheel: does a good case already exist?
- Do you have a lead and need?
- Are the lead and need really a good match? Is there a better educational context for the story or possibly a better lead to make your educational point? If yes: wait and search for something else!
- Do you have a personal and ideally very specific learning objective for this case writing project?

The matching process might very well be a quick, intuitive process of seemingly divine inspiration (such as some of the situations described earlier). Maybe you already knew when writing down the long lists of needs and leads which combination could work very well. In that case: congratulations!

Sometimes, the identification of the learning objective for your case might, however, require a more systematic review (or massaging) of your needs and leads. We suggest approaching this forced matching process from both ends (needs and leads) in iterations until you find the winning formula for your learning objective.

Narrowing down your need for an own case study

We recommend starting with the case needs. As mentioned before: most cases from inexperienced case authors tend to have better leads than very clear needs, i.e., they often lack a specific learning objective. To avoid this trap, rather start by critically assessing your self-identified educational (content and context) needs – and postpone your excitement about the long list of wonderful case leads for later.

How to prioritize and identify the educational need

You might want to use the following list to prioritize and identify the most pressing educational need. You will also find these questions in the case writing workbook in easy-to-use tables, but you can of course use your own notebook or electronic document. Take the time; it will pay off!

- Out of all the sessions you teach, for which session do you most urgently need your own case study? That is, where do you see:
  a) the biggest benefit for your own case, and
  b) where is the biggest gap between how you currently 'fill' this session and an ideal world?
- For this specific session:
  – What exactly are the educational content needs (i.e., what concepts, theories, issues, tools, frameworks, etc. are you not yet able to deal with in class adequately)?
  – What exactly are the educational context needs (i.e., what is the specific configuration of context factors that would need to be matched in the lead, e.g., geography, industry, gender)?
- Sketch out briefly the types of participant enrolled in this course/attending this session.
- What kind of case setting is likely to achieve the biggest learning impact (driven through their excitement or by your understanding about the most important aspects of this subject)?
- Write down the main learning objectives of this group and session.
- Identify two or three potential topics for your new case (not yet specifically related to any of your leads).
- In a nutshell: what is your need? (How will addressing this need fill a gap [content or context]? Why do you want to have this case?)

In essence, think about your target participants and check your leads for the one lead that will be most likely to help them learn – which usually means: a case that will allow them to deal with situations that they are likely to experience in their professional futures.

Remember our 'patient in the room' analogy from the spotlight chapter. Ultimately a case study is the patient in the room that should allow your participants to discover and experience new situations and apply their knowledge and intuition to gain a deeper understanding of relevant theories, concepts, and frameworks.

Narrowing down your lead for your own case study

After having prioritized and specified a need, use this particular need as a lens to revisit the long list of possible case leads. Which of your leads (if any) could be massaged to match this case need? How would you need to present the case to match the need? Think about the case lead as something like an object with many different sides: Is there a way to turn the lead around so that the side that you will show to your participants will match the need specified above? An interesting merger and acquisition story (for which you might know a key player in the transaction) can for example be turned around in many ways: from the buying or selling side; focusing on finance, strategy, marketing, or postmerger integration; looking at the organizational hardware or rather looking at the human dimension of the deal, etc. These few aspects alone highlight that the main point of a great case is not the underlying story but the way in which you present the lead so that it really matches a meaningful learning objective.

 From theory to practice with Urs

I sometimes conduct an executive education format that I call 'Retail strategy city walk.' I take a group of executives and we talk about strategy on the basis of a couple of interesting and innovative retail formats in Berlin. In this city walk, I have occasionally involved the founder of one such store format as a guest speaker after an explorative shopping exercise. I just love the idea and the founder is an inspirational person, who agreed to serve as the protagonist of a case. I believe that I have a really interesting lead. But how can I match this lead to a meaningful need?

I could present the case in many different ways, all of which would address fundamentally different educational needs, and I struggled to find the most meaningful learning objective for myself. I considered the following aspects:

- Ideation: How did he come up with the idea? How did it change early on?
- Finding seed money: How did he get the necessary financial basis to start with the format?
- Managing rapid growth: How did he cope with the enormous early success of the format?
- Cash management: How did he deal with cash in a rapidly growing organization with high investment needs?
- Dealing with copycats: The format was quickly copied by others. How did he deal with that?
- Organizational forms of growth: Should he adopt licensing and franchising models to continue his growth path – especially given the copycats?
- Dealing with setbacks/downsizing: After two years of enormous success, the organization had to close a few of their stores and started to fall behind their initial growth plans. How did he deal with this setback?
- Dealing with investors: How did he manage shareholder satisfaction despite the setbacks? How did he convince them about the need to introduce an online channel that required massive investment?
- E-commerce: How did he build up e-commerce capabilities on the basis of a store-based retail format? Can the key organizational resources and capabilities be transferred to the new business?
- David vs Goliath: Given the entry of financially much more potent new (online only) players in his domain, can he survive in a niche?

You can probably easily imagine many more possible ways to turn this complex lead into an interesting case.

After having detailed your educational need much more specifically in the last section, now review your leads. Out of all the leads, which one of them is probably easiest to present in a way that will achieve your learning objective? Pick this lead first and go through the following questions. You will also find these questions in the case writing workbook:

- My overall lead (the story I would like to cover) in a nutshell (quickly write down a few bullet points about the story).
- What are the most obvious dimensions of the lead? Think divergently! How could you turn this case? And what would be the matching learning objectives if you presented the case this way?
- Which of these different aspects of the lead is (most closely) in line with the learning objective specified above?
- How close would this dimension of your lead be to your learning objective?
- What could you do to make the fit of lead and need even greater?
- Why and how will this story be relevant to achieve the learning objectives/fit into the course?

If after reflecting on these questions you do not find a way to make your specific lead really match to your learning objective, just pick the next lead and go through the questions again. Sooner or later you will probably find that at least one of your leads can be massaged to meet your need. Alternatively, think about the lead that came closest to your need and do some research: is there a different but similar lead that you didn't initially have on your list that would meet the need better/easier? Then just pick this new lead.

If you found a matching pair, congratulations! But, before you get carried away, you need to do one more test: do you really want and need to write this case?

 When not to write your own case

To be clear: Sometimes it is not a good idea to write your own case. For example, do not spend time reinventing the wheel. There are thousands of great cases – and one that addresses your teaching requirements may already exist (and could be better than the one you would write yourself; it is not easy to write a great case).

Do your research carefully – and do not waste time writing your own case if someone else has already written a perfectly good one.

In addition (and contradicting to/complementing the list of benefits from teaching your own case), some teachers are more effective in the classroom when teaching cases written by another author. There are at least three known pitfalls when using own cases in class:

(1) You might be too in love with your lead and become biased (selling and preaching instead of teaching; defending a protagonist or organization in class etc.).
(2) You might know too much about the case and try to squeeze too much of that into a specific session or course. Using your own cases can sometimes tempt you to introduce aspects into the class discussion that you happen to know about and find exciting – but that are not needed to achieve the learning objective.
(3) In cases written by others, you sometimes see more options regarding the possible courses of action/decisions of the protagonist. When using cases that were written by others you are structurally closer to the position of your students when reading the case for the first time. This can make you more willing to use truly participant-centered teaching methods (instead of championing a solution that you might be excited about).

Only you can decide if any of these pitfalls are true for you and your current case idea. But please reflect on your possible biases before continuing the work on the case!

Having said that, we absolutely encourage you to write your own cases. It is an exhilarating rollercoaster journey that we cannot recommend highly enough.

3. Strategic decisions

To get a truly great (sticky) case, you must knead the lead and need together. You are done with the preparation and can now start. From now onwards, the reflections, notes, and text elements that you will perform or produce will flow into the final set of materials of your case. So, take the time to really produce text blocks as you work your way through the next sections. Later, you will be able to copy and paste almost all of these text blocks into the case study or the teaching note.

Structuring the need into a session

We will start with the educational need and now focus on how this need would work out in a specific session. Focus on one specific setting first. If the case works well in this setting, you can later explore possible additional use cases of the material in class.

Defining the target participants

It is important to write the case for one specific course/participant group first! Your case will be much more targeted to achieve your desired learning objective. Having a very specific target reader in mind will result in a case that is spot on for this target group – and will probably still be equally good for others.

Use the case writing workbook or any kind of document to answer the following questions on the target audience:

- Describe your participant group: consider aspects such as program type and position of session in program, participant age, previous education and experience, cultural background, and language.
- What is their previous knowledge regarding the topic of your course/session?
- What are they likely not to know cognitively that you want them to know?
- What skills and abilities do they possess? What are some important skills and abilities that they might be missing?
- What is their likely attitude and motivation when coming to your course/session? What will they be looking for? Which of these expectations do you consider to be legitimate and plan to meet? Which of these expectations do you intentionally (but with good reasons) plan to disappoint? How can you explain to your participants that and why you will not meet a specific expectation that they might have?

You do not need to write down a lot of text at this stage. We just recommend having a specific target audience (possibly with faces and names) in mind when working further on the material.

Defining the underlying issues and learning objectives

Great cases are characterized by an intriguing combination of underlying and immediate issue(s). Accordingly, you as a case author will need to clearly define (and conceptually separate) the two early on in the case writing process. The importance of the distinction between underlying and immediate issues is discussed in the first chapter ('The Case Method in the Spotlight').

The gradual exploration of a topic by the participants during the case discussion is the most exciting element of case-based learning and at the heart of the success of the case method. As in a murder mystery the participants explore an academic domain through curiosity, application of critical and creative thinking, and usage of prior knowledge, research, and readings, as well as debating with others. As we all know, the thrill of the murder mystery is the successive development of the story. If we know the murderer and killing method right from the beginning, we do not have a murder mystery. And if there is no progression from one issue to another, from one topic to another during a case-based session, we do not have a case study.

Wouldn't it be great if your participants were sitting at the edge of their chairs, biting on their fingernails, their eyes wide open and following the entire session with full attention and energy? Case discussions have the potential to evoke such experiences, but only if the case study itself and the session design offer 'a voyage of discovery—and even some interesting surprises' (Abell 1997). With growing experience in case teaching and writing you can orchestrate increasingly complex flows of themes in the session. At this point of the case writing process we do not yet need to have the full or final flow. For now, it is just important to think about the main issues of the case.

We will look in greater detail at the question of the *immediate* issue a bit later as the selection of the immediate issue is closely related to the timing of the case and the protagonist(s) – aspects that we do not yet need to address. Instead we propose that the *underlying* issues need to be defined first – and this is usually the easier task anyway.

The underlying issues should be based on your educational needs, for example key topics, theories, frameworks, and knowledge that you want participants to discover and learn for themselves. These issues will usually only emerge during the case discussion and be critically important in the development of a well-substantiated response to the immediate issue. In stark contrast to the immediate issues, the underlying issues should not be obvious when reading the case.

Have a look back at the sections on educational needs (see page 137) and learning objectives (see page 140). Write down those aspects from before that you chose to address with this particular case and – voila – you are already almost done! This will be particularly easy if your educational need was a content need rather than a context need; in that case, the underlying issue will probably be this particular educational content need. If necessary, add others that you find relevant to adequately deal with the lead.

Then move on to specify the general learning objectives for the usage of this case. Learning objectives should describe what kind of learning effect you intend to achieve with the case. Learning objectives might be closely linked with the underlying issue but might go significantly beyond the underlying issues, especially when your objectives are related to skills and attitudes rather than to knowledge.

Now quickly review the list of underlying issues and learning objectives. If they overlap heavily, combine them into one single list. If they are quite different, keep the lists separate and add a few sentences to highlight the reason for their difference. In either case, you can copy this description of the underlying issue and learning objective into a respective section of the teaching note later.

To maintain clarity and focus, avoid overloading your case with too many underlying issues or learning objectives. When writing the case (or using it in class for the first few times) you will probably realize that your initial draft covers many more issues than you originally planned for. But be disciplined and try to resist the temptation to include all of them in the final case. Most of the really great cases are tightly focused on one specific or only a few underlying issues and a narrow set of learning objectives. This pays dividends in the classroom. It helps to keep your learning objectives in focus and makes it less likely that your participants will go 'off topic' during the discussion. So quickly review your lists and delete individual aspects right now – as this will help you to write a more concise case later!

> **From theory to practice with Martin**
>
> When writing my case study 'Driving Digital Transformation at Faurecia' I was struggling with narrowing down the learning objectives as digital transformation is such a vast topic. I finally settled on the following learning objectives. This is of course just an example and maybe you have ideas to further narrow them down or to make them even more explicit.
>
> - Understand how strategy informs the organization and management of information technology.
> - Understand the drivers of digital transformation.
> - Explore the elements of digital capability (business model, customer experience, operations, employee experience, digital platform).
> - Shed a light on the digital transformation road map of a global automotive supplier.
> - Explore the constant struggle between central and decentralized forces when driving a major change initiative.

Structuring the lead into a case

'Every block of stone has a statue inside it, and it is the task of the sculptor to discover it.'
— Michelangelo

Almost every good lead provides lots of possibilities – just like Michelangelo's block of stone that could be turned into many different statues. It will be your task to determine where and how you want to form this lead into a great case study – and for that purpose it is key to never forget the learning objective. Everything that follows is a question of your choices – all of which you should take deliberately and cautiously.

 In the next four sections, we will describe the four most important decisions case authors need to take about their case lead, namely (1) the case direction, (2) the timeline and cutoff points, (3) the immediate issues, and (4) the protagonist and other actors. On the basis of our experience, case authors should go through these questions in the suggested sequence, but feel free to jump to the next section as soon as you are getting stuck. Just do not forget to go back to choices that you were not ready to take earlier.

Defining the direction (prospective vs. retrospective)

Where do you want to go? Your choice of the case's narrative direction will substantially impact the type of discussions you will have in the classroom and your ability to realize the intended learning outcomes. Cases can be prospective or retrospective. Prospective cases are cases for which the in-class discussion will mostly look at developments after the point at which the case study text ends. Prospective cases most typically have a decision at their core which a protagonist needs to take. At the time of the case this is prospective, even though the relevant developments after the case might very well be in the past for you. Conversely, retrospective cases might, e.g., tell the full story of a person or organization and the subsequent discussion will try to make sense of the described developments or decisions. Both types can work very well in classrooms – but you need to choose which type is a better match to your defined educational needs and objectives.

To make this decision, you might want to consider the below questions. Take the time to write down your answers. You will also find an easy-to-fill table in the case writing workbook.

- Does your learning objective call for a decision? This will obviously be true if the participants' ability to make choices and decisions is part of your desired learning outcome.
- For your own teaching: do you feel more comfortable with prospective or retrospective case studies?
- Considering cases authored by others and that you like particularly well: are they prospective or retrospective cases?
- Might a (possible) contact person in the organization be interested in having participants reflect on the possible future of the organization? Was this how you generated your lead in the first place, e.g., if they asked you to write a case about them?
- Given the content of the case, is there any decision involved or at stake?

After reflecting on these questions, make a choice about the direction of the case – and, if you are still ambivalent, consider the topic of the timing first and then revisit this question a bit later.

Defining the timeline and possible cutoff point(s)

It is all in the timing! Almost all great cases have a very specific date at their core – and the choice of the timing is crucial.

The ability to select the right timing for a case – the optimal point to locate the case in the time continuum – is absolutely critical, possibly even the single most impactful decision after having chosen your lead. Even slight alterations to the cutoff time (i.e., the specific time at which the case is situated), especially where you start and end the case text, can make huge differences to classroom discussions and will probably massively affect the achievement of your learning objectives.

Most good cases allow participants to 'step into the shoes' of the case protagonist – and that implies that there is a specific time to take into consideration. This is important when drafting and writing your case, as your case accordingly should only include information that was available to your protagonist at this specific point in time. Do not include information about anything that happened after the point in time at which you end your case.

 From theory to practice with Martin

For example, a case may include a decision on whether or not to enter a new market. Your chosen timeline is important because it will affect the type and amount of information that can be made available in the case. So, depending on your learning objectives, the timing of the case could be:

- Six months before the decision. The main purpose of this case would be to analyze the company and discuss options. Entering a new market might be just one of these options.
- On the day of the decision. This case would focus on the need to analyze the immediate situation and decide if the company should enter the new market or not.
- After the decision was made. Sometimes, even a week can make a big difference as more information and the consequences of the decision begin to emerge.

It is a good idea to sketch out a full timeline before you start writing your case and even before making a final decision about the timing. We have had good experiences with using a large piece of paper in landscape format on which we organize the main developments of our lead over time from left to right. This timeline should include the dates and times of all the key events and turning points in the story. Try to map which underlying issues/learning objectives might be best achieved at each major event. Next to ensuring the link to your learning objectives, there are at least three additional benefits from investing effort into the timeline: (1) It will help you to ensure that you get the timing right and do not forget major developments; (2) it helps to provide a clear structure for your case (e.g., for the description of the organization's or protagonist's history); and (3) it might later be – partially – used as a timeline in a case exhibit on in additional material for other instructors. We frequently add a description of the developments after the cutoff point into a separate section of the teaching note – so, again, nothing that you do here will be a loss of time.

Below you find an example of the timeline that Urs developed for his case series (cases A to D) on IKEA ('Corruption in Russia: IKEA's Expansion to the East,' Case-Reference no. ESMT-716-0169-1 for the A case).

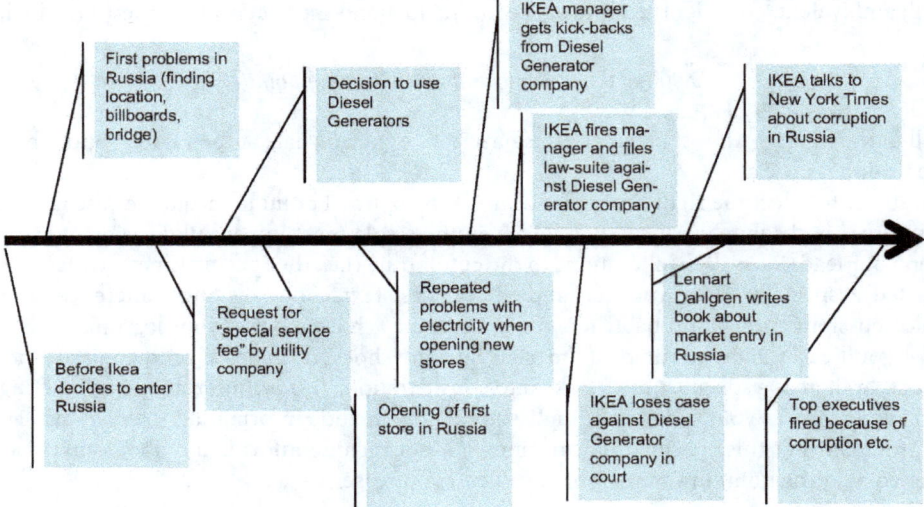

Figure 25: Example timeline with possible cut-offs for "Ikea in Russia" case study.

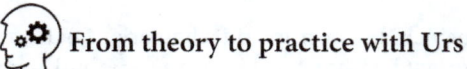 **From theory to practice with Urs**

Timing has been tricky for almost all of my cases.

A good example of this is my case 'Vodafone in Egypt: National Crises and Their Implications for Multinational Corporations (A),' cowritten with Shirish Pandit. In retrospect, I think it would benefit from different timing.

The case deals with the Egyptian government's orders (during the buildup to the Egyptian Revolution of 2011) to first shut down mobile telephone and internet services and later to send out progovernment text messages.

(Continued)

> Initially, I was thinking about a case series where the request to shut down the services would be case A. The request to send text messages would be case B – and the outcomes would be case C. In class, however, I realized that the discussions of cases A and B in class were too similar and repetitive.
>
> Accordingly, I merged both decisions into one case – and, although the two orders occurred a couple of days apart, in the case I deliberately left out the precise timing of the order to send text messages to enable a combined discussion of both events.
>
> However, having taught the case many times, I now think this was a mistake.
>
> If I were writing the case now, I would set it in the short time period between the two orders. This would have allowed a discussion about how the three cellphone operators reacted to the first order (all complied), followed by a discussion about how the cellphone operators should react to the second order (their responses varied) – i.e., instead of writing a clearly prospective case, I would have included a stronger retrospective perspective plus a prospective decision that needed to be taken.

Selecting the immediate issue(s)

The immediate issue is the 'hook' that will spark your participants' interest and (most of the time) kick-start the classroom discussion. It is usually best if the immediate issue is closely linked to the protagonist in the case, so participants can begin to imagine they are in the protagonist's shoes. For example, the immediate issue can be a key question that the protagonist explicitly asks in the opening and/or closing paragraph.

The immediate issue should be pretty clear in the case, but the 'solution' or the protagonist's actual choice should not be obvious. The immediate issue should be nonobvious, be controversial, and offer good material for debate and disagreement.

Ideally, the opening question when teaching the case should be closely related to the immediate issue. The aim is to provoke an instant reaction from participants and force them to take a position, especially when writing a classical decision case.

For example, one participant might say, 'I would do X; I would never do Y,' which then gives another participant the option to disagree and propose a different course of action. The subsequent discussion around these different perspectives of the immediate issue will reveal the critical need to understand the deeper and usually more difficult challenges that are affecting the immediate issue. These are the underlying issues.

 From theory to practice with Martin

The immediate issue or 'hook' in my case 'Team WIKISPEED: Developing Hardware the Software Way' (cowritten with Linus Dahlander and Eric Morrow) is whether to cut and weld an existing axle or to develop an entire axle from scratch as part of a product development process. This immediate issue is quite easy to grasp and provides an easy transition to the underlying issues that are explored in the case: whether a waterfall or agile approach should be taken to product development.

In order to make your choice regarding the immediate issue, have a look at the timeline and ask yourself the following questions:

- Which decisions, questions, or challenges might the possible protagonists of your case have been pondering at the different possible cutoff points? Which of these decisions, questions, or challenges are nontrivial and is likely to provoke the highest level of controversy in the classroom?
- Which person would be the most natural protagonist at each of the cutoff points?
- Which of the underlying issues would need to be addressed to deal with the immediate issues at the different possible cutoff points?
- How easily could the class discussion move from the immediate issue at the various cutoff points to your real interest – the underlying issues/learning objectives?

Identifying the protagonist(s) and other actors

As already said a couple of times: Cases are educational vehicles that allow students to 'step into' the shoes of someone facing a key challenge or decision. The aim is to prepare participants for the real-life situations they will face during their careers. This is why it is so important to pay close attention to how you choose and present the protagonist of your case. The success of your case will largely depend on your protagonist. It is vital to get this right.

For most leads, several actors could possibly serve as the protagonist – and you need to choose wisely. Kassarjian and Kashani (2005: 109) suggest distinguishing between three different types of actors in cases: *drivers*, *passengers*, and *bystanders*:

> **Drivers**
> Drivers are very close to what we label as protagonist, but also other main actors closely related to the immediate issue in addition to the protagonist might be real drivers of the story/events. The opening and closing paragraphs of your case will focus on your protagonist(s) and their problem, dilemma, or challenge. Drivers are the organization's 'key decision makers' and 'own the problem or decision' your case is about.
>
> **Passengers**
> Passengers will often be colleagues of the protagonist(s). They offer 'additional contexts' and an 'alternative perspective,' often 'fill in the blanks,' and can provide additional 'facts and figures.'
>
> **Bystanders**
> Bystanders may be from within the organization but could also be any other individual related to the case (e.g., customers, consultants, or any other stakeholders). They are usually outside 'the decision-making locus of responsibility,' might 'provide 'objective' external points of view,' or offer insights that protagonists and passengers will miss.

First, we recommend making a long list of actors that are connected to the lead. This should include all actors you know to have been connected, but you should also think about actors that might possibly have been involved but that you just are not yet able to identify. For this exercise it is not yet important to know the real persons and names – unless you have them already. At this time, it might be sufficient to just list job titles, functions, or categories of actors that could be represented in the case. You will find easy-to-use tables to complete in the case-writing workbook.

Second, we suggest using the following four questions to choose which person connected to the lead should fall into which of the three categories identified by Kassarjian and Kashani:

- Which of the players in the lead had which role for the developments (retrospective cases: for the developments *until* the cutoff time; prospective cases: for the developments *after* the cutoff time)? The different level of involvement in the decisions, developments, etc. should allow you to roughly allocate all actors to the three categories.
- If you look at the lead from the perspective of the different possible actors: which of them might be most logically connected to your choice of (or just to the most interesting) immediate issue?
- How easily can you get access to this person? How likely will this person collaborate with you?
- Can you describe this person with the required richness as a real human being? (A particularly important question when writing a case solely on the basis of public information.)

Ernest Hemingway was talking about writing novels when he said that 'a writer should create living people; people not characters. A character is a caricature' (Ernest Hemingway, *Death in the Afternoon*). This observation is equally applicable to case writing. No one wants to read about a caricature, much less 'step into their shoes.' In order to allow transfer and impact of the lessons learned it is essential that the participants consider the case to be realistic and the selection and portrayal of the protagonist is key for that.

Whether your protagonist is a real or fictitious person, they must come across as a living and breathing human being: someone your participants can empathize and identify with. The easier readers can identify with the case protagonist (right now or as an option for the future), the more immediately relevant the case discussion will be for them overall. Think about your target audience and ask yourself whether all or at least a part of your audience can identify with the potential protagonist. Over the duration of a whole course, do you have diverse protagonists so that everyone in your target audience might find a protagonist that they can identify with? But be careful: there might also be good reasons to have some cases that participants have a hard time identifying with. Learning to step into the shoes of someone that you cannot easily identify with can be a learning in itself.

 From theory to practice with Martin

As in every good story, people come alive through their actions and words. I always try to describe the actions of my protagonists very precisely and resist the temptation to 'edit' their activities.

I also try to include as many direct quotes as possible (which means taking full and accurate notes during interviews). Direct quotes are an excellent way to capture someone's personality.

Additional background information about individuals featured in the case can also help. For example, in the case I wrote about Bosch ('Global Product Development Strategy at Bosch: Selecting a Development Site for the New Low-Cost ABS Platform') I included a paragraph about each main character based on their CVs in the exhibits of the case study.

Choosing your protagonist

You should decide early on who will be your protagonist – this is true whether you are writing a field-based case or one from published sources.

If you are writing a field-based case, it is a good idea to make your key contact at the organization (or the person from which you generated the lead) your protagonist; maybe this is even a given. By building a good relationship with them you can establish trust and mutual respect. This makes it more likely that they will open up to you and be honest about their mistakes and failures, as well as their successes. You will then have a far greater chance of writing a convincing and effective case that will excite and inspire your participants.

Working closely with your key contact in this way will also help to create goodwill within the company and make access to other key figures much more straightforward. It should also speed up the final signing-off process.

However, be prepared to change your protagonist if you discover while writing the case that the perspective and experiences of a different protagonist would work better (or if your contact leaves the organization while the issue is ongoing and still relevant). Changes in the protagonist could be needed if the immediate issue from the perspective of a different player would just be much more relevant and exciting. So, do not get hooked on your personal connection. Consider making your contact/lead generator a 'passenger' or 'bystander' if this person wants to be included in the case.

Multiple protagonists?

Some cases, whether field-based or written from published sources, work very successfully with two or more protagonists. However, be aware that this can make writing your case more challenging; you will need to incorporate various perspectives and interests, and perhaps differing levels of seniority. When writing a field-based case, bear in mind that multiple protagonists will slow the sign-off process as more people will need to be involved, and more political massaging will probably be necessary.

However, do not automatically dismiss the idea of having more than one protagonist. It can reflect the complexity of a particular scenario. Multiple protagonists also offer the opportunity for role-play and simulation exercises in the classroom. And do not be afraid to experiment and be creative (and undogmatic)! With multiple protagonists, you could write the entire case as dialogue between the protagonists, as if you were writing a theater play.

 From theory to practice with Urs

A few years ago, two colleagues of mine and I were in discussions with an alumnus about writing a case. The alumnus was member of the board of a rapidly growing technology company and personally responsible for the organization's strategy. During guest talks on one of my programs, he mentioned that the organization was not sure about the future direction, especially about its future business model. Should they keep their integrated model, focus only on the high-tech hardware, move to the role of a systems integrator and rather focus on engineering and programing, or focus only on the supply of certain components?

(Continued)

> When we started to discuss a possible case study, we realized that as head of strategy he was not the final decision maker. Then we also learned that there was some uncertainty and even disagreement within the board. At that time, we had an idea: How about bringing the board together to discuss the future strategic direction and to turn this dialogue into a multiple protagonist case study that would almost have been like a theater play. I still think that this would not only have been possible but possibly even a great case. Unfortunately, we could not get the board to agree to this idea.

4. Tactical choices

The identification of target participants, underlying issues, case direction, cutoff points, immediate issues, and protagonists in the last section was key to deciding the most important strategic dimensions of your case. If you make changes to any of these strategic decisions later, you will have to redo a lot of the work – both for the case study as well as for the teaching note. This is why it is important to get these decisions right. The next set of choices can be changed more easily along the way, which is why we refer to them as 'tactical choices.' They are, however, equally important for the overall success of your case.

Specifying the case

In the previous three sections of this chapter we started with the educational needs aspects (which belong more in the teaching note) before looking at the lead side (which is focused on the case study itself). This can now change. After having made your strategic decisions, the educational context is already firmly embedded in your case writing project. We recommend keeping it in mind, but in this section we will first focus on five tactical choices related to your lead.

Defining the structure of the case study

First, we suggest getting back to the timeline of your case. Earlier you plotted the full series of events of your case lead. If you mapped possible cutoff points in the story with different immediate and underlying issues, you can now think about the best way to structure your material. The same story can be told in many different ways depending on your learning objectives. This is not only true for the choice of your protagonist and cutoff time but also for the type of case study you want to write. Review your timeline and ask yourself which case study structure will fit best to your learning objectives:

- a single case,
- a case series,
- several separate cases,
- one or several (connected or independent) cases plus a technical/industry note,
- simulation or role-play cases – these can include, for example, a general overview for everyone in the class plus confidential briefing material for different groups to use during the role-play or simulation exercises.

- The same/similar "story" can often be told in very different ways
- Key question: For what purpose do you want to use your case?
- Accordingly you can split your case in very different ways, e.g.:

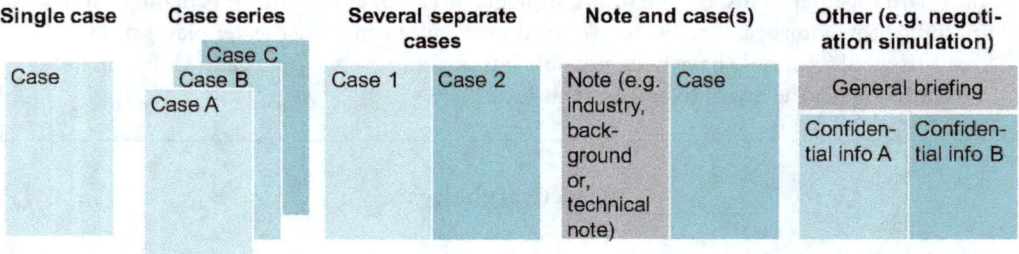

Figure 26: Possible case study structures.

Your choice will depend on your educational need and on the learning objectives you plan to address with the case. In order to make your choice, consider the following aspects:

- Traditional (decision) cases usually call for a single case. For case writing novices in particular, this is a safe bet and much easier. You can then still consider providing an update about later events in a case B – or (our advice) include this update in the teaching note.
- If your educational need requires the description of a longer series of multiple decisions or historical events, a case series might be appropriate, but see Urs's heretic view below.
- If you have established a good relationship with an interesting company and/or individual, it might make sense to write a number of separate cases. These could be totally independent of each other or deal with related issues from different perspectives. This is also an excellent way to avoid the beginner's typical mistake of attempting to kill too many birds with one stone by trying to cover too many different learning objectives in a single case. But if this is your choice: start with the one case that addresses the biggest educational need – and postpone all others.
- Technical notes (e.g., about industries, geographical settings or companies) can be used separately to bring reality into the classroom. But they can also be used to include optional background material to the case if required. This might help enormously to make the case shorter and less onerous to read.
- Specific educational needs might call for separating the case into a general introduction/description of the situation or organization plus additional cases that only describe individual aspects/perspectives. This is, e.g., applicable when using cases for negotiation classes or if the educational need calls for role-play elements – for both of which you need to ensure informational asymmetry across the participants in the classroom.

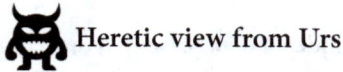 Heretic view from Urs

I made the mistake myself and have often seen others at least tempted to do it: don't plan to structure your material into a case series even though there are some really great examples of highly successful case series!

(Continued)

> I wrote several cases with two parts, where case B was essentially nothing else than an update about the events after the cutoff point so that the instructors could share them (possibly with some additional detail) with the group after the session. But three of my (mostly early) cases are structured into case series of three or even more parts. And I have to admit: I increasingly only use the first part in class – if I use the case at all. And this is not only true for my own case series but also for case series from other authors. Why?
>
> 1. In practice the sheer distribution and reading of the subsequent cases just takes too much time. Distributing parts B, C, D, etc. in class usually just does not work from a logistical perspective. It could work in blocks of several sessions when you can give your participants time for reading between the sessions, but in reality the depth of the reading of the later parts will be much more superficial than for case A.
> 2. Great case teaching requires the orchestration of a well-thought-through line of suspense – from the original puzzle about the immediate issue toward the underlying issues and a closing segment of the session. According to my experience, it is usually much more difficult if not almost impossible to have such a line of suspense on two levels: within the discussion of each of the case parts and simultaneously across all the case parts at the same time.
> 3. Building up the higher-level line of suspense across all case parts is particularly difficult if it relies on additional underlying issues that you only plan to address later. In my experience you will very likely have one super-smart participant who already anticipates and raises the underlying issue that you planned so carefully to discuss with Case C. Yes, you can sometimes park such comments and come back to them later, but that is not really a participant-centered approach. And, yes, you can bury this other underlying issue so well in case A that it will be almost impossible to grasp it initially, but then again this will not feel real, as you would most likely need to eliminate at least some information that the protagonist had at the time from the earlier parts of the case series. I call such cases 'rabbit out of the hat cases' and that's what they are: a lazy trick to cheat your participants.
>
> In a nutshell: Just don't do it – unless this is really your educational need and unless it really works very well in your test classes. Instead of cutting the series of events into multiple case parts (most of which might be prospective in nature), consider combining a longer retrospective section with a prospective ending in one single case. Like this you can still cover two different aspects but avoid the disappointment from investing time and effort into a case series that you will probably rarely use in its entirety.

If you write your first case and if your case lead/need requires the production of a case series (i.e., it really cannot be massaged into one single case): Stop here and first gain case writing experience by writing a simple, short, and more conventional case first. Only then go back to this match of lead and need. If you still want to produce a case series, then go ahead.

Defining the length of the case study

Second, you will also have to choose what length of case you want to write. Long? Short? Somewhere in between?

When deciding on length, you may first wish to consider your intended audience. For example, if the case is aimed at undergraduates, a longer case offering more context and background might be appropriate or even necessary (but bear in mind that undergraduates may be resistant to reading longer cases!).

An executive audience may also be resistant to longer cases but for different reasons; they may already understand the context and background and will probably have limited time outside of work for extra reading.

One solution for executives is to use fewer cases on a course or program, which allows more time for longer cases.

As you can see, deciding on the length of your case can be a bit of a minefield. Ultimately, have the courage of your convictions. If you need to write a longer case, write it. If you believe the case will genuinely benefit from being shorter, make it shorter.

If you stick to the following golden rules, you will not go far wrong:

1. Make your case as short as possible (most audiences will appreciate this), while still achieving your learning objective.
2. Be flexible from the start and adjust the length of your case as you write it. Make it shorter each time you revise it whenever/wherever possible, but do not hesitate to add content if something important is missing. The length of the case is probably the choice that can be changed most easily later on.

 From theory to practice with Martin

You must decide how long your case needs to be. However, there is a growing trend for shorter cases.

My personal opinion is that short cases are more flexible as they can be used in a variety of settings, for example in circumstances where participants may be resistant to longer cases or where it simply is not practical to expect participants to read and prepare a very long case (e.g., due to the lead time between making the material available to the participants and the class itself).

Short cases also reduce one of the most damaging risks of case-based teaching: if participants have not prepared the case before the session, you can give students time to read a short case in class (see also the risks of doing so in our case teaching chapter, page 81).

However, longer cases are equally valid and valuable. I like to use longer cases at around mid-term, or to close a semester or program of study.

And, finally, one more argument for shorter cases: We know that many case teachers use case length as a key search and selection criterion. (The most frequent search option for cases at the Case Centre is cases shorter than 10 pages.) The shorter your case is, the more likely other educators will be to use your work. Watch out for thresholds in the listing and search functionalities of case distributors: some work with any number of pages that educators look for (e.g., The Case Centre); others work in increments of five (e.g., Harvard Business Publishing) or 10 pages (e.g., Ivey Publishing). It would just be a shame to produce a case with 10.3 pages, which is somewhat ironic given the fact that the average length of cases listed at the Case Centre is 12 pages. Then again, do not worry if 10 pages is not enough for you: the average length of the best-selling cases at the Case Centre is 18 pages.

Defining the case complexity

Third, you need to decide how complex you want your case to be. The case difficulty cube by Mauffette-Leenders, Erskine, and Leenders (2005: 12) describes three dimensions of complexity that ought to be considered (see also more detail in our chapter on types of case, page 16) and is a great tool to think about the desirable complexity. The authors differentiate the following three dimensions along which cases can be either more or less complex:

- *Analytical dimension:* What is the problem? This dimension is usually related to the immediate issue of the case but also to the degree to which the underlying issues are hidden. Cases that are quite obvious in this dimension will explicitly state the immediate issue and possibly even present a couple of possible courses of action. For complex cases, on the other hand, not even the immediate issue is very obvious.
- *Conceptual dimension:* What kind of concepts and theories apply? This dimension relates to the concepts, tools, frameworks, and theories that will be needed to properly respond to the underlying issues. Cases that are quite easy in the conceptual dimension might, for example, deal with the criteria for recognizing something as an asset according to IFRS. Cases with higher levels of conceptual complexity might for example deal with the question of an organization's purpose.
- *Presentation dimension:* How is the case presented/written? Cases with low levels of presentation complexity will tend to be shorter, well written, easy to follow and well structured. Cases with higher levels of presentation might present the material in an undigested way – just as it was visible to the case protagonist.

Mauffette-Leenders, Erskine, and Leenders recommend defining your case complexity by specifying a numeric value of 1 (easy) to 3 (complex) for each of the three dimensions. You might not necessarily need to specify a specific value for the three dimensions but you should now make a conscious choice regarding the intended level of complexity for your case. Not surprisingly, this choice should again depend upon your learning objective and the target audience.

- The difficulty of the analytical dimension will typically increase with the participant's experience and then often stay constant at a high level.
- Conceptual difficulty will usually increase over time in courses as well as with the seniority of the participants.
- High levels of difficulty regarding the presentation will frequently be found early or in the middle of courses for rather inexperienced participants, whose ability to separate relevant from irrelevant information you plan to develop.

Our general recommendation: Make your case as uncomplex as possible! As an educator you will be able to increase conceptual and analytical complexity during the session, by asking deep questions. Do not overload your participants unnecessarily – this will just make fewer of them properly prepare for class.

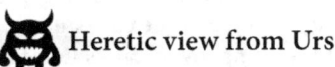 Heretic view from Urs

In specific situations, you might intentionally want to make a case as complex as possible!

One of my clients once asked me to prepare a customized case study for an executive education program. The target participants in this program were highly specialized finance experts of a multinational retail organization (e.g., from treasury, international tax, or financial accounting). The main objective of the overall program was to open the perspective of these finance experts so that they would see the big picture, the business behind the numbers. For that purpose, we wrote a case study (not published) about a possible international expansion of the company into a specific country. The program spanned five days and covered multiple academic disciplines. As preparation for the program, we provided the participants with a 38-page-long case that required them to take the perspective of the head of the internationalization department who had been asked to advise for or against this specific expansion.

(Continued)

> At the end of the five program days, the participants were asked to present their recommendations in groups, but along the way we covered various different topics such as strategy, operations, legal aspects, international taxation, and marketing – even topics such as corruption and the political context. At the end of every program day, we made additional material available to the students – typically about 20 pages with lots of numbers, data, charts, etc.
>
> Essentially, we intentionally aimed to increase the presentation and analytical dimensions of the case to an extreme. This was important to us in this specific context as the participants' ability to differentiate relevant versus irrelevant and to focus on the big picture was a key developmental objective of the overall program.

Irrespective of the case length that you chose earlier, be aware that it will be the case difficulty that will have the biggest impact on the time that your participants will need to properly prepare the case before class.

Thinking early about (preliminary) case release

It might sound premature, but now is a good time to think about case release. As we will explain below in greater detail, you will need a sign-off from the organization or protagonist for your final case as soon as the case contains even the slightest bit of information that cannot be found in the public domain. Ultimately, you (should) want to write a case about a real organization, a real challenge, and a real person. This makes cases typically much better. Accordingly, you should do your very best to get the sign-off at the end of the process. And to get the release you should now consider a couple of aspects that might influence your case writing and that will probably make it much easier for you to get the sign-off later.

We asked you earlier to evaluate the probability of getting case release when selecting your case lead. But by now you should have a much clearer perspective about the case that you are writing – and this might be a good time to (re)assess the sign-off probability and to think about ways to increase the probability.

Please take a few minutes to consider the following questions:

- Is the case describing a success or a failure? (Typically, it will be significantly harder to get release for a case study on failure. Overall, organizations tend to be very reluctant to release cases about really tough challenges and problems, as long as they cannot serve as a shining role model when presenting the outcome of the case study.)
- What is the overall attitude of the company to case studies (are there already cases on the company [check the case distributors], are they a supporter of your institution, did they reach out to you or vice versa…)?
- What is your personal relationship with the company? (How well) do you know the chosen protagonist or other drivers of the story? How senior or powerful are they in the organization?
- Who should you try to get release from? Do you know people in positions that can decide on case release? If not, ask your contact or protagonist who would need to give final release. Sometimes the protagonist is sufficient; sometimes you might need agreement from many individuals or functions, often from the organizational units covered in the case or from central functions such as legal, PR, or marketing.
- Do you have fallback contacts? Whom do you know who might support your quest for case release if, for example, your key contact leaves the organization?

- Do you have other good contacts inside or outside your institution that could help you get the politics done? Are there, for example, more senior colleagues at your school who might have even better connections to the organization?

Just make it a habit to repeatedly mention and discuss the issue of case release as often as possible whenever you talk with representatives of the organization. We have seen many great cases fail because of missing release – a massive loss of time and effort – but we have never heard that an author did not get release because she was talking about release too much.

If you realize that you are unlikely to get case release at the end, review the options of writing a case solely from public sources or to work with disguise/fiction. If neither matches with your educational needs: stop now and do not invest any further effort.

Real or fictional case?

> 'Truth is stranger than fiction, but it is because Fiction is obliged to stick to possibilities; Truth isn't.' – Mark Twain

While considering case release in the last section, you might have concluded that it will be difficult if not impossible to get a final sign-off for the case as you envisioned it so far. Relax: that does not necessarily mean that you need to start all over. There is a fifth and last tactical choice that you might want to use in such cases – or for various other reasons – namely the question of writing a real or fictional case.

As described in the first chapter (see the section in the first chapter, on the typology of cases, page 17), the question of real versus fictional is not a binary decision but rather it represents a spectrum of choices. Sometimes it is easier to get final case release if you change the case type and level of detail in the case. But for you as an educator the main guiding principle should be the following decision criterion: can you achieve your learning objectives if you modify the type of information contained in the case?

We suggest considering three main aspects at this point in the process:

- Factual basis of the case: should the case describe real or fictional events?
- Collaboration with organization or protagonist: should you plan to write the case on the basis of field research (i.e., in collaboration with people and an organization) or just from your desk?
- Level of described detail: how much detail and reality should be described in the case?

Factual basis of the case

Many if not most of the best cases describe real events. That is unsurprising as one of the key benefits of using case studies for educational purposes is to bring reality to the classroom. Accordingly, many authors of books and articles on case writing as well as professional associations (e.g., the North American Case Research Association, NACRA) agree that a case has to be 'a description of a *real* situation' (Naumes & Naumes 2006: 9). On the other hand, we have personally had some exceptionally great experiences when using cases that do not describe real events in class (our own cases and cases from others).

So, let's not be orthodox but rather focus on the main objective of cases: to allow participants to have meaningful learning or development while reflecting and debating the description of a situation. If this learning is triggered by a fictional case, then so be it.

Overall, we think that there are benefits and drawbacks to cases written about real or fictional events. Please have a look at some of them before making your choice:

Real events case

Benefits
- Easy to relate to for your participants (and for you) – they will know that they are dealing with a real-world phenomenon and challenge.
- Familiarity of company or products – it can be much easier if your participants know the organization or product and thus can combine the case with their prior knowledge and experience (e.g., less explanation necessary).
- No need to explain the relevance/context of the case – it is a real case and thus it might happen again in a similar way in the professional future of your participants.

Drawbacks
- Getting access to the company – especially when describing any even remotely controversial behavior of the company or protagonist but also when dealing with organizational failures and tough challenges, organizations might just not respond when you try to reach out to them.
- Need to get case release – unless writing the case entirely on the basis of publicly available information you will need to get release before publishing the case (and possibly it is exactly this not-publicly-available information that makes your case lead so interesting).
- Aging of case – cases on the basis of real events get out of date more quickly, especially if you write a case about an organization that changes rapidly (just think about the possible effects of rebranding, corporate restructuring, bankruptcy, etc. on your case).

Fictional events case

Benefits
- Retaining control – when writing a case on the basis of fictional events, you can present the story the way it fits your educational needs best and you do not need to take reality into account; accordingly, you retain complete control of the setting and content.
- The case as a universe – when using a fictional case, participants need to rely on the information provided in the case (the case text forms an entire universe). They will be unable to use prior knowledge about the firm, industry, or context.
- No distraction from the 'solution' – cases fictional events do not have real-life outcomes. Accordingly, participants will not be distracted by the outcome (often mistaken as 'solution'). If they cannot google the outcome, they will probably be more open minded regarding the possible courses of action.

Drawbacks
- Fiction in the classroom – writing entirely fictional cases thwarts the objective of bringing reality to the classroom.
- Effort and creativity – making up a case from scratch without building upon real events typically requires a lot of creativity and effort.
- Case complexity – in our experience, those few great cases that describe entirely fictional events (i.e., cases that are not only disguised on the basis of real events) are almost always not complex (at least in the presentation and analytical dimension). It is doable to write an entirely fictional short case, but case complexity will almost inevitably go down as fictional cases typically lack detail and information.

As already said, this choice represents a spectrum not a dichotomy. There are what we tend to call gradations of 'fictionality'. The basic story of a case study can be more or less fictional. You could:

- write a case about a real organization and describe the situation and developments as they really occurred;
- add a bit of fiction to a real case, e.g., by changing certain details for either didactical reasons or because this is necessary to get release, but keep the real organization's and protagonist's names;
- start to write a case on the basis of a real story about a real organization with real people, but then present the case as a fictional case in order to avoid (release no longer needed) or ensure (release easy to get as organization is not identifiable) release;
- combine two or three different real situations or developments from one or several organizations into one single case in order to increase case density;
- make up a story entirely from scratch without any relation to real-world developments or situations;

Whatever you choose for your case, beware the ethical pitfalls. Some case authors consider it to be legitimate to add the description of fictional situations, developments, conversations, etc. into the case. We agree that in certain cases a higher level of 'fictionality' might help – but we recommend at least making this visible in some notes to the case or in the teaching note. We do not see that being transparent about modifications could harm the learning experience – and like this you at least do not intentionally say something you know to be wrong in order to mislead others (the classical definition of lying).

Collaboration with an organization or protagonist

As soon as you plan to base your case on real events, you will also need to decide if your case should be based on field research and collaboration with the organization and protagonist or written on the basis of desk research from previously published sources. Again, there are advantages and disadvantages to both.

Cases written through field research in collaboration with the organization or protagonist

Benefits
- Case will probably be a better reflection of the world as it was – and we want to prepare our participants for the real world.
- Case will typically become much richer in detail.
- Collaboration with an organization ensures real-world connection of the case.
- Chance to discover new and original issues and learn for yourself in the process.
- Collected data might be used for (academic) research as a primary or secondary objective of the field research.
- Field research is close to research activity and process – and thus to what you know best.
- Intensification of collaboration with organization for other benefits, e.g., guest lectures, future cases.
- Work on the case might be combined with consulting for client organization, especially when case deals with an acute challenge.

(Continued)

Drawbacks
- It may be tricky or time-consuming to get case release (permission from the company to publish your case will be needed as soon as you include any information gained during your field research).
- The case content will depend on the company: their objectives, opinions, and the extent to which they share information with you.
- Interviews take time and effort to arrange, conduct, and write up.

Case written from published sources

Benefits
- You will have more control over the content of your case.
- Case release is not required; no political considerations are needed and this ensures academic independence.
- The process may be less time-consuming.
- Offers a good alternative when the company involved will not collaborate with you.

Drawbacks
- Your case may have less credibility.
- Participants will not benefit from the 'inside knowledge' of a field-based case.

Realistically, you may just not have the luxury of choosing to write a field-based case. For example, it can be difficult, if not impossible, to write field-based cases on/with:

- controversial businesses (e.g., tobacco, weapons or gambling industries);
- problematic issues and failures (e.g., accounting fraud; ethical or legal transgressions; failures of various kinds);
- highly confidential future plans (e.g., acquisitions, market entries, product developments, numbers for specific projects);
- exposure of personal information about individuals (especially for leadership cases).

But, even if your case is completely noncontroversial, it may still be difficult to get the company's permission to release it. You may receive no or a negative response when you first approach the company or – much worse – it may refuse to release the case after you have finished writing it.

 From theory to practice with Urs

If you do not get wholehearted permission at the start, or if you suspect it will be tricky to get release for your finished case, writing from published sources may be your best (or only) option. If you cannot get the organization or protagonist to collaborate with you on the case early on, there are a couple of other options to consider.

You can:

- use only publicly available information and thus avoid the need for release altogether;
- partially disguise the case which may make it easier to get permission; or
- fully disguise the case so that permission will not be necessary (see below).

(Continued)

> Writing (and publishing) your case solely from published sources may be the best option, especially if you have limited experience of writing cases. Two practical tips:
> - We have sometimes written a first version of the case on the basis of publicly available information and only then reached out to the organization. It might be easier to get their support and collaboration once they see what you have in mind.
> - Document through footnotes or endnotes the sources of your information for every single factual statement in the case – and make sure you save all your sources for later reference (e.g., screenshots/downloads of articles, links to webpages).

Level of described detail

After deciding the factual basis of your case and the required collaboration from the described organization or protagonist, you next need to decide about the level of detail and information in your case – in particular about the possible extent of disguise. As with the previous two decisions, this choice will also heavily affect the probability of getting case release.

Sometimes it might be easier to get final release when:

1. leaving out/making up certain details;
2. postponing the publication of the case to avoid giving away confidential information (some organizations might allow you to use the cases in class but not give you permission to publish the case before a certain deadline); or
3. producing a disguised case.

You should try your very best to avoid the first two options – but you might want to consider them once you hit problems as you write the case. The third option – disguise (sometimes also anonymization or sanitization) – is a frequently used tactic to get release or to ensure confidentiality of critical information. Through disguise, i.e., by changing the description of a situation or development, the author ensures that readers of the case cannot infer the underlying real case.

The *extent of the disguise* can be differentiated between:

- Full disguise: all factual details of the underlying situation or development will be changed except for information that is commonly known and not linked to any disguised organization or individual.
- Partial: certain factual details of the lead are correctly mentioned, while others are only disguised selectively (e.g., in the famous HBS case 'Rob Parson at Morgan Stanley' by M. Diane Burton, most of the information is probably describing the real events behind the case, but the names of certain individuals were changed to protect their privacy).

You should also carefully consider the *scope or object of disguise*, as disguise can affect:

- names and sociodemographic descriptions of individuals (job title, gender, age, education, nationality, professional career, etc.);
- names of organizations (case organization or other organizations, e.g., competitors, acquisition targets, customers, suppliers);
- physical locations – and cultural setting;
- industry settings (to make your life easier, consider at least staying in the larger ecosystem, e.g., by moving into supplier or customer industries as this will probably require fewer adaptations);

- functional setting (e.g., next to changing the name of the protagonist, you could just move her to a different function/department);
- numbers (e.g., certain financial numbers such as the company's WACC or IRR);
- historical setting.

Based on personal experience, we do not recommend fully or partially disguising a case – as long as you can avoid it. Disguising a case is very difficult, painstaking, and time-consuming work. Sanitizing needs a bit of 'lying' and to lie consistently is just not easy.

 From theory to practice with Urs

One of my cases was supposed to deal with corruption. The organization didn't respond to any of my attempts to get in contact. So I wrote the case solely on the basis of publicly available information and submitted it. After a review, a journal accepted the case for publication, but the legal department of the editing house asked for a complete disguise so that readers wouldn't be able to make inferences about the underlying real case – I was expected to present the case as a fictional case.

Initially, I assumed this to be a quick job – just using Ctrl+H to search and replace all the names of organizations, individuals, and locations. But soon I realized that I had to change much more, e.g.:

- Changing the location required adaptations in the description of the cultural context as well as the behavior of the protagonist and other actors.
- The organization's positioning and competitive advantage was important to understand why corruption was such a threat to them – and I had to invent a new story to deal with that.
- Just changing the name of the organization was not enough; it was also important to describe the organization overall in a way that wouldn't allow the real company to be identified. And this was particularly tricky as the industry was characterized by a particularly specific competitive situation.
- The case contained a few numbers – all of which now needed to be changed. Numbers are quite easy to find online, so I had to make them up. But beware: a simple multiplication of all numbers by a certain factor will just not do the job – especially not when you include the three basic financial statements.

So, in a nutshell: unless you are absolutely convinced that you will not get release, spare yourself the effort and try to get release!

Drafting a case teaching plan

By now you have defined the learning objective of your case and taken numerous strategic decisions and tactical choices. The overall design of your case is becoming more and more clear. Now it is time to come back to the educational need for your case. At this point, this means starting to develop a plan on how you want to teach the case in class.

As explained at the beginning of this chapter, we believe that the development of the case study text and of the teaching note should not be done sequentially (neither first the case nor first the teaching note) but that case authors should bring together their lead and need in an iterative process. And, according to our experience, now is the right time to draft a first version of the teaching plan – you will need it soon for your test-teaching anyway.

A *teaching plan* (see also above in the case teaching chapter, page 40, which you might want to read now unless you have already done so) is a structured overview of the flow of a teaching session that usually includes information about:

- building blocks/sections by content in a recommended sequence (including intended learning objectives per building block);
- questions per building block and for the transition from one block to the next;
- learning formats;
- timings; and
- insights you (or others) gained from using the case in class (this last item is not yet applicable right now, but we will come back to it later).

We do not need the full detail at this point of time (much will change in your draft teaching plan as you continue writing the case and after the first test-teachings), but you should now already form an understanding about the rough sequence and rhythm of the session. For that please first refer back to your choice of the immediate issue and of the underlying issues and learning objectives.

Roughly, you should plan to have:

- an intro block that will usually be started by asking a powerful opening question and be linked to the immediate issue of the case;
- a variable number of different discussion blocks that should be linked to the different underlying issues and/or learning objectives;
- a transfer block (ensuring transfer of knowledge/lessons learned); and
- a closure.

For all of these specify at least the approximate duration, the learning format and the main learning points. If you are more specific and detailed, this will rarely be a waste of your time as you can use it in step five when drafting the teaching note further. Even though the plan will most likely change, the individual blocks or certain aspects of the different blocks can probably be used even after the changes (we often just needed to add blocks or to change the sequence of the blocks). At the end, check if your teaching plan truly ensures:

- diversity of learning formats (change of format approximately after every 15 to 20 minutes);
- logical structure of the flow so that participants know where they are in the process and how they got there (i.e., including the method to move from one session block to the next);
- achievement of all learning objectives (please refer back to page 33 above).

You can find tables in the case writing workbook for this exercise. Feel free to use those to write down the intended flow of the session that you have in mind while writing this case.

We believe that writing a case is done best on the basis of a clear idea about the future educational process and context. In a book chapter from 2005, Kassarjian and Kashani also propose thinking early about the 'teaching strategy' (pages 113 and 114). They however suggest not only having one specific teaching plan in mind but instead recommend simultaneously having 'a number of different approaches in mind.' We think that a certain level of flexibility with respect to the final teaching flow can be helpful as it will give you more flexibility and freedom while writing the case. But for first-time authors we still recommend making a commitment to one intended flow of the case discussion. You can always make changes to your teaching plan later.

5. Operational activities for your own case study

Possibly without realizing, you should by now already have produced quite a bit of material and even some text that you can use later for the case study but even more so for the teaching note. However, there is still quite a bit of work ahead. Most of the writing will follow now. So, sharpen your pencils, clean your keyboard – it is time to produce some text!

Drafting the case study

Before you start to write: some conventions

There are some case writing conventions you should observe – and that you should have in mind right from the beginning of your text production. This will not only ensure consistency across all the cases you write but, if your case matches most or all of the conventions, it will probably be easier for others to read and use your case and will therefore maximize your case's appeal to other teachers and facilitators. Most case writing conventions relate to writing style and layout, please find below an overview of the most important aspects.

As you will see, we will present all conventions as strong rules. We really encourage you to stick to all conventions. Even though we are not orthodox about almost any aspect of case writing and case teaching, please follow these conventions – unless you really have extremely powerful counterarguments especially related to your educational needs. Yes, we know that there are great cases that violate some of the following conventions, but they are very rare.

Before jumping into the conventions, please observe that they apply not only to classical text case studies but also to video, audio, or multimedia cases. Your case production process will almost always start with the production of text anyway. Stick to the conventions when writing the script even when planning a different type of case.

Writing style

Use past tense – consistently!

Always write your case in the past tense. We know from experience that many (especially new) case authors struggle with this convention, particularly when writing about information that is current, for example companies that are still in existence, or decisions that have not yet been taken. However, there are several very good reasons for sticking rigorously and consistently to the past tense:

- Past tense is just correct as – in the words of Vega (2013: 3) – a 'case takes place in the past.' Even though the company might at the time you write the case still look similar to the organization that you describe in the case, the situation and developments described in the case will (in almost all cases) be in the past.
- Because things change quickly, your case will quickly look dated if it is written in the present tense and could easily lead to confusion. Using past tense increases the longevity of your case.
- The past tense does not result in confusion for readers, and most will not even notice it. The past tense is commonly used in literature and most readers accept it as a given; it might even make it easier for them to fully dive into the fiction of taking over the position or decision of the protagonist.

There is one exception to the past tense rule: dialogue and quotes should be used verbatim and not changed to the past tense.

Abstain from judgment

Cases should present facts – not your personal judgment.
Are you really excited about your case lead? Do you personally think that the protagonist or organization made a smart, innovative, highly successful decision? Do you like the organization, its products, or protagonist? Are you personally impressed by a turnaround of the organization? Watch out! You are very likely to commit the cardinal sin of presenting your personal opinion and not the case. This risk is particularly high if you plan to write a retrospective case about a positive development or if your case lead heavily depends upon a surprising and successful choice of the protagonist (what we call 'rabbit out of the hat cases').

In cases like these we have seen many case authors using expressions like 'spectacular success,' 'well-balanced and diversified portfolio,' 'the only way to differentiate one's self,' 'culture of underperformance,' 'impressive growth,' 'the margin was meagre,' and 'unique training programme' (all of these just taken from one single – otherwise pretty good – case that we judged for a case-writing competition). But there are many good reasons not to fall into this trap:

- Judgment frequently lacks evidence: Judgment is often just a substitute for more research. Instead of presenting a comprehensive set of data with information about the development of all players in an industry, case authors might just claim that a company was 'growing extraordinarily fast.' But was there really no other player growing even faster – possibly in a related industry? Was something really so unique? Invest the effort to provide the evidence and not your opinion.
- Judgment kills learning: We want our participants to dive into a situation and analyze it critically by using their own reasoning on the basis of the available facts. They should not feel compelled to internalize the case author's personal evaluation.
- Judgment leads to reactance: Overloading a case with judgment can easily provoke reactance, i.e., counterreactions from your participants. When people feel pushed too hard in a certain direction, they will push back for no other reason than to push back. The judgment in the case can then quickly lead to the contrary effect of what you intended.

Again, there is one – but critically important – exception to the rule of abstaining from judgment: dialogue and quotes should use the judgment and evaluation of the person quoted! If you think that some sort of judgment or evaluation is needed to put things into perspective (e.g., if you want to present your protagonist as particularly smart), present it as a statement or opinion of a character in the case (the protagonist, an industry expert, a competitor, a peer, etc.).

Write in the third person

Please write the entire case in the third person. This means you should not use 'I' or 'you' (except in direct quotes) but instead refer to people by their names or as 'him,' 'her,' or 'they.' You might be tempted to believe that cases focus on the perspective of the protagonist anyway, so why not tell the story directly from their point of view and by using their own reflection as the text of the case?

Use active sentences

Use active sentences rather than passive sentences where possible. Active sentences are a much clearer and more direct way of writing. But what is an active sentence? Look at the following two sentences:

The figures were not checked properly (by the chief accountant).

and

The chief accountant did not check the figures properly.

The first is passive, the second is active. You can see that in the active sentence the person responsible for the action is mentioned first in the sentence – and this is usually important so that the readers of the case study can understand who contributed what and how to the current situation or developments.

Formal or informal?

Your case should be easy and inviting to read. Avoid jargon, initials, acronyms, technical terms, and terminology that is specific to a company, industry, function, or culture – and that nonexpert readers will not be able to understand. Remember that participants may not be familiar with the country, business, or products your case is about. Just as an example, some Indian cases use expressions like lakh (for one hundred thousand) and crore (for 10 million). Doing so certainly adds local flavor to your case but non-Indian readers will probably either have to do research to understand the meaning or (even worse) just ignore this aspect and withdraw to a very superficial reading.

You want your readers to be challenged by the issues, not your prose style! If you really believe certain expressions or acronyms are needed (e.g., due to your target audience or to reach the learning objective) – at least explain the terms when using them the first time or consider adding a short glossary in the exhibits of the case. Never assume a reader will know what you are talking about. The only exception to this rule is if your case is solely targeted at an expert audience. If so, it is better to use their shared language and the technical terms that they will be familiar with.

Layout

It is helpful to pay attention to the layout of your case from the very beginning, as this will reduce the effort at the end significantly. The standard of the visual presentation of your case will be seen as an indication of how much effort you have put into the case itself. Even minor imperfections in the layout and visual appearance of your case will reduce the chances of other educators choosing to teach it and will also put students off and significantly reduce their interest in the case.

In our experience, it is always best to have your layout in place right from the start. You may be required to use your institution's template in which case the work has been done for you. But, if not, you should:

- Make sure each page of your case is numbered.
- Include margins that are wide enough for participants to make their own notes.
- Make your case visually appealing and easy to read with well-spaced lines and paragraphs and a suitable font size (avoid pages of dense text, which can be very off-putting – even though this might be a tempting way to reduce the number of pages). You should use at least an 11-point font size and 1.0 line spacing; more would be even better. Spacing before or after paragraphs is very helpful for readers.
- Define your sections and chapters very clearly with clear headings, for example in a different font, bold, or underlined. This will aid reading and enable the reader to quickly scan the text and return to important points more easily.
- Make sure you describe any images in their alt text to make them accessible to screen readers for participants that are visually impaired.
- Limit the use of notes and references. If necessary, add them at the end of the case. Anything important should be included in the body of the text. (Important exception: ensure proper referencing of all factual statements for cases written on the basis of desk research.)

Front page

The front page of your case should always include:

- name(s) of the author(s),
- institution(s) – possibly with a logo,
- case title,
- date of publication (and/or of revision; this will help you to keep track of the different versions),
- copyright statement (including information about where/how to acquire licenses of the case) – or information that the present version of case is only 'work in progress.'

Your institution might have standard copyright text to be used for your case. If not, feel free to word the footer of the case's first page roughly along the following typical content and wording:

This case study was written by <AUTHOR NAME>, <POSITION/TITLE> at <INSTITUTION>. Full responsibility for the content of this case rests with the author.

This case study is not intended to illustrate or endorse effective or ineffective management behavior but is solely meant to serve as basis for class discussion in an educational context.

*This case study includes information that was provided by <PROTAGONIST/ORGANIZATION>, who agreed to the publication of this case study in its present form. / **OR** / This case study was written solely on the basis of publicly available information. / **OR** / This case study was disguised on the basis of a real situation – names of individuals and organizations, locations, industry, and other aspects have been modified to ensure confidentiality of the case.*

Licenses to use this case study for educational purposes can be acquired via <The Case Centre / other CASE DISTRIBUTOR>. Copying or posting of this case study without licenses is strictly prohibited.

Exhibits

> **Conventions regarding exhibits**
>
> Observe the following conventions regarding exhibits:
>
> - Exhibits are included at the end of the case after the closing paragraph (or possibly even only after a page break) so that the narrative flow is not interrupted.
> - Don't show tables, graphs, charts, etc. within the flow of the text – all of that should be in the exhibits section (to allow for the short cycle reading process; see above page 24).
> - Always use the term 'exhibits' (not, for example, 'appendices' or 'annexes').
> - Refer to all your exhibits in the body of the case and use bold font to do so, for example '(See **Exhibit 1**).'
> - Don't include any exhibits that are not referred to in the case text.
> - Arrange your exhibits in the same order as they are referred to in the case – and number them accordingly.

(Continued)

> - For the electronic version of the case – mostly PDF but also for text-based multimedia cases – consider including hyperlinks between the references in the case study text and the exhibit and back; this will make it easier for the readers to jump back and forth.
> - Give all your exhibits a clear title that summarizes the content of the exhibit.
> - Present your exhibits clearly and professionally; a wonky and blurred photocopy of financial accounts, for example, will not create a good impression. A good alternative is to reproduce the data in your own table template.
> - Add sources and references to your exhibits whenever possible.
> - And as mentioned before: be critical with your exhibits. Are all of them really needed to achieve the desired learning objectives? If not, just skip them.

Color or black and white?

Bear in mind that some participants still print their cases in black and white. (This is particularly true in executive education, where we have observed countless participants with big folders containing all the prereadings for a program printed for them by an assistant.) However, this does not mean that you need to avoid using color (especially as an increasing number of cases are being distributed and read electronically). If you do include color, just ensure that the case (especially, for example, any photographs and charts) will print clearly in greyscale and that all data series are easily readable (this is particularly true for all exhibits).

Institutional conventions

Please check with your institution for all existing conventions and regulations for case studies. Next to the layout/template, some institutions have clear expectations about the case (or teaching note). Reach out to your school's publishing department and ask them for all the things that you will need to observe. Failing to do so early will likely result in unnecessary extra work later.

Just as an example: how do you plan to refer to the actors in your case? Do you intend to use their first or last names? Will you include their titles (if any)? We personally tend to use first names, whereas Harvard Business School cases usually use last names.

Developing a draft case title

After internalizing the conventions, get out your case study template and start to write! And we will start with the very top: the title.

The title of your case is its shop window – the first thing your readers (including possible adopting educators) will see. It will need to spark their interest and encourage them to start reading. Your title should therefore offer a brief guide to what the case is about, without giving away too much! Avoid directly mentioning the underlying issues that will be covered in the case.

Do not make the title of your case too long or complex. This can be off-putting and may make your case less appealing when listed online with other cases on similar topics.

Typical case titles include references to:

- the protagonist(s), and/or
- the company, and/or
- the immediate issue.

Even though you might consider the title to be less relevant at this stage of the process: just write down the best title that currently comes to mind. It will also make your interaction with the organization and individuals described in the case study typically much easier.

We recommend starting your case writing with a focused, more traditional single case study, but if you decide – despite our warning – to write a case series, just follow the convention of separating the different cases of the series by adding '(A),' '(B),' '(C),' etc. to the case titles.

Writing the opening paragraph

The opening paragraph (sometimes also called the '(opening) hook'; e.g., Naumes & Naumes 2006; Vega 2013) is crucial; it is the single most important text element of the final case study package. Make sure to get it right – and do not expect to be able to get it perfectly right on the first try; rather, expect to work in multiple iterations! Make sure to include the following information in your opening paragraph (if necessary, this might also be two or three paragraphs):

1. *Immediate issue:* After reading the opening paragraph, the readers need to know what this case is all about. You do not need to be very specific (especially if you want to produce a case that is high in the analytical case complexity dimension; see above page 19), but the opening paragraph should at least inform and guide the further reading of the case.
2. *Name and position of protagonist:* Great cases have a perspective, and this perspective should be clear from the very beginning by clearly specifying the protagonist. But introduce as few people as possible in the opening paragraph to avoid confusion.
3. *Organization, e.g., name, size, industry, and ownership structure:* Again, do not provide too much detail – just enough for the reader to get a feel for the company. You can include more detail later in the case but the reader needs to get an idea about the overall setting right from the beginning.
4. *Timing:* this should be the specific date and time you have chosen as a cutoff point in the timing of your case (see page 147). It is vital to get this right. Your opening paragraph should be set at a single point in time that is then used consistently throughout the case.

 From theory to practice with Urs

I'm sometimes asked to review long and complex opening paragraphs by fellow case writers. I advise them to read through the text and underline each piece of information they have included in the paragraph. Then I suggest they count them up. I have come across examples of 50 pieces of information in opening paragraphs that were up to 1.5 pages long. These are extreme examples, but the point remains: you need to critically assess the content of your opening paragraph, delete all extraneous information, and decide if the information you have removed can be put to good use elsewhere in the case or should be discarded altogether.

The result will be a much crisper and clearer opening paragraph.

Please observe the following recommendations:

- Be concise: The ideal length of an opening paragraph is about 90 to 200 words (Leenders et al. 2010 suggest using no more than six sentences). Keep your sentences short, too; an average length of 15 to 20 words per sentence is ideal but fewer than 15 words is even better. (If necessary, it can be ok to spread the opening paragraph over two or four paragraphs, but: the shorter the better!)

- Make sure your opening paragraph focuses on the immediate issue in the case (see page 21) and is capable of inspiring initial debate in the classroom. Remember that the presentation of the immediate issue in your opening paragraph will shape not only the participants' reading but also the entire flow of the case discussion.
- Depending on the complexity of your case (see page 19), it may also be possible to signpost the underlying issues to be explored. (See page 21 for more information about immediate and underlying issues in case writing.)

> The immediate and underlying issues of your case should be closely linked to your learning objectives. Therefore, we advise that all the content you include throughout your case should support the achievement of the learning objectives.
>
> Having said that, we have to acknowledge that some cases can be used to teach a number of different learning objectives simply by making changes to the opening and closing paragraphs. This highlights the critical importance of introducing the immediate issue in your opening paragraph and we strongly encourage you to focus on achieving this.

- Ensure your opening paragraph creates dramatic interest and draws the reader in. Look at your opening paragraph objectively: Would it motivate you to read on? Is it intriguing? Will it pique the reader's interest and curiosity? Ask critical and honest friends or colleagues for their opinion of your opening paragraph. If they are not inspired to read on, it is unlikely that anyone else will be either.
- Adhere to the conventions listed above, especially: Write the entire opening paragraph in the third person and consistently use past tense. For example:

When Paula Brown arrived at the office on October 23, 2010, two irate colleagues were waiting for her. The two heads of IT and Supply Chain Management challenged Brown, CEO of retailing startup Droogle, regarding her recent decision to outsource the trucking division.

Not:

One beautiful day in October, two colleagues wait for me outside of my spacious office with windows on three sides. My assistant brings them into my room. They briefly greet me, just to tell me how dissatisfied they are with my decision to outsource the trucking division.

Your opening paragraph should:

- present an interesting immediate issue (the 'hook') to generate further interest in the case and spark debate in class,
- specify the protagonist, the organization, and the timing,
- be concise (approximately 90–200 words),
- use short sentences,
- use the third person,
- be written in past tense, and
- create dramatic interest and draw your reader in.

From theory to practice with Urs

Here is an example of an opening paragraph taken from my case 'Norman Nicholls at Seattle Management Consultants':

On October 26, 2004, Norman Nicholls – partner of the consulting company Seattle Management Consultants in London (UK) – received a phone call from Jesper Lind, board member of Telco-Equipment Experts. Jesper told Norman: 'If you don't change your recommendation on the outsourcing job you are doing for Damotel, our business relationship might suffer in the future.'

You can see how this ticks many of the boxes for an opening paragraph: it is short (very short at just 55 words) and written in the past tense and the third person. Despite its brevity, it still includes all the key information about the protagonist and the context necessary to understand the immediate issue. As an added bonus, the case already contains a direct quote from a key player in the case. This helps to bring the case alive and contributes to the dramatic effect. Do you want to find out more after reading this opening paragraph?

Now compare the final opening paragraph with this very first version with 169 words:

Gazing through his office-window on the river Thames, Norman Nicholls hung up the phone in despair on October 26, 2004. The senior partner of the American, but globally acting, top management consulting company Seattle Management Consultants (SMC) had just finished an unpleasant call with Jesper Lind, a senior representative of Telco Equipment Experts (TEE), one of Thomas's largest customers. Norman was responsible for the entire industry group MIHAT (Media, IT, High-Tech & Telecommunication) in Northern Europe (UK, Ireland, Denmark, Sweden, Finland, Norway) and Telco Equipment Experts was not only SMC's third-largest customer in the MIHAT industries, but also pitching for a large-scale outsourcing project for Damotel, which was supported by SMC. Jesper had made very clear that he did not like the fact that a team of SMC consultants had evaluated the offer of Iberola as better than TEE's offer. He had threatened Norman, that SMC would never again get a consulting assignment at TEE if the preference of the consulting team would not switch from Iberola to TEE.

 From theory to practice with Martin

The opening paragraph can be tricky to get right. Even the most experienced case authors will frequently redraft their opening paragraphs at least two or three times before being satisfied with it. Below is a typical example of how an opening paragraph can be gradually improved with a little time and effort. This is from 'Creating Trust in a New Way of Banking: The Case of Lendahand Mesofinance,' a case I wrote with my coauthors Andre Nijhof and Maria Nikolaidou. Here is the first draft of our opening paragraph:

It was 15th of September 2008, when Peter Heijen received an urgent email from his company in which he was informed about the bankruptcy of Lehman Brothers, the fourth largest investment bank in the US. The message was brief:

(Continued)

'Dear colleagues, we would like you to be extremely cautious with your clients regarding the selection of their portfolio ... The upcoming months will be very critical for the financial sector as we are expecting seismic shock and possible hemorrhaging in cash stocks after Lehman Brothers collapse ...'

The same evening it was in the news that Lehman's 25,000 employees were collecting their personal belongings from their offices. Peter Heijen realized that the next morning all those people would be jobless. This was an alert for him, the successful equity analyst, that nothing would be the same anymore in the financial market.

You can see that we wanted to focus on the personal aspects of the situation and on our protagonist, Peter Heijen, to shed some light on what was important to him and what influenced him. However, there were a couple of downsides to this first version.

First, the date (September 15, 2008) is not the date of the case but the date when the story began. I often see this problem in cases: the writer 'begins at the beginning' in chronological order, usually in an effort to explain how the situation started in the first place.

In addition, although we tried to present the protagonist in an engaging way so that readers could identify with him, the paragraph did not include a concrete immediate issue. Something important had obviously happened but it wasn't clear from the first version what this meant for Heijen. The paragraph was too vague and lacked a specific immediate issue.

So, taking all of these points into consideration, we wrote a second draft:

Peter Heijen jolted awake in the middle of the night. He sat up and glanced through the window, whipping his forehead with the back of his hand. The speed of the last day's events would not allow him to fall asleep, his head was spinning. Earlier that afternoon he received a phone call from Manila, where he was informed that one of the local partners of another crowdfunding platform went belly-up. This was an extra hit to the already tense crowdfunding environment, where clients started to ask questions about the risk of crowdfunding companies going bankrupt and investors losing their invested money. While Lendahand was not working directly with the company that was affected, Peter felt like he had to do something. He thought about preparing a press release explaining the situation. Another option could be to contact all of his existing investors directly through a newsletter. Or was he exaggerating and would no reaction be the best reaction? Weighing the pros and cons in his bed, he finally fell asleep undecided.

You can see that we have removed the confusing date.

Equally important, we have introduced an immediate issue. To achieve this, it was necessary to interview Peter Heijen again so we could ask him about concrete events, actions, or decisions that were difficult for him and that kept him awake at night.

You may have spotted that a specific time is missing from this version. Here is the third and final version of our opening paragraph:

Peter Heijen jolted awake in the middle of a late October night in 2014. He sat up and glanced through the window, whipping his forehead with the back of his hand. The speed of the previous day's events would not allow him to fall asleep. Earlier that afternoon he received a phone call from Manila, where he was informed that one of the local partners from another crowdfunding platform went belly-up. This was an extra hit to the already tense crowdfunding environment, where clients started to feel insecure and asked about the risks they were facing

(Continued)

> *if a crowdfunding company goes bankrupt, causing the investors to lose their invested money. While Lendahand was not working directly with the broken company, Peter was wondering about what to do to prevent a possible runaway of sceptical clients in the upcoming days. He struggled with whether he should act proactively and take some necessary steps to calm down potentially frightened clients. His first thought was to send out a press release explaining the situation and differentiating the position of Lendahand from the bankrupt company. Another option was to forward a newsletter to all of his existing investors. The use of social media for informing his network regarding the situation in the crowdfunding market through regular posts was also an option he thought about. Or was he exaggerating and would no reaction be the best reaction? Weighing the pros and cons in his bed, he finally fell asleep with an even more fuzzy mind, still undecided for the next day.*
>
> We have included the specific point in time and added more detail. We aimed to dramatize more effectively and explicitly the choice between taking no action and being proactive.
>
> Reading this introduction again after some time, I feel it can still be improved. For example, would a sentence about Lendahand, a company that is not widely known, be useful? Does Peter's role for Lendahand need to be clarified? What could be done to shorten the opening paragraph to the target length of 200 words maximum (currently 256 words)? Maybe you have ideas? How else could the immediate issue be presented, e.g., to increase the dramatic interest in the story? We welcome feedback!

Borrowing from movies (and books): cold opening, narrative hook and flashback

When writing the opening paragraph: think of movies! Many (especially older) movies start with the opening credits (names of movie and actors etc.) and then present the narrative in a chronological sequence. There are, however, techniques that are frequently used to increase tension and interest right at the beginning of the movie – and these techniques also work very well for case studies. So, think back to movies and write the opening paragraph as if this were the opening of your favorite thriller or horror movie.

The first technique you could use is called 'cold opening.' This is when the viewer is dropped immediately into the story right at the start of the film, even before the opening credits. A cold opening is opposed to traditional (lengthy) narrative expositions/introduction of characters, timing, etc. The idea is to involve the viewer straight away and vastly improve the likelihood that they will carry on watching. This is exactly the effect to aim for in the opening paragraph of your case. Present your opening paragraph so that it is not a boring introduction but that the readers find themselves immediately at the core of the developments and events!

As part of a cold opening, movies (just like novels, short stories, etc.) often present a so-called 'narrative hook.' For example, the movie *The Matrix* opens with the following (phone) conversation:

> *Yeah.*
> *Is everything in place?*
> *You weren't supposed to relieve me.*
> *I know, but I felt like taking a shift.*
> *You like him, don't you? You like watching him.*
> *Don't be ridiculous.*
> *We're gonna kill him. You understand that?*
> *Morpheus believes he is the one.*

After these 45 words we do not yet have a full understanding about the content and context of the movie – but the tension has built up. Obviously, there is some surveillance/observation going on and a possibly special person ('he is the one') might get killed or at least attempted to get murdered ('We're gonna kill him'). And, if you are anything like us, this will have stimulated your curiosity and interest in finding out (by watching the entire movie) how this story evolves further. This is the effect of the narrative hook. And the hook of a case study should ideally be your immediate issue. Revisit your immediate issue and identify the most suspenseful way to present this issue to your readers.

The opening paragraph should present the immediate issue and be written from the perspective of the cutoff date (this is especially true for what we called prospective cases; see page 17). Almost inevitably you will then need to use a third well-known technique from movies and books: 'flash-back' or 'cut-back.' Just like movies, many well-written cases jump back in time instead of telling the story chronologically. After presenting the immediate issue (as present time of the case), the following case sections move back in time and describe the events and developments that lead up to the situation at the cutoff date. In the next section of this chapter, we will discuss the sequencing of the remaining content of the case – for now, just beware: avoid too many jumps in the flow of time. Too much of a back-and-forth might just overstretch the readers' ability to follow.

One reminder: James Bond movies are famous for their elaborate precredit openings. They are usually extremely well composed and sometimes even the most memorable parts of the movies. But when writing your opening paragraph you need to deviate in one crucial aspect: James Bond precredits are mostly (very) long. You should stick to the convention and limit yourselves to 90 to 200 words!

Do you have any great examples of opening paragraphs? Please share them in the forum of the website to this book (add link symbol). Feel free to also comment on these opening paragraphs and state their strengths and weaknesses.

Outlining a possible case study structure

After having developed a draft title and written the opening paragraph, do not immediately jump to producing more text. First pause and define the overall case structure. Ask yourself what information in which structure you really need to allow for the type of case discussion that you want to have (review section 'Structuring the Need into a Session' from above, page 33). These reflections should lead you to a 'case study outline' – a very important document that you can put to multiple uses.

A case study outline is a short document (ideally already in the target case study template/layout and observing all conventions listed above) specifying:

- name(s) and institution(s) of case author(s) (for easier sharing);
- the preliminary case title (see above);
- the full opening paragraph (see above);
- a complete overview of all chapters/sections of the case study, including per section:
  - a preliminary section title (start with more generic titles first; change to more literary section titles later if you wish; already format the section title as a heading to allow for easier changes in the flow as you go);
  - a bullet point list of the desired content (not many more than five to 10 bullets per section);
  - an indication about the approximate length (expected number of pages); and
  - a list of the information needed (differentiating between information you already have and information that you will [probably] need);
- a closing paragraph (see below); and
- a list of exhibits (see below).

You absolutely need a clear outline for your case before starting to write. The outline should not be set in stone but rather allow for some flexibility as you write your case and further investigate the lead. Writing a case study outline will allow you to reap multiple important benefits, namely:

1. *Focus on your educational need:* According to our experience, case authors tend to get carried away by the excitement of their case lead! We have produced quite a few cases with text sections that we found exciting at the time – but that are not touched upon during the case discussions and that are also irrelevant for achieving the desired learning outcomes! Do not make this mistake. Critically reflect on what is really necessary to achieve the learning objective first.
2. *Easy identification of what information you really need and what you do not need:* Case authors (including ourselves) sometimes display the behavior of prehistoric hunters and gatherers: We feel great when collecting as much information as possible. Especially when we do not have a clear idea of the final case, we will happily take whatever we can. But in doing so we easily overstretch the protagonist's and organization's time, effort, and goodwill (and also waste our own time). So, try to be modest and only list information in the outline that you will really need (including whom to talk to and where or from whom to get the information).
3. *Cooperation easier with coauthors/support authors:* As soon as multiple individuals are involved in the production of one case study, the case study outline is of critical importance in coordinating the work of the different contributing parties. This is not only true for cases with several coauthors. Especially when making use of supporting authors that are not usually involved in educational activities such as students or professional writers (see also below page 246), the case study outline is critically important – and allows you to legitimately claim coauthorship even though you might not produce vast amounts of text.
4. *(Preliminary) case release:* The case study outline can also be used to get early buy-in from your protagonist or the company as your case outline will give them a good understanding of what they will be signing up to. As soon as you have the case outline, share it with your protagonist and ask them if a case along this outline will get their release (see also below 'Getting Preliminary Release,' page 196).
5. *Overcoming blank page fright:* And last but not least, creating an outline can help to overcome the dreaded blank page/screen stage of writing a case as you will immediately have something in writing – a small but important first step will have been done! *Small extra tip:* Produce your case outline in the final case study layout and use this document for the case going forward. Writing the case study will now just be about 'filling' the sections according to your outline – just keep properly track of the different versions.

How to structure a case so that it matches your learning objectives? There are some commonalities in the structure of case studies. Just use these commonalities as inspiration or templates for your own case.

Here is a typical case outline as suggested by Kassarjian and Kashani (2005: 111–112) and which we map – for illustrative purposes – to the best-selling case 'Reinventing Nespresso? The Challenges of a Market Leader Under Attack' by Kamran Kashani, Dominique Turpin, and Fang Liu from 2013 (Case number IMD-5-0790):

1. *Introduction: a dilemma, a problem, an action called for*
   - This section corresponds to what we called the 'opening paragraph.' As mentioned above, the opening paragraph (most frequently not labeled as a separate section, but just the first text after the overall case title; please do not call it 'Introduction' as this will make the case much more technical and boring) will usually present a dilemma, a problem, or a decision that needs to be made (the immediate issue or hook). Use the opening

paragraph to introduce your protagonist, i.e., the specific person who has to take a decision. As already described above, the problem will usually vary between different possible actors and thus it is important to describe the protagonist and their perspective.
- ➢ Nespresso case: The case begins with four short opening paragraphs (with a total of 274 words, which is a bit longer than we would usually recommend) that describe on almost one full page the organization (Nespresso), the protagonist (Nespresso CEO Jean-Marc Duvoisin), the product (Nespresso coffee capsules), the time/cutoff (April 2013), and the immediate issue (how to react to increasing competition from copycats). Additionally, the first page features a picture of the product and a quote from a former Nespresso CEO.

2. *Company background*
- After the opening paragraph, you need to describe the context and provide information to allow a discussion of the case study with the required level of depth and sophistication. The first thing is often some background about the organization. This can include information about the product, the history of the organization, the organizational setup/governance, the ownership structure, the management team and key people, or the current and past (economic) performance. This information will frequently be supported by exhibits (see below page 182) such as extracts from financial statements or organization charts.
- ➢ Nespresso case: The first case section after the opening paragraphs (titled 'Success against All the Odds') describes the history, business model and success of Nespresso starting in 1974 on two full pages. Very much in line with the comments above, this section refers to four (out of seven) exhibits.

3. *External context: market, industry, etc.*
- This section covers the context beyond the limits of the organization. It could include information about the industry, geographical factors, general economic climate, or political and cultural setting. The position of this section within the overall flow can sometimes vary upon the author's preferences or educational need (below you will find more recommendations regarding sequencing the flow of the case outline). Occasionally this section might be placed before the company background.
- ➢ Nespresso case: The second case section describes the 'competition' (which is also the section title). For the specific purposes of the Nespresso case this competitive landscape is exactly the relevant external context – as the immediate issue of the case is the challenge of defending the position of a market leader in a competitive industry, especially vis-à-vis copycats that emerge as Nespresso gets more and more successful.

4. *Company context: the evolution of the case problem*
- The next section will then often contain a description of how the immediate issue(s) in the case (i.e., the challenges for the protagonist) evolved over time within the organization. Dependent upon the desired level of analytical complexity of the case (see above on case complexity, page 19), this section will be more or less 'predigested.' Especially when aiming at high conceptual complexity, it can be adequate to fairly explicitly state the key issues (i.e., to be low on analytical complexity).
- ➢ Nespresso case: The description of the company context within the Nespresso case is relatively short (a bit more than half a page). The respective (third) section of the case, called 'Nespresso's Initial Response,' describes the initial strategies Nespresso adopted to deal with the copycats that emerged after Nespresso's great success in the market. In particular, this section provides quotes about the strategy from the former CEO.

5. *Drilling down: issues and actions that have a bearing on the decision*
   - The last content section will typically provide an overview of the factors that need to be considered before a decision can be made. This could also include a list of the possible alternatives. Dependent upon what has been covered so far, this section might be a summary of aspects already (implicitly) discussed or introduce new aspects.
   - ➢ Nespresso case: The next, fourth section, called 'Consumers,' describes consumer reactions on social media and via (blind) product tests on a bit more than one page. At the end of this section, it is getting clearer that the former CEO's initial response to rely on product quality might not fully match the consumers' perception.

6. *Conclusion: decision points*
   - You will need a compelling closing to your case. This can either be done via a full, separate case section or through the closing paragraph (see below more on the closing paragraph, page 183). This part of the case serves as the springboard for the classroom discussion: What are the pressing issues that need to be addressed? What decisions need to be made? What should the protagonist do next? A carefully crafted conclusion will leave your participants fired up and ready to go.
   - ➢ Nespresso case: The fifth and last section of the case is called 'Tough Choices' and summarizes all the decision points and alternatives on a bit more than two pages. The section opens with an overview about the opportunities and limits of geographical expansion, provides some more detail about the effects from copycats in Nespresso's home market, Switzerland, and closes with a list of five specific strategic options that Nespresso could adopt. Then the case closes with two paragraphs. The first shifts the focus back to the protagonist, the newly appointed CEO. The second paragraph is a closing quote from the CEO that introduces some of his personal perspectives on the possible future directions for the organization. A very elegant way to bring the protagonist to the forefront of the case, despite the fact that the case was written solely on the basis of publicly available information.
- *Exhibits* (not part of the overview by Kassarjian and Kashani but an important element of any case outline)
  - Exhibits (see also below) provide information (often data or visuals, less frequently text) that are important, but do not fit into the flow of the case study text. Think carefully about what information might be needed for having an intelligent discussion about the immediate and underlying issues of the case. Which visuals will help the participants to get the key points of the case?
  - ➢ Nespresso case: There are a total of seven exhibits (the case differentiates between six exhibits and one appendix, something that we do not recommend) on seven pages. Four of the exhibits (timeline, revenue development as chart, picture of products/system [and competitors], and overview of competitors [including prices]) are linked to the first full section, with background information about the organization.

This generic case study structure and flow is very helpful guidance as it condenses the structure of many great cases. It works well – and especially for your first case(s) you should seriously consider it as the basis for your case outline. It is, however, by no means a skeleton that you have to follow. There are probably more cases that have largely different structures than cases with this flow – even if we only look at great cases. Accordingly, you should consider Kassarjian and Kashani's structure only as a rule of thumb: in the absence of other considerations, just follow it. Whenever you have good reasons to deviate, feel free to use a different flow.

First define the building blocks in your outline. Then label the different sections (i.e., titles/headers), sketch out the content per section (bullet points), specify the expected number of pages for each section, and add a list of information to be included per section (with an indication of where you expect to be able to find/get the information from). Finally, consider different possible sequences (see also below), e.g., by moving the sections up and down (consider using the outline function of your word processing software) and critically evaluating the fit of the different possible flows to your learning objectives. You will find an easy-to-use table in the case writing workbook to help with this.

Never forget that you will be telling a story in your case. Be inspired by great literature and make use of tried and tested techniques that help to produce good writing:

- Make sure your story has a clear narrative structure, flows smoothly, and is easy for your reader to follow. Tension and drama should usually be highest at the beginning and end (opening and closing paragraphs). Move the more technical content to the middle of the case.
- Make good use of headings and subheadings to break the text up and help guide your reader through the case. This is not only important to allow your participants and other educators to apply the short cycle case study screening method (see above, page 24). It will also make reading easier, especially for longer cases that participants might not read in one go. (Rule of thumb: if a section is longer than two pages, consider adding subsections.)
- Ensure to provide enough space in your case to bring your characters to life as fully rounded human beings with desires, emotions, prejudices, ambitions, faults, and character traits. This can be done in a separate section or by making the protagonist reappear in many different sections. In either case, plan for that in the outline by listing where and how the protagonist will play a role.
- Cases benefit from a lively and engaging writing style, which can easily be achieved by adding quotes. Plan for possible quotes in your case outline.

Although you are telling a story, do not become too creative:

- Always keep your teaching plan in mind.
- Stick to the issues.
- Don't embroider the facts.
- Avoid being over-descriptive.

And, finally, be flexible with your case outline. It should be a living and breathing document – and not cast in stone. You will almost certainly include information in your case that you did not list in the first version of your outline, and you will also leave out information that you initially thought you would include. You will usually be able to make final decisions about what needs to be included when you come to test the case in the classroom.

Sequencing the case flow

As with any story, your case must have a clear narrative and a well-defined beginning, middle, and end (see also Vega 2013: 3), but there are many possible flows that can work well for the middle section. Earlier we presented a prototypical case structure as suggested by Kassarjian and Kashani (2005). But there are sometimes good reasons to deviate from this flow.

You will have to pay particular attention to how to organize the information in your middle section. These are some of the most commonly used options:

- broad to specific,
- chronological,
- based on a business process.

These options are not necessarily mutually exclusive but can be combined, for example, by using one for the main overall structure of your case, and another for one or two specific sections within it.

Broad to specific

One option to structure the middle of your case is to begin with some general information about the wider economic environment and then gradually drill down into the industry as a whole, followed by the particular company you are writing about, and, finally, the specific challenge(s) or problem(s) that need to be addressed. Therefore the flow would be:

- wider economic environment,
- industry as a whole,
- company,
- specific challenge or problem.

Compared to Kassarjian and Kashani's flow, in this option the section about the company is moved further toward the end. This is particularly often the case if the wider context is critically important to understanding the organization and its challenge. This might be true for cases that describe the formation of a typically less known, young, or small company that results from developments in the larger economic context or industry.

Chronological

You can also structure the middle of the case chronologically. Such a structure is particularly helpful if the case setting is not very complex, i.e., for situations in which not too many factors led to the emergence of the decision. After describing the immediate issue in the opening paragraph, you could just go back in time (as in movies or novels using a cut-back/flashback technique) and begin at the chronological beginning. Explain what triggered the situation and what took place next. Events may have occurred in several phases, so make sure your chronology is correct as you explain what happened. End your middle section by bringing the situation up to date, i.e., to the cutoff point at which a decision needs to be made. In summary:

- Explain what happens in time and date order.
- End the sequence of events at the point when a decision has to be made (which will usually be the same point described in the opening paragraph).

Review your case timeline (see the section above on 'Defining the Timeline and Possible Cutoff Points,' page 147) for the key events and developments within your case and try to bring them into line with your case outline (e.g., by using a new section for each key event). Your timeline will also help to make sure that your case does not move backward and forward in time (too much). It will also ensure that you do not include events that happen after the time at which you end your case.

Based on a business process

Sometimes, for example, in operations management cases, it can be enormously helpful to write the case based on a business process (for example, the flow of a production process).

An example for this might be the famous and best-selling 'Sport Obermeyer, Ltd.' case by Janice H. Hammond and Ananth Raman (1994). On the macro-structure the case flows from the opening paragraphs to a description of the company background. But then the structure deviates from Kassarjian and Kashani's flow and presents 'The Order Cycle' – a section that flows from 'The Design Process,' via 'Sample Production,' 'Raw material Sourcing and Production,' 'Retailer Ordering Process,' 'Shipment to Obermeyer Warehouse,' to the 'Shipment to Retail; Retail Replenishment Orders.' The reader of the case is imaginatively walked through the entire process from the very beginning to the end.

A case study structure that follows a business process can be particularly effective if the process is complex with several elements occurring simultaneously. But bear in mind that the structure should ease the reading process – so avoid making it even more complex and only use this structure if it really helps your readers.

Exhibits

Exhibits are information of different types that complement or illustrate different aspects of the case study. They provide important and helpful additions that are usually not included in the main case because they are presented in the form of a diagram or table or are longer pieces of text or other background materials such as company documents, CVs, and emails. Exhibits are usually presented at the end of the case study text so as to not interrupt the flow of the participants' reading.

Typical exhibits include:

Text	Data	Visuals
• CV(s) of protagonist(s) • Excerpts from speeches • Excerpts from annual reports • Dialogue that is relevant but too long or detailed for inclusion in the case itself • Company history (this could e.g., be formatted as a timeline with or without illustrations) • Company documents (e.g., policies, internal reports, mission statements)	• Company financial information (often over longer periods of time) • Information about competitors, customers, markets, industries, sociodemographic data, other country level data etc. • Product descriptions (including e.g., characteristics, customer evaluations, test results)	• Organization chart • Images of protagonists, offices, factories, retail outlets etc. • Images to aid understanding of technical products (e.g., technical drawings) • Maps to flag up key countries and locations • Process charts and descriptions (e.g., of the flow of products, information, decisions)

When making your choice of exhibits, we suggest following a 'green field' approach: We have frequently observed heavy overloads of cases with plenty of unnecessary exhibits. Do not get distracted by all the material that you have already compiled. Case authors are sometimes afraid to have produced 'waste' if they do not add an exhibit (sunk-cost fallacy) or might want to include several exhibits to allow for different learning objectives and use cases of the case. Instead, follow the opposite approach. For any possible exhibit that you have produced or have in mind: Will this really substantially change the participants' understanding of the case? Can they still get the main points and have a meaningful discussion without the case? Leave out everything that does not pass this test!

To help with the accessibility of the exhibits make sure you complete detailed descriptions of images, graphs, diagrams, etc. in their alt text to ensure screen readers used by participants who are visually impaired can decode them.

Writing a closing paragraph

Your closing paragraph (s) should be written with as much care as your opening paragraph. In many ways it is a beginning more than an end – a catalyst for the participants having a passionate debate in the classroom. In the language from movies and literature, the closing paragraph is the cliffhanger at the end of the case. Your closing paragraph should:

- 'Close the loop' of the case. In other words, your final paragraph should link back to your opening paragraph.
- Restate the issues that your protagonist(s) must now address (but do not make the underlying issues too obvious; rather focus on the immediate issues).
- Resist the temptation to summarize the entire case: keep your closing paragraph short and crisp.
- Emphasize that immediate action must be taken (if applicable).
- Communicate a sense of urgency so that participants in the classroom feel compelled to take ownership of the problem.
- Present the immediate issue in a way that the response is not obvious but will instead stimulate controversy and debate.

 From theory to practice with Urs

Here is an example of a closing paragraph from my case, 'Corruption in Russia: IKEA's Expansion to the East (A)':

Finally, a few weeks before the grand opening of the first IKEA in Russia in 2000, the local utility company reportedly approached the company's management and gave an ultimatum: Lennart Dahlgren, general manager of IKEA in Russia, could either pay a special service fee or proceed without electricity. Already under pressure from the previous challenges associated with the grand opening, Dahlgren had to act fast. Could IKEA afford to postpone or even completely cancel the opening in Khimki? Or should he just pay whatever was required?

In fewer than 90 words the closing paragraph reminds the reader of the immediate issue (to pay the service fee or not), the name and position of the protagonist (Lennart Dahlgren, general manager), the company (IKEA), the city (Khimki), the country (Russia), and the cutoff time (2000), as well as 'previous challenges' and the call for immediate action. At the same time – a clear weakness of the case – the paragraph reemphasizes that the case is based on secondary data (note the word 'reportedly').

 Recycling the opening paragraph for the closing paragraph

The requirements for the opening and closing paragraphs overlap significantly. In some cases, it is possible to use a slightly modified version of the opening paragraph as your closing paragraph (a trick we learned from Michiel R. Leenders and Louise A. Mauffette-Leenders

(Continued)

in a case writing workshop many years ago). For example, for the closing paragraph of my case 'Norman Nicholls at Seattle Management Consultants' I used an only marginally modified version of the opening paragraph to reemphasize the immediate issue. Just to remind you, here is the opening paragraph again:

On October 26, 2004, Norman Nicholls – partner of the consulting company Seattle Management Consultants in London (UK) – received a phone call from Jesper Lind, board member of Telco-Equipment Experts. Jesper told Norman: 'If you don't change your recommendation on the outsourcing job you are doing for Damotel, our business relationship might suffer in the future.'

And here is the closing paragraph:

When Norman Nicholls was called by Jesper Lind, board member of TEE, on October 26, 2004, he was anticipating a discussion about the ongoing strategy project for TEE. But very soon he realized that Jesper had another objective: 'If you don't change your recommendation on the outsourcing job you are doing for Damotel, our business relationship might suffer in the future.' Then Jesper abruptly ended the call. With the telephone still in his hand, Norman Nicholls wondered what to do.

Know when to stop! Do not tell the reader too much. Leave your participants with some work to do in the classroom. Make sure your case reveals nothing more than exactly (1) what the protagonist knew at the time and date that the case is set and (2) what is needed to address the immediate and underlying issues in class. Your participants must feel as if they are stepping into the shoes of your protagonist, and this will not be possible if they have the advantage of more information or the benefit of hindsight.

Fail fast pit stop: confirming or rejecting the case outline and immediate issue

If you actually started producing a case in parallel to reading this chapter (as recommended), you will so far probably have invested much more time on reading this book than on actually writing/working on the case. The entire process of bringing case lead and need more and more together in iterations up to the first full case outline, including opening and closing paragraph, should not take much of your time. A couple of hours should have been enough to get you so far. Following the good old 'fail fast' philosophy, you should now make one more check and see if your case is really going to fly. If you stop your project at this point, you will not have wasted too much of your time and effort. The next phase of the case writing process – the information collection – will require heavy investments (mostly time, but possibly also financial resources) from you and should only be initiated if this is really a case that you will produce and publish.

We recommend the following pragmatic check: Give your entire case outline – i.e., title, opening paragraph, description of case study structure and planned content per section, the closing paragraph and a preliminary list of possible exhibits – to several people (students, colleagues, peers, etc.) and ask them the following questions:

1. Does this opening paragraph and case study outline make you interested in reading more/the entire case? (Ask for a ranking from 1 [no interest] to 5 [very interested].)
2. How would you respond to the immediate issue (i.e., what would you do if you were in the position of the protagonist – and only on the basis of the very limited information available from the case outline)?
3. What do you think are the intended learning objectives of this case?
4. Do you have any suggestions, feedback, or recommendations regarding the case outline?

Then, first check if there is sufficient interest in your case. Would the test readers of the case outline like to read more? If no, did you get any suggestions to present the lead in a possibly more appealing way? If your test readers are not really excited and if you do not get suggestions on how to present the case in a better way, seriously consider dropping this particular case lead overall! Instead of investing more time into researching and writing the case, actively look for a better case lead instead! Go back to step 2 and revisit 'Narrowing Down Your Lead for Your Own Case Study.'

If you believe on the basis of the feedback that the case lead is overall good enough, you should then critically assess if your choice of the immediate issue is strong enough to provoke debate and controversy in the classroom. Look at the suggested responses to the immediate issue. How similar are the different responses? If all test readers suggest the same or even very similar decisions or actions, you should revisit step 3 (selecting the immediate issue). This is especially true, if the test readers' responses converge toward the decision or action that the protagonist or organization really chose. A case along this case outline would probably lead to a very boring case discussion, all would agree and there would be little surprise at the end (unless you intend to write a 'rabbit out of the hat' case, where the protagonist's or organization's action turned out to be bad). So, go back to the sections 'Defining the Timeline and Possible Cutoff Point(s)' (page 147) and 'Selecting the Immediate Issue(s)' (page 149).

Information collection

With the production of the case outline, you should have assembled a comprehensive list of information that you already have and information that you still need to finish the case. Now you need to go on the hunt! Most of the investigation and research that you will need to do for your case study will be:

1. desk research, or
2. interviews.

Much more rarely, other types of information collection might also be applicable (but usually only in specific situations).

Just by researching publicly available information and talking to the key stakeholders (especially the protagonist) of your case study, you should be able to put together most of the case.

Desk-based data collection and research

> 'Research is to see what everybody has seen and think what nobody has thought.' – Albert Szent-Györgyi (in Bioenergetics, 1957, modifying a quote from Arthur Schopenhauer)

Collect as much *relevant* data as possible. You will not need to include all this information in your finished case but you should do intensive desk research first. With more background knowledge, you will then be more informed and authoritative when:

- interviewing key figures in the case,
- writing the case,
- teaching the case.

The need to do research and collect data applies to all types of case – whether you plan to write a field-based case in close collaboration with a company and individual(s), a disguised case based on a real situation, or an entirely fictional case based on general experience, sometimes called 'armchair' cases. All cases benefit from being grounded in reality.

Why do the work?

Your case must be strongly related to or based on reality. Why? Because participants in the classroom who are studying your case must be able to anticipate and analyze situations and challenges that they will come across in real life. So, after preparing your case outline, your next step should be to carry out in-depth research into the larger context of the case. This is true even if your initial lead comes from a real person. Do not immediately jump to relying on your protagonist as the sole or main source of investigation. You should instead first qualify your lead by conducting background research and data collection. As in any good research project, be critical with your data and sources of information!

Always complete your desk-based data collection and research before interviewing key players in the case, including, most importantly, the protagonist(s).

Researching the organization and industry before doing interviews also means you will not waste valuable interview time. (Remember: your interviewee will frequently be high-level players with very limited time to spare.) Avoid asking questions that can easily be answered via online searches. This is even true for information about the protagonist (or other actors) as a person: Look for the CVs of your protagonist(s) on social networks such as LinkedIn or on organization websites or personal blogs. Speaker biographies prepared for conferences are often a useful resource.

Finding information

Very often, especially when writing about large organizations and/or prominent and topical subjects, a wealth of information will be available in the public domain (easily accessible, especially online) or in special databases.

Resources for your background research may include:

- Company information including websites, press releases, annual reports, environmental statements (corporate social responsibility or sustainability reports), and product brochures (*extra tip:* do not miss the investor relations sections of company websites, which often include extremely insightful presentations to investors).
- Financial analysts' and consultants' reports about the company or industry (the company's investor relations webpage will frequently list all analysts covering their shares).
- Studies, whitepapers, or databases published by different types of associations in the larger environment of the organization (e.g., industry, country, employer associations).
- News reports including print and online articles and features (check if your school has access to news databases such as LexisNexis), TV documentaries and current affairs programs, and blogs and other social media content.
- NGOs (nongovernmental organizations) or other stakeholder groups, for example: customer/consumer interest and/or protection groups; Transparency International for corruption issues (www.transparency.org); Greenpeace for environmental issues (www.greenpeace.org); the ILO, unions, and work councils; special shareholder groups; or other special interest groups such as participants in class action lawsuits.
- Academic research (this can be a good way to ensure your case will meet the educational need you have identified).
- Existing cases: check out other cases that have been written about the same company; same protagonist (this is rare!); same industry; same geographical region; and similar issues. This will also ensure you are not 'reinventing the wheel' by covering the same ground that is already explored in another case.

For all of these sources of data, also consider researching other organizations in the ecosystem of the organization (e.g., competitors, suppliers, customers).

From theory to practice with Martin

Very often, the initial data-gathering stage of writing a case can get out of hand because of the sheer amount of material available. You may start to feel bogged down and a little panicky.

However, this is where your case outline can be put to very good use as a filter. Continuously refer back to your case outline as you do your initial research and ask yourself the following questions:

- Is the information you are reading relevant to the specific issues you want to address?
- Is the timing of the information correct? You don't need to do in-depth research about events that happened after the timeline in your case (or significantly before the time of the case).
- Is it likely that the information would (or at least could) have been available to your protagonist(s)? If not, don't spend too much time on it.
- Last but not least, will the information make a positive contribution to the class discussions?

Always be wary when doing your research. The downside of having access to so much public information is that not all of it is reliable or trustworthy – particularly online. You must use your judgment and carefully verify all the data you use in your finished case. This is also true for information you collect from the organization itself (via webpage, other material, from your protagonist, other actors): whatever you get from there might very well be biased and reflect a desirable state of affairs rather than the organizational reality. Do not write fiction just to please the organization – ensure that you stay in the position of a neutral and critical observer.

Types of data to be collected through desk research

You must be judicious when selecting information to be included in your case. Below are some typical examples of data that can be useful to include. These will often be in the form of exhibits at the end of the case, frequently provided as background information rather than as part of the case itself:

- company's financial performance (frequently over a longer period of time to show trends leading up to the case scenario);
- organization chart (often used to show the relative position of the case protagonist);
- history of the company – it can be useful to present this as a timeline (see the section above on 'Defining the Timeline and Possible Cutoff Point(s)', page 147);
- process descriptions (for example, flow of products in the production process, flow of information, and approval or control processes);
- product descriptions;
- information about competitors, markets, industries, geographical locations;
- CV of protagonist;
- maps, for example factory locations, global reach and major markets;
- images to help bring the case alive, for example protagonists, products, offices, factories, and sales outlets.

Having done your desk research, it may be possible (and usually desirable) to draft a first version of your case before carrying out interviews. Just make sure this is not 'set in stone': your case may completely change in the light of your interviews! But by immediately translating your desk research into text you are getting in the habit of filling the sections of your case outline bit by bit.

References and citations

Cases that are written in collaboration with organizations usually do not need to cite the sources. This is because the validity of the information will be testified through the case release and because most of the information contained in the final case will be gathered during your interviews.

However, you will need to provide references for certain types of information you wish to include. For example, you will need to cite the sources of all your exhibits, especially for exhibits like pictures, graphs or tables.

Be clear about the difference between cases and academic papers: Academic papers include numerous citations throughout the text, but when writing a case it is necessary to strike a balance between academic rigor and readability. The main body of your case should not be sprinkled with references and citations. However, your teaching note will benefit significantly from detailed and comprehensive references to relevant literature. If needed, move references as endnotes to the very end of the document – avoid references in the text and footnotes as these tend to interrupt the flow of reading the case.

 A first case draft based on your research may offer a 'fallback' option if the organization you are working with decides to end their involvement in the case (for example, if your protagonist moves to another company while you are still working on the case). If this happens, the time you have spent on research may not have been wasted as you can now write your case based on the publicly available information you have already collected. However, make sure you keep track of all your sources from the start; this will ensure you do not include information in your case that is not publicly available.

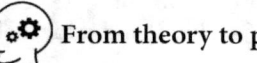 **From theory to practice with Urs**

If you copy the insights gained from your desk research into the case study outline, you might well have a quick and dirty version of the case that you could use in (low-risk) class contexts even before conducting interviews and without getting (preliminary) release. Sometimes, I just copy the main points from the case study outline into a presentation deck and use it as a short ad hoc case (i.e., without prereading by participants) as a very early test use (see page 212 below). Remember: fail fast to fail cheap! The earlier you can use your material in a test, the better!

While doing your desk research…

– Gather as much data as possible through desk research – but only information that you will really need (use your case outline as a filter!).
– Make sure your research is relevant.
– Do your research before interviewing key contacts.
– Be wary of public information: always double-check the facts.
– Consider writing a first draft based on your desk research.
– Don't despair if your contacts pull out – you may still have enough data to write a case.

Interviews

> 'The reason why we have two ears and only one mouth is that we may listen the more and talk the less.' – Zeno of Citium as quoted by Diogenes Laertius in Lives of Eminent Philosophers

Interviews with the key stakeholders – namely the protagonist(s), other key figures in the case, and other experts – are usually the single most important source of information. The thought of interviewing someone – especially someone in a senior position – can be a daunting prospect, particularly if you are an inexperienced interviewer. In your academic work you will probably have only a few opportunities to conduct interviews, unless you do qualitative field research. However, you will not go far wrong if you prepare thoroughly. Your ability to conduct a good interview will be of critical importance for your case – and this is why we will be quite specific and detailed about interviews (the following sections build upon Kassarjian and Kashani 2005; Leenders et al. 2010; Naumes and Naumes 2006; and Vega 2013).

Who should you interview?

First identify possible interviewees, then prioritize and categorize them. It is important to be selective and limit the number of potential interviewees as much as possible for several reasons:

- Fewer individuals from the company have to donate their time and effort.
- Lower opportunity costs for the company.
- Selected interviewees will feel good about having contributed if they are among the 'chosen few'.
- If you interview fewer individuals, you are more likely to actually use their input (and mention them) in your case.

As already mentioned, we find Kassarjian and Kashani's (2005) differentiation of case actors into protagonists/drivers, passengers, and bystanders particularly helpful. First, we recommend revisiting (and, if needed, amending or modifying) the full list of case actors as identified earlier (see the section 'Identifying the Protagonist(s) and Other Actors,' page 150). Then review the list of needed information (as identified while producing your case outline; see page 176). Finally, you should (tentatively) match the different actors to the information that you need.

It can be a very good idea to interview one or two passengers and bystanders first. You might learn some key background information that will help you ask the protagonist(s) more relevant and searching questions.

Before the interview

Prepare a list of questions that you want to ask for each of the interviews. You might find it useful to divide these into questions that you must ask (those that are critical for writing the case and to meet your learning objective) and those that are less important but would be useful to discuss or might help to add new perspectives.

Use a few easy questions to get the interview going but make sure you leave plenty of time to ask your important questions!

Do not waste your interview time with questions that can be easily answered via other channels or for which you could have done desk research! Minimize the total time you will need for the interview as much as possible. Concentrate on questions that only your interviewee will be able to answer with authority and that will provide key information for your case.

Always be clear about the date, time, and location of the interview and confirm the details with your interviewee (or, even better, with their assistants). Ideally, arrange to meet at your interviewee's office. In our experience, viewing offices (also have a look at the canteen!) and observing the real location at which a decision was taken can provide lots of additional information about an organization's culture (intangible, but helpful to know).

And, last but not least, ensure in your request for an interview that you explicitly state the context and objective of the interview and already specify the type of information that you seek and possibly also what kind of questions you plan to ask.

First impressions

Make sure you 'look the part' when turning up to interview someone. Dress smartly, smile, offer a friendly handshake and – this cannot be stressed enough – turn up on time. The people you are interviewing will be busy, perhaps only half-convinced that they want to take part in your case (the bystanders in particular will typically be less excited about the case production than the prominently featured protagonist). Do not add to their doubts. For the same reason, never overrun your allotted interview time – unless your interviewee specifically invites you to do so. Overall, make sure every aspect of the way you present yourself is professional.

Starting the interview

Concentrate on making your interviewee relaxed and willing to share information – do not forget, they may also be nervous. Concentrating on the other person will help your nerves too.

It is good to start the interview by (again) explaining your learning objectives and the purpose of a case.

Bear in mind that many if not most of the people you interview will not be familiar with case studies or case teaching. You might need to explain to them what a case study for educational purposes is and is not. Take a few minutes to explain that cases are purely pedagogical tools. They are used as a basis for classroom discussion about a specific business or management situation to help management students and executives apply theoretical knowledge in a real-life context. You can invite your interviewee to see the finished case being taught, and even take part and interact with students if they wish. It might be helpful to take a few sample cases with you to show your interviewee.

It is also important to manage the interviewee's expectations. Explain that a case concentrates on a specific problem or challenge; it does not aim to analyze the current state of the whole company or offer 'best solutions'; and it is not a marketing tool solely aiming at promoting the company or at presenting the individuals in the case as management heroes.

If possible, highlight the positive outcomes that writing and publishing the case might result in for the company (but be clear that these are not the main focus and may not be achieved). Some possible benefits that you might highlight could include:

- free input, advice, and insights from a management expert (share testimonials if appropriate);
- free publicity for the company;
- raising awareness among top-flight management students who may be potential employees.

You will be on a much stronger footing if your interviewees understand that they may benefit as much as you, if not more, from taking part in the case.

Explain the sign-off and release process. Be clear that the case will not be published without the company's written permission. This will help to put your interviewee at ease as they will feel more in control of the process. (But do not tell them that every single interviewee will need to give release! One release needs to be enough.)

Never forget that many interviewees will feel anxious at the sight of someone taking down notes as they speak; it is up to you to do all you can to put them at ease.

During the interview

Always be flexible with your questions. You do not have to stick with your original list and flow if your interviewee's responses provoke a different and more interesting line of inquiry. It is important to be able to think on your feet when interviewing.

Having said that, it can be easy to allow the interviewee to take over the interview so that all the time is spent discussing interesting topics that are nevertheless irrelevant to your case! Gently lead your interviewee back to the matter in hand. You can say, for example, 'I'd really like to come back to that point, but you hadn't quite finished explaining X, Y and Z to me.'

Be mindful during the interview that you will be hearing a mix of fact, opinion, and emotional responses. Make your notes as detailed as possible to record and reflect this (see also below on 'triangulation' in the section 'After the Interview,' page 193).

Bear in mind that a seemingly unimportant remark may take on more significance later; this is another good reason for taking plenty of notes throughout the interview (or if agreed upon even record the interview).

Note down what the interviewee says in their own words rather than your interpretation of their responses. This will ensure your record of the interview is as accurate as possible. It also means you will be able to use direct quotes in your case, helping to bring your protagonist(s) and other actors alive on the page.

Making a record of your interviews

Unless you are proficient at shorthand, taking full and accurate notes during an interview is an undeniably tricky business. However, it is a vital skill to develop. There are a few different options to explore:

- Take written notes.
- Use a note-taker.
- Take notes on a laptop, tablet, cellphone, or similar.
- Record the interview as audio or video.

There is no perfect solution, and the option you choose will depend on the individual circumstances and your preferences. However, beware of the following benefits and disadvantages of each of the options.

Taking written notes

It can be very difficult to conduct a conversation and take notes at the same time.

Do not forget to maintain eye contact as much as possible. Body language is very important. Ideally, your interviewee will be doing most of the talking and you will be doing most of the listening. But it is very off-putting to be speaking to someone who is permanently bent over a notepad, writing down every single word you say. You must strike a balance. You must engage with your interviewee and demonstrate that you are listening carefully with appropriate responses such as nodding, humming, echoing, or smiling.

Bringing a note-taker with you

This may seem like a luxury option but can also have its drawbacks. For example, you will need to be sure that you can trust your note-taker to record all the information you need, and in a format that you will be able to understand. Make sure that your note-taker clearly understands your educational need, the purpose and content of the intended case (see case outline, page 176), and what you hope to get from the interview.

Also, your interviewee, who may already be wary and nervous, might be intimidated by the presence of a silent note-taker, and it may be more difficult to build up trust and a good rapport.

When writing a case together with coauthor(s), you could split the roles of interviewer and note-taker either within one or across multiple different interviews.

Taking notes on a laptop, tablet, or mobile phone

Make sure your interviewee understands that you are taking notes and not replying to emails or surfing the net while they are speaking! Also, check that your equipment is in good working order and that your battery is not about to go flat. Always take a pen and notepad as backup.

Recording the interview

Making an audio or video recording of the interview can be a great idea. You will not have to worry about taking notes and you can concentrate on the interview. Plus, audio and video material can become excellent supplementary teaching materials (see also the section below on 'Additional Material for Facilitators,' page 233). However, bear in mind that some interviewees will not take kindly to being recorded or filmed. Always ask for permission in advance; do not just turn up with the equipment and expect everything to be fine.

Always get permission from your interviewees before using audio or video recordings in the classroom when teaching your finished case.

Small practical tip: When planning to use an audio or video recording also as supplementary material (or when producing a video case), ask your interviewee to respond to questions in full sentences that do not depend upon the question. For example, to the question 'How many years have you been with this organization?' they should not simply respond 'Seven years' but rather 'I've worked for ABC for seven years.' This will make the usage of the video quotes much easier, e.g., as a video supplement or when producing a video or multimedia case study.

Combined approach

You may sometimes find it useful to use two or more interviewing methods. For example, you may choose to take written notes while also making an audio-recording of the interviewee. This can be a good way of capturing key points while having the luxury of knowing that everything else is also being recorded for later reference.

Having a written note of key points will also make it easier to select the best sequences from your audio/video material for use in the classroom. (Practical tip: especially when conducting longer interviews, occasionally write down the time on your notepad, this will make finding the corresponding video or audio sequence much easier without the need to do a full transcript.)

Ending the interview

Save a few minutes toward the end of the time to give your interviewee an opportunity to add information by asking a couple of very open questions, for example 'Is there anything else you would like to add?' 'Which questions did I forget to ask?' or 'Is there anything we didn't address?'

As already mentioned, make sure you do not overrun your allotted time. If necessary, ask for a second meeting rather than go over time. Ask if you can contact your interviewee at a later date, for example via email, if you want to have additional information or need to clarify anything said in the interview (make sure you have their contact details, especially when the interviews of passengers and bystanders were arranged by your protagonist). Clarify the next steps with this particular interviewee, e.g., regarding follow-up interview or meeting (already try to fix dates and times) or regarding additional information/documents the interviewee promised to provide you during the interview. Then explain clearly what will happen next. For example, your next step might be:

- a further meeting with your current interviewee,
- interviews with other people in the company or stakeholders,
- site visits,
- additional background research, or
- continue to work on the case.

Being open and transparent about your activities will help to develop trust and good working relationships.

Reassure them that anything they said in confidence will not be divulged and that no information from the interview will be published unless the company has given its written permission.

At the very end, thank your interviewee – and highlight a few of the things that you learned during the interview – this will demonstrate that you listened but (more importantly) that the interview was a valuable investment of the interviewee's time.

After the interview

Make sure you write up your thoughts and notes in detail as soon as possible after the interview. You will be amazed at how incomprehensible they can become if you leave them for a week or two before going through them again. There is nothing worse than going back to your interview notes a while after the interview and realizing that you cannot decipher your own writing or make sense of your 'e-notes.'

Practical tip: use files with the exact same layout as your case outline to capture your notes electronically; this will make your life easier when later copying material to your case.

As already said, the insights you collect during an interview are likely to be a mix of fact, opinion, and emotional responses. Your interviewees might provide incorrect or misleading information because they might miss information, because they want to present themselves as heroes, for political reasons etc. – or you might just have misunderstood them. This is why the so-called 'triangulation' (see also Naumes & Naumes 2006) is of critical importance. Use later interviews to confirm or disconfirm the validity of information that you collected during earlier interviews. Do so by adding questions that will help you to check both information that you suspect to be not entirely factual but also selectively for information that you believe to be true.

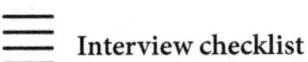 Interview checklist

Interview checklist: prepare – and be professional

- Decide (and carefully select) who you need to interview on the basis of the information deemed necessary in your case outline.
- Prepare your questions (but be flexible during the interview).

(Continued)

> - Decide how you will take notes during the interview.
> - Ask in advance for permission to do an audio or video recording (if necessary).
> - Make a professional impression and do not be late or overrun.
> - Put your interviewee at ease and explain the benefits of taking part.
> - Explain the release process.
> - At the end of the interview tell your interviewee what will happen next.
> - Write up your notes as soon as possible after the interview.
> - Use collected information to refine questions for other interviews ('triangulation').

Other types of research

Desk-based data collection plus interviews with key players will usually provide all the information you need to write an excellent case. However, be aware that other types of research are also possible and can occasionally be used to enhance the content of your case and/or teaching note if appropriate. This might, e.g., include:

- Direct personal observations, for example of customer behavior and product use, or the timing of company processes.
- Questionnaires and surveys (e.g., of company employees or customers. These could be carried out by the company or organized by you).
- Workshops or focus groups with any type of stakeholder groups.

After the information collection: does your case still fly?
At any time doing the information collection (most likely during the interviews), you might realize that the intended immediate issue or flow of the case (according to your case outline) is not really adequate anymore. The immediate issue might be too small compared to other (more pressing) issues at the organization. The way in which your contact/protagonist might have described the situation might differ too much from the perspectives of other interviewees. During the analysis of collected data, you might find massive inconsistencies, or the organization (which previously you considered to be a shining star) might be close to bankruptcy. Things like these happen! Instead of just rolling on, you should now jump back to your strategic decisions (see above page 144) or to your tactical choices. Do not try to bend the original idea to fit to the new reality too much. Critically reflect on whether pursuing your lead and writing the case along your earlier plans is really worth it. Of course, you can revise any of your earlier decisions, but will this really lead to a great case? Consider dropping the lead all together, before investing even more time and energy into a case that you will not really fit your educational needs.

Merging your research results into the case outline

The next challenge will be to transform your desk research and interview notes into the first draft of your case study text. You might be overwhelmed by the plethora of insights and information – and feel lost. But, thanks to the attention we previously paid to the learning objectives, translating the information into text does not need to be difficult. The key element to do so without a lot of effort will be the case outline!

We recommend using the following approach to merge your research results into your case outline:

- After having conducted your desk research, all interviews and possibly other types of research: write up your notes in electronic format.

- Use one or several separate file(s) to capture your research insights and use headers and sections to divide between the different interviews or sources of information.
- Include insightful quotes from your interviewees (especially when having made audio or video recordings).
- Also include tables, visualizations, etc. that could later be used for exhibits.
- Use the same template as for your case study text (i.e., the template/layout you hopefully already used for your case outline).
• Review all your material and search for inconsistencies and gaps.
• If needed, conduct follow-up research and interviews or ask for clarification.
• Amend your notes, if necessary, after doing more research.
• Then, reconsider the overall case outline and structure:
  – Does the intended case structure and flow reflect the real development or structure of the issues?
  – Did you find a possibly more interesting or exciting immediate issue, protagonist perspective, or cutoff point?
  – If necessary, add, delete or move sections; possibly revisit earlier steps of the case writing process. Jump back to the earliest process step for which you now decided to take a different route.
• Finally, go through your notes and copy bits and pieces into the respective sections of the case.
• Transform your notes successively and as needed into text.
• Fill in the blanks between the pieces of information within all sections of the case. Start from the beginning of the case and work your way to the end – like this it will be easier to ensure a clear narrative and flow in the text.

After having copied your notes into the outline and amending the text per section, you should now have the first draft of your case study. Congratulations!

Referencing and observing intellectual property rights

While copying the results of your research into your case study outline, you will need to pay close attention to proper referencing and avoiding infringements of intellectual property rights.

> 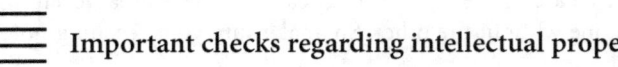 **Important checks regarding intellectual property rights**
>
> Did you make sure to:
>
> • observe all licenses and copyrights for material used in the case (this is especially important for visualizations in the exhibits; try to limit your search from the beginning to material in the public domain or with respective licenses [e.g., Creative Commons] – *practical tip:* Google image search offers filters by usage rights; most information from Wikimedia Commons can be used when following proper attribution);
> • ensure to avoid self-plagiarism (also applicable to teaching note!);
> • properly reference quotes and information from literature or other sources;
> • keep copies of all sources that you use, especially when writing a case about a real organization/person solely on the basis of publicly available information?

Getting preliminary case release

There is really only one way to proceed from a case study draft to a great final case study: You need to test it in class (see page 212 below)! However, to use a case in class you need to give it to your participants for their reading and reflection. As this will make your case (semi)public, it requires at least a preliminary release. Even though you will probably only need to get the signed release form later (when publishing the case), you should aim to get preliminary case release on the basis of the current case draft.

By now, you should have already had multiple discussions about release with your protagonist or the organization. They should therefore know what is expected from them and what they are entitled to. The best way of getting final release is to seek a preliminary case release along the journey! Use your current case draft (the version that you would like to share with participants for your test-teaching or with colleagues to get their feedback) and send it to the protagonist or organization. Then ask them to confirm in writing (e.g., in a short email) that they intend to give you final release as long as the case will broadly follow the provided material and that they are ok with using the current version in class or showing it to a limited number of people.

For that purpose, consider the following questions:

- Whom do you plan to ask for preliminary release?
- How do you get their buy-in (e.g., consider involving this individual during the test use of the case)?
- Is this person in a position to also give you final release – or do you need to (additionally) involve anybody else?
- Worst case: can you still finish and make meaningful use of the case (possibly also for the test use) without getting (preliminary or final) release (i.e., can you either write the case solely on the basis of public information or disguise the case if even preliminary release is not granted)?

Drafting the teaching note

'I touch the future. I teach.' – Christa McAuliffe

Your teaching note is at least as important as your case because it distills the learning objectives – the entire reason to write a case in the first place! Great cases have great teaching notes, and we believe you cannot have one without the other. So, make sure your teaching note is as carefully crafted as your case.

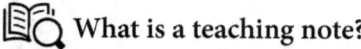 **What is a teaching note?**

The teaching note (sometimes also called 'instructor's manual'; e.g., Naumes & Naumes 2006; Vega 2013) is a document that describes the author's suggestions (and experiences) on why, when, and how to use the case study in the classroom. The teaching note is a document that targets other educators and should never be shared with participants. As well as the learning objective(s), it will (next to other aspects) include at least:

- a teaching plan;
- a thorough analysis of the issues of the case;
- explicit references to the theories, tools, frameworks and concepts that can or should be applied to achieve the desired learning outcome.

But, as you will see below, it will usually include additional items.

There are many good reasons to produce a teaching note:

- *Service to your colleagues:* The primary objective of the teaching note is to enable other faculty to teach your case successfully and to achieve the intended learning objectives. Writing a good teaching note can help them tremendously. Think back: Have you ever used a case without a teaching note? Designing a session using a case written by someone else without a teaching note is usually very difficult.
- *Increased demand:* Your case will have a much greater chance of being selected for use by other educators if it has a great teaching note. Without a teaching note it is sometimes really hard to know which learning objectives the author might have had in mind and thus how to use the case in class.
- *Formal requirements:* Most of the case distributors, such as Harvard Business Publishing, Ivey Publishing, and the Case Centre, will not accept cases into their collections unless a teaching note is included. The same is also true for most of the case study journals (they sometimes might not publish the teaching note but they expect you to have produced one). And, finally, at many schools, colleges, and universities the existence of a teaching note is a prerequisite for its acceptance and publication (and/or toward counting as a publication for your personal targets).
- *Improvement of own teaching:* Probably most importantly, writing a teaching note will also be of great benefit to you personally as it will help to clarify its educational use in your own classes. Through this process of reflection you will improve not only the respective sessions for this particular case but probably also your case teaching in general.

Take the time needed to produce a great teaching note!

At their most traditional, teaching notes are written documents that accompany a case. While these remain extremely effective if done well, it is important to realize that teaching notes are increasingly available in different and exciting formats that have been made possible by new technology. The following are just two examples:

- Two case writers, Senior Lecturer Ruth Gilleran and Associate Professor Erik Noyes, of Babson College, US, developed *video teaching notes* as a great way to engage faculty (see Gilleran & Noyes 2013; Reference no. BAB706VTN).
- Pierre Chandon, L'Oréal chaired professor of marketing, innovation and creativity at INSEAD, is the driving force behind his school's innovative use of *case websites*, designed to offer a wide range of additional information and materials about individual cases to case teachers. These may typically include an enhanced teaching note; video clips of the case protagonists or company advertisements; marketing or financial materials relating to the company; and even a video of the author teaching their case.

But do not be intimidated by these examples, especially if you are a fairly new case writer. A traditional, written teaching note, if done well, remains invaluable. And, once you have mastered the skill of writing a solid, well-structured teaching note, you will be perfectly placed to follow in the footsteps of these teaching note pioneers should you wish to do so.

Writing style of teaching note

Be careful with the writing style. The style in which you present your teaching note should be different from your case. The case will usually be written in a literary style. However, a teaching note is very different. A teaching note is targeted at educators and researchers and the style and content should more closely resemble academic publications. Your teaching note should be written in a very clear, factual, and straightforward way; feel free to use technical terms and jargon specific to your discipline. And, when providing background information about theory that is relevant to the case learning objectives, you will also need to reference and possibly quote relevant research in the field as in your other research activities.

Always remember that the teaching note is a peer publication in the sense that it will be read solely by other educators and researchers. Make sure your teaching note provides sufficient depth and background on the theories, concepts, and tools that underpin the learning objectives of the case.

Work in iterations and learn by doing

Possibly without noticing, you will already have done some work on three aspects of your teaching note: identification of target participants (see page 144), description of underlying issues and learning objectives (see page 144), and the teaching plan (see page 164). Alongside our case development funnel, we will not only revisit these three aspects but also work on some additional parts. Several additional aspects and the finishing touches of the teaching note will follow later – after test-teaching the case (see the section 'Finishing the teaching note,' page 225).

It is important to remember that you will not be able to finish a truly effective teaching note until your case has been tested in the classroom several times. Ideally, this process will include at least one session where you are able to observe your case being taught by someone else.

> We heavily recommend starting with certain elements of the teaching note even before test-using the case! However, a quick way to produce a big chunk of your teaching note might be to ask a colleague (or assistant) to observe and take notes during one or more of your case testing sessions. Alternatively, you could make a video or audio-recording of your session. Then you can use the overall flow and – much more importantly – your best questions from the session as building blocks for your teaching plan. If you followed our suggested process and have already drafted a teaching plan (see above page 164), you might want to use the notes or the recording as a basis for the further refinement of the teaching plan or analysis.

Whichever way you proceed and structure your work, be aware that your teaching note should be understood as a living document that is worked on in iterations and that only needs to be of publishable quality just before the publication. For now, feel free to leave many blanks, to work with bullet points (as opposed to full text), to use notes and comments, to have contradictions, etc. Right now, it is only important to get an increasingly clear idea on how to use the case in class, so if you see fit just pick some of the teaching note sections that we recommend below and leave the others blank for now, only coming back to them later during step 7 of the case development funnel: 'Finishing the Case and Teaching Note' (see page 218).

Structure

There is no consensus about how you should structure your teaching note. Just look at some sample teaching notes available from any of the large case distributors and you will immediately see that different case authors use different structures successfully. You can decide for yourself how you wish to structure your teaching note. However, despite differences in the specific structures and in the nomenclature, there are significant overlaps in what is typically covered in a teaching note. Have a look at the following list – either to use this structure or just for your inspiration:

> 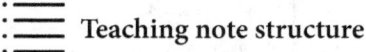 **Teaching note structure**
>
> The final teaching note could comprise the following content or sections (as distilled from many of great and best-selling cases as well as from other case writing guides, especially from Austin 1993, Heath 2015 [pages 92–93], Leenders et al. 2010 [page 140], Naumes and Naumes 2006 [page 86], Vega 2013 [page 83], and Weatherford 1995 [page 2]):
>
> 1. Case summary (sometimes also called synopsis, abstract, or overview).
> 2. Keywords.
> 3. Learning objectives and key issues.
> 4. Target participants and course context (should also contain information about prerequisite knowledge or skills of the participants).
> 5. Suggested participant assignments.
> 6. Analysis (can be included in the teaching plan and could come before or after the teaching plan).
> 7. Teaching plan (including discussion questions and suggested timings).
> 8. Board plan (can also be included in the teaching plan).
> 9. Teaching suggestions for online/hybrid teaching.
> 10. Recommended additional material for participants.
> 11. Sources and additional material for facilitators.
> 12. Other:
>   a. Outcome of the case (sometimes also called: Epilogue).
>   b. Alternative teaching plans.
>   c. Examination and grading.
>   d. Exhibits.
>
> You do not need to use these exact categories or headings in your teaching note but make sure you include all of the content (e.g., by merging or adding sections). Feel free to change the sequence if necessary.

Check whether your institution or the specific distributor or journal that plans to publish your case has additional or different requirements regarding the content or structure of the teaching note.

For now: create a new document in the desired final layout/template for your teaching note. Then copy the 11 (+4) section titles listed above into this document; feel free to merge, add, or omit as you see fit for your case. In the following sections, we will briefly introduce those sections that you should work on now. The other sections (which are less relevant for your own test use) will only be dealt with later. The following table lists again the 11 (+4) sections with an indication of the point at which you should work on them:

Teaching note section	When to work on	See more on pages
1. Case summary	Now: copy opening paragraph from case development funnel step 5; refine if needed in step 7	225
2. Keywords	Case development funnel step 7	226
3. Learning objectives and key issues	Now: copy from step 3 and refine in iterations if needed in step 7	227

Teaching note section	When to work on	See more on pages
4. Target participants and course context	Now: copy from case development funnel step 3 and refine in iterations if needed in step 7	229
5. Suggested participant assignments	Now	230
6. Analysis	Now	230
7. Teaching plan	Now: copy from case development funnel step 4 and refine now and after every test use in iterations	231
8. Teaching suggestions for online/hybrid	Now	232
9. Board plan	Now	233
10. Recommended additional material for participants	Case development funnel step 7	233
11. Sources and additional material for educators	Case development funnel step 7	233
12. Other		234
a. Outcome of the case	Case development funnel step 7	234
b. Alternative teaching plan	Case development funnel step 7	235
c. Examination and grading	Case development funnel step 7	237
d. Exhibits	Case development funnel step 7	237

1. Case summary

The case summary is a particularly important element of your teaching note as other instructors will use this to quickly decide if your case is a potential candidate for use in their courses. A poorly written case summary will drastically reduce the probability of other educators choosing your case. As well as being used in your teaching note, the summary should be provided to case distributors as part of your case's accompanying metadata.

Your opening paragraph already contains most of the important information that other educators need when considering whether to use your case: the immediate issue, the name and position of the protagonist, the organization (name, size, industry, etc.), and the timing of the case. When done well, you can now use the opening paragraph as the nucleus of your case summary (as creatively recommended by Leenders et al. 2010: 117).

Fill out the first section of your teaching note, by copying the opening paragraph into the case summary section. Then consider adding more information (e.g., about the context, the outcome, the underlying issues, or the overall learning objectives) as necessary for other educators.

 From theory to practice with Urs

This is an example of a teaching note case summary for one of my cases (coauthored with Johannes Habel) in which I 'recycled' the opening paragraph of the case study text and added a bit of context:

Around 6:00 p.m. on May 31, 2007, Urs Mueller and Christoph Burger from ESMT European School of Management and Technology were preparing for the presentation. In about an hour they would present their proposal for an executive education programme to the CEO of Energie

(Continued)

> *aus Deutschland Systems (EAD Systems) and two of his senior HR managers. Sitting in the lobby of a hotel in western Germany next to the main entrance of EAD Systems' headquarters, Urs scrolled through his notes and recalled the pitching process.*
>
> *ESMT's pitch to EAD Systems describes the efforts of ESMT European School of Management and Technology to acquire EAD Systems as a client for an executive education programme. The case study comprises two parts, A and B, which allow a comprehensive review of sales management in a professional services firm.*
>
> *We strongly encourage all potential users of the case study to carefully study this teaching note. The case has been written from the perspective of the case protagonist, who—as you will see in the analytical parts of the teaching plan—misses quite a few points.*
>
> *The appendix to this teaching note provides an overview of the case's main actors and the timeline.*
>
> The first paragraph is just copied and pasted from the opening paragraph. The three following paragraphs provide more information and guidance for possible other instructors.

2. Keywords

Do not worry about the keywords and leave this section empty for now – we will get back to it in step 7 (see page 218). But, if you already have a few keywords in mind, just write them down without investing a lot of time yet.

3. Learning objectives and key issues

The teaching note should summarize the learning objectives and describe the immediate and underlying issues of the case.

Revisit your earlier work (from step 3 'Defining the Underlying Issues and Learning Objectives'; see page 144) and copy it into this section of your teaching note. Unless you have changed them while working on your case, just leave them as they are right now. We will come back to them in step 7 (see page 218).

4. Target participants and course context

As mentioned above, we recommend that you prepare your case for a specific course context (see the sections above on 'Narrowing Down Your Need For Your Own Case Study,' page 141) and with a specific audience (see the section 'Defining the Target Participants,' page 144) in mind. This will ensure that you really need the case yourself. For the description of the target participants and course context in the teaching note, you will need to revisit these earlier decisions. But this can wait. For now: just copy and paste your earlier decisions and descriptions into this section of the teaching note. In step 7 you can then rewrite them in a broader way.

5. Suggested participant assignments

The overall purpose of providing assignments for participants is to create curiosity, suspense and anticipation, and to help participants focus on specific aspects of the case as they read and reflect on it. Participant assignments can help the participants to:

- better identify and understand the immediate issue (less so the underlying issues);
- anticipate the topics to be discussed in class;

- go through the 'short cycle case study screening' (see page 24); and
- prepare their own contributions for class (this is especially important for more introverted participants and for nonnative speakers who might need a bit more lead time).

Every teacher uses cases slightly differently. Some ask students to prepare the case before coming to class while others do not hand out the case until the start of the session. If your preferred teaching style is to hand out cases at the start of a class or jump immediately into the discussion without any prior guidance, you should still include suggested student assignments in your teaching note for those teachers who like their students to prepare before class. Teachers can then decide which approach they wish to take and will also have the option of adapting the assignments to their specific needs.

Importantly, the assignment questions should only be included in the teaching note, not within the case itself. This gives other instructors the flexibility to choose which questions to use with their own classes.

We recommend that you use participant assignments (especially questions) for your test-teaching. Accordingly, you should start working on this section now.

Guiding questions

Many educators like to give their participants a list of guiding questions to support their presession reading of the case (these questions will frequently be part of a course syllabus). These help students focus on certain aspects of the case and will point them in the right direction. We therefore strongly encourage you in every teaching note to provide a few questions that can be given to the participants together with the case. Most great teaching notes/cases have about three to six guiding questions.

Usually, the list of guiding questions starts with questions that address the context or the immediate issue. Then there will frequently be questions that transcend the immediate issue and point toward the underlying issue – usually without giving it away directly.

Consider sequencing the assignment questions roughly along the planned flow of the session (e.g., one question per building block of your teaching plan). The following sections of the teaching note, 'Analysis' and 'Teaching Plan,' can follow the same logic – resulting in an overall coherent structure and flow of your teaching note.

 From theory to practice with Martin

These are the assignment questions I included in the teaching note for my Bosch case:

a) As Stefan Tammler, would you bring the development of the new ABS system for the low-price vehicle segment to Yokohama or to Suzhou?
b) How would you assess the overall performance of the Suzhou development site and how would you characterize its role within the Bosch global product development strategy?

You will notice that the first question is a closed question: the answer is either Yokohama or Suzhou. This can be useful if the teacher wishes to take a poll at the start of the session to gauge opinion. There is, of course, also an implied expectation that the student will have thought about the reasons for their response!

Other participant preclass assignments

In addition to assignment questions, you also might want to include other types of assignment in your teaching note. Other preclass assignments are a good way to ensure that participants prepare properly in advance for the case session. Participants could be asked to:

- write an answer to a specific set of questions;
- prepare a case write-up;
- conduct additional research (e.g., about the organization, an industry etc.);
- view (online) videos;
- read additional material in connection with the case study (e.g., academic articles, textbook chapters, notes, news);
- perform certain analyses (especially applicable for highly quantitative case studies);
- create a PowerPoint presentation for the company's next board meeting;
- post comments and replies in an online forum;
- discuss the case with others in small groups; or
- prepare a role-play between case protagonists.

Particularly when writing a case in a rather quantitative domain, you might want to specify which analysis or calculations the participants are required to perform before coming to class.

6. Analysis

Cases that are complex in the analytical dimension (see the section 'Defining the case complexity' page 18) especially require guidance for other instructors. In the analysis part of your teaching note, you should perform a sample analysis on your own case that other instructors can then use as a springboard for their own use of the case in class.

Your analysis should provide comprehensive answers to both the immediate and underlying issues explored in the case. Remember: this does not necessarily mean either single right/wrong answers or the 'solution' that the protagonist/company finally chose.

You will need to perform a critical analysis of the issues at hand before being able to test-use your case in class anyway. We do not yet need a literary masterpiece (right now we are only producing the analysis for ourselves) but take your time right now and fill out this section. Make sure your analysis is detailed and thorough – at least to the standard of what you would expect from your very best students. And one final word of advice: before starting to write down text (even if only high-level notes), you should decide whether to present your analysis in a separate section or to weave it into the description of the teaching plan.

Separate or integrated analysis and teaching plan?

You can integrate your analysis of the case into the teaching plan section or present it as a separate section. We frequently merge these two aspects into one combined section, but there are sometimes good reasons to keep them separate:

- Writing a separate 'analysis' section might be particularly useful if the analysis of the case is complex and extensive. In such cases a lengthy presentation of the analysis as part of the teaching plan would disrupt the flow of the teaching description. Especially for highly quantitative cases it will often be more convenient to present the analysis first and then provide a quite short teaching plan, focusing on flow, timings, and key questions only. In such cases the teaching plan can sometimes be reduced to a single, short, and simple table.

- On the other hand, your teaching note may be easier to read and use if you manage to integrate the case analysis into the teaching plan if the analytical effort is not too high or if the analysis follows the journey from the immediate to the underlying issues.

 If you opt to separate the (extensive) analysis and the (brief) teaching plan, use the suggested student assignment questions to structure your analysis section. Sequence the assignment questions along the anticipated flow of the session of your initial teaching plan. Then you will probably not need a lot of additional work on the teaching plan that you already developed.

Frameworks, concepts, and theories

The critical benefit of including the case analysis in your teaching note is to highlight the frameworks, concepts, and theories that are relevant for your case. This is an important part of your teaching note to get right.

If understanding a particular (especially abstract) management tool is one of your learning objectives, you must include references to it in your teaching note. The same applies if your case is designed as an exercise/application of theories, concepts, and tools that have already been introduced before the session (for example, during previous sessions or through prereadings).

List all the applicable frameworks, concepts, or theories with a brief explanation and proper references to the relevant academic or managerial literature. Clearly explain why each is relevant and which aspects of the case demonstrate its potential application in practice. If combined with a teaching plan you might also want to include comments on how to distill (or apply) the concepts, tools, or frameworks successively out of the case discussion.

Quantitative analysis

If your case includes quantitative data, you should suggest ways in which this information can best be used. You should also include details of any quantitative analysis you have carried out. This analysis could then be shown in even greater detail in supplementary material to your case (e.g., spreadsheets) or in the exhibits to the teaching note.

 Be nice to other facilitators. We have seen numerous colleagues who have struggled to follow the quantitative analysis provided in teaching notes. Make sure that the data is complete and correct. Be detailed and specific in the description of the analysis to allow others to follow even if they are not deeply similarly familiar with the case, its setting, or the underlying tools, frameworks, concepts, and theories, e.g., consider using Microsoft Excel's comment function to explain certain formulas or the overall logic of the spreadsheet. Also consider asking a colleague or expert to perform the necessary calculations from scratch without having seen yours.

7. Teaching plan

The teaching plan will explain your suggested approach for teaching the case and how to orchestrate the classroom discussion. You already developed a first draft of the teaching plan for your case (see the section 'Drafting a Case Teaching Plan,' page 164).

 As a starting point: Just copy and paste your initial teaching plan (the table with the main building blocks of the session) into this section of your draft teaching note. Then consider the following recommendations and suggestions to improve the original teaching plan in iterations, especially when moving beyond the presentation of the teaching plan as a table. Consider producing text with a particular focus on questions, sequencing, and transitioning. Try to be quite detailed and specific. Every minute that you invest into improving your teaching plan right now will likely improve the effectiveness of your test use of the case.

> 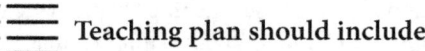 **Teaching plan should include**
>
> The teaching plan of your teaching note should include:
>
> - building blocks/sections by content in a recommended sequence (including intended learning objectives per building block);
> - questions per building block and for the transition from one block to the next;
> - learning formats;
> - timings; and
> - insights you (or others) gained from using the case in class.

Building blocks/sections by content in a recommended sequence

The most important part of the teaching plan is a breakdown of the session into smaller building blocks. There is no (and should not be a) standard structure. The building blocks and their sequence will vary from case to case and heavily depend on the overall learning objectives. Also, think about it from the participants' perspective: How much would you be interested in attending an entire program or course with multiple case study discussions, all of which have a similar or even the same structure? It is key to compose a structure of building blocks that is truly right for your individual case and the learning objectives you are trying to achieve.

You will need to specify the type, number, and flow of building blocks as well as the intended learning objectives per block for your teaching plan by yourself and there is only limited guidance that we can provide:

- *Type of building blocks:* On a very generic level, successful case-based sessions will usually have a beginning, middle, and end:
  - Beginning: The opening of the case discussion could be done in one or spread over several blocks. The beginning is usually oriented around the immediate issue but could also (usually first) link to the context of the case setting or of the overall course context. Typical activities in opening blocks could include (see also the section 'Opening the Case Discussion' in the case teaching chapter, page 54):
    - votes or discussions around the immediate issue;
    - reflections about larger context (e.g., about industry, country);
    - references to the personal experience of participants (with similar issues, the organization, etc.);
    - provision of additional material (e.g., lectures, videos); or
    - discussions around the larger context of the case.
  - Middle: The middle section will usually try to go deep! This is when you will engage the participants in activities that target the underlying issues and learning objectives more directly.
  - End: The closing blocks of the case discussion should aim to reinforce/anchor the learning and, especially in cases for executive education, allow for a transfer to the participants' reality. This can be done within the session or beyond, e.g., by including reflection or transfer activities after the case session (see also phase 4 of the 'four stage learning process,' page 42). If applicable, there will probably also be one short block toward the end to inform the participants about the outcome of the case, e.g., through the distribution of a follow-up case, via a short lecture, or a video.

- *Number of building blocks:* How many building blocks should you plan to have? There is no clear answer but, as mentioned in the case teaching chapter (see the section 'The Teaching Plan,' page 40), we recommend changing the learning format about every 15 to 20 minutes. As changing a learning format is most easily done when changing from one block to another, you might want to consider having *at least* four to six building blocks (plus possibly intro, transfer/debrief, and closure) for sessions of 60 to 90 minutes.
- *Flow of the building blocks:* The flow of the building blocks will very much depend upon the content of the case. But there are a few things to be considered in general:
  - *Immediate to underlying issue:* Most typically the flow of the blocks will move the discussion from the immediate issue in the opening blocks to the underlying issues in the middle or end blocks.
  - *Convergent to divergent discussions:* Very frequently you will start with building blocks of a more convergent nature (e.g., how to respond to a specific set of options regarding the immediate issue) and then move to more divergent blocks, i.e., to blocks in which participants can develop broader sets of possible actions addressing the underlying issues. Toward the end you might (if suitable for the subject and learning objectives) then come back to more convergent blocks toward the end.
  - *Case series:* When writing a case series or a case for use in multiple sessions, you will need to consider where and how to move from one case part or from one session to the next. This decision will usually be influenced by the lengths of the follow-up cases: if they are short, you can distribute (or summarize them orally) in class. If they are longer, you will probably need to synchronize the split between the sessions with the split between the case parts.
  - *Variable sequences:* Case teaching is supposed to be participant-centered. Accordingly, you cannot (and should not) fully predict and define the flow of the entire session. To leave sufficient flexibility while at the same time staying focused on the learning objectives, you can specify which building blocks should be followed in a fixed sequence and which could follow the participants' comments.
- *Content and intended learning outcome of building blocks:* Make sure to clearly state the content and clarify the intended learning outcomes per building block.
  - For each building block, state the content you want to cover (e.g., which issues, tools, concepts, frameworks, theories should be dealt with in this particular building block).
  - Mention the learning objectives that should be achieved in this block before moving on.

 From theory to practice with Urs

The teaching note for my case 'Anna Frisch at Aesch AG' (together with Ulf Schäfer) might serve as an example for the required session blocks including a variable sequence in the middle sections:

We typically assign the case with assignment questions as pre-reading, allowing the instructor to comprehensively cover the case in a 90-miniute classroom session. The session contains four major building blocks, with the core discussion (phase 2) allowing an in-depth discussion of important aspects in more detail:

1. Emerging into the case: Is Anna's change initiative justified? (10 minutes)
2. Analysis of reasons for failure (60 minutes for all 4 aspects and summary)
  – A. Anna's management of stakeholders and her understanding of the political context of her change initiative (20 minutes)

(Continued)

> - B. Anna's personality and influencing preferences (10 minutes)
> - C. Anna's communication (10 minutes)
> - D. Anna's vision, strategy and a plan forward (10 minutes)
> - E. Summary of failures (10 minutes)
> 3. Outlook discussion on what Anna should do next (10 minutes)
> 4. Update, summary and closure (10 minutes)

Questions for each building block and for the transition from one block to the next
Many of the best teaching notes are little more than a list of great questions. And, in keeping with the participant-centered philosophy behind the case method, it is really helpful to include a number of questions that will help other facilitators to:

- kick-start the debate;
- keep the discussion moving forward (especially to ensure a smooth transition from one building block to another);
- prevent the session from going off topic; and
- bring the session to a meaningful close.

How to come up with good questions? Please refer back to the section 'Asking Great Questions' in the chapter on teaching a case-based session (see page 61) for some inspiration on types of questions you could use for the teaching plan in your teaching note – and of course also for your test-teaching. Then develop a few questions for each building block – and pay particular attention to creating questions that will help you to transition (secretly or at least smoothly) from one block to the next.

Later, when test-teaching the case, observe (1) which questions worked well, (2) which might not have had the desired effect, and (3) which questions you came up with spontaneously that worked well. Then refine the questions on the basis of your practical experiences with the case in class.

Learning formats

It will usually be difficult if not even impossible to maintain tension, interest, and attention over 60 or even 90 minutes by just conducting one long full-class case discussion (particularly when dealing with large classes). Yes, there are a few world-class case teachers who can succeed like this but, if you are anything like us, you should plan to include changes in learning formats after approximately 15 to 20 minutes to be successful.

How do you do that? Review our section on 'Learning Formats' in the case teaching chapter (page 83) to get some inspiration about possible learning formats and their advantages and disadvantages. Then come back to the overview of building blocks. For each block try to find matches. Which learning formats will allow you to best (most effectively or most efficiently) achieve the desired learning outcomes? Just as a reminder, you have plenty of choice, e.g., class discussion, role-play, group work, student assignments in the session, or formats for consolidating the learning.

Timing

Last but not least, the teaching plan should include approximate timings for each of the building blocks. This is extremely helpful and important: When an instructor teaches a case written by someone else for the first time, it is usually quite difficult to plan the timings well. Before using a case in class, we just do not yet know how long a certain exercise will need, how long participants will need for a small-group assignment in class, or how quickly they will come up with certain ideas.

Of course, your suggested timings cannot be exact and will probably not be followed diligently, but rough timings will help other instructors using your case for the first time, especially with respect to emphasizing the different facets of your case: The timing that you allocate to the different building blocks should generally reflect the importance that you assign to the various learning objectives. More important learning objectives should be given more time – and do not forget to reserve sufficient time for reflections and transfer.

Approximate timings will also enable the educator to make informed choices about which parts of the case discussion to skip if time is limited, e.g., due to different session durations, other activities that they might want to include in the session, or on the fly as soon as they realize that they need more time than anticipated for a specific building block.

Practical considerations

You might also want to consider the two following aspects when writing your teaching plan:

- Do any of the suggested learning formats require special material (e.g., spreadsheets for calculations), technology (e.g., computer, printer, sound, etc.), or a particular room setup (e.g., group tables)? If yes, specify and highlight them so that you are well prepared for your test-teaching, but also so that other instructors are warned.
- How much time will students need to spend studying the case and related material? How much time will they need to do the participant assignments before coming to class? Sometimes this is useful additional information. You will know when to send out preassignments and readings for your test-teaching. And other instructors might want to use the expected preparation time as a criterion for their case selection.

8. Teaching suggestions for online/hybrid learning

Online learning is an integral part of business education. And cases as a very versatile educational method have proven to work very well in an online setting. Cases are being used in a vast number of online learning formats like (this list is most likely not exhaustive):

- pure online or hybrid formats;
- for entire programs and courses – or just for individual sessions;
- for synchronous and asynchronous session formats;
- for interactive and noninteractive formats;
- using hand-made e-learning solutions or highly sophisticated platforms; and
- with a few or many participants.

Given this diversity, it will probably be impossible to create a single, suggested section in your teaching note to cover all these different use options. However, you can still make your teaching note 'online learning friendly' by adding some or all of the following:

- Explicitly mentioning the use of online collaboration tools like Miro, Mural, Google Sheets, or tools that are integrated into Zoom, MS Teams, Google Meet or the like (on the general use of boards and how to describe their use in the teaching note, see the next point, 'Board Plan').
- Description of a possible online forum/discussion board structure including questions to stimulate the discussion (suitable for use with or without a synchronous online session).
- Description of possible small-group assignments that participants can work on synchronously or asynchronously, face to face or online in preparation for a distance learning session.
- Description of possible asynchronous elements before or after a synchronous case discussion session (and when/how to split these from the synchronous discussion).

- Description of (and adaptation of your case for) learning formats that can easily be used in distance learning with cases such as:
  - online polls/votes,
  - online (quantitative) exercises,
  - individual work assignments,
  - online role-plays (per video or via chats),
  - online tests/exams (e.g., knowledge tests before, during or after case session),
  - word clouds, or
  - discussions in pairs (just to name a few).
- Description of possible mini-lectures (e.g., video clips of you as the case author or by other facilitators teaching the case) that could be made available publicly (e.g., YouTube) or uploaded to an LMS/e-learning platform.
- Description of possible peer evaluation and feedback formats for asynchronous learning (specially to ease grading of online classes with large number of participants).
- Description of questions that are suitable for different types of online learning, for example:
  - Open questions for asynchronous formats (e.g., discussion boards/forums) or for sessions with only a few participants or hybrid settings.
  - Closed questions for synchronous formats with many participants as this is a good way to help manage time.

 From theory to practice with Martin

In the teaching note for my case 'Driving Digital Transformation at Faurecia' (together with Joe Peppard) I added a section called 'Ideas for online teaching.' This section had two main parts. In the first part I made general comments on using case studies in an online setting. In the second part I gave specific examples on teaching the case study online. Below are some examples of suggestions that we gave:

- The first discussion can be led in exactly the same way as with an in-classroom session. We recommend not sharing any slides and to have the gallery view to see as many participants as possible (perhaps consider having a second screen). The instructor should take some notes on a second device like a laptop or tablet computer where we advise using a simple table (three columns like the board layout in the exhibits), either in a MS PowerPoint or MS Word document.
- To kick-start the discussion of the second question, the instructor can announce that they want every participant to share one specific initiative (and only one) in the chat. One fun way to do this is to say that the participants have one minute to think and chose their favorite initiative. Nobody is allowed to write in the chat yet. After one minute you ask everybody to type in their choice but not hit the enter button yet. By counting down from three, you ask everybody to hit the enter button at zero and all answers will appear at the same time. The instructor can then quickly check if everybody has participated and potentially encourage those who have not. After this the instructor can pick different initiatives and ask the participant who submitted it to quickly explain the initiative and why they think that it was important.
- To change the format again, we suggest having a quick group discussion in randomized breakout groups of four participants. The task should be: How do the initiatives launched by René at Faurecia match with the capabilities framework of Bonnet/Westerman? And this question should be discussed in these breakout groups.

Please feel free to share with us innovative approaches of using case studies online with us for future editions of this book.

9. Board plan

The board (blackboard, whiteboard, flipchart, metaplan, electronic note board, screen on which you can write, and of course also the many available online boards like Miro, Mural, and Google Sheets) is a simple yet extremely powerful tool in the classroom. The board can:

- bring structure to the discussion;
- be used to distill the underlying frameworks, concepts, theories or tools out of the individual contributions of the participants;
- serve as acknowledgment of the participants' contribution;
- offer a reminder to the teacher as they move the discussion along; and
- provide a basis for a permanent record (e.g., if students wish to take pictures at the end of the session or if you can send them notes from electronic boards).

Accordingly, your teaching note should include hints and tips on how best to use the board when teaching your case. You should start drawing your board plans now. This way you can use them for the teaching note, and as preparation for your first test use of the case.

The board plan section of your teaching note will usually be little more than a graphical representation of how you recommend using the board. But you can also add a bit of descriptive text that, for example, mentions which parts of the discussion you typically capture or do not capture on the board and why.

It is also helpful to explain how to fill the overall board plan structure. You might want to specify not only what to capture where but also how: Do linear lists work best at some points during the discussion? Or simple notes to capture the main thoughts and ideas? How do you organize and present two sides of an argument? Or the pros and cons of different alternatives?

 From theory to practice with Martin

Below is a very simple example of my suggested use of the blackboard for initial classroom discussions when using my Bosch case ('Global Product Development Strategy at Bosch: Selecting a Development Site for the New Low-Cost ABS Platform'). This summarizes the pros and cons of each potential development location:

Suzhou	Yokohama
• Close to the target market, customer insight	• Proven track record (development of motorcycle ABS platform)
• Engineering capabilities (low-cost engineering, low-cost mindset)	• Strong technical expertise
• Highly motivated team	• Size of the development site (300 engineers compared to about 70 engineers in Suzhou)
• Li Chen (native-born Chinese, deep product knowledge, good access to Chinese customers)	• Robert Hellwach (head of engineering), German-born, long tenure within Bosch, good networks to lead development
• Labor costs (the average cost of an engineer in China in 2008 was 40% of the average cost of an engineer in Japan)	

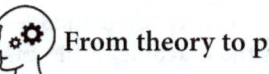 From theory to practice with Urs

I just love to use the board to distill the intended learning outcome of participant comments. Whenever using certain frameworks, theories, or tools that have a visual representation, I frequently write down participant comments alongside the anticipated concept. Later, I can then introduce the concepts or ask the participants to make sense of my notes. Here is an example of a quite complex board plan from the teaching note of my case study 'Magellan versus Quesada: To Mutiny or Not to Mutiny?'

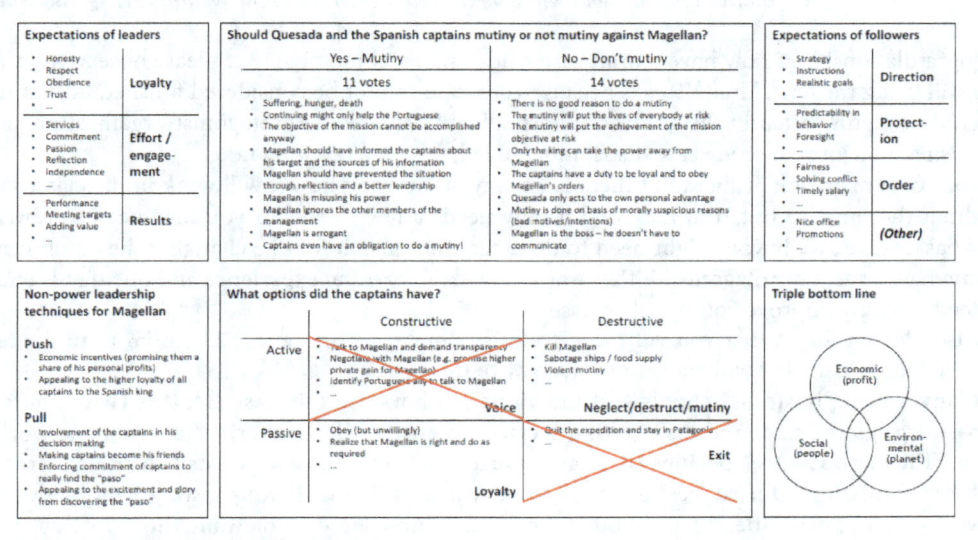

Figure 27: Example for board plan.

You can include your board plan either as part of the main teaching plan, or as a separate section. Some case authors also just refer to the board plan in the teaching plan and then add a graphical representation of the board plan to the exhibits in the teaching note. Just make sure to include some ideas about visualization and note-taking – many case teachers make heavy use of board plans found in teaching notes, so do not disappoint them.

All the other sections ('Recommended Additional Material for Participants'; 'Sources and Additional Materials for Educators'; 'Other') will be dealt with later in step 7 of the case development funnel. You do not need to invest a lot of time on this right now.

The teaching note: a checklist

- Start early: write your teaching note and case in parallel.
- Have a clear structure to ensure you include everything.
- Work in iterations and fill out the different teaching note sections as you go.
- Write in 'teaching note style' (remember: your audience is usually fellow academics and educators).
- Grab photos of whiteboards and flipcharts after test sessions (consider video- or audio-recording the entire sessions as the basis for great questions in the teaching plan section).

(Continued)

> – List all the management tools, frameworks, concepts, and theories that relate to your case.
> – Include extras such as an update about the outcome of the case, exhibits, or notes for online teaching and exams.
> – Check back regularly to ensure references and links are up to date when publishing your case.

6. Test-use case in class

'We all need people who will give us feedback. That's how we improve.' – Bill Gates

Congratulations! You now have a draft case study and teaching note. But please observe that we are still using the term 'draft.' This is because your case cannot be considered finished until it has been thoroughly tested in the classroom, formally released by the protagonist/organization, and published in a journal or via case distributors together with a teaching note.

Your case may look brilliant but there is no way of knowing how it will work in the classroom without the practice test. You may find it only needs a few tweaks or you may need to rewrite key passages. Possibly you might need to do bigger modifications, like changing the cutoff time, immediate issue, or protagonist. Either way, it is a great learning experience and one that is guaranteed to vastly improve your finished case.

Also, do not forget that you will need to finish your teaching note. Classroom testing offers invaluable insights that will help enormously with this task.

 Many leading business schools and individual authors use the Case Centre's (www.thecasecentre.org) global sales and distribution services to ensure their materials are available worldwide. The Case Centre specifies that cases must be comprehensively tested in the classroom before submission. Our suggestion: start as early as possible with your testing; you might not have many opportunities to use your case in class and we do not want this to delay your publication unnecessarily.

Select a safe environment to test your case

Alongside our rapid prototyping philosophy, we highly recommend that you start testing your case as early as possible, but, on the other hand, cases that are not yet finished obviously increase the risk of failure. You should therefore actively search for the earliest possible low-risk opportunity to use your case. But what exactly is a low-risk opportunity or safe environment?

At most schools you will be able to identify teaching opportunities that have less visibility and thus lower risk for your professional standing and reputation. These could include:

- alumni meetings (alumni usually come back to their schools with a positive attitude and mood; they might even know you personally and thus be more open to serve as guinea pigs; also, they probably did not pay for the meeting and might therefore have no/lower expectations);
- extra-curricular sessions for regular students on a voluntary basis (e.g., as evening session);
- replacement sessions (i.e., sessions where you jump in for a colleague with short notice);
- sales events (e.g., MBA fairs – especially events for less experienced students/participants);
- events for the general public (e.g., open house days);
- mandatory courses for less experienced students; or

- in the middle of well-running programs (most educators or course directors try to ensure teaching excellence especially at the beginning, to get into the right mood and flow, and at the end of a program or course, to make sure the last impression is positive; in-between it is less harmful if a session does not absolutely rock);
- teaching at other institutions (ask colleagues in the same domain to allow you to take over one of their sessions); or
- pro bono teaching (e.g., to NGOs, smaller executive education customers).

Use any of these to test early ideas of your case as often as possible!

An important consideration when using any such opportunity will be whether or not to tell your participants that you are using them as guinea pigs. In our opinion it is better not to mention this explicitly so that the participants focus on the learning and class dynamic and are not distracted by meta-considerations about the case. However, especially when only using a slide deck version of the case (as a very early test and without prereading), we have occasionally told our participants that we were considering turning it into a new case study – and this never led to a negative experience. You might also want to consider only informing your students about the test use after the case discussion at the end of the session. Either way, your students will probably infer that this particular case is not yet finished, e.g., because your case text might be marked as 'work in progress' or just because it slightly deviates from other cases they have read (e.g., no full copyright text, very recent date, no case number). We have never experienced any adverse reactions from students with either approach.

How to test your case draft

By now we have hopefully convinced you of the importance of testing your case draft as early and as often as possible. But how can you actually do this? Over the years we have tested our own case drafts in a number of ways, and we have also learned from workshop participants how they have tested their drafts. Here is a nonexhaustive list and we are of course interested in learning about more possibilities:

- Letting participants explore the story themselves (flipped classroom),
- Using source material (newspaper article, video, blog…),
- Short presentation,
- Case outline/mini-caselet.

Letting participants explore the story themselves (flipped classroom)

The earliest way to test your case draft or idea is to let students explore the case idea themselves by actively searching for information themselves before coming to the next class session. When the session starts, you can then test your opening question, how controversial the topic is, and in general the flow of the session.

Using source material (newspaper article, video, blog…)

Another possibility for testing your case draft is to use an existing, publicly available source, such as a newspaper article, a short video or documentary, a blog entry, or the like. Think back to where you got the initial idea for the case study. There might be a quick way to use the original source material that triggered the idea for a test. For example, the idea for the case study '"Do You Really Think We Are So Stupid?" A Letter to the CEO of Deutsche Telekom' (Korotov, Müller, & Schäfer 2009) resulted from an article quoting the entire letter; a quick test of this article in the class environment confirmed the controversy of the material and the interest of participants.

Short presentation

With a little more work, a short (PowerPoint) presentation, that is, a few slides, could be generated. Instead of using the original sources, a very short presentation (in our experience, this does not need to be longer than four or five sides) could be created that presents the key fact of the story, already structured in a way that will help in starting and moderating a discussion. This short presentation (as opposed to just an article, etc.) allows the instructor to make use of visual materials (pictures, organizational charts, tables with data, process presentations, etc.) – various elements to be considered as possible exhibits for a final case study. The case outline that you have already produced can be the blueprint for the presentation, with one slide dedicated to the problem, one to the background of the company, to the industry or wider context, and one final slide to present options or to serve as a kind of wrap-up. Depending on the topic, more details on numbers and background can be offered. This creates a level playing field for the discussion and you can shape the presentation to fit your learning objectives.

Mini-caselets

Another format to test case ideas in the classroom is to use the case outline as it is, or to turn it into a so-called mini-caselet. Mini-caselets focus on the problem description and just offer some basic background information. The level of detail is quite high, and authors do not provide a lot of data or exhibits. Again, the idea is to just deliver the basics to ensure an informed discussion, but things such as quotes, various perspectives, and detailed figures are not added.

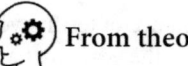 **From theory to practice with Urs**

As rapid prototyping is part of our case writing philosophy, I have often even used several of formats for one single case idea over time. For the case 'Deutsche Bahn AG: The Heartless Train Conductor' (Schäfer & Müller 2015) I conducted a first test-using the original newspaper article. For the next teaching opportunity, with a bit of additional background information, I transformed the article into a short presentation and then finally drafted the first mini-caselet. This way, I could test the idea several times in different formats to gain insights into how students reacted and engaged with the material.

Who should test-teach the case?

This is a matter of personal preference. You may prefer to personally 'test-drive' your case in the classroom, or you may find it more useful to observe someone else teaching it. Our recommendation is to use the case first by yourself. But please find below a few considerations to help with your choice. Pick whichever method works best for you.

Advantages of test-teaching yourself

- Personal experience of the touch and feel when using the case as educator.
- Increased familiarity with the case itself might help to improve the class session, e.g., through spontaneous explanations or additions if you only realize during the session that some information is missing in the case.
- No need to explain the planned flow of the session to a colleague when the teaching note is still a very rough draft.

Advantages of test-teaching by others

- Increased ability to take notes (especially regarding questions and responses).
- Mental switch from case author to participant of a case class.
- Additional input for the finishing touches of your teaching note: what was clear to your colleague from reading your draft teaching note; what was unclear/needs additional explanation.

How many times should I test the case in the classroom?

Cases are a bit like expensive business shoes – the more you wear them the more comfortable they get. And the more often you have used (and refined) a case the better the final product will be. But, on the other hand, who wants to walk around with worn-out shoes that have holes in the sole? Make sure to let go of your case at some point and just publish it. If necessary, you can still submit a revised version later on.

Sometimes great leads are picked up by several case authors simultaneously. Make sure you are the first to publish the case, but test your case at least three or, better, five times before giving the case and teaching note its final polishing! But, when you have time, you will probably still be able to improve the case and teaching note even after having tested it many more times.

Overall, make it a habit to refine your case and teaching note drafts immediately after every test-teaching. This has two main benefits:

1. You capture the necessary changes with a fresh memory of the improvement needs.
2. You will frequently only invest a little bit of time and effort per iteration, which helps you to cut the overall effort into small chunks and also helps avoid too much work for a case that might finally never get published.

What to look out for

When testing your case in the classroom, make as many notes as you can during (e.g., while engaging participants in group assignments or buzz groups) and after the session. Pay particular attention to the following aspects:

- Is key information missing from the case?
- Does it need to be longer or shorter?
- Is the structure or timing in the case confusing or misleading?
- Is there too much information, e.g., information that you don't use in class or information that might make the case too 'easy'?
- Have you chosen the right protagonist?
- Can participants identify with the protagonist?
- Does the case need another character's perspective?
- Does your opening paragraph work well (immediate issue vs. underlying issue)?
- Are participants keen to start the discussion?
- Are the issues controversial, interesting and relevant? Is there sufficient controversy and debate in the class?
- Is the case accessible for people of all backgrounds and cultures?
- Does the case take too long or too short a time to teach?
- Would the case work better as a case series?

> 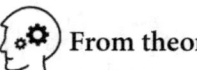 **From theory to practice with Urs**
>
> A fun example of what you can learn when test-using your case in class:
>
> As already mentioned, I wrote a case about the Portuguese sailor and explorer Ferdinand Magellan. A Portuguese MBA student (in an extremely international program) once complained that I had used the English version of the name, Ferdinand Magellan, instead of the Portuguese, Fernão de Magalhães. When confronted with this comment, I initially belittled it in my mind and didn't even remotely consider any change to my case.
>
> About half a year later, I then again used the case in a program in Brazil. All participants were Brazilian and I taught in English. Only one of the approximately 20 students used a simultaneous translation. The class went well – and I was happy, until before the next session one of the 19 students without translation complained: 'Why didn't you tell us that the case was about Fernão de Magalhães?' Only the student with translation really knew about whom we had been talking for 90 minutes. I finally accepted my first student's suggestion and added the Portuguese name at the first mention of Magellan in the final version of the case.

 Actively invite your participants to give you feedback. You are likely to get hints about typos, language issues, inconsistencies, misunderstandings, missing information, cultural specificities, etc. You might even consider involving smart students who gave you valuable feedback in the further work on the case as coauthors. At least be open to any criticism your case receives and do not take it personally. Use the feedback as a gift that will likely make your case even better!

Learning from test use for the teaching note

When actively collecting feedback from participants you are likely to significantly improve the case study itself. However, most of the learning from the test use will flow into the teaching note. The test use is mainly a practice test for your teaching plan and the validity/reachability of your learning objectives.

Immediately after every test use consider the following:

- Overall evaluation
  - Did the case discussion fulfill the learning objectives? Did the participants take away something meaningful?
  - Did the case match your expectations in terms of excitement, engagement and learning outcomes?
  - Did the discussion allow for the discovery, application, critical review of the expected theories/concepts/frameworks?
- Timing
  - Was the timing realistic (globally but also looking at the timing of individual building blocks)?
  - Which building blocks took longer? Which building blocks were done faster? Which building blocks did you have to skip due to lack of time?
  - Was the timing in class better or worse than planned?
- Content
  - Was there too much content, was there too little content, or was the quantity just about right?
  - Unpack next time if needed (i.e., if you did not cover all content) and just leave out some topics.

- Write down topics that came up unexpectedly and should be added to the teaching note.
- Questions (and responses)
  - Which questions worked well by advancing the discussions, which didn't?
  - Write down great additional questions that came to your mind while teaching or afterwards.
  - Also note down some of the most remarkable, unexpected responses.
- Flow and sequence
  - Did the flow from one section to another feel natural or did you need a heavy transition?
  - Could rearranging the flow of building blocks help to ease the transitions?
- Participation
  - Did many different students contribute to the case discussion?
  - Were they engaged and excited?
- Learning formats
  - Which of the learning formats (e.g., votes, group work, role-play, full-class discussion) worked well and for which part of the session? Which did not work well?
  - What other learning formats could be used?
- Materials
  - Did the material add value to the discussion?
  - Did your note-taking on the board make sense (when you look at it critically)?

As already mentioned before, it is a good idea to grab a photographic record of all the notes made on a board during your case testing sessions. These will be a good aide-memoire and can provide an excellent basis for your teaching note. Additionally, you might want to consider asking someone else (a coauthor, assistant, colleague, etc.) to sit in and take notes or to just video-record the entire session to properly review the strength and weaknesses of the case, the case discussion and your teaching style.

Did the case really result in the type of discussion and achieve its intended learning outcome?

By now you will have probably invested quite some effort into your case and teaching note. But the good old 20/80 rule also applies to cases: with only 20% of the effort, you will have achieved an 80% result. (Do not pin us down on the numbers; you will likely have invested more than 20% of the effort at this point, but you will get the idea.) During the next steps, you will still need to do a lot of work – but the final product will change less visibly. So, this is a good time for a final 'fail fast pit stop': If through critical reflection you realize that this is not going to end in a final product that you will be proud of and that you will (frequently) use in your own classes, stop now! But, once you have successfully tested your class a few times, you should also go the last mile and ensure you get it published.

From theory to practice with Urs

I once needed to design a new session about ethical issues and digitalization for an alumni meeting composed of senior executive education participants. Just a few weeks before, I had come across a story (in a newspaper) that intrigued me: An e-book publisher was criticized for having published a thriller from a serial rapist and murderer, who somehow managed to smuggle the book text out of prison. With a few weeks of delay, this led to a big public outcry, and many people called for boycotts of the publisher. This lead would allow me – I thought – to discuss the ethical implications of value chain reconfigurations with the elimination of intermediaries (as also relevant for organizations such as Uber or Airbnb.) I had a need and a lead.

I reached out to the organization through various channels to get information from someone who was involved in their final decision to delist the book, despite the fact that they continued to sell many other controversial books, such as Adolf Hitler's *Mein Kampf*. But I never got a response.

Given my pressing need, the low-risk context of the session, and my intellectual excitement about a truly puzzling issue, I decided to quickly produce a PowerPoint presentation, roughly at the level of detail of what we described as a case outline earlier – and used it as an ad hoc case in class. Overall, the class went extremely well and I got lots of new ideas for how to refine the case.

After the first test use, I reached out to several colleagues who – I hoped – could open the door into the organization for me. One of them strongly advised me not to pursue the lead, given the extremely violent back story and cultural sensitivities. I nevertheless gave the case another try in a very different setting: younger participants (regular students) and a much higher ratio of females in the room. Even though the discussion still went ok, I now realized that the case was probably just too drastic for a wide use and finally decided to bury it in a special folder on my hard drive called 'Dead cases.'

Testing your case in class

Checklist: Testing your case in class
- Choose a 'safe environment' to test your case.
- Test your case at least three times – ideally with different types of classes.
- Be positive about negative feedback: do not take it personally.
- Make lots of notes about the test use immediately after the session.
- Grab a photographic record of whiteboard and flipchart notes.
- Make quick changes to your case study and teaching note drafts – always only with as little effort as needed for a next, improved test use.
- If you face pushback or if the case just does not fly, stop here.

7. Finishing the case and teaching note

'I'd made it this far and refused to give up because all my life I had always finished the race.'
— Louis Zamperini, Devil at My Heels

You are getting closer to the finishing line of this long-distance run! Block a day or two in your calendar to get the prize for all the work you have invested so far. You now just need to wrap up by giving all documents the final touch.

Finishing the case study

'Begin at the beginning,' the King said, very gravely, 'and go on till you come to the end: then stop.'
– Lewis Carroll, Alice in Wonderland

Word of advice: do not get lost in endless iterations of improvement. At some point you need to let go – and remember: Your case study is first and foremost a vehicle for class discussion and learning. Your test-teaching proved that your case could achieve the intended learning objectives and this already makes it good enough.

But to be legitimately proud about your work and get the case published you should now:

- Make your case short!
- Check your timings.
- Get the title right.
- Conduct a final step-by-step review.
- Perform (or ask someone to perform) a final copyedit.
- Get final case release.

Make it short!

We strongly recommend you make your case as short as possible. This can take repeat editing – and it can be difficult to cut away sections of text that you may have spent a long time researching and writing. But the end result will be worth it – a diamond does not sparkle until it is cut.

And do not forget – none of the work you do while writing your case will be a waste of time. Information you leave out may be useful for the teaching note, as background information when you teach the case, or as a basis for a separate case or teaching note supplement.

Ensure that you do not cut out key information when editing your case to make it shorter. Include everything necessary for an informed and intelligent class discussion. If you have left out important information, this should become clear when you test your case in the classroom. Participants may point out information that they feel is missing from the case – but only add it to your final version if you are absolutely sure it is necessary.

After all, making decisions in business without knowing all the facts is a common and often necessary occurrence. These can be facts that the manager knows exist but cannot obtain, as well as facts that the manager is totally unaware of. This can be an important lesson for participants. The missing information can become part of the class discussion with questions such as: Is there any information that would help you make up your mind or change your opinions? How could the protagonist have collected this information?

Check your timings

Go through your case with a fine toothcomb and eliminate all information that:

- relates to events that occur after the point at which your case ends, and/or
- the protagonist will not have had access to at the time of the case.

We frequently observe problems with timing, especially in relation to information included in the exhibits. Many case authors try to use the most recent information in their exhibits, for example the latest financial statements. However, be aware that the timing of your case may mean that you need to use earlier financial statements, for example if your case is set before the end of the financial year or the publication of the annual report. Do not allow the credibility of your case to be undermined with timing errors of this kind.

Get the title right

Review the working title of your case. It is amazing how hard it can be to get just a few words right! You can start by asking yourself the following questions:

- Is it too long or complex?
- Does it give away too much, for example potential solutions?
- Is it subjective or judgmental?
- Does it create immediate interest?
- Is there just enough information to make participants want to read more?

- Will educators be intrigued and want to know more?
- Does it clarify the general direction the case discussion should take?
- Does it include other relevant information to create interest, for example the country, company name, industry, or protagonist?

Typical case titles that work well include reference to the protagonist, company, and/or immediate issue. Here are some good examples of case titles from several best-selling case studies (note how the colon punctuation mark improves the clarity and visual appearance of these titles):

- IKEA's Global Sourcing Challenge: Indian Rugs and Child Labor
- Amore Frozen Foods (A): Macaroni and Cheese Fill Targets
- BP: Putting Profits Before Safety?
- Thomas Green: Power, Office Politics and a Career in Crisis
- GE's Two-Decade Transformation: Jack Welch's Leadership
- Michelin Fleet Solutions: From Selling Tires to Selling Kilometers

Use these – and others that you came across and liked – as sources of inspiration. Then decide upon your final case title.

Final step-by-step review (by yourself and others)

Great case studies have a 'light' and easy appearance but are nevertheless not only the result of a great amount of effort (which should not become visible) but also simultaneously fulfill multiple, sometimes seemingly contradictory requirements. For that reason, we have compiled a list of criteria that you might want to use to perform yet another check. In this way you will be able to ensure you have not left out any vital elements.

Consider each of the following items carefully (building upon Abell 2003 and assessment criteria that are frequently used in different case writing competitions). You should be able to respond positively to many of them, even if a wholehearted 'yes' is not always possible. However, if you end up with a low overall level of compliance, your case may need a little more work.

Step-by-step review

1. Is it really a case and not just a story? Typically, a story can be characterized as one-dimensional; the aim is to simplify and offer a clear message. However, a case should offer different perspectives, have a certain level of complexity, and be a catalyst for rich discussion in the classroom.
2. Does the case tackle a relevant, important and current issue? This applies to both the immediate and the underlying issue(s). Both can quickly become out of date – but your case needs to be current and relevant. Consider shifting the timing of the case if the immediate issue has lost its current relevance. More drastic measures may be needed if your underlying issue has become outdated. You should consider writing a totally different case, although you may still be able to focus on the same organization and protagonist, which would allow you to possibly recycle substantial amounts of text and research effort.
3. Does the case have a strong opening paragraph? Is the opening paragraph strong enough to draw the reader in? Does it contain the necessary information about the setting and the immediate issue?

(Continued)

4. Does the case have a clear decision focus? Does it call participants to action?
5. Does it provide a voyage of discovery – and even some surprises along the way? Does it allow movement from a more obvious immediate issue to one or several truly interesting underlying issues?
6. Does the text of the case study have a clear beginning, middle, and end? Is there a narrative structure that is easy to follow and has a logical flow?
7. Is it controversial and likely to prompt participants to come to different conclusions? Does it at least offer multiple perspectives that can be validly argued?
8. Does it contain contrasts and comparisons? Does it, for example, show different types of behaviors, contexts, and strategies to allow participants to weigh the pros and cons of each?
9. Does it provide currently useful generalizations? In other words, while a case should be about a specific issue or issues, it should also offer the opportunity to learn some wider lessons, for example insights that can be applied to (ideally several) other situations, companies, or industries.
10. Does it have all the data required to tackle the problem? Not too much or too little? This should have become clear after testing the case in class.
11. Does it have a personal touch? Will readers be able to relate to the protagonist and 'step into their shoes'? Have you selected the right protagonist and provided enough background information to make them believable?
12. Is it well structured and easy to read? This includes various aspects such as the meaningful use of sections and headers, the layout, and the (usually almost literary) language.
13. Is it short? (By now it should be; see above!)
14. Is it innovative in terms of content (company, industry, subject area, issues)? What is really new about your case?
15. Does it use formats other than just text? Does the final pack (i.e., including cases B, C, D…, teaching note supplements, exhibits, etc.) include material in other formats such as video clips, visualizations, or interactive elements?
16. Is the information included in the case accurate, consistent, and based on reliable research? Did you check all data thoroughly?
17. Does the case have longevity? Will it be useful for a long period of time? (Unless your case is specifically designed to be used for a limited number of teaching sessions.)
18. Does the case allow the achievement of a well-defined learning objective? Is the learning objective realistic with this material? Is the case all over the place and not sufficiently focused with respect to the learning objective?
19. Is the timing of the case well chosen to maximize learning and provide the most interesting immediate issue? If a case series, is the overall story split at appropriate points in time?
20. Will it be enjoyable for yourself but also for other educators to use this case in class?

When you are satisfied with your case after going through the entire checklist, you should then get it reviewed by others. In some organizations and for some possible journals/distributors this will be a required step in the process. But, even if you do not need to get a review for formal reasons, we encourage you to actively seek it, as we have almost always experienced how significantly such a review has enhanced our own case studies.

Why not ask some trusted friends or colleagues to carry out this step-by-step review for you? Give them the case and the checklist from above and ask for their feedback. They will have a fresh pair of eyes and will be more objective. Make a point of asking them if they would like to use the case in their own classes. If the answer is no, ask them what you need to do to make them change their minds. Do not be disheartened: this is an invaluable opportunity to improve your case writing skills.

Finding the right reviewer is not an easy task. It is important to link up with someone who shares your passion for teaching and more specifically, for the case method. Ideally, find someone who uses cases regularly in their classes. Your reviewer should also be deeply knowledgeable about the topics covered in your case. And, of course, you should feel comfortable working with them. Another option is to split the task between two or more colleagues, asking each to focus on a different aspect of your case.

Final copyediting

You will need to give your case a final polish. Our opinion is that professional copyediting is invaluable. This is particularly important for the two of us as English is not our first language, and if English is not your native language we strongly recommend professional copyediting.

Even native English speakers will benefit from this. Not everyone is a great writer, and an objective professional editor can make a huge difference to the readability and appeal of your completed case. As well as style, spelling, grammar, and punctuation, they can ensure that the flow of information is logical and that even a nonexpert can easily understand your case. Ideally, they should also look out for inconsistencies in the formatting and layout (e.g., usage of currencies).

Check with your institution: usually there are a few internal or external copyeditors within every school's network. Your marketing, press, or publications departments may be able to point you in the right direction. If not, ask some trusted colleagues from other institutions who have written cases and might be able to recommend a good copyeditor. And you can always try searching online for professional copyeditors.

Finalizing your case

- Make it short!
- Check the timings in your case.
- Get the title right.
- Carry out a step-by-step review – or ask friends or colleagues to do it for you.
- Give your case a final polish – seriously consider using a professional copyeditor.

Getting final case release

By now your case is ready for publication – but still subject to the final release from the protagonist or organization. You should already have had multiple respective conversations and ideally already obtained preliminary release. But getting final release is sometimes still a big hurdle – a hurdle at which even many experienced case authors (including ourselves) occasionally fail. Make it easy for the organization to say 'yes' by submitting the final version only after copyediting, proper formatting etc. Like this the organization knows it is being represented in a professional context.

We cannot stress this enough: if your case is based on field research, the company you are working with must formally release the finished case (and possibly any other documents) as soon as it contains any information that is not publicly available.

Case release means that someone with appropriate authority in the company (possibly, but not necessarily, your protagonist) must give their signed permission for the case to be published and distributed. Their permission will need to cover all elements of the case package that are not already in the public domain, including items such as video material and supplementary information. You do not need (and should not ask for) release for your teaching note unless it contains additional, nonpublic information that is not already included in your case. More on the teaching note below.

We have touched upon the importance of getting case release at various points in the book. Alongside the case writing development funnel, getting case release is not a single point or moment in time but rather an iterative approach, and different activities that will ultimately lead to getting release should be done at different steps. Nevertheless, we will now give you the complete list of golden rules for getting case release, although you should have done some of them by now. This will make it easier for you to come back here to see all the activities from the different chapters in one place.

A few golden rules

There are a few golden rules to follow to increase the probability of getting release:

- Find out who has the necessary authority to give their signed approval for case release as early as possible (ideally already at the start of the case writing process). Remember that this may or may not be your protagonist.
- Bear in mind that your main case release contact may no longer be available when your case is finished, so always aim to establish a second (or even third) case release contact as 'backup'.
- Discuss the process with your case release contact as soon as possible. You can show them a copy of the case release document that they will need to sign when the case is finished (see page 224 for a case release template). Explaining the process and showing the document has an additional advantage: it reaffirms to your contact person that nothing will be published without their approval.
- Obtain initial approval from your case release contact to research and write the case. This is particularly important if your case release contact is not your protagonist but a gatekeeper to the people you plan to interview.
- You may need to explain the purpose of writing the case and the potential benefits for the company (see page 190).
- Once you have written your opening paragraph and an outline of the case, show it to your case release contact to make sure they are still happy to proceed. Keeping them in the loop throughout the case writing process will make it much more likely that they will quickly agree to release the case when it is finished. They will have agreed to different stages of the case, making it much more difficult for them to say 'no' at the end.
- Always be open to criticism and ask for input when double-checking facts and figures. This will help to build trust and smooth the way for case release.
- Once you have completed your research and interviews with key players, write the case as quickly as possible. Bear in mind that your case release contact may leave the company, or a restructure may mean they no longer have the necessary authority to release the case. The faster you can get their sign-off the better!
- If you feel that case release might be a problem, mark all those parts in the case that are based on interviews or insights you got from the company. If then you run into problems regarding the case release, you can check if the case is still strong enough without those parts (typically mostly direct quotes and exhibits). If it is strong enough you could consider publishing the case based on secondary and published sources.

> ### ☰ Case release made easier
>
> - Identify your case release contact (not necessarily your protagonist) plus one or two backups.
> - Discuss the case release process with them as early as possible.
> - Explain the purpose of the case and potential benefits for the company.
> - Show them a copy of the case release document at the beginning.
> - Get initial approval to research and write the case.
> - Show your case release contact the opening paragraph and outline.
> - Get preliminary release for the case version you will use for test-teaching.
> - Ask for input when double-checking facts and figures.
> - Finish your case and request final case release as quickly as possible.

Reminder: Try to avoid the need for release of the teaching note

You do not need case release for your teaching note unless it contains additional, nonpublic information that is not already included in your case. We even think that you should not reveal the teaching note to your contact or the company. Remember, the teaching note is only addressed to your peers and is part of your academic work and freedom.

It is best to avoid the need to get case release for your teaching note. Write a 'case B' or some sort of case or teaching note supplement instead! If you feel that recent developments, an update, or additional information are really important for others using the case and this information needs a release, think about producing a separate document for which you then ask for release.

Case release template

You can use the template below to request case release.

Check with your school or institution – it may have its own case release template.

> I [add the name and title of your case release contact, and the name of the organization] authorize [add the name of your school or institution] to use the case [add the name of your case; mention other materials if necessary, e.g., supplements such as videos or texts] for:
>
> - educational purposes
> - distribution to other educational institutions and/or individuals (including via third-party providers)
> - publication.
>
> The case is a fair and accurate description of the situation.
>
> I acknowledge that the case and all accompanying materials will remain the copyright of [add the name of the respective copyright holder, which might be you or your institution] and may not be reproduced without prior written consent.
>
> [*Signature of case release contact, plus name, date, location*]

If you do not get case release...

Do not despair if at the last minute, and despite your best efforts, the company refuses to release your case. It has happened to almost all case authors – and it might quite likely happen to you. It is possible, though, to grab victory from the jaws of defeat by (1) converting your case into one written from published sources or by (2) disguising your case. So all that preinterview research will not have been a complete waste of time!

If you have to *convert* your field-researched case into one written from published sources, you must be scrupulous in removing all the information you gained via interviews with company personnel or through documents that were given to you in confidence. Double-check that all the information that you use is publicly available.

Another potential solution could be to *disguise* the case. In the worst of all situations, i.e., if the confidential information cannot just be removed while still achieving your learning objective, keep the confidential information but change everything so that it is impossible to identify the organization and/or any of the individuals in the case.

Please remember that it is usually tricky to disguise a case (see the section 'Level of Described Detail,' page 163). You might initially think that this is little work but you will soon realize that, while it might be easy to 'lie,' it is difficult to 'lie' consistently and coherently. It will often not be sufficient to just change a few names; you will likely also need to modify many other aspects to ensure that the individuals and the organization can no longer be identified.

Finishing the teaching note

In step 5 we described the overall structure and main content of a good teaching note. If you followed our case development funnel, you should have already done a substantial part of the work. We did, however, advise you to only work on or finish several of the teaching note sections after having test-used your case in class. Now it is time to finish this important document. We will walk you through the necessary steps.

1. Case summary

In step 5 you already 'recycled' (and possibly enriched) your opening paragraph into a case summary. Now it is time to give it the finishing touches.

All major case distributors and journals require a case summary (or 'abstract' or 'synopsis') that will be used to describe your case in their catalogue. Always follow the instructions of distributors when writing your case summary – otherwise you might be forced to write it multiple times, one for the teaching note and several others for the case distributors or journals. For example, the Case Centre advises a maximum of about 200 words written in one continuous paragraph with no line breaks or bullet points. It then allows the addition of separate information such as learning objectives, topics, and settings. Look for the most restrictive requirements from all the distributors or journals that you target with your case. Then make sure that the case summary for the teaching note stays within the requested word limits.

The summary should include a brief description of your case and its context and should allow readers to get a quick overall idea of what your case is all about.

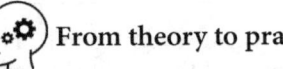 **From theory to practice with Martin**

Below is an example of a case summary. It is taken from my case 'Global Product Development Strategy at Bosch – Selecting a Development Site for the New Low-Cost ABS Platform.'

The case is set in February 2008. Stefan Tammler, head of the chassis systems control division (CC) of the German technology (and specifically automotive) supplier Robert Bosch GmbH (Bosch), has to make a decision about the location for the development of the new anti-lock braking system (ABS) for the low-price vehicle segment (LPV).

(Continued)

> *The case begins with a short introduction outlining the situation. It gives a detailed background on Bosch, especially the chassis systems control division. The main part of the case focuses on the global product development strategy, highlighting especially the two development sites in Suzhou, China; and Yokohama, Japan. Furthermore, the Chinese car market is described in detail, with special emphasis on the LPV segment.*
>
> *The case concludes with Stefan Tammler having to decide where to develop the new ABS system for the LPV segment.*
>
> *The case concludes with Stefan Tammler having to decide where to develop the new ABS system for the LPV segment.*
>
> Why is this a good case summary? It includes in a clear and concise format:
>
> - the date when the case is set,
> - the name and job title of the protagonist,
> - the decision to be taken by the protagonist,
> - the name of the company plus type of industry and geographical locations, and
> - a summary of what is included in the case.

2. Keywords

Keywords are very important as they will help people to find your case, particularly when searching online collections such as those held by the Case Centre or other distributors. Despite the fact that they are more important for the final listing in the databases of the distributors or journals, many case authors also add them into a separate section in the teaching note. This is good practice as it allows other educators to quickly get an overall idea about the case and the resulting sessions.

> 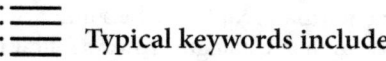 **Typical keywords include**
>
> Typical keywords will include:
>
> - the (academic) discipline (e.g., accounting, finance, strategy),
> - specific topics within this discipline (e.g., pricing, supply chain management, competitive strategy),
> - more specific information about topics, tools, concepts, theories, or frameworks underlying the case (e.g., skimming, strategic alliances, corporate social responsibility),
> - the industry,
> - the geographic region, or
> - the type of organization (multinational corporation, family business).

Aim to have three to 10 keywords (the Case Centre accepts a maximum of 15 keywords, which they call 'topics') for your case and do not only add them to the description of your case in case catalogues (distributors or journals) but also as a separate section within your teaching note.

 Some of the major case distributors require case authors to select keywords from set lists or might have limitations with respect to the maximum number of keywords that can be used. Familiarize yourself with these requirements to avoid extra or wasted work. Example: Harvard Business Publishing (currently) uses the Synaptica Taxonomy for keywords and topics (clustered into discipline/subject, geography, and industry). If you plan to publish your case via Harvard Business Publishing (usually only possible if your institution has an agreement with

HBP), you should try to use this taxonomy as the basis for your keywords right from the beginning to avoid extra work.

 From theory to practice with Martin

A good way to come up with keywords is to think about how I would search for a suitable teaching case that has the same learning objectives and course setting as my case.

Typically, I look for a case that fits into a specific course that I teach (discipline) and for a specific session. I will often look for a certain industry (because I know which industries I have already covered in the other sessions), and a specific region as I aim to have at least one or two cases that are based in the country that I'm teaching in.

Accordingly, you should include all those keywords that others might use in situations when they could well use your case.

3. Learning objectives and key issues

In step 3 of the case development funnel you specified your learning objectives and issues. In step 5 you copied them into the respective section of your teaching note, without much further work. But, after having used the case multiple times in class, you will now have gained a much better understanding about what can really be achieved or not achieved when using the case. You might also have discovered that there were issues and possible learning outcomes that you did not anticipate when starting the case (e.g., through great student comments or by reading more literature about the specific field of interest). It is therefore time to revisit and finish this section.

You can integrate the description of learning objectives and key issues in one single section (as recommended by us) or separate them into two (or even three) different sections (as suggested by Leenders et al. 2010 or Naumes & Naumes 2006). We believe that these are two sides of the same coin and accordingly find it easier to combine them into one section of the teaching note to avoid redundancy and overlap.

 From theory to practice with Urs

Why do we believe that the description of the learning objectives and the immediate and underlying issues should be combined? Let me present an example: In the teaching note for my case study 'Norman Nicholls at Seattle Management Consultants' I differentiate between 'teaching objectives,' 'immediate issues,' and 'basic issues.' But, even though I tried to draw a fine line between these three sections, the overlap between them is so large that I would now instead merge all of them into one single section of the teaching note as 'Learning objectives and key issues.'

Under 'Teaching Objectives' I list, e.g.:
- *Make students/participants aware of ethical dilemmas in business,*
- *Offer an opportunity to discuss corruption and blackmailing in business settings.*

Under 'Immediate issues' I list, e.g.:
- *How should Norman Nicholls respond to Jesper Lind's call, asking him to change the supplier evaluation in the outsourcing tender of Damotel?*

(Continued)

> And under 'Basic issues' I list, e.g.:
> - *Dealing with ethics in business in general,*
> - *Dealing with corruption and blackmailing attempts in business.*
>
> Are these bullet points so different that they merit separate sections? I do not think so anymore.

Review your descriptions of the learning objectives and the underlying issues and of the immediate issues. How much overlap do you see? If you see a value added from separating them into different sections of your teaching note, just do so. If not, follow our recommendation and merge them into one section.

Other educators (the main audience for your teaching note) will be looking for cases that match their educational needs. A proper description of the learning objectives in your teaching note will make it much easier for them to decide whether your case fits their needs or not. Accordingly, we believe that the learning objectives are the most important aspect in this section of your teaching note – and this is why we will start with them.

The description of the learning objectives should be as specific as possible. A typical list of learning objectives will usually include desired outcomes on at least two different levels: knowledge and skills. However, whether the emphasis is on knowledge or skills will inevitably vary according to the educational need that led you to write the case in the first place. An example of knowledge might be something specific such as 'learning about the pros and cons of diversification,' or your knowledge objectives may relate to:

- theories,
- concepts,
- industries,
- geographical regions,
- types of companies (family, smaller companies, multinationals, etc.).

 From theory to practice with Martin

The Bosch case previously mentioned focuses more on the 'knowledge' dimension of learning. Here are the learning objectives:

- to examine the role of low-cost markets for high-tech companies;
- to illustrate the growing importance of low-cost segments, not only in developing countries (especially the so-called BRIC countries) but also in developed markets like Europe and the United States;
- to explore the challenges of organizing R&D on a global scale;
- to discuss the different roles of home-base-exploiting and home-base-augmenting R&D sites;
- to examine the linkage between business strategy and technology strategy and how this is managed on a global scale.

Your learning objectives can (and possibly should) also cover the specific skills that your case will help to develop. These may include, for example, analysis, persuasion, judgment, presentation, public speaking, creativity, and critical thinking.

In addition to this rather broad-stroke differentiation between knowledge and skills, you might also want to (implicitly or explicitly) refer to the elaborate taxonomy of learning teaching and assessing, following Benjamin Bloom, as for example proposed in Anderson and Krathwohl (2001), who differentiate between six levels (see also section 'Question types by learning objectives' page 64):

1. Remember
2. Understand
3. Apply
4. Analyze
5. Evaluate
6. Create

For many courses you might have to state the 'assurance of learnings' criteria as part of your institution's ongoing monitoring of standards (often in the context of obligations resulting from accreditations). These could provide a good basis for the description of your learning objectives – and, if you need to use specific terminology, other possible users of your case might also need the same language. Standardized terminology can make their lives much easier.

 From theory to practice with Urs

As I teach and write cases mostly in the field of business ethics, many of my cases focus on skills (although there are of course important knowledge aspects). Let's take my case 'Axel Springer and the Quest for the Boundaries of Corporate Responsibility,' written together with Anna Hofman and CB Bhattacharya as an example of learning objectives that instead focus on skills:

The case exposes students to a complex situation that requires crucial decisions that might have the potential to severely backfire: Should Axel Springer feel responsible for the tainted resources used in electronic devices (especially electronic reading devices) that are needed to display Axel Springer's news digitally? Should they get involved in the issue of conflict minerals or not, and if so, how? Would Axel Springer's self-made association with conflict minerals cause the public to wonder about the actual linkage between Axel Springer and conflict minerals? To what extent would such an engagement have a negative impact on Axel Springer's digitization success?

Dealing with these questions and those below, the case is designed to enhance students' ability to:

- *weigh the pros and cons of engaging in a highly disputable situation and argue for or against action,*
- *identify and analyze stakeholders,*
- *put themselves into other stakeholders' shoes,*
- *assess and sketch scopes of responsibility,*
- *develop strategies going forward, and*
- *measure the success of CR activities.*

4. Target participants and course context

If you test-used the case in several different settings (e.g., with respect to different levels of experience/seniority of participants, in different countries/cultural settings, in different courses, or with different group sizes) you will have developed a much better judgment about the setting in which the case works best. Now it is therefore the right time to get back to this section of the teaching note and to rework the definition of the target participants and course context.

In this section of the teaching note, explain who your case is aimed at in relation to:

1. Experience/seniority of participants (e.g., undergraduates, graduates, MBA students, executives, or a combination of these).
2. Field of study/domain (e.g., business administration, economics, healthcare management, international policymaking).
3. Course context, including information about:
   - the general type of program (e.g., generalist or specialist programs);
   - the type of course (e.g., mandatory/core course or elective);
   - the relative position of the course within the program (e.g., beginning, middle, or end);
   - the relative position of the respective session within the course (again: beginning, middle or end).

   Examples: 'introductory case study for first session in core course on sales management,' 'summary case for elective course on mergers and acquisitions.'
4. Prerequisites in terms of knowledge and skills (e.g., ability to read financial statements and to perform ratio analysis)

This section could also include comments about your experiences gained during test-use of the case with any of the target audiences. If you observed relevant differences with different contexts and audiences, describe how the context influenced the flow and outcome of your sessions, and when and how other facilitators might need to adjust the flow of their session.

5. Suggested participant assignments

> ### Questions regarding participant assignments
>
> We recommend that you get back to your initial student assignments and update if necessary.
>
> Ask yourself:
>
> - Are the assignments still applicable if you changed the case, e.g., the learning objectives, the immediate issue, the cutoff point, the protagonist, or the level of detail in the case?
> - Which questions worked well in class? Which didn't?
> - Which other effective questions did you come up with in class that could also be given as assignment/guiding questions?
> - Is there a need to perform analysis or extra research before being able to discuss the case meaningfully in class?
>
> Then edit your assignments as necessary.

6. Analysis

Please review your analysis section (or the relevant passages of a merged analysis and teaching plan section) critically and modify if necessary. Consider especially the following aspects:

- changes to the case (different numbers, different level of detail);
- insights during the test-use (e.g., surprising discoveries by your participants);

- ease of understanding (can other educators easily follow your analysis and understand the link to the relevant concepts, tools, theories, and frameworks?);
- language and style: while it was sufficient to use acronyms, bullet point lists, etc. while drafting the first version of this section, you should now polish the language.

7. Teaching plan

Before finishing the teaching plan section of your teaching note, revisit your notes and refresh your memories from test-using the case. Then carefully review this section – changing or adding content as needed. Pay special attention to:

- timing and number of building blocks,
- general usability of teaching plan/building blocks,
- passing on experience.

Timing and number of building blocks

As for almost all of the previous sections of your teaching note, please revisit the suggested timings after having taught your case a couple of times. You will probably observe a need to modify some of the timings as certain blocks will have taken more or less time than anticipated.

Especially when realizing that you planned too many building blocks, you might want to decide to eliminate certain blocks. But that does not necessarily need to be a loss of work or ideas: you should instead consider moving these building blocks to a different section of the teaching note, namely to the 'alternative teaching plans' (see page 235).

General usability of teaching plan/building blocks

While you can (and should) be very creative and open with respect to learning formats that you use in your own classes (also for your own cases), you will – unfortunately – be more limited in the selection and description of the learning formats in the teaching note. Sometimes the way in which you teach your own case might be drastically different from the teaching plan in the teaching note. So far, the work on the teaching plan has focused on your own use of the case – legitimately so. But before the publication you should now critically reflect possible changes that are necessary when other educators want to use your case.

 From theory to practice with Urs

Let me share a few examples of learning formats that I use from my own cases that will typically be difficult to reproduce for others and that are therefore not reflected in the teaching notes of these cases:
- Visits: Do you plan to include visits to a special place in the usage of your own case? This will probably be impossible for others.
  - Example: I coauthored a case study about a snack stand in Berlin (Müller & Etzold 2012, 'Waltraud Ziervogel at Konnopke's Imbiss: Re-inventing a Berlin icon'). When teaching the case myself (and in Berlin), I tend to start on campus with a group exercise before going to the location of the case study. After enjoying their product, I then debrief the

(Continued)

> case on site. This requires a fundamentally different teaching approach (noise, no blackboard, bystanders, etc.). The teaching note therefore describes a session flow that is structured around specific frameworks/concepts/tools and is much more convergent than the explorative learning formats that I use myself when using the case.
> - Guests: Closing a session by bringing in a guest, ideally the protagonist, is usually a great idea – but most likely impossible for others.
>   - Example: I once cowrote a case (Müller & Habel 2015, 'ESMT's Pitch to EAD Systems') in which I am the protagonist myself. Accordingly, I'm usually easily available to bring the protagonist's perspective into the class and to update the participants about the further developments. Obviously, this will be different for other instructors – including for my coauthor. To bring the protagonist's perspective into the classroom we therefore conducted a video interview which is now available as supplementary material.
> - Samples/artifacts: Sometimes it is a great idea to take products, samples, or other artifacts in order to bring the case to life in the classroom, but it might be difficult for other instructors to obtain these things, especially whenever they are located in different countries.
>   - Example: I have a physical share of the German football club BVB including the coupons. Whenever teaching my case 'Defining the Purpose for Borussia Dortmund GmbH & Co. KGaA' (coauthored with Ulrich Linnhoff and Bernhard Pellens), I circulate the share and use this to quickly discuss the logic of shares in general before moving to my core learning objectives. It will probably be difficult (or too costly) for other instructors to use this learning format if anybody else chooses my case for their class.
>
> Therefore, you should critically reflect on all of your proposed learning formats to determine which will really work for others – and not only for your own usage of the case.

Passing on your experience

The final revision of your teaching plan is also your chance to share in greater detail your own experiences with teaching the case. Obviously, this is something you can only do well once you have taught the case a couple of times. But by now you have done so and might want to include a few descriptions of your own experiences with the case. This may include, for example:

- typical reactions from participants (helpful to prepare other instructors about what type of responses they should expect);
- potential areas of misunderstanding or difficulty (e.g., where did some participants simply get something wrong?);
- questions teachers should probably avoid (e.g., because they tend to lead in 'wrong' directions);
- how to tease out more obscure comments and remarks; or
- points where the discussion tends to go off topic and how to remedy this.

8. Teaching plan for online/hybrid

Similar to the teaching plan just above, you can now, after having potentially test-taught the case draft online, revise this section. You can also go into more detail and elaborate on topics like:

- What kind of technical setup did you choose?
- Did you experience any technical difficulties that you can share so that others can avoid them?
- Which specific online tools worked well, which worked not so well?
- Was the case teaching embedded into a learning management system?

9. Board plan

If you followed our recommendation and took pictures of your boards after every test use of the case, you should by now have a nice collection of pictures. Use these to improve the first version of your board plan from step 5.

10. Recommended additional material for participants

The more prepared participants are for the case discussion, the better their learning experience and the higher quality the case discussion will be. Therefore, it is important to provide a list of additional material that might improve participants' understanding of the case context and the issues at stake. This will be of use to your intended audience and will also enable facilitators to use your case with a wider audience who may be less familiar with some aspects such as the industry, geography, or legal context. The extra materials you recommend in your teaching note should help participants fully understand the case, its context, and the underlying theories and concepts.

Your recommended list of additional material for participants could differentiate between:

- additional material for (1) the preparation of the class or (2) for follow-up study after the session, and
- (1) optional material and (2) required material.

Typical additional material to be listed in your teaching note may include (not an exhaustive list):

- textbooks (chapters),
- academic or managerial articles,
- press articles (online, newspapers, magazines, etc.),
- company commercials,
- videos (e.g., YouTube),
- publicly available interviews with key players in the case, or
- company and trade reports.

It is important to get the balance right. In reality, it is often difficult to persuade participants to just read the case in advance of the session, so do not expect them to read a lot of additional material as well. However, easy-to-digest items such as short video clips (whether created by you or publicly available) are a good way to create even more interest.

11. Sources and additional material for facilitators

Make your teaching note as useful as possible for educators. A list of additional background information is an important part of this. This section should include a list with proper references of various kinds of material that will help other educators. Think about your own teaching: When using cases from others for our own teaching, don't we occasionally run into the same issue? We pick a case on the basis of key words, learning objectives, excitement about the immediate issue, etc., but realize during the preparation that, e.g.,

- there are individual concepts, theories, tools, or frameworks that we have never heard so far;
- we are missing knowledge about the (cultural, historical, industry-specific) context/setting of the case;
- we are afraid that our participants (especially when using a case in executive education) might know more about the case than us.

Help your colleagues to deal with such challenges, by including references to additional material! This section can potentially include a wide variety of materials, for example:

- relevant academic or managerial literature,
- textbooks (focus on the most commonly used),
- other books,
- background material to understand the context of the case (including reports, presentations, webpages, etc.),
- journal and newspaper articles,
- a case website (if you plan to set one up), or
- video clips.

 From theory to practice with Urs

I wrote a case study about a (possible) mutiny against the Portuguese sailor and explorer Ferdinand Magellan that happened in 1520 ('Magellan versus Quesada: To Mutiny or Not to Mutiny?'). This is obviously a rather special context and other educators might not know much about the overall story of the expedition or might be afraid of having history geeks in their class. At the same time, the case invites for the discussion, the application or introduction of many different concepts, theories, and frameworks from multiple different domains. It is therefore unlikely that other educators can simply use the case following my teaching note. Accordingly, the teaching note has almost four pages of lists of novels, books about expeditions, academic and managerial articles, webpages, etc. to help fill knowledge gaps of other educators should they wish to do so.

 Make sure you include clear, traceable and proper references and links to all the additional material you are recommending in your teaching note. It is vital to check back every so often to ensure that all the references and links in your teaching note are still up to date and working. For example, a book may have gone into a new edition or be out of print, and website links may be broken or the pages no longer available.

12. Other

There are a number of other sections that you could include in your teaching note, for example to cover the outcome of the case and/or alternative ways to use the case. All of them aim at increasing the variability of using the case – and thus will ultimately increase the probability of other educators using your case in their classes.

a. Outcome of the case

Participants frequently want to know what happened in 'real life' – what the outcome of the case was. But our fundamental belief is that the discussion and reasoning that takes place in the classroom is far more relevant than the actual outcome or developments after the cutoff time.

And, because participants sometimes mistakenly believe that the actual decision taken by the protagonist was the 'right' or 'best' solution, we sometimes choose not to reveal what happened (of course, we are aware that the information may be available online).

However, each facilitator who uses your case must be able to decide if they wish to reveal the real-life outcome, and so we believe this information should be included in the teaching note (or, alternatively, in a separate case B [which would require the purchase of licenses for use by others] or in a separate teaching note supplement [which you could then offer free of charge to other educators through the educator log-ins of the various case distributors]).

Remember that you can only add an update to your teaching note if the information is publicly available. If your case is field-researched and it includes information from the company that is not included in the case itself, you will have to get release for the teaching note as well! This is best avoided – because the protagonist or company might want to have a say about the analysis. This, however, is part of your academic work and should not be subject to third-party consent. Instead, it may be worth using any supplementary information you have from the company to write a case (B) or a separate teaching note supplement (see below).

b. Alternative teaching plans

Throughout this entire chapter, we have encouraged you to produce your case mainly to address your own needs. Hopefully, this will result in a case that works very well in your courses and classes and that achieves the desired learning objectives. Your teaching note, however, targets other instructors who might want to use your case in their class. And for them your teaching plan might just not fit exactly. Probably you have had similar experiences when teaching cases from others: In order to successfully use existing cases from case repositories, there is usually a need for some sort of adaptation and modification in teaching the case compared to the described teaching plan in the teaching note. This is usually due to one or both of the two possible drivers of changes:

- alternative timings (especially session durations etc.),
- alternative learning objectives (which can be driven by different settings or audiences).

To make the lives of other instructors easier, we invite you to quickly sketch out alternative teaching plans in your teaching note.

Your teaching note is an excellent marketing tool. And providing more than one teaching plan is a great way to maximize the appeal of your case. This demonstrates how it can be easily adapted, enabling other educators to use it for their own purposes with minimal effort.

Timings

The length, number, frequency, etc. of class sessions varies widely across academic institutions. It is helpful to sketch out how your case can be used in different settings. Many schools have standard session durations between 60 and 90 minutes. You will probably have used your institution's standard for the timing in the teaching plan. Now think about different settings and describe possible modifications, when using your case:

- in sessions of different lengths (longer or shorter), or
- over different numbers of sessions.

When reviewing other authors' cases for potential use in our own sessions, we frequently struggle with adapting the suggested timings. That is why we strongly recommend you suggest alternative timings for various scenarios. For example, offer a teaching plan for a single 90-minute session, and two alternative suggestions:

- one for teaching it over two sessions, and
- one suitable for a single 60-minute session.

The alternative two-session plan can include suggestions for making meaningful use of the extra time, for example by deepening the investigation of certain topics through additional learning activities such as group work, role-play, and presentations.

The 60-minute plan could suggest which of the building blocks are most easily shortened or omitted.

Learning objectives

As already mentioned, the overall purpose of the teaching note is to enable other faculty to teach your case successfully and achieve the intended learning objectives. However, always bear in mind that their intended learning objectives might be slightly different from yours. Because they will use your case in a different setting (different types of participants, different country, different course context, different position of session in course, different accompanying material, etc.), other instructors will probably have different learning objectives in mind.

To deal with this, you could provide alternative teaching plans, each highlighting a different learning objective. Alternatively, you just might want to point out what other learning objectives could be achieved when using the case and how this would affect the teaching plan.

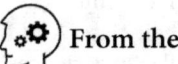 **From theory to practice with Urs**

An example of providing alternative teaching plans to accommodate different learning objectives might be the teaching note I created with Ulf Schäfer for the case 'Who's Responsible for the Drawbridge Drama?'

The teaching note offers different ways in which the case can be used to achieve no fewer than up to nine different learning objectives:

The case discussion may address one or several different issues and of course depends heavily on the learning objectives and time available. Out of the broad range of possible topics, we will focus on the following six aspects:

1. *The role of ambiguity in leadership contexts*
2. *The effect of reference frames*
3. *Working with cases/learning from case discussions*
4. *The psychological need to personalize responsibility*
5. *The idea of responsibility in business*
6. *The seemingly limited power of reason in moral debates*

If time allows (for example, if the case is used in the context of an extended programme or a session on business ethics or responsible leadership) the debriefing may go significantly beyond the scope of the case by introducing helpful terminology and models that might become more relevant in subsequent sessions. In Appendix 1 we will briefly present three alternative or additional debriefing options:

7. *Two types of ethical reasoning (deontological vs. consequentialist)*
8. *The 7 Cs (by Derek Abell) to avoid ethical dilemmas*
9. *Katz's debrief of the case in the context of anti-racism training*

The teaching note to this case then describes (in the appendix) didactical approaches for each of these additional objectives.

b. Examination and grading

In case-based courses, case studies are sometimes also used as the basis for exams. It can therefore be very useful to include some suggestions in your teaching note about using your case in an exam, and about how the exam should be graded. It has to be admitted, however, that this is not a standard element of most teaching notes; i.e., consider adding this section especially if you used your case for an exam yourself. (See page 123 for more on grading case-based courses.)

Instructions on how to use your case for exams and grading in the teaching note could include:

- instructions about when to read the case (before the exam; during the exam);
- allowed materials;
- closed questions that can be used to validate comprehension of the case (possibly including multiple-choice responses);
- closed questions to test the understanding of specific tools, theories, and concepts illustrated in the case (you could include sample responses);
- open questions to set an essay-type exam to assess analytical capabilities (you could include sample responses and the draft of an exam evaluation rubric);
- suggested total time for the entire exam and/or for individual questions;
- a grading/scoring rubric, i.e., information about:
  - expected/sample answers,
  - relative weights for the different questions and answers.

Make sure your suggested exam questions are not just duplicates of the assignment questions you have suggested as part of the coursework, for at least two reasons:

1. If your case is quite long and participants need to read it before the exam, the participants might just google the assignment questions and standard responses.
2. The suggested participant assignment questions should be written with the class interaction in mind. They will frequently be very open-ended, whereas good questions for exams should include some closed questions to ease the grading process.

c. Exhibits

As in case studies, teaching notes can (and frequently do) include exhibits. As with the exhibits in the case study, follow the conventions, i.e., call them 'Exhibits,' number and present them in the sequence in which they are referenced in the teaching note, present them at the end of the teaching note, and do not forget to include sources and references whenever applicable.

Examples of typical teaching note exhibits

Examples of typical teaching note exhibits include:

- tables, data, results from exemplary analysis (especially for quantitative cases);
- (visual) frameworks filled with information from case (analysis) (e.g., five forces or SWOT analysis);
- process flow diagrams;
- decision trees; or
- information (quantitative or qualitative) that is expected to be collected by participants as part of an assigned background.

d. Teaching note (or case) supplements

Finally, you might want to consider adding teaching note (or case) supplements. These are additional but separate documents that accompany your teaching note. There are multiple possible types of teaching note supplements, most of which we discuss at other places (mostly below), e.g.:

- presentation slide decks for use by other instructors in class,
- separate updates about the outcomes of the case,
- any other type of text document,
- videos.

When/why and how should separate teaching note supplements be used? Simply to help other educators, e.g., by providing more information. There is, however, also another reason: The use of cases from others usually requires the purchase of a license. These license fees are most frequently collected by the large distributors on a per participant and document basis. If you just write one single case study, other educators will just need to buy this one license multiplied by the number of participants on the course. Sometimes a case pack might include multiple documents (e.g., case plus update about case outcome, or – as frequently for negotiation or role-play case studies – case plus confidential information for multiple parties). In such situations, the cost of using your case increases drastically – and this might make other instructors less likely to use your case just because of cost considerations.

Digital instructor materials (teaching notes, teaching note supplements, etc.) are provided free to registered educators by case distributors. In this situation, a teaching note supplement (or sometimes also offered as case supplement) might be a possible solution: produce one main case (for which licenses need to be acquired) and move everything else to case or teaching note supplements that can be downloaded free of charge through the educator log-in of the large case distributors.

An added benefit of moving the outcome of the case into a separate teaching note supplement: You will not need to get release for your teaching note (as it now does not contain confidential information). And, given that the teaching note should be considered part of your academic work, this is how it should be!

8. Publishing the case and teaching note

Congratulations, you have finished your case study and the accompanying teaching note. Well done! This was the main purpose of the case writing section of this book. But we have two more optional steps left in the case development funnel: publishing and promoting your case study.

Some of you might only want to use their own case study and do not care about publishing it. But we suspect that, for most of you, once the bulk of the work is done, it makes a lot of sense to invest just a little bit more energy to publish the case and teaching note. And we promise, compared to the time and energy that you have already invested, this almost final step is not very time-intense and complicated, especially if you have followed our case development funnel along the way.

There are fundamentally three ways to publish your case, and these are not exclusive and can potentially be mixed:

- in your school's case collection,
- with a case distributor (the Case Centre, CPMA, Ivey Publishing, Harvard Business Publishing, etc.),
- in a journal (*Case Folio, Global Journal of Business Pedagogy, IMA Educational Case Journal, The CASE Journal, International Journal of Teaching and Case Studies*, etc.).

There are pros and cons for each of those and the requirements might be very different not only for each of these categories but even between the different options within a category. The only way to find out is to identify potential outlets and then go to the respective websites and check the requirements.

Here we will describe the process for publication with the Case Centre as one example. But even this might change over time, and it is best to check on www.thecasecentre.org/submissionrequirements for the most up-to-date information.

The Case Centre offers an online submission process. The following information/documents must be submitted:

- the case study as a PDF document,
- the teaching as a PDF document,
- data source (e.g., field research, published sources, generalized experience),
- subject category (e.g., entrepreneurship, marketing),
- topics (at least one, no more than 15),
- learning objectives (at least one, no more than five),
- abstract (it suggests around 200 words),
- author and copyright ownership information.

Important requirements:

- A signed case release form has to be supplied for all field-based cases.
- Case, teaching note, and all metadata must be provided in English. Additionally, translations can also be submitted.
- The case has to have been tested at least twice in the classroom (you will need to give full details of course title on which the material was taught, name of the institution at which it was taught, details of the educator who taught it, date when it was taught, and number of students in the class).

When the online submission process is complete the case will be available worldwide! It will also be listed in the monthly email update service. Congratulations!

9. Promoting your case study

'Publicity can be terrible. But only if you don't have any.' – Jane Russell

Your case is ready to be unleashed into the world! It has been edited, tested, polished, perfected, and published. So, what is next? How can you make your case stand out from the crowd?

We know many case writers who are happy to simply use their case with their own students. However, we would argue that, having put in the considerable time and effort to write an effective case, it would be a shame not to get more mileage out of it. We believe you deserve it! So, what can you do?

Spread the news

Here are a few suggestions and recommendations to spread the fame of your new masterpiece:

- Start with the basics: Spread the news about your case within your institution. Tell your colleagues about it and invite them to see you teaching it in the classroom.
- Do you have a blog, personal website, or official online profile? If so, do not forget to add details about your case.

- Are you on Twitter, LinkedIn, or any other social media site? Again, share news about the launch of your case. If your case has been published, make sure you tag the case distributor – they will often amplify your news through their channels.
- Does your institution maintain a database of faculty expertise? Make sure your profile includes details of your case-writing activities and related company/industry in-depth knowledge.
- Be sure to tell your institution's PR and marketing teams about your new case. They may be able to promote it on your behalf and will also bear you in mind when contacted by journalists looking for an expert in your field.
- Proactively contact newspapers, magazines, and journals that cover cases.
- The Case Centre regularly features a number of cases in its online newsletter (www.thecasecentre.org/connect), which goes to thousands of subscribers worldwide. Suggestions for inclusion are always welcome, so be sure to submit yours for consideration.

Give it a try: case competitions can greatly enhance your case's visibility

There are many case competitions held every year and a full list can be found at www.thecasecentre.org/casewritingcompetitions. If successful (and you will not know unless you try – we recommend entering as many competitions as possible), you will gain credibility in the classroom and among your peers, raise your profile (often internationally), and get some great publicity for your case and school. Most case writing competitions offer a financial reward to the winners – a great added bonus!

Enhance the appeal of your case

As well as actively promoting your case as outlined above, you can also take steps to make your case more immediately appealing to colleagues and educators at other institutions worldwide. One sure way to achieve this is to enrich your case with supplementary material.

Cases that include additional elements, such as slides, software simulations, video clips, extra tools such as frameworks and questionnaires, and dedicated case websites, are always far more appealing to educators than a simple standalone text-only case. Supplementary materials give potential users of your case more confidence as they will be armed with additional background information and a variety of materials to use in the classroom.

Most case distributors are pleased to distribute supplementary material alongside your case and teaching note.

Broaden your potential audience: translate your case into other languages

Many programs that are not run in English are now increasingly frequently using case studies. Consider publishing your case in other languages than just English. This can be for your own needs or to reach additional audiences. But be aware that the translation might need to specify content that is context-specific (e.g., currency, political situation, geography, company background, etc.). And, last but not least, do not add new information that would require you to get a new case release.

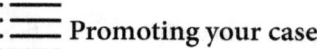 **Promoting your case**

–Spread the news: Do not keep your new case to yourself!
–Share the news online via your blog, website and social media.

(Continued)

- Tell your marketing and PR people.
- Proactively submit your case to newspapers, journals and newsletters.
- Enter case competitions.
- Enhance the appeal of your case with supplementary material.

Developing alternative format case studies

'Technology is anything that wasn't around when you were born.' – Alan Kay

Why a plain case might not be enough

As we have already discussed, the main purpose of a case is to create interest, foster curiosity, and stimulate thought and discussion in the classroom. Or, to put it another way, a good case offers the opportunity to embark on a journey of discovery.

This can, of course, be successfully achieved with a traditional text case study. However, we now have many other options available that can enhance or even replace traditional case formats. These options include various media that are commonly available such as audio, video, blogs, websites, online quizzes, games, and simulations.

From the inclusion of a basic video or website link to, at the other end of the spectrum, 'virtual world' cases created and taught online, technology is a fundamental component of many cases now being created.

However, in our view, technology should be the means and not the end. Always ask yourself whether the use of technology genuinely enhances your case and whether it would really be poorer without it. Do not add lots of multimedia 'bells and whistles' to your case just because you think you should or because you hope it will impress your students.

Also, be aware that technology changes quickly. For example, using or making reference to websites or other online resources might mean that you will have to revise your case much more frequently.

There are also challenges associated with distributing alternative format cases to a wider audience. You will need to discuss possible options with each case distributor.

Reasons to incorporate new technologies/media

Your target audience

In the section about 'leads and needs' in case writing we explained the necessity of having a clear target audience in mind for your case. In addition, you should also reflect on which media your target audience uses, how it is used, and whether there is easy access to it. You do not want to alienate your target audience: the aim is to further increase engagement among participants by using popular and familiar technology.

It is important to note that technology can also 'level the playing field' in the classroom by accommodating students with different learning styles, and by offering less confident students nontraditional forums in which to participate and have their say. For example, online voting tools offer all participants an equal opportunity to have their say in a less visible forum than the classroom. And asynchronous online discussions give participants more time for individual reflection before making their contribution, instead of being overwhelmed by the speed of a classroom discussion.

The topic

Your case may be an ideal candidate for the inclusion of multimedia if the topic is relevant, for example if the learning objectives include references to digital transformation, digital media, or social media.

> **From theory to practice with Martin and Urs**
>
> In 2014, we wanted to write a case about the digital transformation of the big German media company Axel Springer. While discussing the learning objectives, we immediately decided that the case itself should also be an example of digital transformation and not only incorporate new technologies but potentially be completely based on new technology.
>
> As a result, we initially decided to create the case as an 'app'. However, although this was a great idea, we unfortunately never finished the project for a number of reasons. The situation at Axel Springer was moving very quickly, and we were not quite comfortable with using an app format. Nevertheless, we have included this story because we feel it illustrates the huge potential that multimedia has. The app idea was exciting and inspiring and would have been perfect for the case we planned to create – it just wasn't right for us at that time.

Personal choice

Your approach to case writing should always reflect your personality and you should feel comfortable with the technologies that you want to use to produce the case. If you are not comfortable and confident using multimedia in the classroom and ultimately multimedia to produce the case, then it will not work for you or your participants.

It is good practice to build up a broad portfolio of cases that you can teach in your area of expertise. This may be a mix of your own cases and those of other authors, and you may wish to make sure that you have at least one or two multimedia cases in your portfolio. But they do not have to be your own.

Advantages of using technology

Using technology enables you to seamlessly incorporate different media formats such as audio and video into your case. This can be as simple as including links to online materials in your case or at the other extreme may involve creating a dedicated website for your case where students can find additional information and materials.

Dedicated websites (or potentially even apps) might also offer an additional advantage. While a traditional paper- or PDF-based case leads the reader through the story, online formats can break with this linear approach: participants can decide for themselves how to browse and explore the information and in what order, going back and forth much more easily and naturally than when dealing with traditional text.

Finally, technology can increase the complexity of the case, especially in its presentation. In a more traditional case, the participants are more likely to see all the relevant information after going through it from start to finish. With an online multimedia case this might be more difficult and challenging as content is linked and embedded differently.

Ways to incorporate technology and different media

Adding on

The easiest and most obvious way to use different media in your case is to keep the traditional format as a base and add multimedia materials as a valuable enhancement. There are a few different ways to do this:

- provide URLs in the text of the case;
- incorporate hyperlinks or QR codes;
- list online resources at the end of the case;
- provide your own video (or audio) material (for example interviews or site visits) digitally or make the material available online (you could create your own YouTube channel);
- provide links to additional online material such as commercials, video material aimed at employees, publicly available media interviews or company promotions.

Participants can also be invited to create and upload their own videos as part of the mix, perhaps making a short presentation 'in character' as the case protagonist, or to simply share their views about the issues to be discussed in class. This is one way to encourage students who are less confident in class to participate.

Fully embracing new technology

Instead of simply adding different media to your case, you could dispense with the traditional written component altogether and create a wholly online case. There are many ways to do this, including:

- video case,
- case in the form of a website,
- case as an app,
- a simulation,
- a virtual/augmented reality case.

The case method's effortless embrace of technology and multimedia in all its forms is testament to its flexibility and adaptability.

However, when considering creating a fully multimedia case it is important to think about the additional resources (technical, financial, etc.) that you will need. Some schools are well set up to support case writers who wish to explore this option and you should speak to the learning designers and technical team at your institution. It is also key to give thought to the support that may be needed to use the case in class – for example, will you need members of your IT team to be on call?

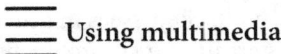 **Using multimedia**

- Make technology the means, not the end.
- Use multimedia to enhance your case, not to impress.
- Always keep your audience in mind.
- Remember: multimedia aspects of your case may need frequent updates.

Typical mistakes in case developments

'You must learn from the mistakes of others. You can't possibly live long enough to make them all yourself.' – Sam Levenson

Of course, there are any number of mistakes that you can make when writing a case and we cannot possibly list them all here. However, we can cover some of the most common errors that are very easy to fall into. Even experienced case writers are not immune. We are often too close to our own work to spot its weaknesses, and that is why it is very important to get independent feedback from a trusted colleague. Equally vital is the process of testing your case in the classroom, as we have already discussed.

Here are the main pitfalls to be aware of as you draft and refine your case:

- overloading your case with facts, figures and detail;
- including too many issues;
- being biased toward or against your protagonist and company;
- preaching instead of teaching;
- giving away too much;
- using too much jargon and industry-specific language.

Overloading your case with facts, figures and detail

Whether your case is based on field research, published sources, or a mix of both, you will have spent a lot of time and effort gathering all the information you need. We can pretty much guarantee (from personal experience) what happens next:

- You are unwilling to leave out any of the information because it was such hard work to get it in the first place.
- You do not know what to leave out and what to keep in.
- You are tempted to leave too much in rather than make the mistake of taking too much out. Kassarjian and Kashani (2005: 110) put it very nicely: 'You must resist the temptation to find ways to include everything you found: you are not trying to prove your diligence at data collection, but trying to compose a learning script, one that has clear focus and can hold interest of the reader.'

This is where the discipline of case writing kicks in. First of all, it is very useful to remember that none of your research will be wasted. The information you leave out will serve as great background detail when teaching the case and will enhance your status as an authority on the topic. Also, some of the material you exclude from the case will be very useful for your teaching note.

Your case should include only the information that is directly relevant to the issue or issues you want to discuss and the learning objectives you want to achieve.

Spare a thought for your reader: They do not want to wade through pages and pages of research that may or may not have a bearing on the key issues in general or on your session in particular. Your aim is to engage, excite, and inspire in your classroom discussion. You must be objective and ask yourself: is this interesting and relevant, or just interesting? Everything you include must be both interesting and relevant.

 However, this does not mean that you must strip your case to the bare bones. This is particularly important when one of the learning objectives for participants is to discriminate between which information is relevant and which is not (see the analytical dimension of the case difficulty cube, page 19). As an additional challenge, this may even involve the inclusion of contradictory information.

You can see there is a fine balance to strike when deciding which information to include in your case. To help you decide, it is vital to keep your learning objectives in mind.

Including too many issues

During your research, a number of issues may arise that you feel should be included. However, do not be tempted to squeeze them all into a single case. A case with multiple issues will be impossible to teach effectively and it will be very difficult to focus on specific learning objectives.

A good solution is to write a case series if the issues are linked, or separate cases if the issues are not related in any meaningful way.

 From theory to practice with Martin

For executive education programs we are sometimes asked to write a single, topic-heavy case covering multiple issues. The idea is that participants will cover each topic in turn as they move through the course.

However, in our experience, the results are rarely satisfactory. This is because it is difficult to prevent participants from discussing more than one topic from the case without looking as though we are trying to control the class discussion too much. This is demotivating for participants, and they start to disengage.

A far better solution is to write a case series or separate cases about the same company with each case covering a discrete topic and featuring different protagonists.

Being biased toward or against your protagonist and company

As you research and write your case, you will inevitably form opinions about the course of events and the people involved. However, you must guard against allowing your personal viewpoint to color the way you present the issues.

It is essential to ensure that your account of the situation is balanced and neutral. Never include your personal opinions or commentary in your case. It is also necessary to guard against more subtle forms of bias, such as giving one character more 'airtime' than another or selecting information that puts one person or company in a good light and another in a bad light.

 The following representative extract is a type of bias we very often see:

The company made an excellent choice when it acquired ...

The word 'excellent' needs to be removed as this reveals the writer's approval of what took place. It is simple to make this information neutral, with the added benefit that you also make it shorter:

The company acquired ...

'Excellent' is, of course, an adjective. The use of adjectives is a warning sign that subjectivity may have crept into your case; be very careful when using them.

Writing to convince instead of writing to engage

There is no point in using your case to 'prove' your theories or share your in-depth diagnosis of a situation. If you do, we can almost guarantee that this will lead to resistance and participants will probably go to great lengths to prove you wrong. A case should not be used to prove something but should act as an invitation to discuss and explore the issues – always keep this in mind when writing your case.

Your aim is to encourage debate and discussion and to guide others toward a plausible solution in the circumstances, not to present your solution at the start and wait for everyone's agreement.

To help with this, refer to the case difficulty cube (page 19). Do not make your case too easy from an analytical or conceptual perspective. Participants will then be empowered to make discoveries for themselves.

Giving away too much

We like to say that writing a case is like telling a story. However, perhaps we need to be more precise: you should tell a story but leave it unfinished. Do not give too much away or there will be no work left to do in the classroom. Follow the example of typical TV dramas – they always leave you guessing at the end of each episode to ensure you return for the next one.

Write a story but end with a cliffhanger. The reader should always be left with the question 'what happens next?' And, more importantly, you will be in the position to ask your participants: 'what should happen next?'

Using too much jargon and industry-specific language

If you are familiar with an industry or market sector, it is very easy to forget that others may not understand the acronyms and jargon that are part of your everyday vocabulary. This can be very alienating and may reduce the wider appeal of your case.

Always try to use everyday language in your case, avoiding technical expressions and specialist terminology. This will help to ensure that your case reaches as wide an audience as possible.

Avoiding common mistakes

- Ask a trusted colleague for feedback.
- Always test your case in the classroom.
- Don't dump your data.
- Focus on a specific issue.
- Stay neutral.
- Teach, don't preach.
- Don't give away too much.
- Avoid jargon and specialist vocabulary.

Resourcing: getting support for your case development

'Alone we can do so little; together we can do so much.' – Helen Keller

Writing a good case and teaching note is a lot of work, although there are a number of steps you can take to reduce the work involved. But to be clear from the start: There are some aspects of writing a case that cannot (or at least should not) be delegated. Only you (together with your coauthor(s) if you are collaborating) can:

- write your case outline (see page 176). This is a vital stage of case writing and your sole responsibility,
- test the case in class, or
- write the teaching note.

However, there are many ways you can lighten your workload and save time by calling on the help of others. This works best when it becomes a mutually beneficial process. For example, by asking a student to draft all or part of your case, you will save time and benefit from a fresh perspective, while your student will gain knowledge and fresh insights as well as honing their writing skills. This is a win–win situation (and makes your case a great learning tool in more ways than one!).

Never lose sight of the fact that this is your case, and you need to stay in overall control of every aspect of the writing process, including the final editing/review stage. Irrespective of the type and level of support, as an author you are responsible for the final product, and you need to ensure adequate representation of the contribution of others.

Who can help?

There are several people who may be able to help in various ways with your case. Where this involves financial outlay, you will need to decide if you can justify the cost within the overall budget you have set aside for writing your case. Here are a few key people and resources you may be able to call on:

- students,
- research and teaching assistants,
- the publishing department at your institution,
- the company your case is about,
- professional writers and copyeditors,
- consultants working in the business or industry you wish to write about.

What can they do?

Their support activities may include:

- sharing expertise and/or key contacts,
- supplementary desk-based research,
- researching relevant literature,
- number-crunching and analytics,
- transcribing interviews,
- drafting the text of all or part of your case,
- proofreading and copyediting,
- observing and taking notes when you test your case in class (these notes can be invaluable when creating the teaching and blackboard plans for your case, particularly relating to the questions you ask and the responses that can be expected).

In addition, human resource, communications, or investor relations departments at the company you are working with should be able to provide key information such as a company history, CVs for your key personnel, and descriptions of processes and policies.

Financial resources

How much money will you need to write your case? You need to think about this in advance and create a realistic budget. Be clear about how you will finance various aspects of your case. Here are a few of the main costs you may need to factor in:

- travel expenses in relation to interviewing or site visits;
- professional copywriting, editing, and proofreading fees;
- translation fees (for both the case itself and all the related materials);
- creation of multimedia materials (for example, videos, dedicated web pages);
- general administrative and office costs.

Some institutions set aside budgets specifically for case writing, but this is fairly rare. It is good practice to reduce costs by combining your other professional (and even leisure) activities with case writing. For example, if you are traveling to a conference or to teach at another institution, take the opportunity to carry out interviews or make site visits. Similarly, the development and preparation of a teaching program can often be combined with case writing activities.

One of the best ways to control your financial costs is to stick to your case writing schedule. If you allow the case writing process to drag on, your costs will inevitably increase.

Support and resources

– Even if you get support, if you are the (co)author you need to be in control and are responsible!
– You must at least write the case outline and develop the teaching plan by yourself.
– You must test the case in class.
– Stay in control from start to finish.
– Decide who can help with what.
– Make workload sharing a win–win situation.
– Create a realistic budget.
– Control costs by sticking to your schedule.

Structured approach to developing your own case studies

Writing your first case and developing a case portfolio

We hope you become a keen case writer and eventually build up your own collection of cases. As a regular case writer, you will need to find some way to keep tabs on everything; you may have a mix of published cases, cases in progress, and cases out for approval. Your cases may also cover different topics and subject areas. It can be a good idea to create a framework that offers an instant visual summary of the status of all your cases.

 From theory to practice with Urs

Case framework

I like to use a Venn diagram to organize all my cases. You can see that this simple layout provides a lot of information in a single glance, including:

- the current status of cases (color-coded to denote published, in progress, out for review or unable to publish);

(Continued)

- which topics they cover (one, two or all three of my main subject areas);
- if they are competition winners or best-sellers;
- the order in which they were written (as numbered).

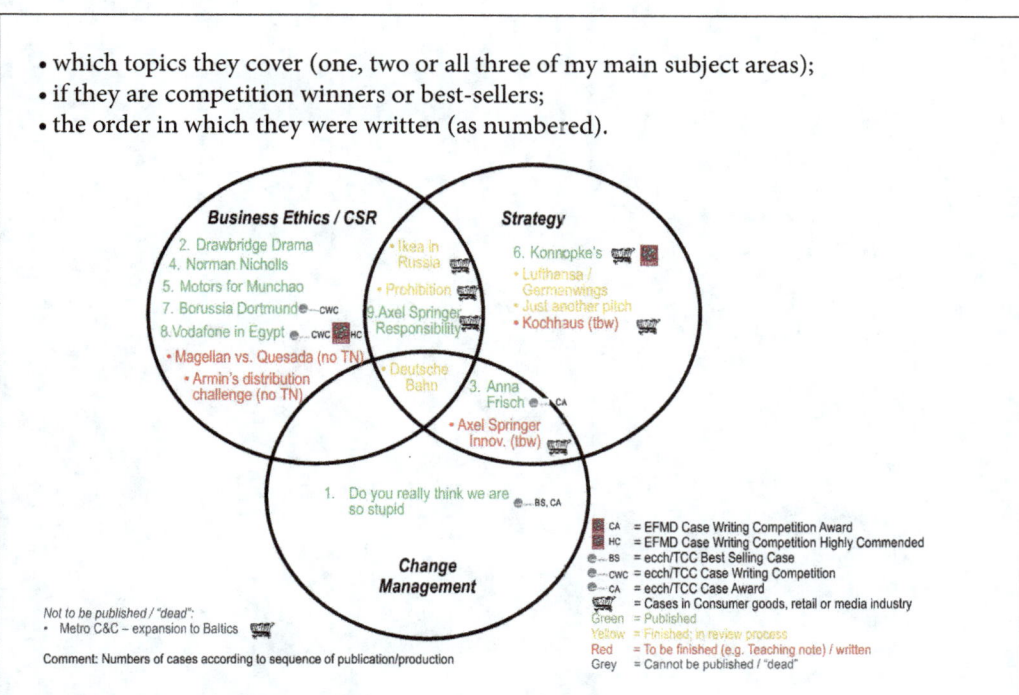

Figure 28: Sample framework for production of cases.

References

Abell, D 2003 *What makes a good case?* IMD Technical Note (IMD-3-0731).

Anderson, L W and Krathwohl, D R (eds.) 2001 *A taxonomy for learning, teaching, and assessing: A revision of Bloom's taxonomy of educational objectives.* Allyn and Bacon.

Hammond, J H and Raman, A 1994; 2006 Sport Obermeyer, Ltd. Harvard Business School Case study. 9-695-022. Available at https://www.thecasecentre.org/products/view?id=45743.

Kassarjian, J B and Kashani, K 2005 Writing an effective case for executive programs. In: Strebel, P and Keys, T *Mastering executive education: How to combine content with context and emotion – The IMD guide.* Harlow: FT Prentice Hall, pp. 105–117.

Leenders, M R, Mauffette-Leenders, L A, and Erskine, J A 2010 *Writing cases.* 4th ed. Richard Ivey School of Business.

Mauffette-Leenders, L A, Erskine, J A, and Leenders, M 2005 *Learning with cases.* 3rd ed. Richard Ivey School of Business.

Naumes, W and Naumes, M J 2006 *The art & craft of case writing.* 2nd ed. Armonk, NY and London: M.E. Sharpe.

Roch, W 1992 *Case writing.* Technical Note (UVA-G-0364).

Vega, G 2013 *The case writing workbook: A self-guided workshop.* New York, NY: M.E. Sharpe.

Index

A

academic journals
  case discussion 9
  publication of case studies 164, 197, 199,
     212, 238, 240, 241
       case summaries 225
       keywords 226
        See also publication and
         case release.
  research cases 3–5
  supplementary materials 97, 98, 234
  teaching cases 35
       case leads 139
acoustics 77, 95, 100
age of cases 39
  participants who know the outcome 60
alternative format case studies 241
  incorporating new technologies/media
       advantages 242
       methods of incorporation 243–244
       participant groups 241
       personality and personal choice 242
       topics 242
  See also technology use.
alternative teaching plans 235
  learning objectives 236–237
  timings 235–236

assessment and grading 123–124
  assignments and submissions 126–127, 128
  case-based exams 127–128
  checklist 128
  ethics and ethical considerations 129
  participation and contribution 124–126
  teaching note 237
assignments 101
  assessment and grading 126–127
  group assignments 28, 67, 215
  late submission 120
  presession assignments 52, 53, 59,
     203, 208
  teaching notes 199, 201–203, 230–231

B

background cases 20
best practice cases 21
board plans and board use 95
  preparation and review 51, 53
  teaching notes 44, 46–48, 210–213, 233
  teaching plans 41, 46, 100, 199
  teaching style 95–96
broadening questions 68
business and management studies 2
  types of cases 4
bystander role 150

C

Case Centre   8, 18, 34, 35, 156, 197, 212, 225, 226, 239, 240
case development funnel   198–200
  case origin   136–143
  classroom testing   212–215
  finishing the case study   218–229
  finishing the teaching note   225–233
  learning objectives   140–212
  operational activities   166–176
  promoting the case study   239–247
  publishing the case study   238–250
  strategic decisions   144–145
  tactical choices   153–156
case discussion. *See* discussion
case flow   180–181, 182, 188, 194, 206
case leads   106, 136, 138–140, 141, 242
  learning objectives   141–145
  structure   146–155
case method
  business and management studies   1–2
  criticisms   8–9, 121
    incorrect syllogisms   9–10
    positivity bias   10–12
  law schools   1
  medicine   2–3
  origins   1
  participant-centricity   128
  philosophical research and instruction   1
case platforms from individual business schools   35
case portfolios   32, 188, 167, 242, 248
case repositories   34, 35
case series   18, 148, 149, 153, 154, 154–155, 171, 206, 221, 245
case structure   176–180
  broad to specific   181
  business process basis   181–182
  case flow   180
  chronological   181
case study defined   2
case study selection   40–41
  age of cases   39
  case-based courses   118–137
  checklist   40
  copyright   39
  educational objectives   38
  non-traditional case material   37–38
  screening   37
  search options and quality indicators
    authors   36
    experience   36
    institution   36
    prizes and awards   36
    recommendations   36
    use of the case   36
  searching for cases   34–40
  traditional text-based case studies   34–39
case summaries   60
case teaching. *See* case-based courses
  preparation. *See* presession preparation
  selection of cases. *See* case study selection
  teaching plans. *See* teaching plans
case-based courses   62
  case study selection   118–119
  content and method   116
  core courses versus elective courses   114–115
  grading   123–124
    assignments and submissions   126–127
    case-based exams   127–128
    checklist   128
    participation and contribution   124–126
  learning objectives   114
  overall program, relationship with   115–118
  participant groups. *See* participant groups
  part-time versus full-time   115
  structure and flow   116–117
  weekly versus blocked courses   115
  See also case-based sessions.
case-based sessions   32
  case-based courses compared   113
  identifying the right course   32–33
    checklist   33
  identifying the right session   33–34
    checklist   33
  learning objectives   33–35
    checklist   33
  See also case-based courses.
class size   50, 98–99
classroom layout   99–100
classroom testing   106–107, 212–213, 213, 215–216
  existing, publicly available sources   213–214
  learning from test use   216–219
  mini-caselets   107, 214
  objectives of testing   107–111
  participant exploration   213
  short presentations   107, 214

test-classroom testing multiple times   215
when and where to test   110–111
who should test-teach   214–215
closed-ended questions   56, 62–63, 64–66, 202, 209, 237
collaboration with organizations or protagonists
  field research   161
  published sources   162
collecting material for case writing   105–106, 184, 185–188, 244
  desk-based data collection and research   185–189, 194
  interviews   189–194
company or site visits   19–20
complexity of cases   38–39, 109–110, 157, 160, 220
  analytical dimension   18, 21, 157, 178, 203
  conceptual dimension   18, 157, 178
  presentation dimension   18, 21, 157, 242
convergent topics   41–42, 47, 116, 206
copyright ownership   25, 34, 35, 39, 169, 195, 195–196, 224, 239

D

decision cases   20, 149
deep learning   6, 91, 119
Delta Leadership   35
direct personal observations   106, 194
discussion   42
  checklist   61
  classroom layout   100
  closing discussion
    generalizing questions   71
    relating questions   70–71
    summarizing questions   70
  closure   88–90
  leading discussions   78–79
  managing participants
    participants surfing the net/texting   83
    participants who are too quiet   80–81
    participants who are too vocal   80
    unprepared participants   80–82
  managing transitions   79–80
  opening case discussions   55–56
    opening questions   55–65
  questionnaires   59
  setting the scene   54–55
  small-group presentations   59
  supplementary materials   98
  types of questions   61–62
    broadening questions   68
    checklist   72
    closed-ended questions   62–63
    learning objectives, questions related to   64–67
    learning process   67–68
    open-ended questions   63–66
    special situations   71–72
    transition questions   69–70
  votes on a specific question   59
distance learning. *See* online teaching
divergent topics   41–42, 47, 116, 206
Donham, Wallace Brett   1
driver role   150

E

echoing   77
  benefits of echoing   77
  developing echoing skills   77–78
  overuse of   78
educational needs   136
  content versus context   137–139
  learning objectives   140–142
effective case studies   12
  amount of data   14–15
  cases as unfinished stories   12
  checklist   15–17
  controversiality   13
  discovery of underlying issues   13
  length of case   15
  opportunities to draw wider lessons   14
  personal touch   15
  substantive and relevant issues   13
  use of contrasts and comparisons   14
  well structured and easy to read   15
ethics and ethical considerations   128
  grading issues   129
  hindsight bias   129
  mutual respect   129
  opportunity to participate and contribute   129
  participant-centricity   128–129
exercise cases   20
exhibits   14, 107, 169–170, 179, 182–184
  references and citations   188
  teaching note   237–238
expectations and excitement
  communications with participants   52
  supplementary materials   98

F

factual level of information   74, 159
   fictional events case   160
   real events case   159–161
fake/sanitized cases   17, 60, 107, 164
feedback   102–103, 125
fictional events cases   2, 17, 37, 118, 159, 160, 185
field research
   collaboration with organizations or protagonists   161–163
field visits   19–20, 109–116
flexibility
   case teaching   57, 69, 91, 243
      breaking down traditional power relationships   30
   case writing   156, 165, 177
   group work   84
   teaching plans   30, 79, 129
focus groups   194
formats of case studies   19
   See also alternative format case studies; learning formats; teaching formats.
full-class discussions   84

G

generalizing questions   71
group work   84–85
   classroom layout   100
   flexibility   84
   group composition   85–86
guest participation   15, 84, 87, 142, 161, 232

H

Harvard Business Publishing   34, 35, 156, 197, 226
Harvard Business School   1, 2
Harvard Law School   1
Harvard-style case studies. See traditional text-based case studies
hindsight bias   10, 21, 128, 129

I

immediate and underlying issues, differentiation between   13, 22, 43, 227
immediate issues   9, 13, 20, 21, 22–23, 43, 56, 109–110, 171, 176, 183, 185
   analytical complexity   157
   checklist   23

learning objectives   144–145, 201, 206
   selection of   149–150
   teaching notes   201, 227
incident cases   20
INSEAD Publishing   17, 35
intellectual property rights   25, 34, 35, 39, 169, 195, 195–196, 224, 239
interactive teaching and learning   5, 7, 99, 123, 208, 221
   See also alternative format case studies; technology use.
Ivey Publishing   34, 35, 197

K

knowledge input
   learning cycles   42–43, 43

L

Lancaster model of learning   42–43, 43–44, 116–117
Langdell, Christopher Columbus   1
leads and needs   136–137
   case leads   138–140
   educational needs   137
      types of case needs   137–139
   See also case leads; educational needs.
learning contracts
   checklist   120
   explicit learning contracts   119–120
   implicit learning contracts   119
learning cycles   42–43
   case-based courses   117
learning formats   208–209
   checklist   88
   field visits   19–20, 87
   full-class discussions   84
   group work   84–85, 100–101
      group composition   85–86
   guest participation   87
   lectures   86
   quizzes and polls   88
   role-play   67, 80, 86–87, 152–154, 153
   teaching plans   207
   video clips   54, 60, 87, 197, 221, 233, 240
learning objectives   33–35, 140–146, 198
   alternative teaching plans   236–237
   breadth and depth   109
   case development funnel   140–146
   case leads   141–145
   case-based courses   114

case-based sessions   33–35
case development funnel   140–146
   educational needs   140–142
   immediate issues   144–145, 201, 206
   teaching notes   201, 227–228, 228
   teaching plans   33–35, 206, 236–237
   underlying issues   144–145, 206
   writing case studies   140–146
learning outcomes   19, 33, 85, 132, 133, 147, 196, 206, 207, 211, 217
lectures   86
legal studies   1
length of cases   15, 18, 38, 155–157
level of detail   163–165
levels of communication   73–74
   appeal message   76
   factual information   74–75
   relationship message   75–76
   self-revelation message   75
listening
   case teaching   61–62
      checklist   78
      echoing   76–78
      exchange of information   73–76
      responding to contributions   68–69
      things not said   76
live cases   19

M

medicine   2–3
   types of cases   3
mini-cases   19, 107, 213, 214
mistakes to avoid   90–92
motivations of contributors   73
multimedia cases   19
   See also technology use.
multiple cases   43, 153
multiple protagonists   152–153

N

newspaper articles   19
nontraditional case material   37

O

online teaching   100–101, 208–210
   grading participation   126
   teaching formats   100–101
   teaching notes   208, 232
open educational resources (OERs)   35
open-ended questions   63–66, 64–66, 237

opening questions for case discussion   55–59
   cold call   58
   examples   57
   open call   58
   warm call   59
open-source educator portals   35
organizational elements
   checklist   25
   faculty and teaching support   25
   HR matters   24–25
   student preparation   23–25

P

participant groups   38, 48, 144, 198
   age groups   49
   business and employment experience   49
   checklist   50
   class size   50–51
   corporate cultures   93
   gender   50
   level (undergrad, graduate, executive...)   50
   managing participants
      participants surfing the net/texting   83
      participants who are too quiet   80–81
      participants who are too vocal   80
      unprepared participants   81–82
   nationality and culture   49
      cultural diversity   92–93
      language   92
   preparation   50
   teaching notes   201
participant-centricity   128–129
passengers   150
personality and teaching style
   board use   95–96
   experimentation and adapting case sessions to personality   31
   media and technology use   242–243
   supplementary materials   96–98
   technology use   94, 94–95
philosophical research and instruction   1
positivity bias of case studies   10–12, 19
presession preparation   51–52
   checklist   52, 53
   communications with participants
      communication channels   53
      content   53
      expectations and excitement   52
      tone and style   52
   See also teaching.

promoting case studies 239–241
prospective cases 17, 20, 146–147, 149, 151, 155, 176
protagonist role 150
   choice of 152
   drivers/passengers/bystanders 150–152
   guest participation 87
   interviews 189–194
   multiple protagonists 152–153
publication and case release 222–226, 238–239
   case release template 224–225
   See also academic journals.
purpose of case studies 6
   facilitator benefits 7–8
   multifunctionality of cases 6
   online learning 7
   participant benefits 7

Q

questionnaires and surveys 194
quizzes and polls 194

R

real events cases 159–161, 161
reflection
   learning cycles 42, 43
   relating questions 70–71
relationship between speaker and listener 75–76
research cases 3–6
retrospective cases 17, 20, 146, 149, 155
reviewing performance 103–110
   checklist 103–110, 220–224
role-play 67, 80, 85–86, 152, 153
Rotterdam School of Management (RSM) Erasmus University 35

S

self-assessment 125
self-improvement 101–102
   reviewing performance
      checklist 103–110, 220–224
self-revelation level of communication 75
simulation 153
single case studies 18, 153, 154
situation cases 20
Socratic Method of question and answer 1, 32
summarizing questions 70

support and collaboration 25, 246–249
syllogisms
   error and simplification 9–10

T

target audience. *See* participant groups
teaching 3, 27, 32
   behavior 66–67
   breaking down traditional power relationships 29–30
      exploring topics together 30
      flexibility 30
      take students seriously 30–31
   collecting material for case writing 105–106, 185–188
   experimentation
      adapting case sessions to personality 31
      observation and feedback 31
      trying out new learning formats 32
   listening 61
      responding to contributions 68–69
   orchestrating class discussion 61
   preparation 48
      checklists 23, 51, 52, 53
      familiarization with case and materials 51–56
      introducing case method to participants 120–123, 120–124
      participants 48–51
      preclass preparation for participants 51–52
      reviewing teaching and board plans 51
      supplementary materials 98
   prioritizing the method over the content 116
      ensuring psychological safety 29–30
      importance of nontechnical content 28–29
      social dimension of learning 28
testing case ideas 106, 213, 215
   learning from test use 216–219
   objectives of testing 107–110, 107–111
   participant exploration 213
   test-teaching multiple times 215
   using existing, publicly available sources 213–214

using mini-caselets   214
  using short presentations   214
  when and where to test   110–111
  who should test-teach   214–215
  See also classroom testing.
 testing knowledge   65–66
 testing skills   66
 typical mistakes   90–91
teaching formats   5–6
 checklist   88
 field visits   19–20, 87
 full-class discussions   84
 group work   84, 84–85, 85, 85–86
  group composition   85
 guest participation   87
 lectures   86
 online teaching   100–101
 quizzes and polls   88
 role-play   67, 80, 85–87, 152, 153
 video clips   54, 60, 87, 197, 221, 233, 240
teaching materials   5
 checklist   43
 dimensions of case material   16–20
 formats of case studies   19
 prototypical case types   20–21
 supplementary materials   38, 43–44
  exhibits   182–184
  facilitators   233–234
  participants   233
  types of material   97–98
  when to use material   96–97
teaching notes   38, 196
 analysis   203–204, 230
  frameworks/concepts/theories   204
  quantitative data   204
 assignments   201–203, 230–231
 benefits   197
 board plans   46, 210–213, 233
 case summary   200–201, 225–227
 checklist   211
 collecting data   110
 course contex   229–230
 course context   201
 examination and grading   237
 exhibits   237
 immediate issues   201, 227
 keywords   201, 226–228
 learning objectives   201, 227–228, 228
 online/hybrid courses   208–210, 232
 participant groups   201, 229–230

 structure   198–201
 supplements   238
 teaching plan   204–209, 231–233
 underlying issues   201
 writing style   197
teaching plans   40–41, 164–165, 198
 alternative teaching plans   235
  learning objectives   236–237
  timings   235–236
 board use   46–48
 building blocks   205–206
 checklists   205
 context and potential constraints   41
 flexibility   30
 flow of sessions   41–42
 key elements   44–46
 learning cycles   42–43
 learning formats   207
 learning objectives   33–35, 206
 preparation and review   51
 teaching notes   204–209
 transition questions   207
teaching style. *See* personality and
  teaching style
technical notes   20, 154
technology use   94
 add ons   243
 advantages   242
 checklist   243
 embracing all forms of technology   243
 participant groups   241
 personality and personal choice   242
 topics   242
 See also alternative format case studies.
text-based case studies. *See* traditional
  text-based case studies
timings   219
 alternative teaching plans   235–236
 position in course   147–150
 teaching plans   207
traditional text-based case studies   5–6, 16,
  19, 34–37, 241
transition questions   69–70
 managing transitions   79–80

U

underlying issues   21, 43, 198
 checklist   23
 learning objectives   144–145, 206
 teaching notes   201

unprepared participants
  encouraging preparation
        pull techniques   82
        push techniques   82
    establishing reasons for lack of
        preparation   81
    long-term solutions   82
    short-term solutions   81

V

video cases   19
video clips   54, 60, 87, 121, 197, 221, 233, 240

W

workshops   194
writing case studies   131–133
  benefits   134
  case origin   136–140, 136–143
  case writers' mistakes   244–247
  classroom testing   212–219
  closing paragraphs   183–185
  copyediting   222
  finishing the case study   218–230
  finishing the teaching note   225–243
  institutional conventions   170–171
  layout of case   168–170
  learning objectives   140–145, 140–146
  opening paragraphs   171–178
  operational activities   166–231
  pitfalls   134–136
  promoting the case study   239–241
  publishing the case study   238–239
  references and citations   188–189
  strategic decisions   144–156
  tactical choices   153–170
  writing style   166–168

www.ingramcontent.com/pod-product-compliance
Lightning Source LLC
Chambersburg PA
CBHW051147290426
44108CB00019B/2642